Report on the American Workforce

U.S. Department of Labor
Alexis M. Herman, Secretary

1999

Preface

This is the fourth *Report on the American Workforce* to be issued by the Department of Labor. The three themes covered in this edition—workplace responses to an increasingly competitive global environment, the central role of improved skills for all participants in the labor market, and the balance of work and family—will be central concerns for policymakers, researchers, and American workers and their families well into the 21st century.

The *Report's* basic direction and context is established in an introductory message from the Secretary of Labor. Each of the three subsequent chapters investigates one of the analytical topics. An updated compendium of statistical tables completes the volume. The completed *Report* as it appears here reflects the work of many people—economists, statisticians, data development experts, editors, visual information specialists, computer programmers, and others. Katharine G. Abraham, Commissioner for the Bureau of Labor Statistics, established the strategic direction of this series of reports. Deborah Klein and Richard Devens provided overall direction for this year's report.

Information in this report is available to sensory impaired individuals on request. Voice phone: (202) 606-7828. Federal Relay Service: 1-800-877-8339. This material is in the public domain and may be reproduced without further permission. Appropriate citation is requested.

Acknowledgments

Chapter 1 is a case study of two pivotal industries: the automobile-manufacturing cluster and the temporary help supply industry. The members of the team that wrote the chapter were Kent Kunze, Kenneth Lavish, Lois Plunkert, Cynthia Engle, Paul Kern, Virginia Klarquist, Shannon Martin, Francisco Moris, and Thomas Wedemire. The automotive industries are competitive leaders in adopting "just-in-time" production technologies, whereas the temporary help supply industry exemplifies the growing competitive importance of a "just-in-time" staffing concept that already challenges employment and training policy.

The second chapter explores the concept, measurement, and growing importance of worker skills and skilled work. It is the product of a team consisting of Harriet Weinstein, Larry Rosenblum, Pamela Frugoli, Linda Moeller, Jane Osburn, Brooks Pierce, Carolyn Veneri, and Pat Wash. The chapter starts with a discussion on the various definitions of skill and the effect of changes in the economic environment and their effect on skill. This sets the backdrop for an analysis of changes in the education and work experience of the Nation's workforce, occupational patterns and evidence of skill upgrading, the relationship of skill and earnings, and occupational shortages.

Chapter 3 addresses the demands that evolving labor market forces have placed on workers' time. The chapter was written by the team of Anthony Barkume, Howard Hayghe, Mary Joyce, Larry Rosenblum, William Wiatrowski, Thomas Beers, Sasha Eidelman, Randy Ilg, Curtis Polen, Hector Rodriguez, Jay Stewart, Linda Stinson, and Stella Cromartie. The chapter works to untangle the influences of changing demographics, family structures, and work arrangements on the way the American workforce uses its time.

The *Report* was edited, designed, and composed by Monica Gabor, Jacqueline Gadt, Margaret Jones, Phyllis Lott, and Irma Mayfield under the supervision of Eugene Becker.

Contents

Contents—Continued

Contents—Continued

Message from the Secretary of Labor

The U.S. economy over the past few years has performed above and beyond our highest expectations. Real growth in the Nation's output was roughly 4 percent last year, while productivity grew by over 2 percent. The Nation's unemployment rate averaged 4.5 percent for the entire year of 1998, the lowest in almost 30 years. With a rate of inflation of just 1.6 percent last year, we have achieved a combination of low inflation and low unemployment that many had thought was impossible just a few years ago. And wages have consistently outpaced inflation, providing America's workers with real wage gains averaging almost 2 percent a year for 3 consecutive years.

Furthermore, the prosperity of the past few years has been very widely shared. Unemployment rates among minorities and high school dropouts have fallen to some of the lowest rates on record for those groups; and real wage gains among these groups have exceeded the national average.

Still, some areas of concern remain. The gaps in wages between more- and less-educated workers that widened so dramatically in the 1980s and early 1990s remain large. Families that once could have lived comfortably on the paycheck of one earner now often require two to make ends meet. And, in a dynamic economy in which the forces of technology and international trade sometimes create job losses, as well as job gains in certain industries, worker insecurity and anxiety have remained high, despite the economy's stellar performance.

Against this backdrop, the 1999 *Report on the American Workforce* presents three chapters that deal with important and timely labor market issues. The first presents evidence on how two very different industries—automobile manufacturing and help supply services—have been affected by the growing competitive pressures on American companies to improve productivity and reduce costs. Flexible production techniques and "just-in-time" methods in autos and other manufacturing industries have raised the need for the "temps" that the temporary help industry provides. But relatively low wage and benefit levels, along with uneven employment opportunities, remain problems for those employed as contingent workers.

In an economy where what we earn very much reflects what we learn, the second chapter provides important new evidence on the kinds of skills that matter in the labor market. A wide range of skills is important in the new economy: Formal education and workforce experience, on-the-job training, and a variety of competencies needed to perform different occupations all are rewarded. Workers must enter the workforce with strong basic and job-related skills, and they must be prepared to learn new skills continuously in their places of employment, over the course of their lives.

The final chapter presents data on trends in the numbers of hours worked by American workers. While the overall number of hours worked has been fairly constant over time, this fact masks several important trends—the rise of hours worked among women, their fall among less-educated males, and the growing use of overtime and non-traditional hours by some in the workforce. Both one- and two-earner families have difficulty balancing the needs of home and children versus those of the workplace.

Together, these chapters highlight a number of important themes. For one thing, a wide range of skills must be provided to U.S. workers in many different contexts. The Clinton Administration has implemented a number of policies that encourage higher levels and improved quality of schooling, such as expanded funding for Head Start and Pell Grants, Hope Scholarships, and School-to-Work grants. The new Workforce Investment Act promises to provide more coherence, quality, and choice to workers seeking job training in local "One-Stop" centers. But now we must ensure that no one is left behind.

Despite the progress of the last several years, certain groups continue to experience weak attachment to the labor market or high unemployment. For instance, African-American teens still suffer unemployment rates of nearly 30 percent, just as they did 20 years ago during an earlier boom. And while welfare recipients have entered the labor market in record numbers, many experience frequent job turnover and low earnings, while those on the rolls increasingly reflect a hard-to-employ population. Programs that raise the skills of these groups and enable them to enter and prosper in the mainstream economy should be among our highest priorities. And those workers who have been displaced by new technology, international trade, and other sources of workplace restructuring must be ensured access to the kinds of reemployment services that will enable them to regain the earnings and employment that they have lost through no fault of their own.

As employment rates rise among the less-skilled population, we also need to ensure that "work pays" for everyone. Expanding the Earned Income Tax Credit and raising the minimum wage have been two key components of our strategy to make this a reality. Furthermore, we need to ensure *equal pay* and equal employment opportunities for all workers, regardless of gender or race. It is unacceptable that women still earn only about 75 cents for each dollar earned by men and that discrimination and occupational segregation continue to limit their advancement. We will strengthen enforcement of our Equal Employment Opportunity laws and educate both employers and workers about how to make equal opportunity a reality once and for all.

Since 80 percent of families now depend partly or fully on the paychecks of mothers, equal pay is not just a women's issue—it's a *family* issue, as well; and helping families deal with the competing needs of the home and the workplace must also be among our highest priorities. Increasing the amount of financial support we provide for child care expenses and the coverage of the Family and Medical Leave Act are two important vehicles through which we could reduce the stress associated with balancing work and family life.

Achieving security for workers and their families requires not only healthy paychecks for employees but also access to a range of important benefits. For instance, only half of all employees today, and well under half of all female employees, are covered by a workplace pension. Yet, our needs for retirement income will continue to rise over time, as medical advances improve our life expectancies and as senior citizens become a larger segment of the population. It is, therefore, critical to ensure adequate pension coverage for all workers, especially lower-wage workers and those who work in small establishments. Making it easier for small employers to establish pension plans is one way to improve this coverage. Of course, reforming Social Security to ensure its fiscal stability throughout the 21st century is another critical piece of our plan to ensure security for all present and future retirees.

Finally, we need to ensure that all employees feel secure during their working lives, as well as in retirement. A Patient's Bill of Rights should make workers feel secure about the quality and coverage of health care benefits they receive. Full enforcement of occupational safety and health regulations would also strengthen that sense of security, by further reducing the hazards and injuries associated with work.

In short, we are enjoying an unprecedented period of economic prosperity and well-being in the United States today. By implementing the right policies, we can ensure that this prosperity is fully shared by all, and that workers and their families enjoy the fairness and security they deserve.

ALEXIS M. HERMAN
Secretary of Labor

Chapter 1

"Just-in-time" Inventories and Labor: A Study of Two Industries, 1990-98

Although the automobile and help supply industries are quite different, trends in both have been affected by the just-in-time supply philosophy that has become commonplace in the decade of the 90s. To set the stage, we review the period of study, 1990 to 1998, from an economic perspective and then explain why these industries were selected. The analysis of the automobile industry follows, with the review of the help supply industry completing the chapter. This chapter draws heavily on economic data produced by the Department of Labor's Bureau of Labor Statistics (BLS).

Economic background

The period 1990 to 1998 began with a downturn in economic growth, marked by a recession from July 1990 to March 1991. The subsequent recovery started slowly but picked up speed in 1992. This expansion was still healthy at the end of 1998 and, at that point, was the longest in the postwar period. While notable for its length, this expansion is not necessarily remarkable for its pace of economic growth. During the period of study, gross domestic product (GDP) grew at an annual average rate of 2.6 percent; and labor productivity for business (business represents about 80 percent of GDP) grew at an annual average rate of 1.4 percent. Both rates of growth are below the 1948 to 1998 average: GDP grew at an annual rate of 3.3 percent, and labor productivity grew at a 2.3 percent rate during this period. Employment during this period increased at an average annual rate of 1.3 percent, compared with 1.9 percent for the period 1981 to 1990. Despite the relatively slow growth in GDP, productivity, and employment, the unemployment rate fell below 5 percent in July 1997 and remained there throughout 1998. The previous period that the monthly unemployment rate remained below 5 percent for 6 months or more was in 1973. Simultaneously, the rate of inflation—as measured by the change in the Consumer Price Index for All Urban Consumers (CPI-U)—averaged less than 3 percent per year for the period 1990 to 1998. Similarly, the change in the Producer Price Index for Finished Goods (PPI) decreased precipitously during this period. The PPI increased at an average annual rate of 1.2 percent for the period 1990 to 1998.

Given this economic environment, we elected to study two industries. Along with the first industry, the motor vehicles and passenger car industry (SIC 3711), we examine its most important supplier industries: motor vehicles parts and accessories (SIC 3714) and automotive stampings (SIC 3465). (For convenience, we refer to the group of related industries as the automobile industry.) The second industry chosen for study is the help supply industry (SIC 7363). The automobile and help supply industries were selected for two reasons. First, many changes in both industries over the past decade are a reflection of the flexible, just-in-time mode of production that many U.S. industries have adopted to reduce costs in a period of heightened worldwide competition. Changes related to this style of production are well documented for the motor vehicle industry. In the help supply industry, the exceptional growth can be traced to the increasing use of just-in-time labor by businesses of all types. In this example, temporary workers provided by help supply agencies met the need for more flexibility in the size of a firm's staff; they are the labor equivalent of just-in-time production factors in the motor vehicle manufacturing industry.

The second reason for selecting these two industries is that they contrast with each other. The automobile industry is an older, established manufacturing industry; the help supply industry is a newer service industry. The automobile industry has nearly the same level of employment in 1998 as it did in 1979, whereas employment in the help supply industry has grown dramatically since 1982 (the year data were first published for the industry). The following sections explore these elements, along with the changes that have taken place in each industry's workforce.

Manufacturing employment has been a declining percent of total nonfarm jobs throughout most of the post World War II period. However, this belies the continuing importance of manufacturing activity on the economy's health. In particular, a host of manufacturing and service-producing industries rely on economic activity in motor vehicle manufacturing and sales. These include input industries such as steel, fabricated metals, chemicals, automotive electronics, as well as automotive dealers and car financing. In addition, the cyclical behavior of motor vehicle output and employment is critical for policy planning and business cycle analysis.[1] For motor vehicle manufacturers, the decade of the 1980s, characterized by foreign competition and trade disputes, gave way to a diverse and competitive industry landscape where quality, lean production, and new supplier-assembler relationships are paramount.[2] In this chapter, we focus on the motor vehicles assembly industry (SIC 3711) and its key suppliers, the motor vehicles parts industry (SIC 3714) and the automotive stampings industry (SIC 3465).[3] These supplier industries were selected, because of the large proportion of their output that goes to the assemblers. (The motor vehicles as-

sembly industry purchases about half of the output of the parts industry and three-quarters of the output of the stampers.)

Motor Vehicles Industry

Lean production and productivity growth

The problems for automobile manufacturers, brought to the fore by increased competition, have been how to reduce costs and maintain sales, while preserving vehicle reliability. The answer has been lean manufacturing techniques. Automakers began selling non-core businesses to focus their efforts on automotive manufacturing and to raise cash. They also began revising their internal structures and processes, in accordance with lean manufacturing principles. This enabled them to boost productivity and reduce costs. However, this process takes significant time and effort.[6]

The first step automobile manufacturers took in the 1990s to remedy their situation was to shift to new, improved methods of production under the heading *lean production*. Lean production is distinguished by its minimalist approach to factory management. Inventories are taken on a just-in-time basis, to reduce handling and to expose defective parts before they accumulate in the warehouse. Additionally, lean manufacturing requires a company to look at each detail of its organization and determine how *tasks* can be best organized, modified, eliminated, or combined for an efficient operation. Indirect labor is pared, and specialized labor is replaced with cross-trained production workers who rotate jobs. Employees also take on responsibility for quality control, repair, housekeeping, and preventive maintenance.[7] Moreover, lean manufacturing dictates that employees be empowered to make suggestions for improvements beneficial to the company.

Quality of the product is an important consideration in lean production, because well-made products reduce rework and warranty costs. All members of a team are authorized to take necessary steps and actions to ensure that quality goals are met. With this type of system, employees act as the quality control staff, thereby removing duplication of effort.

Greater reliance on suppliers

To further reduce costs and improve efficiency, manufacturers turned to their suppliers. One of the early steps taken was to reduce costs in the manufacturers' own parts operations. Typically, manufacturers depended on their in-house parts

6

Long-term Trends, 1987-98

Productivity, output, and hours. The period 1987-98, the years for which BLS has complete measures for labor productivity, output, and total hours for all manufacturing industries, included the end of the expansion of the 1980s, the brief 1990-91 recession, and the current expansion.[4] Labor productivity in the motor vehicles assembly industry grew at an average annual rate of 2.4 percent during the 1987-98 period. (See table 1-1.) Output increased 1.7 percent per year, whereas employee hours decreased 0.8 percent per year.[5] Trends in labor productivity of the motor vehicles suppliers were similar to those of the assemblers. Output per hour rose at an average annual rate of 1.8 percent in the motor vehicles parts industry and 2.1 percent annually in the automotive stampings industry. However, output growth has been more robust in the supplier industries than in the assembly industry. Output of the automotive stampings industry rose at an average annual rate of 3.3 percent. This was nearly double the growth rate in the assembly industry. The motor vehicles parts industry increased production 5.1 percent per year—three times as fast as the assembly industry. The supplier industries also recorded higher rates of growth in employee hours than did the assembly industry. Employee hours increased 1.2 percent per year in the automotive stampings industry and 3.2 percent annually in the motor vehicle parts industry.

Labor productivity and unit labor costs are closely related variables. Whereas productivity measures the hourly output of workers, unit labor costs measure compensation per unit of output. An increase in compensation per hour tends to increase unit labor costs, but an increase in productivity tends to reduce unit labor costs. Therefore, through its impact on unit labor costs, productivity is an important element in the wage-price relationship, because it is an indicator of the extent to which compensation gains can occur without putting pressure on prices.

Unit labor costs. Unit labor costs in the motor vehicles assembly industry increased at an average annual rate of 1.3 percent during the 1987-98 period. (See chart 1-1.) In contrast, unit labor costs were flat in the motor vehicles parts industry and actually declined 0.8 percent per year in the automotive stampings industry.

---

divisions to supply components, and these divisions usually did not have to compete with outside suppliers. However, beginning in the late 1980s and early 1990s, motor vehicles assemblers began to require their divisions to compete with outside suppliers. This put great pressure on in-house suppliers to improve efficiency and lower costs. Similarly, outside suppliers also had to improve efficiency and reduce costs, in order to compete with the larger in-house suppliers for contracts.

Seeking additional cost reductions, motor vehicles assemblers demanded that suppliers assume greater responsibility for design, development, and supply management. The suppliers responded with new product development processes that focused on integrated supply-base management. Expansion of supplier responsibility in design and product development resulted in a greater commonality of components between platforms, reducing time needed to develop new products. Suppliers also reduced costs by standardizing design and tooling. Additionally, suppliers' work-

ers earn substantially less than what major motor vehicle manufacturers' employees earn, resulting in lower labor costs. The most successful suppliers managed groups of individual component suppliers and oversaw the integration of these components into a final assembly delivered to the motor vehicle manufacturer. An example of this shift in responsibility to suppliers is the extended enterprise system of the Chrysler Corporation.[8]

These supplier changes produced entire modules or systems ready to be bolted onto chassis on the assembly line, thereby reducing the amount of labor, complexity of tasks, and costs required for assembly.[9] Whereas the modules themselves usually cost more than the sum of their parts, motor vehicle manufacturers come out ahead in the end, because of fewer injuries, fewer repairs, and lower labor costs.[10]

Materials to hours ratio. Evidence of the shift to greater reliance on suppliers is found by examining data on output per hour and materials per hour of the motor vehicles assembly industry. (See chart

7

1-2.)[11] From 1987 to 1996, output per hour in the motor vehicles assembly industry increased at an average annual rate of 1.8 percent. In comparison, the ratio of materials to hours of production in the motor vehicles assembly industry grew much faster, 3.9 percent per year. When this ratio is restricted to materials purchased from the motor vehicles parts industry, the ratio of materials to hours increased even more rapidly, rising 5.7 percent annually. Thus, the shift of responsibilities to suppliers resulted in an expansion in the use of purchased components or systems by the motor vehicles assembler.

Motor vehicle industry structure

During most of the 1990s, U.S. motor vehicles assembly firms included General Motors, Ford, and Chrysler (the Big Three), and nine foreign-or jointly-owned companies with American plants. The Big Three motor vehicles companies were first, second, and seventh in terms of 1997 worldwide vehicle production.[12] In late 1998, Chrysler Corporation and the German firm, Daimler-Benz AG, merged to form Daimler-Chrysler AG. This new company is ranked number five behind General Motors Corporation, Ford Motor Company, Toyota Corporation, and Volkswagen AG, in terms of worldwide production.[13]

North America, Western Europe, and the Asia-Pacific region dominate the global motor vehicle market, with the United States as the leading producer and consumer of automobiles and trucks. In 1998, the U.S. produced 12 million passenger and commercial vehicles, which represented one fifth of the motor vehicles produced worldwide. The United States is also the largest consumer of vehicles. In 1996, about a third of the 206 million worldwide vehicle registrations were located in this country.[14]

A host of foreign companies have set up shop on U.S. soil, helping to support American employment in the motor vehicles industry. These foreign companies were attracted by several factors, including proximity to the largest automobile market, a skilled labor force, trade considerations, and favorable currency fluctuations. This has resulted in the U.S. market share of imports decreasing. (See table 1-2.) U.S. motor vehicle companies have become global companies, with major production sites in Canada, Mexico, Germany, England, Spain, and Brazil. Overseas production is devoted to both local markets and the U.S. market.

U.S. motor vehicles and parts market. The value of personal consumption expenditures on motor vehicles and parts was $279 billion in the first quarter of 1999, whereas fixed investment in transportation equipment by producers represented an additional $167 billion.[15] Together, motor vehicle and related transportation equipment accounted for 5.8 percent of the GDP.

In 1998, sales of passenger cars and light trucks were 15.6 million units, with 52 percent of these cars and 48 percent trucks[16]. The light truck market includes pickup trucks, minivans and vans, and sport utility vehicles (SUVs). One U.S. market trend during the 1990s is the steady increase of the share of light truck sales, compared to cars. (See chart 1-3.) This trend continues, as U.S.-based factories respond to high demand for SUVs and other light trucks.

The after-tax profits of motor vehicles and equipment companies were $4.5 billion on $96 billion of sales in the fourth quarter of 1998.[17] This profit level is about one-tenth of all manufacturing's profits over the same period. After-tax profits of motor vehicles and equipment companies as a percent of sales—at 4.7 percent—are slightly above the rate for all manufacturing, 4.5 percent.

In 1997, there were 947 plants or installations devoted to motor vehicles assembly in more than 20 States.[18] About two-thirds of employment in these plants was located in Michigan (43 percent) and three other Midwest States: Ohio (13 percent), Missouri (5 percent), and Illinois (3 percent). Outside the Midwest, Kentucky and Tennessee also have emerged as important players, representing a combined 9 percent of the industry's employment. Transplants—foreign-owned motor vehicle assembly plants—have established a manufacturing presence in areas outside the Midwest, including Kentucky, Tennessee, North Carolina, Alabama, and California.[19] Employment is somewhat less concentrated in motor vehicles parts than assembly. Still, three Midwest States employed 49 percent of the motor vehicles parts workers in 1997: Michigan (24 percent), Ohio (13 percent), and Indiana (12 percent).

Workforce profile

Employment and earnings. Nearly a million people, or 5 percent of total manufacturing employment, work in the motor vehicles and equipment industry (SIC 371). More than three-fourths of these employees are production workers. In comparison, 69 percent of the employees are production workers in the manufacturing sector as a whole. The motor vehicles and equipment industry is highly organized, with nearly 36 percent of employees currently members of a union. In comparison, 16 percent of workers belong to unions in the manufacturing sector overall.[20]

Average weekly hours are higher for workers in motor vehicle manufacturing than for all workers in the manufacturing sector. Production workers in motor vehicles assembly worked longer weeks during the 1990s than in the 1980s, with the workweek increasing from 42 to 44 hours. (See chart 1-4.) By 1997, these production workers were on the job more than 45 hours per week. Average weekly overtime grew from 4 hours in the 1980s to over 7 hours in 1994. (See chart 1-5.) A lengthening workweek was also the trend in the motor vehicles supplier industries. Among motor vehicles parts manufacturers and automotive stampers, the workweek grew from 43 hours in the 1980s to 44 hours in the 1990s. Workers in the supplier industries also had more overtime hours in the 1990s than in the 1980s, with average weekly overtime rising from 4.5 to almost 6 hours in the motor vehicles parts industry. Stampers gained nearly an hour of weekly overtime work in the 1990s, compared to the 1980s.

Earnings of production workers in the motor vehicle industry are also significantly higher than the average earnings of all production workers in the manufacturing sector. Earnings in manufacturing, which includes overtime pay, grew at an annual rate of 4.8 percent from 1960 to 1998, compared to a 5.0 percent rate in transportation equipment. Excluding overtime, the annual growth rate in earnings for transportation equipment workers was a tenth of a percent lower than earnings including overtime. This indicates that the upward trend in overtime hours played a role in the increased earnings in this industry. (See table 1-3.) Within the motor vehicle industry, the highest earnings are in motor vehicles assembly. Not only are motor vehicles assembly workers earning more than manufacturing workers overall, their earnings are also rising faster than average manufacturing earnings. The annual growth rate in average hourly earnings from 1960 to 1998 was 5.4 percent for auto assembly workers, compared to 4.8 percent for overall manufacturing.[21]

Wage rates of production workers in the motor vehicles *supplier* industries also are higher than average rates in all manufacturing industries taken together, but lower than rates paid to motor vehicles assemblers. In 1960, production workers in the motor vehicles parts industry earned one fifth more than people employed in all manufacturing industries, but their wage rate was 5 percent lower than motor vehicles assemblers. In 1998, parts workers continued to earn a fifth more than other manufacturing workers but earned a third less than motor vehicles assemblers. Automotive stampers also earn more than the manufacturing sector, but less than motor vehicles assemblers. Production workers in the automotive stampings industry earn a third more than the manufacturing average but a fourth less than assemblers.

Occupational and demographic profile. The age composition and occupational mix of the workforce of the motor vehicles and equipment industry changed little during the 1990s. The largest occupational group in motor vehicle and equipment (SIC 371) is production, operating, and material handling occupations, comprising 73 percent of employment in 1996.[22] A third of production workers in motor vehicle production are assemblers, including precision machine and electronic assemblers, structural metal fitters, and welders and cutters. Machine setters and operators represent another third of these production workers.

Managerial, administrative, and clerical support positions represent about 10 percent of the motor vehicle workforce, whereas 15 percent are employed in the professional and technical occupations (engineering, statistics, computer and physical sciences, and law). These shares are comparable with those for manufacturing overall.

Whereas women held just under half of the total nonfarm jobs and a third of manufacturing jobs in 1998, they held just below a fourth of the jobs in motor vehicles and equipment. However, this share is up from 14 percent in 1978, a peak year in employment for this industry.[23] The age distribution in the industry followed manufacturing and the overall economy, with 55 percent of workers between the ages of 25 and 44 and 35 percent between 45 and 64 years old. Just over 82 percent of motor vehicles and equipment workers were white workers in 1998, compared to 84 percent in the manufacturing sector.[24]

Benefits. Most workers in the motor vehicles and equipment industry (94 percent in 1993) are offered some kind of health insurance coverage by their employers. The comparable coverage rate for total manufacturing was 90 percent.[25] Nearly three-quarters of workers in the motor vehicles

9

and equipment industry are covered by a retirement plan, whereas less than half of total private workers have such benefits. In particular, employers of almost 60 percent of workers in this industry offered a 401(k) plan, and more than 60 percent of these workers contributed to their plans. Over 70 percent of motor vehicles and equipment workers have paid sick leave or sickness insurance, compared to just over half of total private workers. Three-fifths of these industry workers have a short-term disability coverage of 5 to 6 months.

Employment trends

Assemblers. The most recent contraction of employment in the motor vehicles assembly industry began in the mid-1980s and extended into the 1990-91 recession. (See chart 1-6.) The number of employees decreased every year from 1985 to 1991. Bottoming out at 313,200 employees, the 1991 level of employment was only two-thirds of the peak employment level reached in 1978. (The last year that employment dipped below 313,000 was during the 1960-61 recession.)

A weak recovery began in 1992, as assemblers added 1,900 employees to their workforce. Employment grew modestly in 1993, reaching 319,700 workers. Larger additions were made to the workforce in 1994 and 1995. Assemblers increased employment by 6.8 percent in 1994. Another 4.7 percent were added to the roster in 1995, raising industry employment to 357,400 workers. The employment situation in the last half of the 1990s has been mixed. Motor vehicles assemblers cut 11,500 jobs in 1996, but added 1,900 in 1997. In 1998 employment dropped back to 341,800 workers, only 73 percent of the 1978 peak employment.

Suppliers. The employment story of the motor vehicles parts industry has been different from that of the motor vehicles assembly industry. The number of employees in the parts industry rose every year since the 1981-82 recession, except for 1986 and 1990. The parts industry has hired 223,500 workers, an average increase of 3.3 percent per year, from 1982 to 1998. The fastest growth in employment occurred in the 1990s. From 1990 to 1998, employment in the motor vehicles parts industry grew at an average annual rate of 4.0 percent. Employment reached a new high in 1998 of 546,800 workers. The number of people working in the parts industry surpassed that of the assembly industry for the first time in 1981 and has remained higher than assembly employment since 1987.

Employment growth in the automotive stampings industry has been weaker than in the motor vehicles parts industry but stronger than in the motor vehicles assembly industry. Employment peaked at 118,300 workers in 1978, before falling to 94,400 in the 1990-91 recession. The peak level was nearly attained again in 1996, when the number of workers climbed to 117,000. Since 1996, 2,900 jobs have been lost, bringing employment down to 114,100 in 1998.

Increased competition and lower prices

Increased competition. Throughout the late 1980s and 1990s, the domestic motor vehicles industry has been in a state of increasing competition, due to the significant amount of overcapacity in the industry. Executives from the Big Three manufacturers estimate overcapacity equivalent to approximately 80 factories.[26]

Increased competition, due to overcapacity, has caused motor vehicles assemblers to change pricing strategies. Typically, manufacturers increase prices at model year introduction and intermittently throughout the year. This trend has changed. Price increases have been small, and there have actually been some price declines recently, particularly in the passenger car segment. (See chart 1-7.) The Big Three manufacturers have continued to lose market share to transplants and import brands. For example, in 1993, the Big Three held 66 percent of the market; but by 1997, this percentage had fallen to 60 percent.[27]

Light truck manufacturers have also started to feel increased competitive pressure, as more models enter the market. In 1993, there were 429 light truck models offered in the domestic market. By 1998, this number had increased to 573, a 30 percent increase. The largest portion of this increase came from the Big Three, who increased the number of models offered from 383 in 1996 to 456 in 1998. (Imports and transplant manufacturers added seven models during this period.)[28] Even with this large gain in the number of models, the Big Three are beginning to lose market share. From 1993 to 1996, their market share hovered around 86 percent. In 1997, this percentage fell to 84.8 percent.[29]

Incentives have gained importance in the U.S. market, as manufacturers try to lure buyers into showrooms to buy their products. These incentives include low rate financing, as well as cash incentives that lower the overall transaction price to consumers. In addition, incentives can enable a manufacturer's product to stand out from the

10

competition and may sway customers. Dealers, too, are offered incentives, which they can choose to pass on to consumers in terms of lower negotiated prices, without sacrificing profit margins. Even in a period of low interest rates, the contemporary market requires incentives.

A relatively flat market has compounded the competition problem. Light vehicle sales have remained around 15 million units per year for the past several years, with increases in truck sales offsetting declines in passenger car sales. (See table 1-2.) The declining sales of passenger cars are due to several factors.

Consumers are keeping their vehicles longer than they did. According to a report from the International Trade Administration, the ownership period of passenger cars increased from 4.6 years in 1985 to 5.7 years in 1995. A partial explanation of this trend is that as new car prices increased rapidly—outstripping the growth in disposable personal income—many buyers were forced to hold on to their vehicles. (See table 1-4.) In addition, quality improvements in vehicles have enabled consumers to extend the lives of their vehicles.[30] The median age of passenger cars on the road rose from 6.5 years in 1990 to 8.3 years in 1998.[31] Furthermore, in 1997, the median age of passenger cars was 8.1 years.[32]

Price changes. As stated above, increased competition has been a major factor affecting motor vehicle prices. (See chart 1-8.) Motor vehicle prices, as measured by the Producer Price Index, rose sharply in the 1980s and early 1990s before leveling off in the mid-1990s. Vehicle prices increased roughly 14 percent over the period 1990 to 1994, averaging 3.6 percent per year. Increases in 1995 and 1996 slowed to about 1 percent per year. 1997 and 1998 saw a different trend, declining prices, as the PPI fell approximately 1 percent per year.

Lower overall inflation over the past several years, as measured by the Consumer Price Index (CPI) and the PPI, has also benefited automakers. For the period 1990-98, the CPI rose, on average, 3 percent per year. The PPI, on average, rose 1.6 percent per year during the same period. Lower inflation has enabled manufacturers to hold down prices without suffering significant cuts in profit margins. Suppliers have been able to provide components and parts to the manufacturers at constant or lower prices without much price or profit pressure. The prices from motor vehicle suppliers demonstrate this fact.

Prices of motor vehicles suppliers also rose in the 1980s and flattened in the 1990s. Prices of motor vehicles parts rose at an average annual rate of 1.2 percent from 1983 to 1990. Since 1990, the growth rate of prices has been reduced by more than half to 0.5 percent per year. The automotive stampings industry registered a 1.1 percent annual growth rate in prices in the 1980s; but since 1990, prices have risen a negligible 0.1 percent per year. (See chart 1-8.)

Transition and recession, 1987-91

Productivity, output, and hours. A sharp increase and subsequent leveling off of productivity growth in the motor vehicles assembly industry marked the final years of the expansion of the 1980s. Labor productivity grew a robust 9.9 percent in 1988. Assemblers increased output 5.3 percent, despite a cutback in employee hours of 4.2 percent. Productivity, output, and hours changed little in 1989. However, output per hour fell 1.3 percent in 1990, as output and hours plunged 9.3 percent and 8 percent, respectively. Labor productivity of assemblers declined an additional 5.3 percent in the 1991 recession year, as output dropped almost twice as fast as hours. The final years of the expansion of the 1980s were also volatile for the parts industry. Output per hour rose 4.8 percent in 1988. Output grew a robust 10.8 percent, whereas employee hours increased much less, 5.8 percent. Labor productivity declined 5.9 percent in 1989. Although production fell 4.6 percent, hours rose 1.4 percent. The automotive stampings industry registered productivity declines in both 1988 and 1989. In 1988, employee hours grew almost three times as fast as output, resulting in a drop in productivity of 3.7 percent. Output per hour fell another 3.5 percent in 1989. Employee hours rose 0.7 percent, and production decreased 2.8 percent. Suppliers felt the 1990-91 recession less than motor vehicles assemblers. The parts industry recorded productivity growth of 2.1 percent in 1990 and a drop in productivity of 2.5 percent in 1991. Output declined in both 1990 and 1991, 4.1 percent and 3.3 percent, respectively. The decline in output per hour was somewhat greater in the stampings industry, 3.8 percent in 1990, and 3.1 percent in 1991. Sizable drops in output of automotive stampers were accompanied by smaller reductions in employee hours.

Unit labor costs. The motor vehicles and equipment industry experienced highly volatile unit labor costs during the 1987-91 period. After declining 6.4 percent in 1988, unit labor costs of motor vehicle assemblers increased 8.3 percent in 1989 and 6.6 percent in 1990. Unit labor costs skyrocketed 12.9 percent in the 1990-91 recession. Among the supplier industries, unit labor costs increased in the early years of the 1987-91 period and then fell in later years. From 1987 to 1990, unit labor costs grew 3.7 percent per year in the motor vehicles parts industry and 5.2 percent annually in the automotive stampings industry. Unit labor costs continued to rise during the 1990-91 recession, 4 percent in the parts industry, and 7.8 percent in the stampings industry.

Current expansion, 1991 to present

Productivity, output, and hours. The adoption of lean production practices, as well as plant characteristics, such as large-scale production, operating near capacity (at select plants), and automation contributed to the productivity gains registered by the motor vehicles and equipment industry in the post-recession 1990s.[33] Recovering from the 1990-91 recession, motor vehicles assemblers boosted labor productivity 3.4 percent annually in the 1991-98 period. The growth in output per hour reflected a 4.9-percent annual gain in output and a 1.4-percent annual increase in employee hours. The supplier industries also made strong recoveries during the current expansion. From 1991 to 1998, output per hour grew at an average annual rate of 3.1 percent in the parts industry. Parts production increased 8.4 percent per year, whereas employee hours grew 5.2 percent annually. Similar growth rates were recorded by the automotive stampings industry. Labor productivity grew 5.4 percent annually, as output rose 8.5 percent per year; and hours grew 3 percent per year.

Unit labor costs. The motor vehicles and equipment industry reined in labor costs in the current expansion. From 1991 to 1998, unit labor costs of assemblers declined 0.9 percent per year. During the same period, parts manufacturers cut unit labor costs, on average, by 2.0 percent annually. The automotive stampings industry had even greater success in controlling costs, reducing them 4.4 percent per year.

Other cost reduction efforts

Beyond the implementation of lean production methods and the greater reliance on suppliers, motor vehicles assemblers have been gaining greater efficiencies on the production line by reducing the number of model combinations being built. This is accomplished through a reduction in the number of options and packages offered to consumers, as well as a reduction in the number of trim levels of any given vehicle. Reducing the complexity of combinations on the assembly line reduces the cost of production through several means. Line workers become more familiar with the process and their tasks, so there are fewer errors and less rework required. Less inventory needs to be placed at the assembly station and fewer steps are required in the process, because a smaller product mix is offered. This also reduces the amount of space on the line, which enables manufacturers to better utilize factory floor space.

Manufacturers are using other methods of cost reduction, as well. In an effort to speed up the vehicle design process, specialized computer-aided design software in the research and development (R&D) phase is being used. Many of these systems enable manufacturers to see how a design will work and correct problems before actually committing to tooling to build a prototype. Designing a vehicle on a computer also allows manufacturers to reduce the amount of time needed for R&D. This enables manufacturers to get a design to market before consumer tastes change. This process requires fewer employees and allows all divisions of the company to have input into the design before resources are committed. An extension of this is that suppliers also have access to these systems and are able to find less expensive ways to design parts and modules for a particular vehicle—or group of vehicles—which may use common parts.

Manufacturers also are attempting to standardize components, including powertrains, interiors, chassis, and platforms, across models. By designing components that are used on different models (and even in different markets), manufacturers are able to gain production efficiencies and lower costs. R&D costs and the amount of inventory and space needed can be reduced, and production workers are less prone to errors and rework, when a common design is employed.

Conclusion

The United States is both the leading producer and the leading consumer of cars and trucks. Not only do many manufacturing industries depend on the production and sales of motor vehicles (steel, fabricated metals, chemicals, and automotive electronics); but several service industries (automotive dealers, auto repair shops, and the auto financing industry) depend on the vehicle industry. Therefore, policy planners and business cycle analysts closely follow the cyclical behavior of the motor vehicle industry.

Nearly one million people work in the motor vehicles and equipment industry. Their workweek is longer and their hourly wage rate is higher than the averages in the manufacturing sector overall. Insurance and retirement plans cover most of these workers.

From the end of the 1980s and continuing through 1998, motor vehicle manufacturers faced stiff competition, at the same time that demand for their products flattened. The primary reason for the intense competition was that motor vehicle assembly plants were operating well below capacity. Improvements in the quality of vehicles, together with high prices, caused consumers to postpone the purchase of new cars, thus lengthening the replacement cycle. Simultaneously, consumer preferences shifted from cars to light trucks. Minivan sales surged early in the decade, and sports utility vehicle sales grew at the end of the decade. The share of industry receipts from passenger car sales fell, whereas the share of industry receipts from light truck sales rose.

To boost sales, motor vehicle assemblers attempted to reduce costs, maintain quality, and, ultimately, to price vehicles in a way that would attract customers. In their effort to lower costs, the motor vehicle industry adopted lean production techniques. Lean production is a minimalist approach to factory management where cross-trained workers are responsible for quality control, repair, housekeeping, and preventive maintenance, in addition to producing the cars. Further cost reductions are achieved by shifting many design, development, and supply management tasks from assemblers to suppliers. The efforts of the motor vehicles and equipment manufacturers paid off with gains in output above gains in hours, thus increasing productivity. The expansions in output, hours, and productivity recorded by the suppliers was larger than the gains recorded by the assemblers.

Temporary Help in Auto Manufacturing

In this chapter, we have analyzed in detail two very different industries. A natural question that follows is, do these industries interact? Whereas input-output tables of the U.S. economy measure the transactions between the two industries ($274 million worth of services purchased by auto manufacturers from personnel supply in 1992), they do not tell us much about this relationship. Temporary help firms are unable to state how much of their output goes into manufacturing, let alone one industry within that sector.[79] In 1995, a trade journal attempted to gauge the number of temps working in auto manufacturing in Detroit. While two of the Big Three declined to answer, Chrysler Corporation said it had 2,000 *contract* workers.[80] However, a contract worker is not necessarily a temp.

In spite of sparse data on the use of temp help agencies by the auto industry, some insight can be gleaned from efforts related to welfare reform. A number of States began experimenting with new aid programs for welfare recipients before the Federal Government enacted the Personal Responsibility and Work Opportunity Reconciliation Act in 1996, commonly known as welfare reform.[81] The two industries analyzed in this chapter played a part in both the early State efforts and the recent Federal welfare reform program.

The primary functions of help supply services establishments are recruiting, screening, training, and placing individuals in jobs. These skills work well with the objective of welfare reform—to place people who are receiving assistance into the job market where they can earn a living.[82] "Welfare to work makes good business sense, because there are many jobs that are going unfilled and many candidates who want to work," says the CEO of Manpower, Inc.[83]

Beginning in 1995, Kelly Services, one of the largest help supply companies, began working to place welfare recipients into the labor force in Michigan, in an alliance with government and a community college.[84] The Oakland Community College's Advanced Technology Program takes welfare recipients with dependent children and trains them in computer skills, while providing certain benefits and childcare. The 15-week program ends, when the recipient is placed in a high-tech position as a Kelly Services employee at General Motors' Centerpoint facility in Pontiac, Michigan. By late 1998, this program had graduated 87 individuals; overall, Kelly employed more than 300 people at the Centerpoint facility.[85]

13

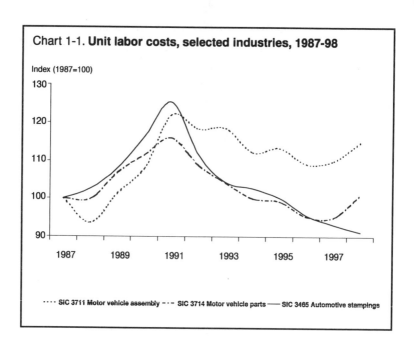

Chart 1-1. **Unit labor costs, selected industries, 1987-98**

Index (1987=100)

···· SIC 3711 Motor vehicle assembly –·– SIC 3714 Motor vehicle parts ——— SIC 3465 Automotive stampings

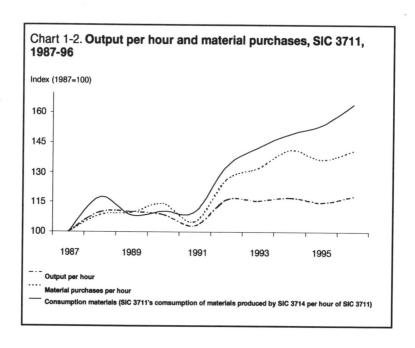

Chart 1-2. **Output per hour and material purchases, SIC 3711, 1987-96**

Index (1987=100)

–·– Output per hour

···· Material purchases per hour

——— Consumption materials (SIC 3711's comsumption of materials produced by SIC 3714 per hour of SIC 3711)

14

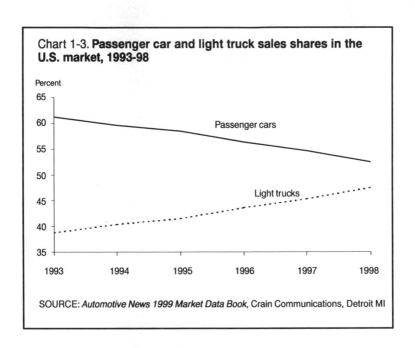

Chart 1-3. **Passenger car and light truck sales shares in the U.S. market, 1993-98**

Percent

Passenger cars

Light trucks

SOURCE: *Automotive News 1999 Market Data Book*, Crain Communications, Detroit MI

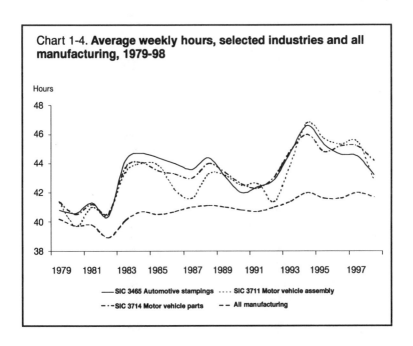

Chart 1-4. **Average weekly hours, selected industries and all manufacturing, 1979-98**

Hours

SIC 3465 Automotive stampings .... SIC 3711 Motor vehicle assembly

—·–SIC 3714 Motor vehicle parts – – All manufacturing

15

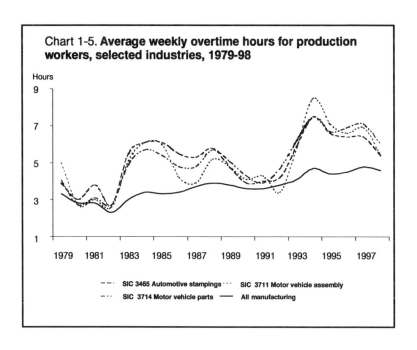

Chart 1-5. Average weekly overtime hours for production workers, selected industries, 1979-98

Hours

- - - SIC 3465 Automotive stampings · · · SIC 3711 Motor vehicle assembly
- · · SIC 3714 Motor vehicle parts —— All manufacturing

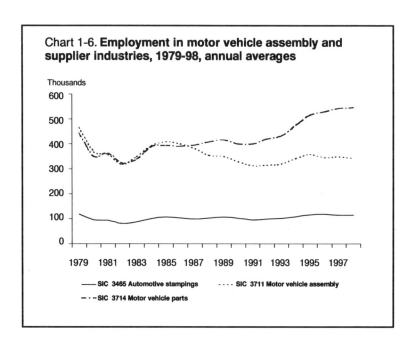

Chart 1-6. Employment in motor vehicle assembly and supplier industries, 1979-98, annual averages

Thousands

—— SIC 3465 Automotive stampings · · · · SIC 3711 Motor vehicle assembly
— · —SIC 3714 Motor vehicle parts

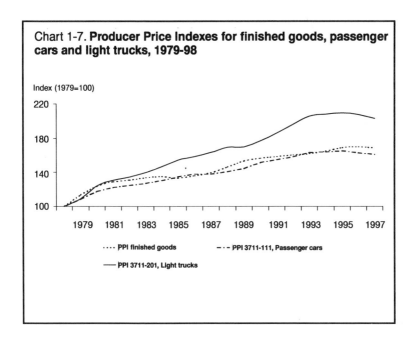

Chart 1-7. **Producer Price Indexes for finished goods, passenger cars and light trucks, 1979-98**

Index (1979=100)

···· PPI finished goods   − · − PPI 3711-111, Passenger cars

——— PPI 3711-201, Light trucks

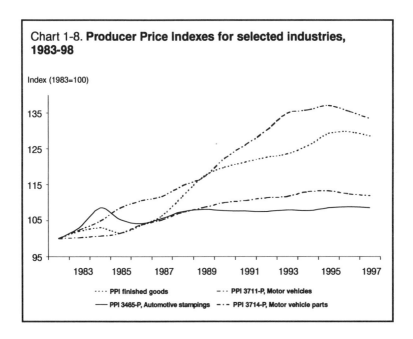

Chart 1-8. **Producer Price Indexes for selected industries, 1983-98**

Index (1983=100)

···· PPI finished goods   − ·· PPI 3711-P, Motor vehicles

——— PPI 3465-P, Automotive stampings   − · − PPI 3714-P, Motor vehicle parts

Help Supply Services

Employers that have flexibility in adjusting labor requirements to meet product and service demands have a competitive edge over those with less flexible human resource policies. The contingent work force that accommodates fluctuations in labor requirements has become an increasing segment of the labor market. Whereas the standard work arrangement remains the full-time, permanent job, variants from that standard to provide just-in-time labor have become commonplace. The definition of this kind of *alternative* or *contingent* labor varies widely.

BLS studies of contingent work have focused primarily on whether a job includes the expectation of long-term employment.[34] The definition of contingent workers oftentimes includes not only persons hired for temporary positions, but also the self-employed, part-time workers, those involved in home-based work, and independent contractors, among others.[35]

One group of contingent workers is distinguished from the others, in that they have agreed to short-term employment contracts arranged through help supply services companies. This group of temporary employees is the only part of the contingent workforce that is identified in the SIC structure. Thus, more data are available for help supply services employees than for other contingent workers. This category of just-in-time employment is the focus of the remainder of this chapter.

Help supply services (SIC 7363) is the largest component of the personnel supply services industry (SIC 736); temporary help agencies dominate help supply services.[36] The help supply industry primarily involves the contracting of labor for short periods of time. The only other significant component of personnel supply services is employment agencies (SIC 7361), which provides permanent placement and recruiting services. Employment agencies accounted for less than 12 percent of employment in the personnel supply industry group in 1998, with this primarily a count of the administrative staff of the agencies. However, the differences between help supply and employment agencies are becoming blurred, because many companies now offer both types of services.

Besides temporary help agencies, help supply services include employee leasing services. However, this is a very small component of the industry.[37] Hence, temporary help agencies dominate both the help supply services industry (SIC 7363) and its *parent*, the personnel supply industry (SIC 736). This fact is important, because the Current Population Survey (CPS) provides demographic detail for the personnel supply industry but not separately for the help supply industry. For this reason, data used in this chapter refer to the personnel supply industry (SIC 736), unless otherwise noted.

Most temporary help workers have full-time jobs and work less than a year in an assignment. The majority do not work indefinitely as temporaries.[38] Even though temporary workers report to clients at a variety of sites, they receive their pay from the temporary help firm, their employer of record.

Increasingly, businesses are turning to personnel supply firms to supplement their work force. Historically, this industry has been associated with staffing for seasonal and fluctuating workloads. However, recent growth has been spurred by competitive strategies to increase flexibility and decrease cost within organizations, increasing growth in project-related assignments, and the use of temporary staffing arrangements as a screening device for hiring potential permanent employees.

Industry portrait–rapid growth

Help supply services employment grew from 0.6 percent of the total private economy in 1982 to 2.7 percent in 1998—a rate of growth surpassing even computer and data processing employment. (See chart 1-9.) Despite its small size, the industry accounts for a large portion of increased work activity over the past several years, and particularly in the years following economic recessions. Help supply service workers (more commonly known as temporaries or temps) are particularly sought by businesses, when increased economic activity is tentative. At these times, firms fear the hiring of permanent staff only to be forced to cut employment later, if the increased activity does not prove sustainable. (See chart 1-10.)

The volatility of the help supply services industry is due in part to its role as a buffer for changes in economic demand, with employers turning to help supply services when they're not certain that an economic recovery is reliably underway. The tendency for this industry to grow rapidly as the economy comes out of a recession is enhanced by a large pool of available labor, with the reverse also true as the economy enters the latter stages of an expansion. (See chart 1-11.) Reliance on the availability of a supplementary labor pool has resulted in significant volatility in the personnel supply industry and possibly less volatility in employment growth for the industries

18

Terms Defining Leasing and Temporary Employees

Employment in help supply services includes a small portion of employment attributed to employee leasing firms. Leasing arrangements provide a cost-effective human resources alternative for small firms. According to the National Association of Professional Employer Organizations (NAPEO), member leasing firms report an average of 14 employees per client work site.[39] Essentially, businesses contract with staffing companies that specialize in human resource and administration functions, leaving managers more time to devote to the activity of their businesses. Employee leasing is similar to the help supply component in that increased use of temporary help supply may also reflect companies' focus on core functions. Employee leasing is different from help supply, in that personnel are assigned to the staffing firm on a long-term, rather than on a short-term basis. Frequently, an employer transfers existing and future staff to the leasing agency's payroll but retains hiring and training functions.

The rapid growth of employee leasing in the late 1980s was related to changes in tax laws affecting the calculation of coverage tests for benefit plans. Amendments to the Employee Retirement Income Security Act of 1984 and the Tax Reform Act of 1986 were instrumental in changing employer incentives to provide benefits.[40] This growth in the number of employees under leasing arrangements had an impact on the industry classification of workers. Leasing agencies are asked to complete a multiple worksite report (MWR) form to identify the industry of each of their clients. If they do not do so, leased workers that previously were counted in the industry of the business site are counted in help supply services. Whereas most leasing firms complete the MWR (83 percent of establishments in 1996), firms that failed to do so add to the employment count in help supply services and diminish it in the industry where the primary work activity took place. Following an initial development period between 1987 and 1990, when the NAPEO indicated that leasing firms quadrupled, employee leasing services have grown at a rate similar to help supply services. Over the last several years, leased employees accounted for 16 percent of employment in help supply services.

it serves. In the most recent recession (1990-91), employment in the private economy, as measured by the Current Employment Statistics (CES) Survey, fell only 1.4 percent over the year, compared to 5.3 percent in the personnel supply industry. Job reductions in help supply in the most recent recession were less severe than in the 1974 and 1981-82 recessions, partly because the 1990-91 recession lasted only half as long; and the overall drop in employment was less steep.

Worker portrait

Demographic makeup. What characteristics do workers in this industry have? Perhaps the single greatest common denominator among personnel supply workers is that they tend to be young. At least half of these workers are under age 35, with only a small percentage over the age of 45. Interestingly, even as temporary help employment has expanded, the age distribution of personnel supply workers has remained unchanged. This has held true, although the rate of growth in the population of the young has declined.[41] Many students turn to staffing services for employment.

(Twenty-one percent of temporary workers in a 1997 survey came to their first assignment as a temporary directly out of school.) Combined with a turnover rate of 393 percent in 1997, an absence of "aging" in the temporary work force also implies that workers are not temping throughout their careers.[42] For many temporary help workers, this is a transition to a permanent career.[43]

Although a majority of temporary help workers are white, the proportion is smaller than among workers in traditional arrangements.[44] Unlike workers in traditional jobs, the majority of temporary help workers are women. Since 1982, however, the percent of help supply workers who are women declined, and the percent of all persons on nonfarm payrolls who are women increased. (See chart 1-12.) Both proportions have been relatively stable since 1994 and stood at 53 percent women in help supply and 48 percent on all nonfarm payrolls in 1998.

Occupational and industrial trends. The proportion of male workers in the personnel supply industry grew, as blue-collar positions surged from 9 percent of all temporary help workers in 1983 to 23 percent in 1993.[45] According to a February 1997 CPS supplement, over 41 percent of male temps are operators, fabricators, and laborers, whereas more than 50 percent of female temps work in administrative-support functions.[46] These proportions were little changed from the original CPS supplement of 1995.[47] Growth in blue-collar occupations was verified by payroll data in a survey conducted for the National Association of Temporary and Staffing Services (NATSS), covering the period that males were increasing their participation in the industry. In 1997, the industrial category represented 34 percent of payroll, second only to the office and clerical segment, as the gap between the two narrowed over time.[48] The technical and professional payroll has changed little in recent years, and the percent of payroll attributed to medical services has declined. (See chart 1-13.)

Identifying the industries supported by temp help is problematic, because temporary help firms typically do not maintain records on the industries of their clients. The large volume and rapid turnover of companies for whom temp agencies provide employees make such data gathering very difficult. Also, temporary help firms have little need for the specific industrial classification of their clients. In contrast, the specific *occupation* for which the agency provides temporary help is very important to both the temp agency and the client firm. Therefore, excellent data exist on occupations of temp help workers but not on the industry to which they are assigned. However, a supplement to the CPS conducted in 1995, and then again in 1997, attempted to identify the industries where temporary employees work. Through follow-up questions to persons who identified themselves—or someone in their household—as a temporary worker, these surveys indicated that the percent of all temporary workers placed in manufacturing was 34 in 1995 and 32 in 1997. Thirty-nine percent of all temporaries were in the services group in 1995, whereas 42 percent were there in 1997. Surprisingly, the percentage of women temporaries placed into manufacturing positions was relatively high—26 percent in 1995 and 27 percent in 1997. Significant proportions of male temps were found in the service sector, 30 percent in 1995 and 31 percent in 1997.[49] Whereas women have a greater association with services and a lesser affinity to manufacturing, male workers reflect the opposite image. Given the small proportion of manufacturing to the overall economy, this would suggest a greater use of temporary services by manufacturing industries.

The migration of males into temporary help occurred coincident to a steady increase in temporary help employment in the category of operators, fabricators, and laborers over the decade. (See table 1-5.) This category contains machine setters, set-up operators, and assemblers and fabricators—occupations that typically are manufacturing-related. Helpers, laborers, and material movers—a very large component of operators, fabricators, and laborers—provide support for a variety of industries. In contrast to the growth in these blue-collar occupations, the share of temporaries in administrative occupations declined, as did the shares in professional specialty and technician occupations. However, the data do not reveal what industries are associated with these declines.

Worker skills. Whereas the occupational data do not reveal the industries being supported by personnel supply workers, they do indicate that the work force is relatively low skilled. The proportion of clerical and administrative workers in temporary help is more than double the proportion represented in the aggregate labor force, and the same is true of the operators, fabricators, and laborers category. Since these two categories comprise about two-thirds of employment in temporary help, one would expect that overall educational attainment would reflect similarly low levels. Since only about 16 percent of *all* employees in administrative support and 5 percent of all operators, fabricators, and laborers are college graduates, one would expect that the educational attainment level of temporary help workers would be low.[50] Surprisingly, 22 percent have a college degree—a rate nearly identical to that of the general population—with only 11 percent having not earned a high school diploma.[51] Among workers in traditional arrangements, 30 percent had college degrees in 1996.[52] The most common level of education reported by a temporary worker was "less than a bachelor's degree."

Although temporary workers in the aggregate have more education than their jobs require, education is only one measure of a person's ability to perform a job. To some extent, a desire for temporary employment also can reflect individual preferences for leisure over work, as some workers do not want the inflexibility inherent in full-time jobs. Temporary workers may also face a period of time when they place priority on other life events. For example, the recent birth of a child is often associated with a desire for flexibility and can increase the propensity for part-time employment.[53] Whereas this is the case for a minority of workers—24 percent of those surveyed by NATSS indicated that they did *not* want a full-time permanent job—the majority would have preferred a full-time position.

Hours and earnings

Do workers in the help supply services industry have lower pay and fewer hours of work each week than coworkers in more traditional job arrangements? The earnings and hours of individuals in temporary work arrangements appear to be determined more by the *type* of work performed than by the industry. In fact, some temporary workers in white-collar occupations are paid more than permanent coworkers.[54] At the other end of the spectrum, some employees of the help supply services industry have experienced problems being paid what Federal law mandates. These situations will be viewed in more detail later in this section.

Another misconception of help supply services employees is that they are primarily part-time workers. Although these workers averaged about 27 hours each week in 1982, by 1996, the average workweek was equal to that of all workers in the services sector. (See chart 1-14.) This, coupled with the huge growth in the number of employees in this industry, shows an increased *intensity* of their use, which may reflect the change in the occupational mix of the industry. However, the *duration* of temporary workers' assignments is very short, compared with traditional employment, as the pool of workers making up this industry's labor force turns over much faster than the pool of those in more traditional work arrangements. A special supplement to the CPS completed in 1995 determined that 42 percent of temps had been at their current assignment less than 3 months, 72 percent less than 9 months, and only 16 percent had spent more than a year in their current assignment.[55]

The unemployment rate of persons who most recently were employed in the personnel supply industry is high--usually three times the rate for all workers in private industry. In 1998, 14 percent of personnel supply service workers were unemployed, compared to 5 percent among all private wage and salary workers. Since those who quit working because they no longer want to work are not counted as unemployed, one must assume that there are other reasons for this unemployment, even though a portion of these individuals may have simply been waiting for their next temporary assignment. At any rate, temporary workers are unemployed with greater frequency than other groups, partly due to the nature of the tem-

porary help industry. Temps appear to be at the mercy of business cycles, far more than the employees of other industries. When the economy enters a downturn, these workers quickly feel the pinch in their paychecks, and average weekly earnings show declines during recessions. As the economy returns to growth, temps make pay gains with equal vigor. This variability can be an attractive feature to establishments considering using the help supply industry's services. The high turnover of temps would be a factor in allowing wages to be responsive to economic conditions.[56] A portrait of earnings *variability* in help supply services is shown in chart 1-15.

When comparing wages of temporary workers to wages of permanent workers, several caveats should be observed. Permanent workers normally have more firm-specific knowledge and on-the-job experience, because they have been at the same establishment for a longer period of time. Consequently, it is reasonable for wage rates to reflect these differences. Also, as wages are only one of several components of compensation, permanent employees receive additional pay in forms other than wages: Health and life insurance, transportation subsidies, paid travel, etc. By comparison, temps generally have few benefits. (This topic is discussed in more detail in a later section.)

In observing hours and earnings, and comparing them to the services industry division, a notable trend appears. Whereas average weekly hours increased for individuals in help supply services to equal those of all services by 1996, earnings moved in the opposite direction. Wage gains over time have not matched those of other service industries. In 1982, average hourly earnings for nonsupervisory workers in the help supply industry were $5.97. This was 86 percent of the level in all services. By 1998, average hourly earnings had moved up to $10.18 in help supply services—less than 80 percent of the wage in all services. Whereas a changing composition of the occupations within help supply services may explain this growing discrepancy in earnings, it is unclear if that is the only factor.

Workers supplied by temp agencies encompass those in high-paid occupations, as well as those in some of the lowest-paying jobs. An example of a premium pay occupation is computer programming. The assignments this type of work generates fit well with help supply services output. For example, when a business is in need of a specific type of programming skill to complete just one task, temps are often the best choice. Because employers pay by the hour and offer few benefits, temporary workers' wages may be higher

Productivity Measures and the Help Supply Industry

Labor productivity for an industry is measured as the ratio of output, the goods or services produced, to labor input—the amount of hours worked—for a specified time such as a year. The total amount of goods or services produced is generally determined by counting the volume of goods and services produced or by deflating the value of goods and services produced with an appropriate price index. Labor input is a count of all hours worked by all employees in an industry during a period of production.

The help supply industry supplies (produces) labor services to other businesses. Output is the number of labor hours supplied to other businesses, and the labor input is the number of hours worked by employees of the help supply establishment who find and place temporary workers in positions. Presently, employment and hours data collected for this industry include both employees who work for the industry, placing the temporary workers, and the temporary workers themselves. As such, neither a correct labor input measure can be estimated from these data, nor can these data be used to estimate the quantity of services being produced by this industry. Furthermore, a deflated value measure of output cannot be calculated at present, because the Producer Price Index for the help supply industry has been calculated for only the past 4 years.

What effect does the help supply industry have on productivity measures of *other* industries which use its output? Has the growth of this industry begun to boost labor productivity, as measured, in the industries to which the labor are supplied, including auto manufacturing? To the extent that temps—whose hours of work are counted as labor input in the service sector–produce output in manufacturing, measured labor productivity in manufacturing will be boosted. However, measures of productivity aggregating a complete set of inputs, called multifactor or total factor productivity, will not be affected by this trend, because multifactor productivity captures the input of temporary workers as purchased business services.

than the permanent computer professionals at the establishment where they are assigned. (*Total* compensation may be less.) One help supply services company's technical workers cost its customers $40 to $200 an hour. These temps include network administrators and programmers, and they can earn more than $100,000 a year.[57] A less obvious example is the physicist employed as a temporary worker. One of the largest help supply services companies offers Ph.D. physicists to its customers in high-tech fields and expects to place these highly skilled people into 6-month to 2-year assignments.[58] These employees are expected to develop new computer chips and types of software. Again, because these temps—even physicists —are paid on an hours-worked basis, they probably will earn more than permanent co-workers.

Many workers in help supply services are at the opposite end of the wage spectrum. These include day laborers. This type of work is relatively unskilled and sometimes subject to abuses by employers. The U.S. Department of Labor is charged with enforcing the Fair Labor Standards Act. In 1996, the Labor Department brought a case against two Massachusetts help supply services firms for not properly following this act. In particular, these firms did not pay 619 of their employees overtime pay when the employees worked more than 40 hours a week. The help supply services firms had classified these workers as independent contractors, but an administrative law judge disagreed.[59] The Labor Department also filed a lawsuit seeking back wages and damages for the employees. Then-Secretary Reich stated, "This case should discourage other temporary employment firms from trying to evade the Nation's wage and hour laws by classifying low-skilled workers as independent contractors."[60] The differences between temporary worker and independent contractor are subtle but very important in determining wage and hour law applications.[61]

Factors spurring temporary hiring

Competition. The corporate work environment reflects a market that is less regulated, more affected by international trade, and more subject to rapid change than ever before. The resultant volatility has led to the desire for a more flexible labor "infrastructure." To meet this need for flexibility, business increasingly is contracting labor for a specific purpose and for a specific duration. Just-in-time in the materials market is being met by just-in-time in the labor market, as expenditures for labor are determined more by the bottom line than by norms and traditions.[62]

Empirical results suggest that demand-side factors, rather than supply-side factors, such as an influx of women into the labor force, have been more useful in explaining variation and growth in temporary employment in the 1980s.[63] A higher-than-average growth in output, growth in the ratio of fixed to variable labor costs, and increased competition in foreign markets are important in explaining the growth of temporary employment.[64] To some extent, increasing amounts of paid vacation for existing staff also increases the use of temps. Costs associated with adjusting a permanent workforce to changes in demand often result in firms incurring excessive labor costs in lower- production periods. The contracting of temps allow firms to respond quickly to changes in production schedules and to eliminate excess overhead. Not only is employment easier to adjust in the short run, but the hours of temporaries also are easier to adjust than in other segments of the labor market.[65]

Increasing fixed labor costs. The increasing cost of providing benefits and hiring and firing workers has made permanent workers relatively more expensive than temporary workers. The incentive to contract out low-paying jobs may have been encouraged by the high share of insurance costs in total compensation costs in these jobs, as well as overall increasing disparity in the growth of benefits to that of wages. (See chart 1-16.) Legally required benefits, which include Social Security, unemployment insurance, and Medicare, are the largest non-wage employer costs. Following these, insurance costs are major portions of compensation packages. Health insurance consumes a large portion of insurance costs, although slightly less than in recent years.[66] Whereas health care benefits are available to about two-thirds of temporary workers, few actually partake of them. Many temporary workers have difficulty becoming eligible for many provided benefits and instead tend to rely on their spouses' or parents' plans.[67] Temporary employees are less than half as likely to be eligible for health coverage as permanent workers, although this is to some degree a function of high turnover and short employment periods.[68]

Health plan costs, as a percent of compensation, are high for low-paid workers. For example, the insurance cost to employers of full-time administrative support averaged 9.5 percent of compensation, compared to 7.1 percent for all white-collar occupations. The relative absence of health insurance costs saves employers more than $1.00 per hour for administrative support positions that in the temporary help industry carried an average wage of only $7.96 in straight-time hourly earnings in 1994.[69] For material handlers, helpers, and laborers, insurance costs also are higher than for the average private worker. The low cost of contracting with temporary workers has led to a contingent workforce that derives few benefits from their employers. For young temporary help workers, this lack of benefits does not seem to be much of a loss, as many decline coverage even when eligible.

A lack of benefits is not confined to the health arena. Other benefits, such as paid holidays and vacations, also require a minimum hours-of-service requirement that many temps are unable to fulfill. In 1989, the occupational compensation survey found that 43 percent of temporary workers had to meet an annual minimum of 900 hours of service to receive paid holidays.[70] Only 36 percent of those surveyed in 1997 received paid vacation days; many temporaries simply don't work long enough to qualify for many benefits.[71]

Cost of flexibility has been reduced. It is easy to see why compensation costs are lower for temporary workers than for permanent workers, especially with the relative absence of employee benefits. But does this cost advantage hold after help supply services establishments include charges to pay for administrative salaries, overhead, and earn a return on their investment? Apparently so, as prices charged in the temporary help supply industry have grown at a slow rate of 1.9 percent on an annual basis since 1995.[72] This data series alone provides limited evidence, since BLS only recently began measuring prices. However, the rate of growth in the price of help supply services has been less than the average rate of growth in civilian compensation over this period. (See chart 1-17.)

A variety of factors in the marketplace may have improved the efficiency of temp help workers. First, temporary workers often are prepared for job assignments through training provided by temporary agencies, and training expenditures by these agencies have increased dramatically in recent years.[73] This job-related training is extremely valuable for workers who are re-entering the workforce, and clerical and administrative workers especially are singled out. Three-fourths of help supply establishments provide instruction in word processing, and computer-based tutorials are widely used. Additionally, some companies provide training that simulates the use of clients' software.[74] Temporary employees have indicated that computer skills are more important than others acquired through employer-based training.[75] Even without help supply firms providing training, the standardization of software and the similarity of existing word processing programs has made it easier for employees to transfer skills from job to job.

The spread of technology has not been confined to work activity itself, as new software programs also have simplified the process of matching applicants to jobs. Software programs have even replaced some of the work of recruiters. Certain programs allow candidates to submit resumes via the Internet and then scan those resumes for target words that may indicate qualification for job openings.[76] These same programs are sometimes tied to the payroll system of employees and often are capable of interfacing with other applications, as well.

A poorly placed worker can impose large costs on a company, whether those costs are "soft," as in the loss of a sale, or "hard," like the abuse of physical inventory.[77] Many employers are finding that the screening services of staffing companies are superior to their own, as many companies simply do not rival the screening offered by temporary agencies. Since the success of staffing firms relies on their ability to provide successful matches, help supply firms invest in a variety of tests, both general and job-specific.

According to the 1998 Salary and Employment Trends Survey conducted by Accustaff, a large temporary help staffing company, the most frequently cited reason for using supplemental staff was to preview potential permanent employees (30.9 percent), followed by staffing for special projects (27.6 percent) and peak periods (23.4 percent). The practice of auditioning permanent employee candidates as temporaries first is the fastest growing segment of the staffing industry, reflecting the desires by employers to observe candidates for a trial period before deciding whether they are the right fit for the job.[78]

Conclusion

A restructuring of the labor market in recent years has resulted in rapid growth in the temporary help supply services industry. Producers strive to make labor as flexible a cost as possible in the production process, with increasing numbers of employees hired for work on specific projects or for specific durations. For example, employers often contract out for tasks that are not an integral part of the firm's mission or for jobs that are seasonal in nature. Employers have greater control over labor costs, when they are free to vary labor use, as product and service demands fluctuate. Temporary workers often are the answer to controlling these labor costs.

The growth of temporary labor represents a shift in the way employers plan staffing needs. This growth has stemmed from the need to drive down costs (especially during low production times). The growing share of benefits in total compensation for permanent employees is increasing the relative attractiveness of the temporary labor market. Additionally, companies preview new employees by contracting with temporary help companies for short assignments with these employees as they evaluate their skills. Also, firms are tapping into the recruiting and screening services of staffing agencies, rather than incurring these costs themselves.

Whereas this shift in hiring arrangements is profitable for employers, many temporaries earn less than their counterparts in other industries, primarily because—as a group—temps do not earn many benefits. Although industry earnings are difficult to interpret due to the transient nature of this workforce, *fluctuations* in temp earnings are more prominent than for all private workers. Finally, compared to traditional work, temporary work is unstable, as temporary employment, hours, and earnings fluctuate with greater intensity.

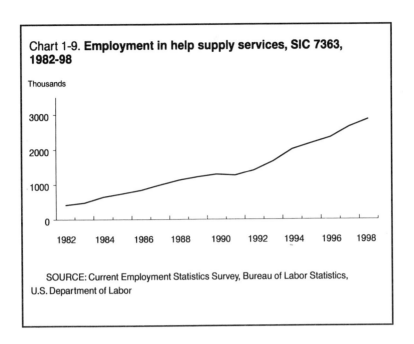

Chart 1-9. **Employment in help supply services, SIC 7363, 1982-98**

Thousands

SOURCE: Current Employment Statistics Survey, Bureau of Labor Statistics, U.S. Department of Labor

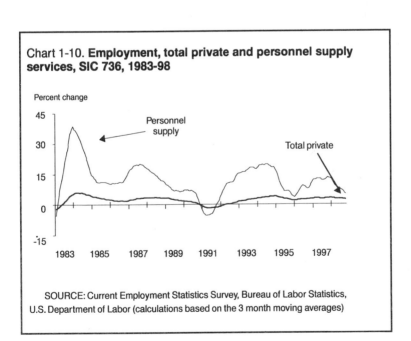

Chart 1-10. **Employment, total private and personnel supply services, SIC 736, 1983-98**

Percent change

SOURCE: Current Employment Statistics Survey, Bureau of Labor Statistics, U.S. Department of Labor (calculations based on the 3 month moving averages)

25

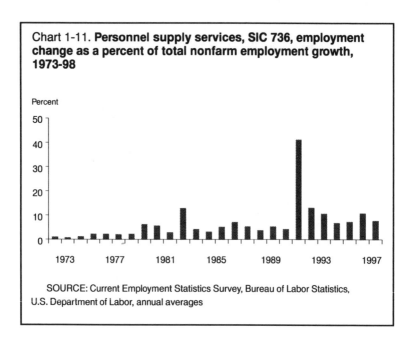

Chart 1-11. **Personnel supply services, SIC 736, employment change as a percent of total nonfarm employment growth, 1973-98**

Percent

SOURCE: Current Employment Statistics Survey, Bureau of Labor Statistics, U.S. Department of Labor, annual averages

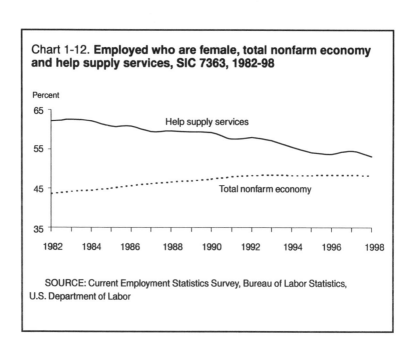

Chart 1-12. **Employed who are female, total nonfarm economy and help supply services, SIC 7363, 1982-98**

Percent

SOURCE: Current Employment Statistics Survey, Bureau of Labor Statistics, U.S. Department of Labor

26

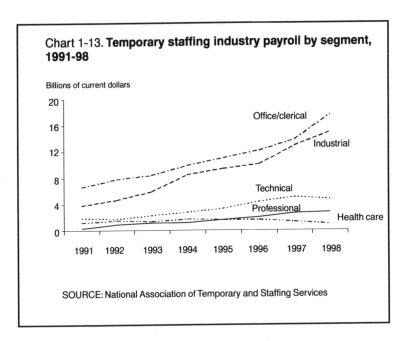

Chart 1-13. **Temporary staffing industry payroll by segment, 1991-98**

Billions of current dollars

Office/clerical
Industrial
Technical
Professional
Health care

1991 1992 1993 1994 1995 1996 1997 1998

SOURCE: National Association of Temporary and Staffing Services

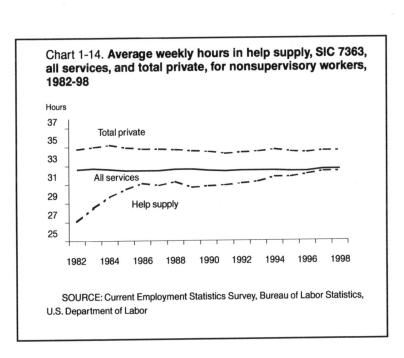

Chart 1-14. **Average weekly hours in help supply, SIC 7363, all services, and total private, for nonsupervisory workers, 1982-98**

Hours

Total private
All services
Help supply

1982 1984 1986 1988 1990 1992 1994 1996 1998

SOURCE: Current Employment Statistics Survey, Bureau of Labor Statistics, U.S. Department of Labor

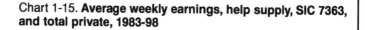

Chart 1-15. **Average weekly earnings, help supply, SIC 7363, and total private, 1983-98**

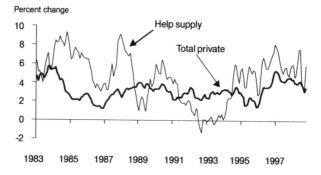

Percent change

Help supply

Total private

SOURCE: Current Employment Statistics Survey, Bureau of Labor Statistics, U.S. Department of Labor (calculated as 3 month moving averages of over-the-year percent changes).

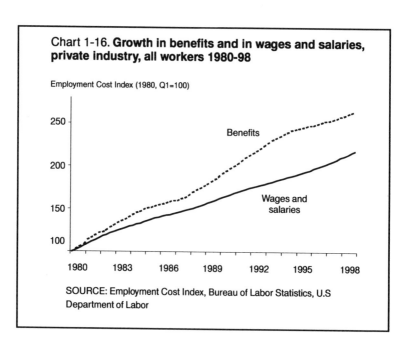

Chart 1-16. **Growth in benefits and in wages and salaries, private industry, all workers 1980-98**

Employment Cost Index (1980, Q1=100)

Benefits

Wages and salaries

SOURCE: Employment Cost Index, Bureau of Labor Statistics, U.S Department of Labor

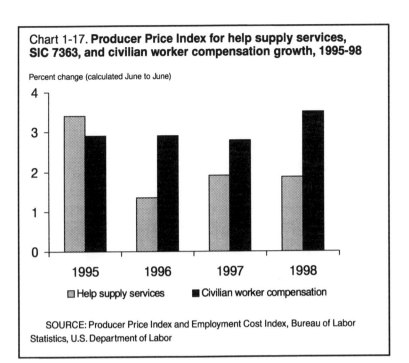

Chart 1-17. **Producer Price Index for help supply services, SIC 7363, and civilian worker compensation growth, 1995-98**

Percent change (calculated June to June)

☒ Help supply services   ■ Civilian worker compensation

SOURCE: Producer Price Index and Employment Cost Index, Bureau of Labor Statistics, U.S. Department of Labor

Table 1-1. **Indexes of output, hours, and output per hour and percent change, selected industries, 1987-98**

Year	SIC 3711 Motor vehicle assembly			SIC 3714 Motor vehicle parts			SIC 3465 Automotive stampings		
	Output	Hours	Output per hour	Output	Hours	Output per hour	Output	Hours	Output per hour
1987	100.00	100.00	100.00	100.00	100.00	100.00	100.00	100.00	100.00
1988	105.26	95.75	109.93	110.85	105.79	104.79	102.14	106.06	96.30
1989	105.23	95.49	110.20	105.76	107.29	98.57	99.28	106.83	92.93
1990	95.47	87.80	108.73	101.41	100.77	100.64	88.23	98.69	89.40
1991	85.81	83.30	103.02	98.07	99.96	98.10	80.65	93.05	86.67
1992	95.23	82.03	116.09	113.31	106.36	106.54	99.04	97.97	101.09
1993	100.91	87.31	115.58	129.40	113.49	114.02	111.53	104.51	106.72
1994	114.73	97.93	117.15	152.25	127.62	119.30	123.61	115.46	107.06
1995	115.88	101.04	114.69	161.40	135.65	118.98	129.66	121.10	107.07
1996	114.41	97.13	117.79	165.09	140.11	117.83	134.83	120.51	111.88
1997	119.39	98.13	121.67	173.84	144.14	120.60	139.58	117.49	118.80
1998	120.03	91.98	130.50	172.27	142.16	121.18	142.99	114.10	125.32
Average annual percent change:									
1987-98	1.67	-0.76	2.45	5.07	3.25	1.76	3.30	1.21	2.07
1990-98	2.90	.58	2.31	6.85	4.40	2.35	6.22	1.83	4.31
1990-91	-10.12	-5.13	-5.26	-3.30	-0.79	-2.52	-8.59	-5.71	-3.05
1991-98	4.91	1.43	3.44	8.38	5.16	3.06	8.52	2.96	5.41

Table 1-2. **U.S. sales and production of light vehicles, 1986-97**

Year	U.S. sales	U.S. production	Import sales	Import share
1986	16,108,392	11,335,241	4,162,191	0.26
1987	14,976,770	10,925,601	4,020,942	.27
1988	15,556,278	11,237,954	3,711,544	.24
1989	14,540,494	10,872,203	3,337,335	.23
1990	13,857,688	9,783,433	3,011,876	.22
1991	12,310,019	8,794,974	2,575,375	.21
1992	12,865,279	9,721,454	2,347,582	.18
1993	13,892,834	10,898,739	2,153,831	.16
1994	15,058,578	12,249,987	2,144,807	.14
1995	14,730,753	11,974,691	1,908,438	.13
1996	15,096,183	11,832,245	1,714,178	.11
1997	15,121,690	12,130,486	1,947,019	.13

SOURCE: *Ward's Automotive Yearbook*, 1996, 1997, and 1998

Table 1-3. **Average hourly earnings of production workers, selected industries, 1958-98**

Year	SIC 3711 Motor vehicle assembly	SIC 3714 Motor vehicle parts	SIC 3465 Automotive stampings	All manufacturing
1958	$2.64	$2.52	na	$2.10
1959	2.80	2.68	na	2.19
1960	2.91	2.76	na	2.26
1961	2.97	2.82	na	2.32
1962	3.10	2.95	na	2.39
1963	3.22	3.07	na	2.45
1964	3.32	3.19	na	2.53
1965	3.45	3.33	na	2.61
1966	3.55	3.44	na	2.71
1967	3.66	3.53	na	2.82
1968	4.02	3.89	na	3.01
1969	4.23	4.11	na	3.19
1970	4.42	4.17	na	3.35
1971	4.95	4.63	na	3.57
1972	5.35	5.08	$5.23	3.82
1973	5.70	5.42	5.47	4.09
1974	6.23	5.81	5.85	4.42
1975	6.82	6.31	6.52	4.83
1976	7.45	6.96	7.36	5.22
1977	8.22	7.80	8.14	5.68
1978	8.98	8.42	8.80	6.17
1979	9.74	8.84	9.40	6.70
1980	10.80	9.42	10.35	7.27
1981	12.29	10.38	11.37	7.99
1982	13.01	10.91	11.62	8.49
1983	13.36	11.61	12.22	8.83
1984	14.12	12.16	12.81	9.19
1985	14.81	12.69	13.60	9.54
1986	14.99	12.71	13.71	9.73
1987	15.33	12.69	13.58	9.91
1988	16.09	13.11	13.99	10.19
1989	16.51	13.26	14.16	10.48
1990	17.26	13.22	14.34	10.83
1991	18.34	13.62	15.05	11.18
1992	18.32	14.22	15.42	11.46
1993	19.44	14.74	16.08	11.74
1994	20.71	15.56	16.47	12.07
1995	20.57	16.18	16.30	12.37
1996	21.06	16.46	16.96	12.77
1997	21.63	16.60	17.06	13.17
1998	21.81	16.48	17.26	13.49

na = Data not available.

31

Table 1-4. **Average new car prices and percent change in disposable personal income, 1988-97**

Year	Domestic car price	Import car price	Disposable personal income	Percent change from prior year		
				Domestic car price	Import car price	Disposable personal income
1988	$14,029	$15,537	$14,881			
1989	14,907	16,126	15,771	6.3	3.8	6.0
1990	15,638	17,538	16,689	4.9	8.8	5.8
1991	16,487	17,795	17,179	5.4	1.5	2.9
1992	17,252	20,552	18,029	4.6	15.5	4.9
1993	17,219	21,988	18,558	-0.2	7.0	2.9
1994	18,360	24,595	19,251	6.6	11.9	3.7
1995	17,174	23,995	20,050	-6.5	-2.4	4.2
1996	16,998	27,441	20,840	-1.0	14.4	3.9
1997	18,199	27,695	21,633	7.1	0.9	3.8

SOURCE: *Automotive News Market Data Book 1998*, Bureau of Economic Analysis, U.S. Department of Commerce

Table 1-5. **Personnel supply services, SIC 736, occupational distribution, selected years, 1988-2006**

Occupation	1988	1990	1992	1994	1996	2006 projec- tion
	Percent distribution					
Executive, administrative and managerial	6.9	6.7	6.4	5.8	5.8	5.6
Professional specialty occupations	6.4	6.6	6.0	5.3	5.3	4.9
Engineers	0.9	0.9	1.4	1.1	1.1	1.2
Health Assessment and Training	4.6	5.0	3.3	2.8	2.8	2.4
Technicians and related support occupations	5.5	5.5	6.0	5.5	5.5	5.4
Administrative support occupations, including clerical	45.4	46.0	41.8	40.1	40.1	35.7
Service occupations	8.6	8.6	8.3	9.5	9.5	9.4
Health technicians and technologists	3.3	3.5	3.6	3.2	3.2	2.8
Engineering and science technicians	1.7	1.6	2.0	1.8	1.8	2.1
Precision production, craft, and repair occupations	3.1	2.6	3.8	5.0	5.0	5.5
Operators, fabricators and laborers	21.7	21.6	24.0	24.8	24.8	28.8
Helpers, laborers and material movers, hand	14.8	15.0	16.4	16.3	16.3	18.5

SOURCE: Office of Employment Projections, Bureau of Labor Statistics, U.S. Department of Labor (not all occupations displayed)

Endnotes

[1] Paul Ballew, Robert Schnorbus, and Helmut Hesse, "The Automobile Industry and Monetary Policy: An International Perspective," *Business Economics*, National Association of Business Economists, Washington, D. C., October 1994, pp. 29-34. See also Oliver Blanchard, "The Production and Inventory Behavior of the American Automobile Industry," *Journal of Political Economy*, Vol. 91, June 1983, pp. 365-400 and Oliver Blanchard and Angelo Medino, "The Cyclical Behavior of Prices and Quantities: The Case of the Automobile Market," *Journal of Monetary Economics*, Vol. 17, May 1986, pp. 379-407.

[2] Christopher J. Singleton, "Auto Industry Jobs in the 1980's: A Decade of Transition," *Monthly Labor Review*, February 1992, pp. 18-27. See also Thomas A. Kochan, Russell D. Lansbury, and John Paul MacDuffie, *After Lean Production – Evolving Employment Practices in the World Auto Industry*, Cornell University Press, 1997, pp. 9-42, 61-83.

[3] For the purposes of this chapter, the motor vehicle industry is composed of motor vehicles and car bodies assemblers (SIC 3711), manufacturers of motor vehicle parts and accessories (SIC 3714), and manufacturers of automotive stampings (SIC 3465). The first two, plus manufacturers of trucks and buses (SIC 3713), manufacturers of truck trailers (SIC 3715), and manufacturers of motor homes (SIC 3716) compose motor vehicles and equipment (SIC 371).

[4] John Duke and Lisa Usher, "BLS Completes Major Expansion of Industry Productivity Series," *Monthly Labor Review*, September 1998, pp. 35-51.

[5] The index of hours is derived from (1) production worker hours, which are based on production worker employment and average weekly hours data; (2) number of nonproduction workers; (3) an estimate of average annual hours paid for nonproduction workers. Production worker hours include all the hours at the plant, worked or paid for, and include paid time for vacations, holidays, and sick leave. Overtime and other premium pay hours are included based on actual time spent at the plant. The estimates of nonproduction worker average annual hours were prepared by the Bureau of Labor Statistics at the 2-digit industry level and were derived primarily from studies undertaken by the Bureau of Labor Statistics. Average hours for nonproduction workers were multiplied by the number of nonproduction workers to obtain total nonproduction worker hours. Indexes based on nonproduction worker hours are subject to a wider margin of error than are indexes involving only production worker hours, because it is necessary to estimate the average hours of nonproduction workers. Errors in such estimates, however, would have a relatively insignificant effect on the trend in hours for all employees. Total hours are the sum of production worker hours and nonproduction worker hours.

[6] Ward's Autoworld, The University of Michigan Management Briefing Seminars, September 24, 1998, p. 2.

[7] Steve Babson, *Lean Work: Empowerment and Exploitation in the Global Auto Industry*, Wayne State University Press, 1995, pp. 6-7.

[8] "Auto Suppliers Handle More Design Tasks, Lower Costs," *Purchasing*, Vol. 124, Number 5, April 9, 1998, pp. 49-50.

[9] Dave Welch and Daniel Howes, "Suppliers Will Help Create New Vehicle Categories," The Auto Industry at a Crossroads, *The Detroit News*, December 21, 1998, pp. 1-2.

[10] Dave Phillips, "New Approaches Threaten Big Labor," The Auto Industry at a Crossroads, *The Detroit News*, December 21, 1998, pp. 1-6.

[11] Materials data are reported in the *1992 Census of Manufactures* - table 7a, Bureau of the Census, U.S. Department of Commerce.

[12] *Automotive News 1998 Market Data Book*, Crain Communications, Detroit, Michigan, p. 9.

[13] *Automotive News 1999 Market Data Book*, Crain Communications, Detroit, Michigan, p.9.

[14] *World Motor Vehicles Data - 1998*, American Automobile Manufacturers Association (AAMA), Detroit, Michigan, p. 8.

[15] *Quarterly Gross Domestic Product (GDP) Report* – First Quarter 1999, Bureau of Economic Analysis, U. S. Department of Commerce.

[16] *Automotive News 1999 Market Data Book*, Crain Communications, Detroit, Michigan.

[17] Quarterly Financial Report for Manufacturing, Mining, and Trade Corporations – Fourth Quarter 1998, Bureau of the Census, U. S. Department of Commerce. Note: All data are in nominal dollars, not seasonally adjusted.

[18] *Employment and Wages Annual Averages, 1997*, Bureau of Labor Statistics, U.S. Department of Labor, December 1998, Bulletin 2511.

[19] For an early study on new automotive sites, see Andrew Mair, Richard Florida, and Martin Kenney, "The New Geography of Automobile

Production: Japanese Transplants in North America," *Economic Geography*, October 1988, pp. 352-373.

[20] Unpublished tabulations from the Current Population Survey, 1998 annual averages.

[21] Hourly earnings in the motor vehicles assembly industry rose from $2.91 in 1960 to $21.81 in 1998. In comparison, workers in all manufacturing industries earned hourly rates of $2.26 in 1960, $10.83 in 1990, and $13 in the mid-1990s.

[22] Occupational Employment Statistics Survey, Bureau of Labor Statistics, U.S. Department of Labor.

[23] Current Employment Statistics Program, Bureau of Labor Statistics, U.S. Department of Labor. Internet site: http://stats.bls.gov/ceshome.htm

[24] Unpublished tabulations from the Current Population Survey, 1998 annual averages.

[25] Data are for employed private wage and salary workers. Unpublished tabulations from the Current Population Survey, April 1993.

[26] James R. Healey and Michelmine Maynard, "Big Three: Auto Firms Will Dwindle," Money Section, *USA Today*, Sep. 24, 1998.

[27] *Automotive News Market Data Book, 1993-99*, Crain Communications, Detroit, Michigan, p. 35.

[28] *Automotive News Market Data Book, 1993-99*, pp. 52-54.

[29] *Automotive News Market Data Book, 1993-99*, p. 35.

[30] Standard and Poor's Industry Surveys, Autos and Auto Parts, January 9, 1997, p. 11.

[31] "The Road Ahead for the U.S. Auto Industry," International Trade Administration, U. S. Department of Commerce, March 1998, p. 2.

[32] *Automotive News 1999 Market Data Book*, Crain Communications, Detroit, Michigan, p. 60.

[33] James Lowe, Rick Delbridge, and Nick Oliver, "High-Performance Manufacturing: Evidence from the Automotive Components Industry," *Organization Studies*, Vol. 18, Number 5, 1997, pp. 783-798.

[34] See Anne E. Polivka and Thomas Nardone, "On the Definition of 'Contingent Work'," *Monthly Labor Review*, December 1989, pp. 9-16, and Anne E. Polivka, "Contingent and Alternative Work Arrangements, Defined," *Monthly Labor Review*, October 1996, p. 3-9.

[35] As an example, see a report by the Economic Policy Institute, available at: http://www.epinet.org/97labex1.html. Also, in "The Rise of the Contingent Workforce: Growth of Temporary, Part-time, and Subcontracted Employment," in the National Policy Association's *Looking Ahead* magazine, Richard Belous includes

consultants, hired business service workers, subcontractors, and life-of-project employees.

[36] Other types of agencies in help supply include: Chauffeur registries, employment agencies (excluding theatrical and motion picture), executive placing services, employee leasing services, labor pools, and modeling services.

[37] Leased employees comprised about 16 percent of employment in help supply services in 1997. These workers are not in contingent employment arrangements, since the employment relationship is expected to be ongoing. Employee leasing generally refers to an assumption of the human resource function on behalf of *all* or *most* of a customer's workforce, rather than of a supplemental workforce. Also, see box note, "Terms Defining Leasing and Temporary Employees."

[38] Bruce Steinberg, "Profile of the Temporary Work Force, 1997," *Contemporary Times*, Spring 1998.

[39] National Association of Professional Employer Organizations 1997 Financial Ratio Survey, Available:http://www.napeo.org/ind-statistics.htm

[40] The law establishes coverage tests that require coverage of a minimum percentage of lower-paid employees. The tax code requires employers to include in their head count certain employees supplied by third-party contractors, when applying the coverage tests. For analyses of TEFRA, see: Leon E. Irish and Richard M. Lent, "TEFRA Brings Sweeping Changes to Pension Plans," *Legal Times*, Sept. 27, 1982; and Leon E. Irish, and others, "Tax Act Makes Important Changes in Benefit Area," *Legal Times*, July 23, 1984, and Edward A. Lenz, "Co-employment, Employer Liability Issues in Third-Party Staffing Arrangements," 1997, National Association of Temporary and Staffing Services (NATSS).

[41] Declines in the population of those aged 20-34 are occurring in the 1990s. *Current Population Reports*, various, Bureau of the Census, U.S. Department of Commerce.

[42] Bruce Steinberg, "Profile of the Temporary Work Force, 1997," *Contemporary Times*, Spring 1998.

[43] The 1995 NATSS survey found that nearly one-third of former temporary employees said their permanent job was a direct result of their temporary job, and 72 percent of former temporaries had found a permanent job. "Growth in Temporary Help Reduced Unemployment," July 1, 1998 news release.

[44] Sharon Cohany, "Workers in Alternative Employment Arrangements," *Monthly Labor Review*, October 1996, pp. 31-45.

[45] Lewis M. Segal and Daniel G. Sullivan, "The Temporary Labor Force," *Economic Perspectives*, March/April 1995, p. 11.

[46] Sharon Cohany, "Workers in Alternative Employment Arrangements: A Second Look," *Monthly Labor Review*, November 1998, table 6, p.10.

[47] Sharon Cohany, "Workers in Alternative Employment Arrangements," *Monthly Labor Review*, October 1996 pp. 31-45.

[48] Surveys done for NATSS define industrial occupations as: Assembler, carpenter, construction, driver, electrician, food service, inventory, laundry, machinist, maintenance, mechanic, painter, picker, plumber, printer, production line, shipping, warehouse worker, guard, and welder.

[49] Cohany, "Workers in Alternative Employment Arrangements" and "Workers in Alternative Employment Arrangements: A Second Look."

[50] Unpublished detailed occupational and industry employment tables, 1996 annual averages from the Current Population Survey, table 10, employed persons by occupation, years of school completed, sex, race, and Hispanic origin.

[51] Since 1989, slightly more than 20 percent of the population has completed a bachelor's degree, with the percent of college graduates highest among those age 25- 29. The level of educational attainment of help supply service workers may reflect their relative youth. Younger adults, on average, have more education than older adults. Available: http://www.census.gov/population/pop-profile/p23-189.pdf

[52] There was a small increase in the percent of college graduates between the February 1995 and 1997 supplements. "Contingent and Alternative Employment Arrangements, February 1997," December 2, 1997 press release.

[53] Donna Rothstein, "Entry into and Consequences of Nonstandard Work Arrangements," *Monthly Labor Review*, October 1996, p. 78.

[54] Two economists of the Federal Reserve Bank of Chicago in analyzing BLS Current Population Survey data found that. "...full-time hourly white-collar SIC 736 workers earn 2.4 percent (standard error 1.4 percent) *more* than their non-SIC 736 counterparts." From: Lewis M. Segal and Daniel G. Sullivan, "The Temporary Labor Force," *Economic Perspectives,* March/April 1995, Federal Reserve Bank of Chicago, pp. 2-19.

[55] Cohany, "Workers in Alternative Employment Arrangements," pp. 31-45.

[56] In another study Segal and Sullivan found that in Washington State, "...the average duration is approximately two quarters and that approximately three quarters of temp employment is accounted for by spells of four quarters or less." From: Lewis M. Segal and Daniel G. Sullivan, "Temporary Services Employment Durations: Evidence from State UI Data," *Working Paper Series Macroeconomic Issues Research Department (WP-97-23),* Federal Reserve Bank of Chicago, December 1997.

[57] Marianne Kolbasuk McGee, "Just Don't Call Them Temps" *Informationweek,* May 12, 1997, issue 630, pp. 38-40.

[58] G. Pascal Zachary, "Looking for a Real Rocket Scientist? Manpower to Offer Physicists as Temps," *Wall Street Journal,* Eastern Edition, New York, November 27, 1996, p. A4.

[59] U.S. Department of Labor; Employment Standards Administration press release: "Massachusetts Temp Firms Ordered To Pay $150,000 In Civil Money Penalties For Willful Violations of Federal Wage & Hour Law," Available: http://www2.dol.gov/dol/opa/public/media/press/esa/esa96233.htm

[60] "Employment firms face $150,000 fine for wage violations," *Wall Street Journal,* Eastern Edition, New York, June 13, 1996, p. C19.

[61] In *Martin v. Selker Bros., Inc.,* 949 F.2d 1286, 1293 (3rd Cir. 1991) the court set some factors for deciding whether or not a worker is an independent contractor. Specifically they are: 1) the degree of the alleged employer's right to control the manner in which the work is to be performed; 2) the alleged employee's opportunity for profit or loss depending upon his managerial skill; 3) the alleged employee's investment in equipment or materials required for his task, or his employment of helpers; 4) whether the service rendered requires a special skill; 5) the degree of permanence of the working relationship; 6) whether the service rendered is an integral part of the alleged employer's business. From: DOL/OALJ REPORTER: U.S. Department of Labor Administrative Review Board, *Reich v. Baystate Alternative Staffing, Inc.,* 94-FLS-22 (ARB Dec. 19, 1996), Available: http://www.oalj.dol.gov/public/mtrad/decsn/94fls22c.htm

[62] Richard S. Belous, *The Contingent Economy: The Growth of the Temporary, Part-time and Subcontracted Workforce*, National Planning Association, Report 239, Washington, DC, 1989.

[63] Lonnie Golden and Eileen Appelbaum,"What Was Driving the 1982-88 Boom in Temporary Employment?" *American Journal of Economics and Sociology*, October 1992, pp. 473-493.

[64] Lonnie Golden, "The Expansion of Temporary Help Employment in the U.S., 1982-1992:

A Test of Alternative Economic Explanations," *Applied Economics*, Vol. 28, No. 9, pp. 1127-1141.

[65] Work hour flexibility is more pronounced among temporary help workers compared to labor in other industries. "The Expansion of Temporary Help Employment in the U.S., 1982-1992: A Test of Alternative Economic Explanations."

[66] In 1994, health insurance averaged 6.7 percent of total compensation for private workers, compared to 5.4 percent in 1998. Bureau of Labor Statistics, U. S. Department of Labor, *Employer Costs for Employee Compensation, 1986-97*, Bulletin 2505, August 1998, table 54. . 1998 data are from the July 9, 1998 press release, table 5.

[67] Because of minimum hours-of-service and contribution requirements, only about 10 percent of temporary employees that are offered insurance actually participate in health plans sponsored by the temporary agency. Of those that participate, half were required to pay the entire cost. Bureau of Labor Statistics, U.S. Department of Labor, *Occupational Compensation Survey: Temporary Help Supply Services, November 1994*, Bulletin 2482, August 1996, p. 4 and table 26.

[68] "Employment-based Health Insurance," GAO report 98-184, p. 16. And Edward A. Lenz, "Flexible Employment: Positive Work Strategies for the 21st Century," *Journal of Labor Research*, Fall 1996, Volume 17, No. 4, pp. 555-567.

[69] In 1994, administrative support positions averaged a cost of $1.32 per hour for all forms of employer insurance, whereas health insurance averaged about 90 percent of those costs. Bureau of Labor Statistics, U.S. Department of Labor, *Employer Costs for Employee Compensation, 1986-97*, Bulletin 2505, August 1998, table 58. And "Flexible Employment: Positive Work Strategies for the 21st Century," table 1.

[70] Bureau of Labor Statistics, U.S. Department of Labor, *Industry Wage Survey: Help Supply Services*, Bulletin 2430, October 1989.

[71] "Profile of the Temporary Work Force."

[72] The price mentioned here is a Producer Price Index, the amount that help supply firms are charging customers for the use of a temporary help worker. BLS began measuring these producer prices in mid-1994.

[73] The National Association of Temporary and Staffing Services (NATSS) estimates that the industry spent $866 million training temporary employees in 1997. That figure is 2½ times the amount spent in 1995. From NATSS press release, "Temporary Help Revenues Show Big Boost," September 4, 1998.

[74] Kelly's PinPoint CD-ROM offers this training at no cost to employees. "The Greening of the Kelly Girl," *Staffing Industry Review*, Volume III, No. 4, July/August 1998, pp. 39-44.

[75] "Profile of the Temporary Workforce."

[76] See http://www.skilmatch.com for an example.

[77] While an industrial worker may work for less than $10 an hour, mistakes can result in damages to costly equipment. "Skills Testing for Light Industrial Candidates: Can You Afford Not to Test?" *Staffing Industry Review*, May/June 1998. Vol. III, No. 3, pp. 88-92.

[78] "Surveys Find More Employers Relying on Staffing Firms," *Staffing Industry Review*, September/October 1998, Vol. III, No. 5, pp. 42-48.

[79] Fred R. Bleakley, "Is Manufacturing Job Loss Overstated?—Use of Temporary Workers Is Distorting U.S. Figures," *Wall Street Journal*, Eastern Edition, September 20, 1996 p. B5A.

[80] Frank Washington, "The Underground Workforce," *Ward's Auto World*, August 1995, Volume 31, Issue 8, p. 20.

[81] Full text of the act is available online at: http://thomas.loc.gov/cgi-bin/t2GPO/http://frwebgate.access.gpo.gov

[82] Kenneth L. Deavers and Anita U. Hattiangadi, "Welfare to Work: Building a Better Path to Private Employment Opportunities," *Journal of Labor Research*, Fairfax, VA; Spring 1998, Vol. 19, Issue 2, pp. 205-228.

[83] Success stories from "The Welfare to Work Partnership" website http://www.welfaretowork.org./success/large.html#14

[84] "Twelve Local Residents Graduate from Oakland Community College Model Welfare to Work Training Program, Receive Jobs with Kelly Services," press release from Kelly Services Public Relations Department, Troy, MI. October 13, 1997

[85] Diana Dillaber Murray, "OCC Gains Acclaim for Welfare Training Program," *The Oakland Press*, April 29, 1998 p. A-3. And "Eleven Pontiac Residents Graduate from Oakland Community College Welfare to Work Training Program Received Jobs with Kelly Services" press release from Kelly Services Public Relations Department, Troy, MI. October 5, 1998.

Chapter 2

The Many Facets of Skills

Major changes in the Nation's economic environment have fostered an increasing need for information on both the supply of skills and the demand for them. Over the past few decades, the country's economy has moved from an era of industrial production to the "information age." New industries have been created and older industries have declined dramatically. Success in this new economy depends primarily on a workforce that can adapt to constant change and adopt the new technologies to make production more efficient.

To make informed decisions, different groups look at skills in the labor market in different ways. Policy makers, for example, want to know if the current labor force is highly skilled and versatile enough to sustain economic growth. Employers will want to evaluate the skills of their workers to identify needs for training or new hires. Employers and compensation specialists want information that will help them determine the wages they must offer to be able to hire workers who have the skills that they require. Individuals want to know what specific skills they will need to acquire to obtain their first job, to qualify for and succeed in their intended career, to gain a promotion, or to continue functioning effectively in their current job in a changing environment.

Employers are increasing their demand for workers with specialized skills. Although education has always been valued, employers are seeking to hire highly trained workers and are providing training on both basic skills and new techniques to their current workforce. As a result, the pay gap between highly skilled workers and less trained workers continues to grow.

At the same time, many new and old service establishments do not require specialized skills. Instead, they depend on convenience, choice, quality, and price to satisfy their customers. Workers in many of these jobs do not need a college education or advanced training.

Using a variety of historical BLS data and some new BLS measures, this chapter explores the following topics:

- Alternative dimensions of skill

- Changes in the economic environment and their effects on the skill composition of the labor force

- Broad measures of change in the education and work experience of the labor force

- Changes in average skill levels resulting from shifts in employment by industry and occupation

- Trends in occupational education and training requirements

- Relationship between skills and earnings

- Occupational shortages

Defining Skills

There are different dimensions to the concept of skill. In a labor market context, skill refers both to the abilities, or human capital, of *workers,* as well as to the specific requirements of individual *jobs (*or jobs classified into the same occupation category). The real distinction in looking at the skill of workers, as compared to the skill requirements of occupations, is that workers can be viewed by their potential. Skills, abilities, and knowledge that workers possess indicate what they can do. Skills are learned over time, through instruction and practice. A young labor market entrant with little schooling, by definition, is unskilled. A worker with some education but no practical work experience becomes more skilled through practice, on-the-job training, and continuing education. Therefore, both education and accumulated work experience contribute to the skill with which a worker performs a job and the wage rate that he or she can command, so long as the prior schooling and work experience are relevant to the current job.

The skills people bring to the labor market have changed over time. In addition, changes in average skill levels in the overall economy can result from changes in: 1) The industrial composition of employment, 2) the occupational composition of employment, and 3) changes over time in the av-

erage skill requirements of given occupations. That is, employment growth (or decline) in certain industries and shifts over time in the types of workers needed within a given industry alter the number of workers required in certain occupations.

Occupational requirements can also change over time, but to track these changes requires detailed information. Occupations are classified based on their required tasks and duties, which can be further defined in terms of the skills needed to perform those tasks. Workers also must possess certain skills and knowledge in order to qualify for entry into different occupations. The Department of Labor has developed the Occupational Information Network, or O*NET (see box), to provide this type of information.

Among economists, the concepts of skill differentials and wage rate differentials are closely related. The value of a worker's time depends on the usefulness of his or her skills in the production process. It is assumed that employers will not pay employees more than the value that they can produce, and that employees will not work for less than the wage rate they could earn elsewhere. Thus, wages are often used as an operational proxy for skill level.

This chapter uses several different measures to examine changes in the skills of the labor force and the skill requirements of occupations. The definitions of these various measures will be explained as they appear in the course of the analysis.

The Economic Environment

The economic environment provides the context for our discussion of work skills of the labor force. Since 1983, the United States has enjoyed two long periods of sustained economic growth, interrupted by a single and relatively mild recession. The current economic expansion has lasted

---

Occupational Information Network—O*NET

The Department of Labor's Employment and Training Administration released the O*NET 98 database and viewer to the public in 1998, along with a user's guide and data dictionary. O*NET is a comprehensive database of occupational requirements, including information on required knowledge, skills, tasks, and machines, tools, and equipment, as well as data on worker requirements and characteristics, using a common language to define and describe the various elements. The flexible design and electronic database format of O*NET are intended for rapid capture of changing job requirements. These technological enhancements will remedy the drawbacks of the precursor to O*NET, the static *Dictionary of Occupational Titles*, which first came into use in the late 1930s and was updated through new editions roughly every 10 to 15 years.

longer than any other in the post-war period. Per capita increases in stocks of "broad capital," that is, stocks of both physical and human capital, have resulted in increased worker productivity and increased output per person.[1]

Several economic forces have underlying effects on the skill-composition of the workforce. Shifts in the demand for skill stem from technological change, and increased "globalization" of production. At the same time, long-run changes in education, training, and work experience, as well as long-run shifts in the sex and age composition of the labor force and the impact of immigration have redefined the skills that workers bring to the labor force.

Technological change. New technologies have reshaped the skill needs of today's labor force, either in the restructuring of the requirements of individual jobs or the distribution of employment across jobs. The changing face of the labor force did not occur overnight; in many establishments, both old and new technologies are used simultaneously. This effect of technological development is not uniform for all jobs. For some, the required skill level has increased, for others it is reduced, and for yet others it has remained unchanged.

The content of a given job may have changed through technological innovation, although the job title remains unchanged. This is highlighted below in the description of drafters in the 1966-67 and 1998-99 editions of the *Occupational Outlook Handbook.*

Drafters today still do the same work as they did 30 years ago; they just use additional, more complex skills to perform their tasks.

The widespread use of microprocessors has led to a restructuring of factory and office jobs throughout the economy. Several work tasks, previously completed by unskilled and low-skilled

Drafters

Characteristic	1966-67 duties	1998-99 duties
Nature of work	Draws detailed working plans from the ideas, rough sketches, specifications, and calculations of engineers, architects, and designers. Might also calculate the strength, reliability, and cost of materials and plans.	Prepares technical drawings and plans.
Tools	Uses instruments such as compasses, dividers, protractors, and triangles, as well as machines that combine the functions of several devices. May also use engineering handbooks and tables to assist in solving technical problems.	Uses technical handbooks, tables, calculators, and computers. Most drafters now use computer-aided drafting (CAD) systems to prepare drawings.
Recommended education or training	High school or post-high school courses in mathematics and physical sciences, as well as in mechanical drawing and drafting. The study of shop practices and shop skills are also helpful.	Postsecondary training including a solid background in computer-aided drafting and design techniques as well as communication and problem-solving skills.
Qualifications for success	Ability to visualize objects in three dimensions and to do freehand drawing.	Well-developed drafting and mechanical drawing skills, a knowledge of standards, mathematics, science, and engineering technology.

workers, now may be handled through automated machines. With the elimination of repetitive, routine tasks, the remaining workers are called upon to perform tasks of increased complexity. The skills requirements of some jobs have increased (as demonstrated in the drafter example above), whereas the level of skill required for some low skilled jobs has either been reduced or the job eliminated entirely. For example, sales clerks may no longer need to key in the price of an item, but can either scan the product or point to a picture of the item.

In addition to restructuring the requirements of specific jobs, firms also can change their staffing patterns or the mix of occupations they employ over time. In the cigarette manufacturing industry, for example, between 1989 and 1995, the share of production workers decreased by 12 percentage points (from 66 percent to 54 percent), while nonproduction workers increased in share by 14 percentage points (from 32 percent to 46 percent). Even though overall employment declined in this industry between 1989 and 1995, nonproduction workers increased numerically as well as in share, partially offsetting the overall decline in the number of production workers.[2]

According to one BLS study, a large part of the modification of the content of jobs can be attributed to technological change. "Although job titles frequently remain the same while innovation is taking place, over time, employers have less demand for manual dexterity, physical strength for materials handling, and for traditional craftsmanship. In the printing industry, for example, electronic composition methods have replaced long-standing craft skills, and employment of compositors and typesetters has declined sharply."[3]

Globalization of production. Shifts in the industrial composition and organization of production constantly cause changes in the skill mix of the U.S. labor force. During the first half of this century, many manufacturing industries shifted away from small artisan shops toward the use of assembly-line techniques. These technological changes may have contributed to general declines in wage rate differentials between skilled and unskilled U.S. workers over the period 1930-50.[4] More recently, U.S. multinational corporations have relocated a significant portion of their low-skilled production sites to foreign countries where wage rates for unskilled workers are even lower. Moving more jobs abroad decreases the demand for low-skilled labor within the United States,

while increasing the demand for higher-skilled workers who coordinate or oversee foreign production.[5]

Export-oriented manufacturing plants account for a significant portion of the increasing earnings differential between more and less skilled workers in manufacturing.[6] Technological improvements in computer efficiency and telecommunications have clearly lowered the costs to U.S. multinational corporations of production abroad, as well as the costs to foreign multinationals of production within the United States.[7] Indeed, a number of studies have found that rising capital per worker and information technology in particular leads to an upgrading of the workforce toward better educated workers and white collar jobs.[8] Thus, technological change and foreign outsourcing may well be the complementary, not conflicting, forces behind increases in skill differentials within the United States.[9]

Education. The population of the United States is large and diverse. We are a Nation of immigrants for whom education has served both as a means of social integration and as a source of literacy and numerical skills.[11] Education is widely viewed as an investment that will provide prospective workers with the skills required to obtain good jobs and to earn high wages. The average schooling levels of men and women in the workforce have been approximately equal, increasing steadily, since the 1930s.[12] But children enter U.S. educational systems from a variety of backgrounds, and the income and schooling levels of their parents are known to have an important influence on their school performance.[13] Therefore, it is perhaps not surprising that, compared to other large industrialized countries, the U.S. workforce includes a larger percentage of adults with relatively low verbal and quantitative skills, as well as a larger percentage of adults with relatively high skills.[14]

Training. While schooling itself is an important source of skills, workers devote considerable time to training as well. Roughly 70 percent of establishments report that they provide formal training on the job, and roughly 95 percent of large establishments provide some worker training. Except for the construction industry, there appears to be little difference in training rates by industry.[15] Among young new hires, nearly a third of time at work is spent in formal and informal on-the-job training.[16] There is some evidence that union members are more likely to receive company training, as well as training from business institutes and school sources, than comparable non-union workers. Therefore, declines in union membership rates may reduce the likelihood that blue-collar workers will receive structured training on the job.[17]

Work experience. The accumulation of relevant work experience is a prerequisite for most higher-skilled jobs. The amount of work experience needed before an employee is fully competent or reaches journeyman status differs by occupation, establishment, and industry. Given the investment made in acquiring skills through work experience, it is not surprising that during periods of economic downturns, employers will lay off less senior workers first. Thus, skills and employment stability both increase with tenure.[18]

Sex. During the past 50 years, many women have entered the labor market. As their numbers have increased, women are taking less time off for child rearing activities. This stronger attachment to the labor force provides women with greater incentives to specialize in job-related fields while in school, and increases the likelihood that they will receive the on-the-job training required for advancement to higher-level jobs.

Age. The current labor force is dominated by a large cohort of well-trained middle age workers. These highly educated baby-boomers have achieved senior positions at work, and may be diminishing the employment prospects of younger, less-skilled workers. As a result, some younger workers may well have fewer opportunities for growth and training.[19] However, the aging of the U.S. population, in combination with increasing female labor force participation rates, is expected to generate significant employment growth in occupations devoted to elder care services in the near future.

Immigration. Estimates suggest that an influx of unskilled immigrants may explain between one-half and one-fourth of the increase in the earnings differential between workers with a high school degree and workers with less schooling over the period 1980-95.[20] An increased inflow of low-skilled immigrants to the United States may decrease both the probability of employment and the wage rate received by low-skilled residents, with whom they compete.[21]

Broad Measures of Change in Education and Work Experience

Concurrent with widespread changes in the distribution of jobs and the complexity of work, over the last 30 years the workforce has evolved in its composition and its preparation for the changing job market. Among the most dramatic changes, the labor force participation of women has risen sharply from 41.6 percent in 1968 to 59.8 percent in 1998, and the share of all jobs held by women increased from 37.1 percent to 46.4 percent of the labor force.[22] The many children born between 1946 and 1962, sometimes known as the baby boom generation, grew up, entered the workforce, and now have accumulated a significant amount of work experience. Overlaying these changes has been a steady increase in educational attainment as the next generation is more educated than the one before.

Changes in the demographic characteristics of the population, as well as the other long-run changes in the economic environment described in the previous section, mean that the skills of an average worker in 1968 are very different from those of an average worker in 1998. The distribution of workers' skills changes slowly. At each point in time, there is a variety of skills among workers in different occupations, and within different levels of each occupation. Acquisition of these skills depends on each person's abilities and opportunities. Persons with relatively more ability acquire skills more quickly and efficiently than persons with less ability. Persons with relatively more resources are more able to invest the time and money required to achieve a given set of skills.

There are a variety of metrics for measuring worker skills, but few that are available for all workers and that provide a consistent picture over time. But if skills are learned over time, through instruction and practice, then years of school completed and years of accumulated actual work experience are one obvious set of indexes of workers' skills.

Hours-weighted averages of years of school completed by men and women have increased, and converged, during the post-World War II period. As shown in text table 1, the average educational attainment of men and women has risen from about 10 years in 1948 to more than 13 years today. The declining share of hours worked by those without a high school diploma is clear. In 1948, men without a diploma accounted for more than 60 percent of all hours worked by men employed in the private sector, and women without

41

Text table 1. **Percent distribution of hours worked by educational attainment, men and women, 1948-97**

Year	Years of schooling completed						
	0-8	9-11	12	13-15	16	17 or more	Mean years
Men							
1948	38.4	21.9	25.2	7.3	4.3	2.9	9.7
1958	31.0	21.0	27.9	9.4	6.2	4.5	10.4
1968	18.7	18.9	36.4	12.6	8.1	5.3	11.4
1978	9.6	13.4	39.0	18.5	11.4	8.2	12.5
1988	5.7	10.1	38.6	19.7	15.1	10.8	13.1
1997	4.4	7.8	34.8	26.0	18.2	8.9	13.3
Women							
1948	30.3	19.5	39.0	7.1	2.7	1.4	10.1
1958	23.5	20.6	41.6	9.0	3.5	1.7	10.6
1968	14.5	18.5	50.4	11.8	3.4	1.3	11.2
1978	6.7	13.2	50.5	18.6	7.7	3.4	12.2
1988	3.4	8.9	45.7	22.8	13.3	5.9	12.9
1997	2.6	6.3	35.8	31.5	17.6	6.2	13.4

a diploma accounted for almost 50 percent of all of the hours worked by women. By 1997, male workers without a high school diploma supplied slightly more than 10 percent and comparable women supplied slightly less than 10 percent of private sector hours. Conversely, men with at least a college degree comprised about 7 percent of the hours of men in 1948, but more than 25 percent of employed hours in 1997. The corresponding figures for women are approximately 4 percent in 1948 and about 24 percent in 1997.[23]

Wage premiums associated with seniority and total accumulated work experience may reflect increased productivity due to on-the-job training, increases in efficiency that come with experience at performing work tasks, and improved knowledge of the organizational or institutional structures at a workplace. Employer-provided training has been shown to provide high returns.[24] Even if a job provides little formal training, many jobs provide opportunities for informal training or learning by doing. Informal training can take many forms, including coaching by a supervisor, demonstrations of how to perform a task by a sales representative, asking a co-worker how to perform a task, or by simple repetition.

The 1995 BLS Survey of Employer Provided Training (SEPT95) is particularly valuable because it surveyed both employers and their employees.[25] Employer records are an excellent source of formal training data, but employees are likely to be a better source for the large amount of informal training that they receive. Not surprisingly, more than 90 percent of establishments with at least 50 employees provide formal training and

nearly 70 percent of employees receive some formal training. Informal training is nearly universal (95 percent).

During the 6-month survey period, employees trained for about 44 hours, with more than 70 percent of that time spent in informal training. The time spent in training represents a considerable investment. Establishments paid an average of $647 in wages while workers were in training. This is more than four times the direct cost per employee of $139 for tuition, instructors, and payments to outside trainers.

Who receives training varies considerably. The youngest employees (24 years or younger) and the oldest employees (55 years or older) are less likely to receive any formal training, and those receiving formal training spend much less time in it. Employees 25-54 years old also receive more hours of informal training, although the distribution of informal training is less skewed. Women are more likely than men to receive formal training, but men receive most of the informal training. Finally, the likelihood of receiving formal training increases with educational attainment.

It was widely thought that newly hired workers received the most training because this maximized the time employers had to recoup their investment.[26] However, the SEPT95 found the reverse. Employees with at least 10 years' tenure received twice as many hours of formal training as an employee with less than 2 years with the firm. Recently hired workers tended to be trained informally as they spent more than twice as much time in informal training as employees with at least 10 years' tenure.

Text table 2. **Mean years of work experience in private business by sex, 1968-97**

Year	Men	Women
1968	19.4	13.0
1970	19.3	13.0
1975	18.3	12.0
1980	17.5	11.6
1985	17.4	11.7
1990	17.8	12.1
1995	18.6	12.4
1996	18.7	12.5
1997	18.8	12.5

Although the SEPT95 provides a glimpse into the importance and the distribution of training, it can not indicate if employers are increasing the amount of training of their workers over time. Instead, economists have approximated the amount of training by the amount of time a worker has been employed. Because data on total accumulated work experience have not been available, many labor economists use potential experience, or years since leaving school, as a broad index of skills acquired at work.

Data on actual work experience are preferable to data on potential work experience for this purpose, because the labor force participation of women is often intermittent. Large sets of confidential administrative record data on employment, from the Social Security Administration, occasionally have been matched to microdata from the Current Population Survey (CPS) to construct data sets that could be used for analytical purposes.[27] The BLS Office of Productivity and Technology maintains estimates of actual accumulated work experience based on these matched records. Text table 2 provides estimates showing that the average number of years worked declined for both men and women in the 1970s, but rose in the 1980s and 1990s.

The patterns of work experience shown in text table 2 are easily understood. Because most men and many women have strong attachments to the workforce, the level of work experience depends primarily on the age distribution of the workforce. The age distribution of the workforce is now dominated by large cohorts of persons born between 1946 and 1962, who began to enter the workforce in the mid-1960s. During the 1970s, as their numbers grew, the average level of work experience declined. By 1980, most of the baby boom generation had completed its entrance into the workforce, and the leading edge of this cohort was approaching middle age. During the 1980s and 1990s, the baby boomers went from being a large group of inexperienced work-

ers to becoming a middle-aged and experienced group, and average work experience levels rose rapidly.

Average levels of education and work experience, weighted by hours of employment, both show that skill levels rose after 1980. But it is difficult to gauge how much impact these changes had on the economy. Therefore, as part of its productivity measurement program, BLS has used data on the education and experience composition of hours of employment to construct a broad measure of changes in the skill composition of the workforce.

As noted above, an hour of work provides a different contribution to output over time as the workforce becomes more or less skilled. BLS constructs an overall index of labor services that reflects both changes in the number of hours worked and in the average skill level of an hour of work, where skills are measured by education and work experience for men and women. In addition, a second BLS index, the labor composition index, removes the effect of changes in the number of hours worked and focuses exclusively on changes in the average skill level of the workforce. The labor composition index generally rises if there is a shift toward more educated or more experienced workers, or if the wage rates commanded by high-skilled workers increase.

BLS compiles data on roughly 1,000 groups of workers, cross-classified by their educational attainment, work experience, and sex, to create a single index that captures changes in the skill-composition of the U.S. workforce. (See box, p. 44.)

The index of labor services grew about 1.9 percent per year since 1968. This growth reflects the more rapid growth of hours employed among highly-educated workers and, especially since about 1980, an increasing share of total hours worked by middle-aged workers who are in their peak earnings years. Of this increase, labor quality contributed about 0.4 percent per year, whereas the annual average contribution of hours was 1.5 percent. Therefore, increases in skills accounted for roughly 19 percent of the growth in labor services.

The contribution of labor composition to output growth is the product of the growth rate of labor composition and labor's share of total production costs. Labor's share averaged 69 percent over this period. Labor quality, or increases in the average skill level of the workforce, therefore, added about 0.2 percent per year to output growth over the period 1968-97.

Skill Composition of the U.S. Workforce

For each category of worker, growth in hours at work is weighted by that category's share of the total wage bill. This weighted average is an index of labor services. An index of total hours, in contrast, implicitly weights the growth rate of hours of each group of workers by its share of total hours, regardless of differences in wage rates paid for different kinds of work. The labor services index differs from an index of total hours because the labor services index places more weight on the hours growth rates of high-skilled, high-wage workers and less weight on the growth rate of hours of low-skilled, low-wage workers.

Changes in the labor composition index are calculated as the difference between this weighted average of hours growth rates, on the one hand, and the unweighted growth rate for the hours of all workers in the private sector, on the other.[28] Conceptually, a 1-percent increase in the labor composition index has the same effect on output growth as a 1-percent increase in hours worked. That is, the rate of growth of total labor services can be viewed as the sum of the rates of growth of labor quantity (total hours) and labor quality (labor composition effect).

Before turning to the estimate of skill change, it is useful to examine the assumptions that the measures rest upon. Besides those assumptions needed for model production, asumptions of competitive capital and labor markets are fundamental to the labor composition measures.[29] These assumptions permit hourly earnings to be used to measure each type of worker's contribution to output and, therefore, as a measure of skill.

Of course, the wages of some workers may not be strictly the result of competitive labor markets. Occupational and industrial wage differentials are persistent over time, even after controlling for differences in education and work experience.[30] A number of explanations for these differences have been suggested; some are consistent with competitive markets while others are not.[31] One of the assumptions that is consistent with the approach discussed here is that industry-specific wage differentials reflect differences in the training requirements by industry for workers whose education and work histories are otherwise comparable. Employers who have invested significant amounts of time and money to train their employees in industry-specific skills will pay enough of a premium to retain them.[32]

Similarly, unionized workers earn more, on average, than nonunionized workers. Nonetheless, competitive firms will attempt to equate the prevailing wage, however it is determined, to the value of the worker's marginal product by adjusting the level of employment or by screening workers to hire only the most skilled. For example, Allen[33] finds that the occupational mix of unionized workers implies that they are more skilled than nonunionized workers in the construction industry and, thus, at least a portion of the union wage differential is offset by higher marginal products of unionized workers. So, while earnings may not equal the value of marginal products for all workers in all periods, it is assumed that any deviations from the competitive market are temporary and rapidly eroded so that hourly wages approximate marginal products.

Text table 3 shows that the labor composition index advanced quite slowly until about 1979 and increases in skills accounted for little of productivity growth. Since then, the baby boom cohort entered their prime earnings years and labor composition growth has advanced much more rapidly. Skills have become a more important source of productivity growth since 1979. Labor composition effects now account for more than a quarter of all growth in labor productivity.

As noted at the beginning of this section, the baby boom generation made its entrance into the workforce in the 1970s, and this large cohort of inexperienced workers largely offset increases in average schooling levels. After 1979, the baby boom generation gained sufficient experience so that increases in educational attainment and experience both contributed to faster labor composition growth. By 1990, the baby boom generaeration joined the ranks of prime age workers, and even the slower growth in average schooling levels was not sufficient to prevent an acceleration in the average skill level.

Today, the baby boom generation has largely entered middle age, the prime earnings period of a worker's career. Members of this cohort are not expected to make substantial new investments in education and training, since the expected benefits

Text table 3. **Labor composition and its contribution to labor productivity in private business, 1968-97**

Period	Average annual growth rates		
	Labor composition effect	Contribution of increased skill to labor productivity	Labor productivity
1968-73	0.09	0.05	2.66
1973-79	.04	.03	1.27
1979-90	.49	.34	1.22
1990-97	.60	.41	1.30

of these investments would only accrue for a relatively short time until retirement. These workers will gain additional work experience as they grow older, but their earnings will not increase as rapidly as they have during the earlier stages of their careers, when they received more intensive training.

It is also noteworthy that currently middle-aged workers have produced a relatively large cohort of children, known as the "baby boom echo". Members of this younger large cohort are now approaching working age, and early signs of their entrance into the workforce are beginning to appear in the labor force data. This new, large cohort of inexperienced workers will increase the share of the labor force with relatively low earnings. The effect of this shift will be to slow labor composition growth as a larger fraction of the workforce once again becomes younger and less experienced.

Skill Change and Shifts in Industries and Occupations

The United States is enjoying the longest economic expansion since World War II. However, growth has been uneven. Employment in some industries and occupations has risen rapidly while in others it has declined. As seen in the previous section, there is evidence that labor force skills are increasing. By examining employment patterns by industry and occupation, we can gain a clearer understanding of the forces driving skill change in the U.S. workforce.

There is evidence of skill upgrading over the last three decades.[34] However, skill upgrading is not uniform across all industries, nor is it uniform for all occupational groups. Changes in the industrial composition of employment and in the occupational composition of employment within industries can change average skill levels in the overall economy, as can changes over time in the average skill level of given occupations.

This section reviews findings on the pattern of skill change from 1989 through 1997, based on data from the BLS Occupational Employment Statistics (OES) survey. Data on occupational employment and wages by industry from the OES were used to measure changes in average skill levels in the United States resulting from shifts in both the structure of occupational employment within industries, and from shifts in the industrial structure of employment.[35] (See box for a description of skill measure.)

Sources of skill change

Skill change occurs through three paths. First, industries vary in their relative need for skilled workers. Changes in employment across industries can lead to increased employment of skilled workers if expanding industries require workers of greater skill than declining industries, even if the occupational structure of each industry remains constant. Next, changes in production methods within an industry can substantially alter the nature of work. The shift between production and nonproduction workers, noted earlier, is one example. Third, some changes are subtle, leading to changes in the mix of narrowly defined occupations, while leaving the mix of broad occupations unchanged. For example, the computer revolution has transformed secretaries into administrative assistants who now perform word processing instead of typing.

The measure of skill change was produced for the economy as a whole, the goods-producing sector, the service-producing sector, and for six Standard Industrial Classification (SIC) industry divisions (not including agriculture, forestry, and fishing). Text table 4 shows this overall measure of skill change, as well as the decomposition of this measure into skill change resulting from shifts in the industrial composition of each sector, and skill change within detailed industries. The difference between the overall skill change

45

OES Measure of Skill Change from 1989 to 1997

The OES skill change index measures changes in the relative demands for occupations of differing skill levels in detailed industries over time. Shifts in the relative demand for an occupation are measured by the change in the portion of the wage bill that firms allocate to that occupation. The change in the portion of the wage bill is used rather than the change in the portion of employment as a means of gauging the true resource expenditure involved. For example, when a firm demands one additional manager, the commitment of resources is greater than the case of demanding one additional janitor, even though the employment change is the same.

This measure of skill change resulting from shifts in the occupational structure is produced for the goods- and service-producing sectors and for each industry within those sectors. The measure is then disaggregated into skill change resulting from occupational shifts within detailed industries of the sector and skill change resulting from shifts in the industrial structure of employment within the sector. The skill measure developed by OES takes advantage of data at the 4-digit SIC level, the most detailed industry level available. Data at this level of industry detail provide a clear distinction between skill change resulting from shifts in occupational employment within industries versus that due to shift in industrial composition.

Changes in an occupation's share of the wage bill are calculated as follows: The wage bill for each industry is first calculated by multiplying the total industry employment of each occupation by its wage rate, and summing across all occupations in the industry. Each occupation's portion of the wage bill is then calculated by multiplying the employment for each occupation by its wage rate, and dividing by the total industry wage bill.[36]

Changes in each occupation's share of the wage bill are then weighted by a measure of the skill level of the occupation—the occupation's relative wage, expressed as a percentage deviation from the industry average wage. Relative wages are used as a measure of relative skill assuming that wages, on average, reflect the value of a worker's production. Workers who earn more are assumed to have higher underlying skills. Summing these weighted changes produces a positive or negative value that serves as a measure of relative skill upgrading or downgrading, respectively. This index is comparable across industries; if the skill index increases 5 percent in industry A and 10 percent in industry B, then industry B exhibits twice the rate of occupational upgrading as does industry A.

This skill change index measures the percentage change in the average wage of the industry that is implied by the pattern of shifts in the relative demands for occupations of differing skill levels (i.e., wage rates). It is an index of the degree to which inter-occupational shifts in relative demand within the industry are biased toward or away from relatively skilled workers.[37]

index (column 1) and the index that measures shifts in the industrial composition of employment (column 2) is the effect of occupational shifts within detailed industries (column 3). The measure of skill change within detailed industries (column 3) uses the same concept of skill, but it represents an average of the measures produced for each 4-digit SIC industry, the most detailed industrial category available.

Overall skill change

Average skill levels in the economy as a whole increased about 1.1 percent over the 1989-97 period. Skill levels rose by 0.2 percent in the goods-producing sector, and by 1.4 percent in the service-producing sector. Across the broad occupational spectrum, there was a shift away from less-skilled workers and toward more highly-skilled workers. This shift was due primarily to industries within the service-producing sector.

For the period from 1989 to 1997, the overall index shows that employment shifts led to an increase in average skill levels of about 2 percent in service industries, 3 percent in finance, insurance, and real estate, and 0.4 percent in manufacturing. Average skill levels fell in all other industries, most notably the trade sector, which had an overall skill change measure of -2.0 percent.

Text table 4. **Skill change by sector and industry, 1989-97**

Industry	Overall Skill change (1)	Skill changes due to shifts—			
		Across industries (2)	Within detailed industries		
			Total within industry skill change (3)	Decomposition of within industry skill change:	
				Among broad occupational groups (4)	Within broad occupational groups (5)
All Industries	1.1	0.1	1.0	0.4	0.6
Goods-producing sector:	.2	(¹)	.2	- .2	.4
Mining and Construction	- 0.8	- .3	- 0.5	- .8	.3
Manufacturing	.4	(¹)	.4	.1	.3
Service-producing sector:	1.4	.2	1.2	.6	.6
Finance, insurance, and real estate	3.0	1.3	1.7	1.4	.3
Services	2.1	- .7	2.8	1.5	1.3
Transportation, communications, public utilities	- .6	- 1.1	.5	.9	- .4
Trade	- 2.0	- .3	- 1.7	- 1.7	(¹)

¹ Indicates value is less than 0.05 percent and greater than -0.05 percent.

Skill change resulting from shifts in industrial composition

A shift in industrial composition increases the measure of skill change if employment shifts toward high wage industries. Conversely, industrial shifts will reduce skill change if employment shifts toward lower paid industries. Column 2 of text table 4 shows the portion of skill change that is due to shifts in industrial composition.

Skill levels rose slightly in the economy as a whole (0.1 percent) due to shifts in industrial composition toward higher-wage industries. This effect was greater in the service-producing sector (0.2 percent), driven by finance, insurance, and real estate, which experienced strong shifts toward higher wage industries. Wage-weighted employment shifts between detailed industries contributed negatively to skill change for mining and construction, services, transportation, and trade, while having a neutral effect on skills in the remaining industries.

The positive effect on skill change within the financial services sector is largely the result of large shifts toward securities and commodities brokers and other credit institutions that have gained in importance as a result of the stock market boom of the last half decade. Depository institutions lost over 8 percent of total sector employment over this period.

Skill change arising from occupational shifts within detailed industries

This section discusses changes in skill levels arising from occupational shifts within industries. Shifts in the occupational structure within detailed industries increase average skill levels in the sector if, on average, there is *occupational upgrading,* or a shift toward relatively highly paid occupations within the detailed industries. Column 3 of text table 4 shows this average measure of skill change for the detailed industries within each sector—total within industry skill change. Skill levels increased in the economy as a whole as a result of shifts in occupational employment within industries over the 1989-97 period, led by services sector industries with an average rate of occupational upgrading of 2.8 percent. Industries in the mining and construction sector, and in trade, had average declines in skill levels as a result of shifts in occupational employment.

Changes in skill levels arising from occupational shifts within detailed industries can be further differentiated into employment shifts *among* broad occupational groups (such as between professional and clerical, shown in column 4) and shifts *within* broad occupational groups (such as between secretaries and data processors, shown in column 5).[38] The "among" effect reflects gross changes in the occupational structure. The "within" effect reflects more subtle alterations to

Text table 5. **Index of skill change for broad occupational groups, 1989-97**

Occupational groups	Skill index		
	All industries	Goods-producing sector	Service-producing sector
All occupational groups	1.0	.2	1.2
Managerial	- .4	.4	- .7
Professional	.7	- .1	1.0
Clerical	.3	.6	.2
Sales	.8	- 1.0	1.4
Service	- .8	- 2.1	- .3
Production I [2]..	.6	.8	.5
Production II [3]...	([4])	([1])	([4])

[1] Indicates value is less than 0.05 percent and greater than -0.05 percent.
[2] Includes production supervisors; inspectors; mechanics, installers, and repairers; construction trades and extractive occupations; and precision production occupations.
[3] Includes machine setters, set-up operators, operators, and tenders; hand working production occupations; plant and system occupations; transportation and material moving machine and vehicle operators; and helpers, laborers, and material movers, hand.
[4] Data do not meet publication standards.

the occupational mix within industries.

This decomposition shows that employment shifts among broad occupational groups worked to increase average skill levels in all industries with the exception of trade and mining and construction. Table 2-1 (at end of chapter) shows that the pattern of employment shifts most responsible for the increase in skills within service sector industries are shifts toward professional workers, who earn relatively high wages, and away from clerical workers, who earn relatively low wages. Although the goods-producing sector mirrors this shift away from clerical workers, there was no shift toward professional workers in that sector.

Skill change within broad occupational groups. Column 5 of text table 4 shows the average amount of skill change within detailed industries that is the result of occupational shifts within broad occupational groups. This measure indicates occupational upgrading or downgrading, or the degree to which shifts in occupational employment within broad occupational groups are biased toward or away from relatively high- or low-wage workers, respectively. All industry groups experienced occupational upgrading within occupational groups, with the exception of transportation and trade. Closer examination of this effect, however, reveals that skill levels did not increase for every occupational group. Text table 5 shows the average measure of skill change for occupational groups within industries in the goods-producing and service-producing sectors. (For more details, see table 2-2.)

Text table 5 shows that the economy as a whole and both the goods-producing and service-producing sectors experienced occupational upgrading in the clerical and production I groups, along with occupational downgrading in the service group. Skill changes for other broad occupational groups were mixed.

Table 2-3 shows the average pattern of relative demand shifts among detailed occupations within the clerical, production I, and service occupation groups. Occupational upgrading among clerks within detailed industries is the result of a shift toward clerical supervisors, who earn relatively high wages, and a shift away from secretaries and data processors, who earn relatively low wages. Occupational upgrading among production I occupations is due to a shift toward first line supervisors and away from inspectors and precision production occupations. Occupational downgrading among service occupations is primarily due to shifts away from service worker supervisors and protective service workers, and toward workers in personal and health services occupations.

Summary

Shifts in employment patterns indicate occupational upgrading over the 1989-97 period. Average skill levels increased for the economy as a whole, driven primarily by increases in average skill levels in both the services and finance, insurance, and real estate industries. Skill levels increased slightly in manufacturing industries and fell in mining and construction, transportation, and trade. By decomposing these figures into skill

Text table 6. **Highlights of occupational employment changes by broad education and training categories, 1986-96**

Education and training category	Growth rate 1986–96 (in percent)	Numerical growth 1986–96	Percent of overall job growth
Total, all occupations	19	21,068,780	100.0
Bachelor's and above	29		
First professional degree	16	201,277	1.0
Doctoral degree	-2	-3,620	(¹)
Master's degree	44	518,917	2.5
Work experience, plus a bachelor's or higher degree	32	2,313,970	11.0
Bachelor's degree	29	3,623,663	17.2
Postsecondary education and training below the bachelor's degree	14		
Associate degree	37	1,130,078	5.4
Postsecondary vocational training	5	413,063	2.0
On-the-job training or experience	17		
Work experience in a related occupation	19	1,202,526	5.7
Long-term OJT	11	1,199,188	5.7
Moderate-term OJT	11	1,888,523	9.0
Short-term OJT	20	8,581,195	40.7

¹ Slight decline.

change resulting from shifts in industrial employment and shifts in occupational employment, it is apparent that occupational upgrading within detailed industries was the primary source of skill change.

Analysis of Trends in the Education and Training Requirements of Occupations

An analysis of trends in the educational requirements of occupations between 1986 and 1996 suggests that technological and other demands of the economy placed a premium on occupations requiring higher levels of education and training. Industry-occupation matrices developed by the BLS Office of Employment Projections (OEP),[39] show occupational staffing patterns over time. The matrices are developed from data on occupational employment by industry collected through the OES survey.[40]

Shifts in industry and occupational employment were analyzed in the context of the classification system developed by OEP that places occupations into 1 of 11 different categories based on the education, training, or experience that usually is required.[41] The 11 categories are distributed to three summary groups (See box).

Overall changes in occupational skill across industry sectors

Total employment in the United States increased 21.1 million over the 1986-96 period, from 111.4 million to 132.4 million. (See text table 6.) Occupations at all education and training levels, except the doctoral degree, experienced increases, with the largest numerical growth (41 percent) in short-term on-the-job training. Employment in occupations usually requiring at least a bachelor's degree grew by 29 percent over the 1986-96 period, considerably faster than the 19-percent growth for all occupations. Occupations generally requiring postsecondary education or training below the bachelor's degree and those that require on-the-job training or experience had slower than average employment growth, 14 percent and 17 percent, respectively.

Chart 2-1 shows the 1986-96 employment changes by broad education and training category and earnings level. Each of the three bars shows the distribution of the increase in employment by earnings above or below the average. For occupations requiring a bachelor's degree and above, 97 percent of the increase was in occupations with above average earnings. In contrast, the percent with above average earnings was lower in occupations requiring postsecondary education and training (below the

49

Occupational Education and Training Categories

Bachelor's degree and above

First professional degree. *Occupations that require a professional degree.* Completion of the academic program usually requires at least 6 years of full-time equivalent academic study, including college study prior to entering the professional degree program.

Doctoral degree. *Occupations that generally require a Ph.D. or other doctoral degree.* Completion of the degree program usually requires at least 3 years of full-time equivalent academic work beyond the bachelor's degree.

Master's degree. *Occupations that generally requires a master's degree.* Completion of the degree program usually requires 1 or 2 years of full-time equivalent study beyond the bachelor's degree.

Work experience, plus a bachelor's or higher degree. *Occupations that generally require work experience in an occupation requiring a bachelor's or higher degree.* Most occupations in this category are managerial occupations that require experience in a related non-managerial position.

Bachelor's degree. *Occupations that generally require a bachelor's degree.* Completion of the degree program generally requires at least 4 years but not more than 5 years of full-time equivalent academic work.

Post secondary education or training below the bachelor's degree

Associate degree. *Occupations that generally require an associate's degree.* Completion of the degree program generally requires at least 2 years of full-time equivalent academic work.

Post-secondary vocational training. *Occupations that generally require completion of vocational school training.* Some programs last only a few weeks while others may last more than a year. In some occupations, a license is needed that requires passing an examination after completion of the training.

On-the-job training or experience

Work experience in a related occupation. *Occupations that generally require skills obtained through work experience in a related occupation.* Some occupations requiring work experience are supervisory or managerial occupations.

Long-term on-the-job training. *Occupations that generally require more than 12 months of on-the-job training or combined work experience and formal classroom instruction for workers to develop the skills needed for average job performance.* This category includes formal and informal apprenticeships that may last up to 4 years and short-term intensive employer-sponsored training that workers must successfully complete. Individuals undergoing training are generally considered to be employed in the occupation. This category includes occupations in which workers may gain experience in non-work activities, such as professional athletes who gain experience through participation in athletic programs in academic institutions.

Moderate-term on-the-job training. *Occupations in which workers can develop the skills needed for average job performance after 1 to 12 months of combined on-the-job experience and informal training.*

Short-term on-the-job training. *Occupations in which workers generally can develop the skills needed for average job performance after a short demonstration or up to one month of on-the-job experience and instruction.*

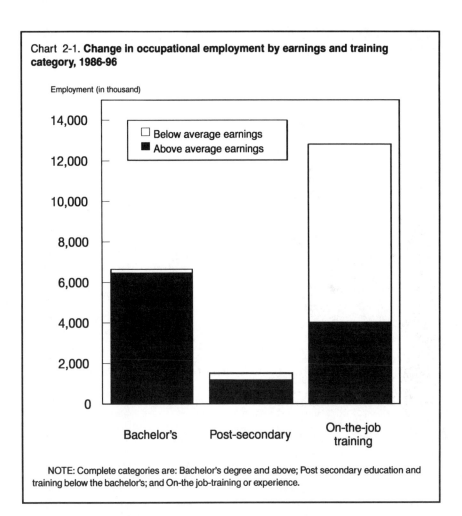

Chart 2-1. **Change in occupational employment by earnings and training category, 1986-96**

Employment (in thousand)

NOTE: Complete categories are: Bachelor's degree and above; Post secondary education and training below the bachelor's; and On-the job-training or experience.

bachelor's) and on-the-job training or experience (77 percent and 31 percent, respectively).

Shifts in the distribution of industry employment are important determinants of shifts in the distribution of occupational skill requirements. The most rapid growth of employment over the 1986-96 period was in the services sector (40 percent). This resulted in faster than average employment growth within services in all occupations in each of the three summary groups of occupations. This reflects the dynamic that when firms grow rapidly enough, the demand for lower-skilled labor can rise, even though some of their traditional duties are being done more efficiently by more highly trained workers or through technological innovation. However, the top group (bachelor's and above) increased its share of sector employment at the expense of the other two groups.

In manufacturing, employment declined slightly over the period.[42] Because overall manufacturing employment fell, only those occupations in the highest education and training category had higher employment in 1996 than they did 10 years earlier. Occupations requiring at least a bachelor's degree increased their share of manufacturing employment as both groups of lower skilled occupations became relatively less important to employers.

These data are indicative of increased relative employment of college educated workers. However, this pattern may arise because employment growth in some education and training categories was driven by the rapid growth of a single occupation or only a small number of occupations. For example, almost all of the growth in occupations requiring an associate degree resulted from growth in a single occu-

Text table 7. **Occupations accounting for the largest share of employment growth, bachelor's degree and above, 1986-96**

Education and training category	Occupations accounting for the largest share of growth (ranked by share)	Industries contributing to growth in category	Number of occupations in category	Earnings
First professional degree	•Lawyers •Physicians	•Health services •Legal services •Agricultural services •Federal/State government	6	Top quartile
Doctoral degree	•Biological scientists	•Drug manufacturing •Federal/State/ local government	4	Top quartile
Master's degree	•Teachers and instructors, all other •Counselors •Speech-language pathologists and audiologists •Physchologists	•Education •Amusement and recreation •Health services •Government	9	Top two quartiles
Work experience, plus a bachelor's or higher degree	•Managers and administrators, all other •Financial managers •Marketing, advertistingand public relations managers •Management analysts	•Business services •Health services •Local government •Education •Real Estate	11	All but 3 occupations in top quartile (one wage not available)
Bachelor's degree	•Teachers, preschool through college, except special and adult education •Computer engineers, scientists, and systems analysts •Management support workers and professional workers, all other	•Education •Business services •Health services •State and local government •Residential care	56	45 occupations in top quartile 9 occupations in second highest quartile 2 occupations with below average earnings

pation, registered nurses. Similarly, the growth of lawyers and physicians drove the growth for occupations that usually require a first professional degree.

Occupational shifts by educational requirements

The following sections discuss employment changes in specific education and training categories. In addition to highlighting occupations accounting for the largest share of employment growth, text tables 7 through 9 show those industries contributing significantly to growth within each education and training category. Job growth can also be stratified by earnings. As part of the analysis of the 1986-96 time series, median hourly

earnings of all wage and salary workers in 1996 by occupation, as measured by the Occupational Employment Statistics (OES) survey, were used to construct earnings quartiles. The last column of text tables 7-9 distributes occupations within each education and training category by earnings quartile. Earnings in either of the bottom two quartiles are below the average.

Bachelor's degree and above. Lawyers and physicians accounted for more than 80 percent of job growth among occupations requiring a first professional degree, but neither of these occupations grew as fast as the average for all occupations. A single occupation—all other teachers and instructors, which includes lecturers, nursing instructors,

Text table 8. **Occupations accounting for largest share of employment growth, postsecondary education and training below the bachelor's degree, 1986-96**

Education and training category	Occupations accounting for the largest share of growth (ranked by share)	Industries contributing to growth in category	Number of occupations in cagetory	Earnings
Associate degree	•Registered nurses •Health professionals and paraprofessionals, all other	•Health services •Drug stores and proprietory stores •Business services	12	11 occupations in the two highest quartiles 1 occupation with below average earnings
Postsecondary vocational training	•Emergency medical technicians •Licensed practical nurses •Secretaries, except legal and medical	•Business services •Health services •Education •Religious organizations	33	25 occupations in top two quartiles 8 occupations in with below average earnings

graduate assistants, sports instructors, and farm and home management advisors—accounted for 65 percent of new jobs at the master's degree level. Teachers, preschool through college, accounted for 886,000, or 24 percent, of the growth of the group usually requiring a bachelor's degree. However, employment of computer engineers, scientists, and systems analysts; all other therapists; physician assistants; and occupational therapists each more than doubled over the period. Nearly all of the occupations requiring a bachelor's degree or above had median earnings in the top quartile.

Postsecondary education and training below the bachelor's. Rising demand for workers in health-related occupations was the driving force behind job growth for occupations included in this group. About three-fourths of the growth in occupations requiring an associate degree occurred in the health services industry. Registered nurses accounted for one-half of all growth in this group. All other health professionals and paraprofessionals, radiologic technologists and technicians, medical record technicians, dental hygenists and respiratory therapists brought the health related share of job growth in this category to about 95 percent. More than one-half of the new jobs generated by the occupations in the postsecondary vocational training category can be attributed to four health-related occupations: Emergency medical technicians, licensed practical nurses, medical secretaries, and surgical technologists. All but eight of the occupations in this category had higher than average earnings. (See text table 8.)

On-the-job training or experience. A little more than one-half of the growth in occupations commonly requiring applicants to have work experience in a related occupation, or long-term on-the-job training, occurred in eating and drinking places, education, State and local government, and business services like personnel supply services. Nearly 60 percent of the growth in occupations that usually require moderate-term on-the-job training occurred in business and health services, grocery stores, and construction. Four occupations accounted for 92 percent of job growth in the moderate on-the-job training category—all other sales and related workers, composed largely of sales workers in wholesale trade and manufacturing; bookkeeping, accounting, and auditing clerks; medical assistants; and human services workers. In general, median earnings of occupations requiring work experience in a related occupation or long-term on-the-job training were higher than the average for all occupations. (See text table 9.) Just 3 of the 107 occupations requiring moderate-term on-the-job training had median hourly earnings in the highest quartile, although slightly more than one-half of the occupations had above average earnings.

The 20-percent growth in occupations that generally require short-term on-the-job training was concentrated in two industry sectors, wholesale and retail trade and services, accounting for about 90 percent of the growth, or about 7.4 million jobs. Occupations that generated at least 100,000 jobs and grew at least twice as fast as the overall average accounted for 49 percent of the

Text table 9. **Occupations accounting for largest share of employment growth, on-the-job training or experience, 1986-86**

Education and training category	Occupations accounting for the largest share of growth (ranked by share)	Industries contributing to growth in category	Number of occupations in cagetory	Earnings
Work experience in a a related occupation	•Service workers, all other •Clerical supervisors and managers •Adult and vocational education teachers •Food and service and lodging managers	•Eating and drinking places •Education •Business services •State and local government •Health services	30	22 have earnings in the top two quartiles 8 have earnings below average
Long-term OJT	•Maintenance repairers, general utility •Cooks, restaurant •Correction officers •Musicians •Telephone and cable •TV line installers and repairers	•State and local government •Eating and drinking places •Construction •Business services •Religious organizations	74	22 occupations in top quartile 30 in second highest quartile (one wage not available) 21 occupations with below average earnings
Moderate-term OJT	•Sales and related workers, all other •Bookkeeping, accounting, and auditing clerks •Medical assistants	•Business services •Health services •Grocery stores •Construction •Wholesale trade, other	107	59 occupations in top two quartiles 48 occupations with below average earnings
Short-term OJT	•Cashiers •General office clerks •Janitors and cleaners, including maids and house-keeping cleaners •Truckdrivers, light and heavy •Salespersons, retail	•Retail trade •Business services •Health services •Educatiion •Trucking, warehousing, and transportation	114	1 occupation in to quartile 15 in second quartile 98 occupations with below average earnings, including 39 in the bottom quartile

growth in occupations requiring short-term on-the-job training. These included cashiers, hand packers and packagers, receptionists and information clerks, home health aides, teacher aides and educational assistants, adjustment clerks, child care workers, counter and rental clerks, bill and account collectors, personal and home care aides, and amusement and recreation attendants. This is the only education and training category with most occupations having below average earnings. Only one, industrial truck and tractor operator, had earnings in the top quartile.

Quality of job growth

Another way to view changes in skills is to examine changes in the distribution of earnings, since most economists associate high wages with a high level of skills. As part of the analysis of the 1986-96 occupational employment time series, median hourly earnings of all wage and salary workers in 1996 by occupation as measured by the Occupational Employment Statistics survey were used to construct earnings quartiles. Median hourly earnings ranged from $60.01 to $5.01 for the 456 occupations included in the 1986-96 time se-

Text table 10. **Employment by earnings quartile, 1986 and 1996**

Earnings quartile	Range of median hourly earnings, 1996[1]	Percent distribution		
		1986 employment	1996 employment	Employment change, 1986-96
Total	$ 5.01-60.01	100.0	100.0	100.0
1	60.00 -115.39	23.9	25.1	31.1
2	15.39 -10.63	24.6	24.6	24.7
3	10.61 -7.51	26.5	25.5	20.1
4	7.47 -5.01	25.0	24.8	24.1

[1] Nominal.

ries.[43] The range of earnings varied among the quartiles and the top quartile had the widest range. (See text table 10.) Employment size significantly affected the distribution of occupations by quartile. Of the 454 occupations in the distribution of employment, the first quartile included 112 and the second, 152. The third quartile contained 134 occupations and the fourth, 56.

The highest earnings quartile's share of growth between 1986-96 was disproportionately high, at 31.1 percent; the lowest quartile's share was 24.1 percent. The first quartile showed the greatest occupational growth and the third quartile, the least. This reflects the different growth rates for occupations in the different quartiles.

The distribution of employment growth by quartile was affected significantly by the concentration of occupational growth. Of the 454 occupations, 16 accounted for 50 percent of the change in employment from 1986 to 1996.[44] Five of these occupations were in the top earnings quartile; three each were in the second and third quartiles, and five were in the lowest quartile.

What do these trends really tell us?

The high rates of growth over the 1986-96 period for occupations requiring at least a bachelor's degree clearly indicate that the economy is placing an increasing emphasis on workers with extensive higher education. This is confirmed by the rapid growth of occupations with the highest earnings, which are highly correlated with educational attainment. Nevertheless, despite employers' growing need for these highly educated workers to handle increasingly complex tasks, 2 of every 3 jobs created over this period were in occupations that do not require a degree. Shifts in employment across education and training categories occurred slowly, since the rapidly growing, high-educa-

tion occupations account for a relatively small share of employment. For example, despite their rapid employment growth, occupations that generally require at least a bachelor's degree increased their share of employment by only 1.8 percentage points over the period, from 20.3 percent to 22.1 percent.

While part of the economy is characterized by industries undergoing rapid technological change, the rest is characterized by activities that change relatively slowly. For these dramatically changing sectors, consumer demand and changing demographics provide a strong impetus for continued growth in lesser skilled jobs.

Relationship between Earnings and Skill

The generally increased skill level of the labor force was the focus of the previous section. We concentrate now on the the more day-to-day concerns of employers and employees on how skills are rewarded. Human capital theory codifies the roles of education and on-the-job training in the acquisition of job skills, and the relationship between these skills and earnings.[45] According to this theory, workers' skills are the primary source of their productivity, although the skills of different individuals may be very different. In the case of the U.S. workforce, these skills are extremely difficult to measure directly. But there is a systematic relationship between education and training, on the one hand, and wage rates on the other, because people acquire skills through education and training. According to human capital theory, firms pay higher wage rates to more educated and experienced workers, all else being equal, because their additional skills raise their productivity compared to workers with less education and work experience. People invest in education and training, both by paying the direct costs and by incurring the opportunity costs associated with these investments, in order to earn a higher wage rate in the future.

To illustrate the relationship between education and earnings, the following tabulation shows the ratio of hourly compensation of college to high school male and female graduates from 1970 to 1997, holding other characteristics constant.[46]

	1970	1980	1990	1997
Men	1:36	1:29	1:51	1:62
Women	1:23	1:32	1:56	1:65

In 1970, college educated men earned about 36 percent more than high school graduates. Starting around 1980, college educated workers began to fare substantially better than less educated workers. By 1997, the gap had nearly doubled to 62 percent. The results are even more striking for women. College educated women earned 23 percent more than high school graduates in 1970 and 65 percent more in 1997.

Similar patterns can be seen in the relationship between experience and earnings. As noted in the section on broad measures of change in education and work experience, BLS has constructed estimates of actual work experience from the Social Security Continuous Work History file. Analysis of these data reveals that the wage rates of more experienced workers have also increased, relative to the wage rates of younger workers. The tabulation below shows the ratio of hourly compensation of men and women having 15 years to 5 years of experience over the period, 1970 to 1997.

	1970	1980	1990	1997
Men	1:47	1:70	1:70	1:64
Women	1:15	1:22	1:28	1:35

The relative earnings of more experienced women have continued to rise throughout the last 27 years. For men, however, work experience commanded increasing premiums until the mid-1980s; those premiums have remained stable since then.

Other researchers have shown that growing wage inequality also arises within narrowly defined categories of industry, sex, age, and schooling.[47] Many of the economic forces that underlie these increases in the variance of wage rates within narrow industrial and demographic categories have been mentioned in the section on the economic environment. But their effects on wage rates are partially hidden when they are analyzed in terms of broad measures of skill such as earning and experience. Consequently, it is useful to examine the structure of earnings, and particularly the relationship between wage rates and more

specific measures of job skills, within broadly defined occupational categories.

Not everyone in a given occupation has the same level of skill, and not all jobs within a given occupation require equal levels of skill. Thus, it is not surprising that wage rates vary within an occupation. Several variables have been identified as having an effect on pay scales—unionized workers generally earn more than their non-union counterparts; pay rates in the north are higher than those in the south; large establishments pay more than small ones; and men earn more than women for comparable work. While these observations are useful for policy makers, they do not explain the pay setting mechanisms used by individual firms.

John Dunlop, one of the first to describe the interplay of the individual firm and product markets in setting wage rates,[48] noted the importance of the salary level of specific "key" jobs for the pay rates of other jobs within an establishment. The role of key or benchmark jobs is paramount to the job classification and compensation setting schemes commonly used today.[49]

A point-factor pay setting scheme is the most common approach used by compensation analysts in setting pay rates within an establishment.[50] It usually starts with a careful evaluation of jobs within a firm based on a set of defined factors, of which skill is one. Jobs are assessed on how much of each factor they contain. Points are then assigned for each factor, and a total point score is compiled for each job. The point score is then translated into a salary level. Different establishments use different factors and different weights for each factor, reflecting the relative value of each factor to the establishment.

The Occupational Compensation Survey (OCS), and the half century of its predecessor programs, compiled earnings data based on a preselected job list. These surveys were aimed at collecting wages paid for specific jobs; the focus was not on the individuals holding these positions. Jobs were selected as key or representative occupations in an area, industry, or for setting Federal pay scales.

Not all jobs in the same occupation require equal levels of skill or ability. The surveys gathered wage data for various levels within an occupation. Skill requirements ranged from trainee to journeyman, and beyond. The number of levels varied by occupation.

The surveys used detailed job descriptions for each job, as well as various job levels within an occupation. (As an example, see box on p. 56 for

Synopsis of major distinguishing characteristics used to determine job level for two sample occupations under the Occupational Compensation Survey

Budget analyst

Level I: Trainee. Clearly defined tasks. Comparing and verifying data. Preparing budget forms. Examining and highlighting deviations in reports.

Level II: Routine, recurring analysis work. Gathering, extracting, reviewing, verifying, and consolidating data. Examining and comparing budget requests.

Level III: Relatively stable operation analysis. Forecasts funding needs. Reviews and verifies data. Formulates and revises estimates. Explores funding alternatives. Certifies obligations and expenditures. Recommends transfer of funds within accounts.

Level IV: Analytical support for budgets requiring annual modifications. May recommend new budgeting techniques. Cost-benefit analysis and program trade-offs studies. Confers on request modifications. Develops procedures for budget requests. Prepares status reports. Recommends adjustments. Advises management. Serves as budget liaison.

Accountant

Level I: Trainee, learns to prepare financial statements.

Level II: Prepares financial statements, working papers and periodic reports following a set of rules and procedures.

Level III: Maintains conventional and relatively stable accounting system or segment. Solves moderately complex accounting problems and makes decisions.

Level IV: Maintains complex accounting system or segment. Makes frequent recommendations for new accounts, revisions in account structures, new types of ledgers, or revisions in the reporting system.

Level V: Work extends beyond accounting system maintenance. Participates in developing and revising accounting systems and procedures. Works with operating managers to explain how changes in the accounting system will affect them.

Level VI: Complete responsibility for establishing and implementing new and revised accounting systems and procedures. Accounting program is complex. Typically a corporate level job.

a brief synopsis of major distinguishing features used to evaluate various levels for two jobs.)[51.] In practice, all the elements in each level definition were considered in making a classification judgment. For example, in some occupations, individuals classified at different levels of an occupation can perform work of essentially the same complexity, but have significant differences in direction received or responsibility for the direction of others.

Table 2-4 shows the proportion of workers at each level for selected occupations surveyed in 1996. Higher level jobs within an occupation require greater skill or knowledge, or both. This higher skill can be a reflection of higher tenure (and associated additional experience and on-the-job training) as well as more education. As shown in table 2-5, earnings also increased for higher levels within an occupation.

Periodic additions and deletions were made to the jobs selected for study in an effort to reflect changing labor market conditions. The definitions and number of levels were also modified from time to time. These changes were relatively slight from one year to the next, but the cumulative effect of these modifications and other changes in the sample design renders it difficult to make comparisons over time.

The OCS survey has been integrated into the National Compensation Survey (NCS), as part of an effort to combine several compensation programs into a single vehicle that can produce local, regional, and national statistics on levels, trends, and characteristics of pay and benefits.[52] Under this umbrella program, the use of a pre-set job list was dropped. In its place, the NCS collects data on randomly selected occupations. BLS economists use a factor evaluation system to

National Compensation Survey: Factor Evaluation System

Factor 1 - Knowledge
1. Knowledge to perform simple tasks, requires little or no previous education/training.
2. Knowledge of commonly used procedures, requires some previous training.
3. Knowledge of standardized rules. Requires considerable training or experience.
4. Knowledge of extensive rules in a generic field to perform a wide variety of tasks.
5. Knowledge of specialized, complicated, techniques. BA/S degree or experience.
6. Knowledge of a wide range of administrative methods. Graduate study or experience.
7. Knowledge of a wide range of concepts or principles. Extended graduate study or experience.
8. Mastery of administrative field to apply experimental theories or new developments.
9. Mastery of administrative field to develop new hypotheses and theories.

Factor 2 – Supervision received
1. Supervisor makes specific assignments, employee closely monitored.
2. Employee handles ongoing assignments, supervisor makes decisions.
3. Supervisor provides objectives and deadlines; employee plans tasks. Review based on conformity to policy.
4. Supervisor sets objectives, employee sets deadlines/plans tasks. Review based on meeting requirements.
5. Supervisor defines mission, employee responsible for all planning. Review in terms of meeting program objectives.

Factor 3 – Guidelines
1. Guidelines are specific and detailed; employee follows them strictly.
2. There is a list of guidelines; employee chooses most appropriate.
3. Guidelines are not always applicable; employee uses judgment in adapting them.
4. Guidelines are scarce but policies are stated; employee may deviate from traditional methods to develop new methodology.
5. Guidelines are broadly stated; employee is a technical authority in development of guidelines.

Factor 4 – Complexity
1. Tasks are clear cut and easily mastered. No decision making.
2. Tasks involve related steps requiring employee to recognize different steps.
3. Tasks involve unrelated methods; employee must recognize them and choose based on relationships.
4. Tasks involve unrelated methods; employee must assess approach.
5. Tasks involve unrelated methods; decisions deal with uncertainty.
6. Tasks involve broad functions; decision making involves undefined issues.

Factor 5 – Scope and effect
1. Little impact beyond immediate organization.
2. Work impacts future processes.
3. Works affects the operation of the program.
4. Work affects wide range of establishment activities or operations of other establishments.
5. Work affects work of other experts or development of major program aspects.
6. Work is essential to the mission of the establishment.

National Compensation Survey: Factor Evaluation System—Continued

Factor 6 – Personal contacts
1. Contacts are with employees in immediate office or with public; highly structured situations.
2. Contacts are with employees in the same establishment (in or out of office) or with public in moderately structured situations.
3. Contacts are with individuals and groups outside the organization. Each contact is different.
4. Contacts are with high ranking officials in unstructured settings.

Factor 7 – Purpose of contacts
1. The purpose is to obtain, clarify, or give facts.
2. The purpose is to plan, coordinate, or advise on work efforts.
3. The purpose is to influence, motivate, interrogate, or control persons or groups.
4. The purpose is to justify, defend, negotiate, or settle matters involving significant/controversial issues.

Factor 8 – Physical demands
1. Work is sedentary.
2. Work requires physical exertion.
3. Work requires considerable and strenuous physical exertion.

Factor 9 – Work environment
1. Work involves everyday risk—normal safety precautions.
2. Work involves moderate risk—special safety precautions.
3. Work involves high risk.

Factor 10 – Supervisory span of control
1. No supervisory responsibility.
2. Group Leader—nonsupervisory person who leads work activities.
3. First line supervisor.
4. Second line supervisor.
5. Third line supervisor.

---

evaluate each job. The system is based on 10 "generic" factors:

- Knowledge
- Supervision received
- Guidelines
- Complexity
- Scope and effect
- Personal contacts
- Purpose of contacts
- Work environment
- Physical demands
- Supervisory duties[53]

A weighted value of each factor is then used to assign job levels. See the box on p. 22 for a summary of the criteria used in evaluating each factor.[54]

The occupational levels used by NCS differ from those in the OCS. Under OCS, the lowest level for any given occupation was set as 1, generally an entry-level position. Both skilled and unskilled occupations were classified as level 1. In contrast, NCS uses characteristics and factors to determine occupational levels. Thus, the lowest level for a given NCS occupation need not be 1.

Different occupational groups have different generic leveling profiles. One useful aspect of the generic leveling data is that disparate occupations can be measured on common scales. Table 2-6 presents modal values of three generic factors—knowledge, supervision received, and guidelines—within broad occupational groups.[55] *Knowledge* captures schooling, work experience, and other training used on the job, and is measured on a scale of one to nine. As measured by this factor, professional and executive jobs require large amounts of skill. Technical, clerical, and precision production jobs involve moderate

59

amounts of this factor, whereas operatives, laborers, and service occupations involve substantially lower amounts of knowledge.

Various occupational groups exhibit differences along other dimensions as well. Thus, table 2-6 also lists modal values for two other factors, each of which is measured on a scale of one to five. *Supervision received* measures the extent of direct or indirect controls exercised by supervisors, such as the degree to which assignment priorities and deadlines are set. *Guidelines* assess the extent to which policies and procedures in the job are made explicit, and the extent to which individual employee judgment in applying policies is required. Occupational groups with higher knowledge measures also tend to have higher measures for these other two factors. Nevertheless, the other factors measure different job attributes that vary independently of knowledge.

Jobs with different levels of the job attributes pay different wage rates, as demonstrated by table 2-7, which shows the mean hourly wage rates for occupations with given levels of knowledge. On average, wages increment by about 30 percent as knowledge increments one level. Other factors, including the other generic leveling factors and other job attributes such as full-time status and occupation, are not held fixed in these comparisons.

Table 2-7 illustrates the substantial differences in hourly wages across jobs within a given occupational category. There is substantial dispersion within the occupational group about the group modal values presented above, and within broad occupational groups. Higher job duties command higher pay. Although there are differences in wages across occupational groups—for instance, Precision Production and Transport jobs tend to uniformly pay more than other jobs with the same level of knowledge—those differences are often small, at least as measured relative to the typical wage differences across adjacent levels of knowledge. Thus, the generic leveling factors capture some characteristics of jobs that are associated with higher wages that are difficult to identify except by recourse to job title. That is, typical professional jobs and typical technical jobs pay very different amounts, but professional and technical jobs with the same level of knowledge pay much the same.

Wage differences across occupational groups for a given level of knowledge partly reflect differences in other job duties or attributes. Wage regression analysis is one way to determine whether this is the case. In essence, regression is

a statistical method that allows one to isolate the effects on wage rates of a given factor or variable, holding other variables fixed. Table 2-8 gives the estimated wage premiums to knowledge from such a regression.[56] For example, the first number in the table, 9.5 percent, indicates that jobs with Knowledge=2 pay about 9.5 percent higher than jobs that have Knowledge=1 but that otherwise appear similar.[57] Generally speaking, a one unit increment to knowledge usually raises wages by about 10-15 percent, holding other factors fixed. This is roughly comparable to the wage premium associated with full-time status, or with union coverage.

The wage premiums associated with knowledge are higher than those associated with the other factors. For example, the premiums for increments to supervision received in the same wage regression are all on the order of 7-10 percent, and similarly so for guidelines. There appear also to be some less substantial premiums for the factors of complexity, scope and effect, and supervisory duties. There are, moreover, relatively negligible wage premiums for the other factors, which include measures of how job incumbents interact with others inside and outside of the establishment, and measures of the physical aspects of the job. Therefore, job attributes relating to interpersonal relationships seem not to affect wages, except insofar as they relate to managerial aspects of work. In addition, physically difficult or dangerous jobs seem to pay about the same as jobs that would otherwise have comparable duties.[58]

In sum, results obtained from the NCS survey indicate that the duties most highly valued by the marketplace are generally cognitive or supervisory in nature. To the extent that these measures of job duties or job attributes reflect individual incumbent worker skills, the results suggest that cognitive abilities are quite highly valued by employers. This result is generally in accord with the findings presented earlier in this chapter relating wages to schooling and work related training.

Occupational Shortages[59]

"Evolving technology, shifts in consumer taste, and innovative business practices are among the contributors to progress over the past 35 years and to anticipated growth for the future."[60] Analysis of historical employment trends has shown that technological and other demands in the economy have placed a premium on higher levels of education and training. BLS develops employment projections for more than 500 detailed occupations, which reveal that higher levels of education are associated with the fastest employment growth and high earnings.[61] For the 1996-2006 period, the rates of growth range considerably: from an increase of 118 percent for database administrators, computer support specialists, and all other computer scientists to a decline of 75 percent for typesetting and composing machine operators.

Among the 30 occupations that are projected to grow the fastest, educational requirements and earnings of workers are quite varied; about half require education or training beyond high school. In fact, all education and training categories requiring at least an associate's degree or higher are projected to grow faster than average and have higher than average earnings.

Projections indicate that occupations requiring a bachelor's degree will grow almost twice as fast as the average for all occupations. The top three fastest growing occupations, which are all computer-related, require at least a bachelor's degree and, in 1996, had median weekly earnings that were much higher than average for all full-time wage and salary workers.

Not all of the occupations projected to grow the fastest, however, are in fields requiring postsecondary education. Six of the top 10 fastest growing occupations require varying levels of on-the-job training. These include occupations such as personal and home health aides, medical assistants, desktop publishing specialists, and physical therapy assistants. Despite the fact that jobs usually requiring an associate degree or higher are expected to grow faster than average over the 1996-2006 period, the majority of occupations with the largest expected job growth will require less than an associate degree.

Whenever there is sustained rapid employment growth, there is potential for concern on the part of employers and others about occupational shortages. Labor shortages occur in a market economy when the demand for labor in a particular occupation exceeds the supply of workers who are qualified, available, and willing to do that job. Jobs go vacant as employers seek to hire more workers than are willing to work at the prevailing wage or salary.[62]

The term "labor shortage" is often used to describe a variety of situations, some of which are not generally considered by economists to be actual shortages. When labor is plentiful, employers become accustomed to hiring workers with specific training or levels of experience. When the labor market tightens, however, the number of job applicants is likely to shrink, and employers may have difficulty finding that same

caliber of candidate. The employers may be able to fill positions by offering higher wages; otherwise, they may have to settle for candidates who do not match their notion of "ideal." Under these labor market conditions, the issue becomes one of the *quality* of job candidates, not necessarily *quantity* of people willing and able to do that job. From the employers' perspective, a shortage of workers exists; from the job market perspective, the existence of a shortage could be questioned because a qualified worker filled the job.

Economists who have studied occupational shortages generally hold the view that in an unconstrained market, supply will equal demand at the "true" market price. If demand exceeds supply, salaries will be bid up until the market clears. Thus, in theory, most labor shortages should disappear as employers increase wages to attract more workers. Different types of shortages resulting from various labor market situations may, however, require very different responses from both employers and workers.

Labor shortages can result from a sudden or persistently rapid increase in demand, which outpaces the job market's capacity to supply workers. Often, this type of shortage results from an increase in demand for particular goods or services. Even though wages and the labor supply also may be increasing, a shortage may result because they cannot keep up with demand. If the supply of labor is flexible enough to adjust sufficiently, however, an increase in demand alone may not lead to a shortage.

Shortages resulting from inflexible supply, on the other hand, can occur in occupations for which demand and the level of compensation fail to attract a sufficient number of jobseekers. When years of education and specialized training are required of an occupation, a lag will continue to exist between supply and demand, even if employers increase wages. This is the case with occupations such as physicians and college or university faculty. A decrease in the supply of labor can also create a labor shortage, especially in tight labor markets where employers face keener competition for workers. If wages are higher in other occupations, workers are faced with more choices, making employment in one occupation or for one employer more or less attractive than another.

A slow reaction or response time by employers or by workers also will slow market adjustment time. It may take time for employers to recognize the difficulty of finding workers or for workers to realize the opportunities available. Also, response time may be slowed by institutional barriers, such as limited enrollment capacity in

61

training institutions or requirements such as licensing and certification.

Reluctance on the part of employers to raise wages often causes, or at least contributes to, a shortage. In some cases, the wage or salary level cannot increase because of a fixed compensation structure within an organization. Employers may also be reluctant to raise wages or salaries because the company places a higher priority on avoiding increases in costs. If wages are increased to attract new employees, the employers may then have to increase the wages of workers already on their payrolls to avoid dissension among longer tenured, more experienced employees.

Besides increasing wages, employers can respond in a number of other ways when faced with the difficulty of filling vacancies, but generally try the least expensive response first. One reaction to a perceived shortage involves an increase in recruiting efforts. This can be accomplished by stepping up advertising campaigns and by expanding the recruiting area, which could involve greater use of employment agencies, rewarding existing employees who bring in new workers, or offering bonuses to new hires for joining the firm.

Employers may handle staffing shortages by increasing the use of overtime, restructuring the workforce, or using workers from one occupation to perform the tasks of another occupation. To illustrate: in response to a shortage of registered nurses in the late 1980s, hospitals asked existing staff to work more overtime and restructured the work to make more use of nursing aides, licensed practical nurses, and other hospital workers.

Employers who have difficulty filling vacancies may also relax or reduce the minimum qualifications for the job or expand worker training, or both (in many cases, the two go hand-in-hand). After relaxing the hiring specifications, employers may find that the work can be completed by conducting additional training to bring less qualified workers up to speed. This may involve providing financial assistance to persons still in school, with the stipulation that they will stay with the firm for a specified time once the training is completed.

No single empirical measure of occupational shortages exists, nor does it appear that one can easily be developed. Data available through the Nation's statistical programs, however, can be used to observe some aspects of supply and demand and assess job market conditions. Research on shortages indicates that available data on employment, unemployment rates, and wages can be evaluated to assess the existence of or potential for a shortage.[63]

By looking at "snapshots" of the labor market over time, it is possible to evaluate changes in demand and supply for a particular occupation. For example, dramatic growth in employment in a particular occupation over a period of time likely reflects a significant rise in demand for that type of worker. Likewise, an uncharacteristically low unemployment rate for a specific occupation may imply the demand of workers exceeds supply. Rapidly rising relative wages in a particular occupation also could be associated with a level of demand that exceeds supply.

Assessing supply and demand in a specific occupation also requires analysis of factors such as educational qualifications, training, and entry requirements. Clearly, job market conditions for occupations such as physician and registered nurse, which require specific academic training and a license, must be analyzed differently than for fast food preparation and service workers, jobs that are often filled by high school students. Data on academic completions collected by the U.S. Department of Education, for example, provide information on the supply of graduates by field of study and level of degree for any given year.

Most research studies emphasize the importance of considering multiple measures of labor market conditions and tracking them over time to determine whether conditions of a shortage exist. Available data should be combined with background information on the occupation and knowledge of the workings of the labor market. Information on supply such as data on demographic characteristics, educational completions by field of study, and employer education and training requirements plays a significant role in completing an analysis of the labor market in an occupation.

As indicated earlier in this chapter, the United States has enjoyed over 7 years of economic expansion, during which the national unemployment rate dropped from 7.5 percent in 1992 to 4.5 percent in 1998, the lowest level since 1969. As the labor market tightened over this period, shortages in certain occupations were widely reported in the media, led by stories of unmet needs for workers skilled in information technology. Groups such as the Information Technology Association of America and the U.S. Department of Commerce's Office of Technology Policy identified what they considered "substantial evidence that the United States is having trouble keeping up with the demand for new information technology workers."[64] Shortages also were reported for construction laborers and craft workers. According to the National Center for Construction Education and

Research, "Sixty-five percent of the contractors responding to its third annual survey in 1997 reported shortages in one or more crafts."[65] Related stories in papers across the country proclaimed the resurgence of a shortfall of registered nurses, a need for qualified teachers, and even shortages of workers such as roustabouts and nannies.

At this time, no specific sources of data exist that provide a measure of occupational shortages. In the absence of any definitive measure, analysts generally rely on labor market data to corroborate anecdotal reports of employers' difficulties in filling jobs. Labor market data, combined with background information on a specified occupation, anecdotal evidence, and factors of demand and supply work in combination to assess occupational shortages.

Conclusion

When change occurs in the production of goods and services both workers and employers must adapt. The types of jobs employers need are dictated in large part by changing consumer demands and international trade, but also by changes in technology, which evoke a restructuring of the nature of work. Workers have responded by acquiring the skills needed through education and job training. Changing family relationships have led women to enter the labor market in increasing numbers. Those workers who have gained skills that are in demand have been increasingly well rewarded. This chapter documents many of these effects.

Skills are, of course, multidimensional. Furthermore, some dimensions of skill are quite difficult to measure. This chapter therefore adopts the pragmatic approach of measuring skills in different ways. At times, schooling and work experience levels have been used as a proxy for skill. At other points, wage rates themselves have been used to measure skill. The main emphasis has been, however, on occupation as a summary indicator of skill.

The most fundamental finding is that skills are rewarded. It is abundantly clear that greater schooling and training tend to lead to higher wage rates. It is also clear that there are substantial differences in job duties and wage rates, both across occupations and within occupations. Occupations have specific competency profiles, and competency pays. This appears to be particularly true for competencies or abilities that might be broadly considered cognitive in nature. The ability to do complex work or manage effectively is also highly valued. Differences in competencies have resulted in wage dispersion within occupations.

By most of our measures, the skill levels of the American workforce have increased substantially in the recent past. This is most apparent in increased schooling levels. It is also apparent in occupational shifts. Most employment growth is in occupations not requiring a postsecondary degree—a set of occupations that spans a large fraction of the jobs in the American labor market—but occupations with higher schooling requirements are growing faster than average. Consequently, employment has shifted toward occupations requiring more education and training.

These occupational shifts are reflected in occupational upskilling, meaning shifts in employment toward jobs that tend to pay higher wages. Conceptually such upskilling can occur through shifts in the industrial structure, or through shifts in occupational composition within industries. The relative importance of these avenues of occupational upskilling differ among industrial categories, at least in the labor market of the 1990s. The primary contributor to the increase in skills is occupational upgrading within industries. Shifts in industrial composition account for a small portion of the overall increase in skill change. In addition, most of the change is due to the growing service-producing industries.

There is no guarantee that the forces causing changes in the recent past will persist into the near future. The value and need for skills will, therefore, likely change in unpredictable ways. "Although employers will continue to require workers at all levels of education and training, those with the most education or work experience usually will have more options in the job market and better prospects for obtaining the higher-paying jobs."[66]

Table 2-1. **Employment shifts among occupational groups averaged over detailed industries sorted by change in share. 1989-97**

Industry and occupation	Wage-weighted employment[1]			
	Percent share in 1989	Percent share in 1997	Change in share	1997 mean wage
All industries				
Professional	24.4	29.0	4.6	$19.01
Sales workers....................................	10.1	10.7	0.6	15.07
Production II[2].....................................	14.7	12.9	- 1.8	10.33
Agricultural	0.4	0.5	.1	9.59
Production I[3]....................................	12.9	11.2	- 1.7	13.84
Service occupations	7.8	8.9	1.1	9.25
Managerial	14.7	13.6	- 1.1	26.96
Clerical	15.0	13.3	- 1.7	10.93
Goods-producing sector				
Production II[2].....................................	30.4	30.7	.3	11.47
Production I[3].....................................	25.5	27.7	2.2	15.34
Agricultural	.3	.7	.4	11.66
Sales workers....................................	3.6	3.7	.1	20.55
Service occupations	.9	.7	- .2	10.20
Professional	16.6	15.1	- 1.5	19.99
Managerial	14.0	13.7	- .3	29.91
Clerical	8.7	7.6	- 1.1	11.94
Service-producing sector				
Professional	28.0	33.6	5.6	18.68
Sales..	13.1	13.0	- .1	13.25
Production I[3]....................................	7.1	5.7	- 1.4	13.34
Agricultural	.4	.4	([4])	9.04
Service occupations	11.0	11.6	.6	8.93
Production II[2]....................................	7.4	7.0	- .4	9.95
Managerial	14.9	13.5	- 1.4	25.97
Clerical	18.0	15.2	- 2.8	10.59

[1] Calculated by multiplying the total industry employment of each occupation by its wage rate.
[2] Includes machine setters, set-up operators, operators, and tenders; hand working production occupations; plant and system occupations; transportation and material moving machine and vehicle operators; and helpers, laborers, and material movers, hand.
[3] Includes production supervisors; inspectors; mechanics, installers, and repairers; construction trades and extractive occupations; and precision production occupations.
[4] Indicates value is less than 0.05 percent and greater than -0.05 percent.

SOURCE: Tabulations from the Occupational Employment Statistics Survey 1989-97, Bureau of Labor Statistics, U.S. Department of Labor

Table 2-2. **Index of skill change within occupational groups, 1989-97**

Industry sector	Skill index						
	Manage-rial	Profes-sional	Clerical	Sales	Service	Produc-tion I[1]	Produc-tion II[2]
All industries	- 0.4	0.7	0.3	0.8	- 0.8	0.6	([3])
Goods-producing sector:	.4	- .1	.6	- 1.0	- 2.1	.8	([3])
Mining and Construction	.7	- 1.0	1.1	- .6	- .1	.7	- 0.8
Manufacturing	.3	.2	.5	- 1.1	- 2.8	.9	.2
Service-producing sector:	- .7	1.0	.2	1.4	- .3	.5	([4])
Transportation, communications, public utilities	- .6	- .4	- .3	- .1	- 1.6	.2	([4])
Trade	.4	.2	.4	.3	1.2	2.2	([4])
Finance, insurance, and real estate	([3])	- .1	.7	- .7	- .5	2.5	([4])
Services	- 1.5	1.9	.1	2.7	- .8	- .6	([4])

[1] Includes production supervisors; inspectors; mechanics, installers, and repairers; construction trades and extractive occupations; and precision production occupations.

[2] Includes machine setters, set-up operators, operators, and tenders; hand working production occupations; plant and system occupations; transportation and material moving machine and vehicle operators; and helpers, laborers, and material movers, hand.

[3] Indicates value is less than 0.05 percent and greater than -0.05 percent.

[4] Data do not meet publication standards.

SOURCE: Tabulations from the Occupational Employment Statistics Survey 1989-97, Bureau of Labor Statistics, U.S. Department of Labor.

Table 2-3. **Employment shifts among clerical, service, and production I[1] occupations within detailed industries averaged across all industries, 1989-97**

Occupational group	Wage-weighted employment[2]			1997 mean wage
	Percent share in 1989	Percent share in 1997	Change in share	
Clerical				
Industry-specific clerical	8.5	10.7	2.2	$10.74
Material recording, scheduling, dispatching, and distributing	14.6	14.7	0.1	10.74
First line clerical supervisors	9.1	10.9	1.8	15.62
Other clerical occupations	2.6	2.9	.3	11.14
Communications equipment operators and mail clerks	1.9	1.7	- .2	9.12
Data-processing and other office machine operators.............................	4.2	3.4	- .8	10.79
Secretaries	59.1	55.8	- 3.3	10.66
Service				
Service supervisors.............................	11.3	9.1	- 2.2	15.00
Protective service	15.6	13.7	- 1.9	10.14
Food and beverage preparation and service......................................	14.9	15.0	.1	8.11
Health services and related	7.0	10.6	3.6	8.92
Cleaning and building service	42.6	41.5	- 1.1	8.39
Personal service..................................	3.2	4.0	.8	7.96
Other service occupations	5.5	6.0	.5	9.70
Production I[1]				
Production, construction, maintenance supervisors	19.0	21.1	2.1	17.77
Inspectors and related	5.6	5.2	- .4	12.42
Mechanics, installers, and repairers	46.3	48.2	1.9	13.01
Construction trades and extractive occupations	14.8	14.7	-.1	14.68
Precision production occupations	14.4	10.8	- 3.6	13.10

[1] Includes the occupational groups listed in the table above and excludes machine setters, set-up operators, operators, and tenders; hand working production occupations; plant and system occupations; transportation and material moving machine and vehicle operators; and helpers, laborers, and material movers, hand, which are aggregated under production II.

[2] Calculated by multiplying the total industry employment of each occupation by its wage rate.

SOURCE: Tabulations from the Occupational Employment Statistics Survey 1989-97, Bureau of Labor Statistics, U.S. Department of Labor

Table 2-4. **Percent distribution of workers in selected occupations by level,[1] 1996**

Occupation	Level							
	I	II	III	IV	V	VI	VII	VIII
Professional								
Accountant	9.1	31.5	36.7	17.9	4.3	0.6	-	-
Accountant-public	20.2	30.3	33.6	15.9	-	-	-	-
Attorneys	9.2	21.9	30.4	25.2	10.9	2.3		
Engineers	4.8	12.3	26.3	29.1	18.7	7.0	1.6	0.2
Administrative								
Budget analysts	6.3	27.4	41.2	25.1	-	-	-	-
Buyer/contracting specialist	14.9	44.2	31.1	9.8	-	-	-	-
Computer programmers	6.9	30.9	38.2	17.3	6.8	-	-	-
Computer systems analysts	17.1	45.5	29.2	7.4	.8	-	-	-
Computer systems supervisors/managers	46.6	43.0	10.4	-	-	-	-	-
Personnel specialists	3.4	27.3	37.9	24.0	6.5	.8	-	-
Personnel supervisors/ managers	35.0	40.1	20.2	4.7	-	-	-	-
Tax collectors	13.5	46.7	39.8	-	-	-	-	-
Technical								
Computer operators..........................	6.4	49.7	35.9	7.4	.6	-	-	-
Drafters	11.4	34.6	36.3	17.7	-	-	-	-
Engineering technicians	2.9	12.5	26.8	33.2	19.8	4.8	-	-
Engineering technicians/civil	9.0	17.5	35.2	27.7	9.2	1.4	-	-
Protective service								
Police officers	96.6	3.4	-	-	-	-	-	-
Clerical								
Clerks, accounting	3.1	49.0	38.4	9.6	-	-	-	-
Clerks, general	3.6	30.8	43.7	21.9	-	-	-	-
Clerks, order.....................................	70.3	29.7	-	-	-	-	-	-
Key entry operators	63.3	36.7	-	-	-	-	-	-
Personnel assistants	7.8	39.6	41.0	11.6	-	-	-	-
Secretaries	16.8	31.7	34.5	14.3	2.7	-	-	-
Word processors	31.0	57.0	12.0	-	-	-	-	-
Maintenance and toolroom								
Maintenance electronic technicians ...	9.6	75.4	14.9	-	-	-	-	-
Material movement and custodial								
Guards	87.6	12.4	-	-	-	-	-	-
Truckdrivers[2]...................................	11.1	26.2	26.3	36.4	-	-	-	-

[1] Occupations included in Occupational Compensation Survey pre-set job list.

[2] Data were compiled for four different truckdriver occupations—Light, medium, heavy, and tractor-trailer. For this illustration, these truckdriver occupations were classified as levels I, II, III, and IV, respectively, because the job duties and skills required increased for each job level.

NOTE: Dashes indicate that the level was not applicable to the occupation.

SOURCE: *Occupational Compensation Survey: National Summary, 1996*, Bulletin 2497, March 1998, Bureau of Labor Statistics, U.S. Department of Labor

Table 2-5. Mean weekly and hourly earnings by level for selected occupations,[1] 1996

Occupation	Level							
	I	II	III	IV	V	VI	VII	VIII
Weekly earnings								
Professional								
Accountant	$523	$626	$811	$1,041	$1,375	$1,734	-	-
Accountant-public	594	641	747	977	-	-	-	-
Attorneys	700	952	1,260	1,647	1,994	2,415	-	-
Engineers	675	805	959	1,167	1,411	1,659	$1,962	$2,343
Administrative								
Budget analysts	585	667	858	964	-	-	-	-
Buyer/contracting specialist	522	662	889	1,085	-	-	-	-
Computer programmers	543	639	788	945	1,095	-	-	-
Computer systems analysts	779	940	1,111	1,321	1,527	-	-	-
Computer systems supervisors/								
managers	1,202	1,408	1,665	-	-	-	-	-
Personnel specialists	515	611	804	1,045	1,362	1,784	-	-
Personnel supervisors/managers	1,160	1,460	1,788	2,253	-	-	-	-
Tax collectors	513	588	771	-	-	-	-	-
Technical								
Computer operators	357	448	576	689	820	-	-	-
Drafters	408	504	640	816	-	-	-	-
Engineering technicians	390	518	650	781	898	1,070	-	-
Engineering technicians-civil	356	489	593	730	865	1,081	-	-
Protective service								
Police officers	770	930	-	-	-	-	-	-
Clerical								
Clerks, accounting	320	379	464	549	-	-	-	-
Clerks, general	289	342	429	493	-	-	-	-
Clerks, order	345	477	-	-	-	-	-	-
Key entry operators	353	414	-	-	-	-	-	-
Personnel assistants	332	409	508	596	-	-	-	-
Secretaries	385	476	557	665	809	-	-	-
Word processors	389	496	610	-	-	-	-	-
Hourly earnings								
Maintenance and toolroom								
Maintenance electronic technicians	11.89	18.14	20.56	-	-	-	-	-
Material movement and custodial								
Guards	7.11	12.14	-	-	-	-	-	-
Truckdrivers[2]	8.53	14.81	13.38	14.24	-	-	-	-

[1] See footnote 1, table 2-4.
[2] See footnote 2, table 2-4.

NOTE: Dashes indicate that the level was not applicable to the occupation.

SOURCE: *Occupational Compensation Survey: National Summary, 1996*, Bulletin 2497, March 1996, Bureau of Labor Statistics, U.S. Department of Labor

Table 2-6. **Modal values of selected generic leveling factors by major occupational group, 1998**

Major occupational group	Knowledge (Scale:1-9)	Supervision received (Scale:1-5)	Guidelines (Scale:1-5)
Professional	6	3	3
Technical	4	3	2
Executive	6	3	3
Sales	2	2	1
Clerical	3	2	2
Precision production	4	3	3
Machine operatives	2	2	1
Transport	2	2	2
Laborers	1	1	1
Service	2	1	1

SOURCE: Tabulations from the 1998 National Compensation Survey, Bureau of Labor Statistics, U.S. Department of Labor

Table 2-7. **Average hourly wage rates by knowledge level, 1998**

Major occupational group	Knowledge level								
	1	2	3	4	5	6	7	8	9
All	$6.68	$8.88	$11.96	$16.12	$18.61	$23.06	$31.15	$46.08	$53.68
Professional	-	-	-	12.39	18.04	23.59	29.76	42.03	-
Technical	-	8.85	11.16	14.60	17.91	23.79	-	-	-
Executive	-	-	-	13.42	15.71	20.69	31.32	49.26	-
Sales	6.30	7.74	10.16	14.62	-	-	-	-	-
Clerical	6.84	9.02	11.58	15.05	16.24	-	-	-	-
Precision production	-	9.36	13.65	18.07	21.89	25.35	-	-	-
Machine operatives	7.37	10.22	13.11	16.51	-	-	-	-	-
Transport	7.27	11.66	14.59	18.17	-	-	-	-	-
Laborers	7.13	9.75	13.33	-	-	-	-	-	-
Service	6.18	7.18	10.65	16.16	-	-	-	-	-

NOTE: Dashes indicate that the level was not applicable to the occupation.

SOURCE: Tabulations from the 1998 National Compensation Survey, Bureau of Labor Statistics, U.S. Department of Labor

Table 2-8. **Estimated wage premiums for greater job duties, 1998**[1]
(in percent)

Level	Knowl-edge	Super-vision re-ceived	Guide-lines	Com-plexity	Scope and effect	Per-sonal con-tacts	Pur-pose of con-tacts	Physi-cal de-mands	Work envi-ron-ment	Super-visory duties
1	-	-	-	-	-	-	-	-	-	-
2	9.5	8.8	6.5	2.6	2.6	-1.2	2.5	-2.3	3.8	1.7
3	18.7	17.1	11.5	7.8	5.4	1.6	3.3	-2.1	5.9	6.7
4	35.6	25.6	21.0	9.1	7.0	6.5	2.9	-	-	14.0
5	57.2	38.2	35.0	14.0	14.0	-	-	-	-	42.4
6	80.5	-	-	28.3	2.0	-	-	-	-	-
7	106.7	-	-	-	-	-	-	-	-	-
8	128.2	-	-	-	-	-	-	-	-	-
9	116.6	-	-	-	-	-	-	-	-	-

[1] The table presents wage differentials between jobs with the given levels of the job attribute and jobs with the lowest level of the attribute. Wage differentials are shown in percent, and are based on a wage regression that controls for other characteristics of the establishment and job.

NOTE: Dashes indicate that the level was not applicable to the occupation.

SOURCE: Regression results from the 1998 National Compensation Survey, Bureau of Labor Statistics, U.S. Department of Labor

References

Abraham, Katherine G. and Henry S. Farber (1987). "Job Duration, Seniority and Earnings." *American Economic Review*, pp. 278-297.

Allen, Steven (1984). "Unionized Construction Workers are More Productive." *Quarterly Journal of Economics*, 99, pp. 251-274.

Arrow, Kenneth J. and William M. Capron. "Dynamic Shortage and Price Rises: The Engineer-Scientist Case." *Quarterly Journal of Economics*, Vol. LXXIII, No. 2 (May 1959), pp. 292-308.

Arulampalam, Wiji, and Alison L. Booth (1997). "Who Gets Over the Training Hurdle? A Study of the Training Experiences of Young Men and Women in Britain. *"Journal of Population Economics*, 10, pp. 197-217.

Autor, David H., Lawrence Katz, and Alan B. Krueger (1997). "Computing Inequality: Have Computers Changed the Labor Market?" National Bureau of Economic Research, Working Paper No. 5986.

Barron, John M., Dan A. Black, and Mark A. Loewenstein (1989). "Job Matching and On-the-Job Training." *Journal of Labor Economics*, 7, pp. 1-19.

Becker, Gary (1964). *Human Capital*, 1st Ed. New York: Columbia University Press.

Ben-Porath, Yoram. "The Production of Human Capital and the Life Cycle of Earnings." *Journal of Political Economy*, August 1967, pp. 352-365.

Bernard, Andrew B. and J. Bradford Jensen (1997). "Exporters, Skill Upgrading, and the Wage Gap." *Journal of International Economics*, 42, pp. 3-31.

Berndt, Ernst R. and Catherine J. Morrison (1995). "High-Tech Capital Formation and Economic Performance in U.S. Manufacturing Industries: An Exploratory Analysis." *Journal of Econometrics*, 65, pp. 9-43

Berndt, Ernst R, Catherine Morrison, and Larry S. Rosenblum (1992). "High-Tech Capital Formation and Labor Composition in U.S. Manufacturing Industries: An Exploratory Analysis." NBER Working Paper No. 4010.

Blank, David M. and George J. Stiger. *The Demand and Supply of Scientific Personnel*. New York: National Bureau of Economic Research, 1957.

BLS Bulletin 2426 (1993). *Labor Composition and U.S. Productivity Growth, 1948-90*, Washington: U.S. Department of Labor, Bureau of Labor Statistics.

Borjas, George J., Richard B. Freeman and Lawrence F. Katz (1997). "How Much Do Immigration and Trade Affect Labor Market Outcomes?" *Brookings Papers on Economic Activity*, 1: 1997, pp. 1-90.

Broadberry, Stephen N. (1993). "Manufacturing and the Convergence Hypothesis: What the Long-Run Data Show." *Journal of Economic History*, 53, pp. 772-795.

Card, David (1998). "Falling Union Membership and Rising Wage Inequality: What's the Connection?" NBER Working Paper No. 6520.

_____. (1996). "The Effect of Unions on the Structure of Wages: A Longitudinal Analysis." *Econometrica*, 64 (4), pp. 957-979.

Cappelli, Peter (1993). "Are Skill Requirements Rising? Evidence from Production and Clerical Jobs." *Industrial and Labor Relations Review*, Vol. 46, No. 3, pp. 515-530.

_____. (1996). "Technology and Skill Requirements: Implications for Establishment Wage Structures." *New England Economic Review*, May/June, pp. 130-154.

"Charting the Projections: 1996-2006." *Occupational Outlook Quarterly*, U.S. Department of Labor, Bureau of Labor Statistics, Winter 1997-98.

Cohen, Malcolm S. *Labor Shortages as America Approaches the Twenty First Century*. Ann Arbor, Michigan: University of Michigan Press, 1995.

Connelly, Rachel and Peter Gottschalk (1995). "The Effect of Cohort Composition on Human Capital Accumulation Across Generations." *Journal of Labor Economics*, Vol. 13, No 1, pp. 155-176.

Dunlop, John T (1957). "The Task of Contemporary Wage Theory," in *New Concepts in Wage Determination*, ed. G. W. Taylor and F.C. Pierson. New York: McGraw-Hill.

DiNardo, John E. and Jorn-Steffan Pischke (1997). "The Returns to Computer Use Revisited: Have Pencils Changed the Wage Structure Too?" *Quarterly Journal of Economics*, pp. 291-303.

Employee Turnover and Job Openings Survey: Results of a Pilot Study on the Feasibility of Collecting Measures of Imbalances of Supply and Demand for Labor in an Establishment Survey. Washington: U.S. Department of Labor, Bureau of Labor Statistics, 1991. (Unnumbered report.)

Employment and Earnings, Vol. 46, No. 1, Washington: U.S. Department of Labor, Bureau of Labor Statistics.

"Employment Outlook: 1996-2006." *Monthly Labor Review*, November 1997.

Employment Outlook, 1996-2006: A Summary of BLS Projections, Bulletin 2502, U.S. Department of Labor, Bureau of Labor Statistics, February 1998.

Evaluating Your Firm's Jobs and Pay. (Brochure) Washington: U.S. Department of Labor, Bureau of Labor Statistics.

Feenstra, Robert C. and Gordon H. Hanson (1997). "Direct Foreign Investment and Relative Wages: Evidence from Mexico's Maquiladoras." *Journal of International Economics*, Vol. 42, pp. 371-393.

Filer, Randall K. (1992). "The Effect of Immigrant Arrivals on Migratory Patterns of National Workers." In *Immigration and the Work Force: Economic Consequences for the United States and Source Areas*, Borjas and Freeman, eds., Chicago: University of Chicago Press, pp. 245-269.

Finegold, David (1994). "The Changing International Economy," In *Something Borrowed, Something Learned? The Transatlantic Market in Education and Training Reform.* Finegold, McFarland, and Richardson, eds. Washington: Brookings Institution, pp. 47-75.

Franke, Walter and Irving Sobel. *The Shortage of Skilled Technical Workers.* Lexington, Mass.: Heath-Lexington Books, 1970

Frazis, Harley, Maury Gittleman, Michael Horrigan, and Mary Joyce (1998). "Results from the 1995 Survey of Employer-Provided Training." *Monthly Labor Review*, June, pp. 3-13.

Frazis, Harley J., Diane E. Herz, and Michael W. Horrigan (1995). "Employer-provided Training: Results from a New Survey." *Monthly Labor Review*, Vol. 118, No. 5, pp. 3-17.

Goldin, Claudia and Lawrence F. Katz (1998). "The Origins of Technology-Skill Complementarity." *Quarterly Journal of Economics*, pp. 693-732;

Goldin and Robert A Margo (1992). "The Great Compression: The Wage Structure in the United States in Mid-Century." *Quarterly Journal of Economics*, Vol. 107, pp. 1-34.

Griliches, Zvi, ed. (1971). *Price Indexes and Quality Changes.* Cambridge, Massachusetts: Harvard University Press.

Henderson, Richard (1979). *Compensation Management and Rewarding Performance*, Reston, VA: Reston Publishing Co.

Howell, David R. and Edward N. Wolff (1991). "Trends in the Growth and Distribution of Skills in the U.S. Workplace, 1960-1985." *Industrial and Labor Relations Review*, Vol. 44, No. 3. (April 1991)

Johnson, George E. (1997). "Changes in Earnings Inequality: The Role of Demand Shifts." *Journal of Economic Perspectives*, Vol. 11, No. 2, pp. 41-54.

Juhn, Chinhui, Kevin M. Murphy and Brooks Pierce (1993). "Wage Inequality and the Rise in Returns to Skill." *Journal of Political Economy*, Vol. 101, No. 3, pp. 410-442.

Kane, Thomas J. (1994). "College Entry by Blacks Since 1970: The Role of College Costs, Family Background, and the Returns to Education." *Journal of Political Economy*, Vol. 102, No. 5, pp. 878-911.

Katz, Lawrence F. and Kevin M. Murphy (1992). "Changes in Relative Wages, 1963-1987: Supply and Demand Factors." *Quarterly Journal of Economics*, Vol. 107, No. 1., February, 1992.

Katz, Lawrence F. and Ana L. Revenga (1989). "Changes in the Structure of Wages: The U.S. vs. Japan." *Journal of Japanese International Economies*, Vol. 3, No. 4 pp. 522-553.

Krueger, Alan B. (1997), "Labor Market Shifts and the Price Puzzle Revisited." Princeton University Industrial Relations Section, Working Paper No.375.

_____ and Lawrence H. Summers (1988). "Efficiency Wages and the Inter-Industry Wage Structure." *Econometrica*, Vol. 56, pp. 259-293.

Levy, Frank and Richard J. Murname (1992). "U.S. Earnings Levels and Earnings Inequality: A Review of Recent Trends and Proposed Explanations." *Journal of Economic Literature*, Vol. XXX, pp.1333-1381.

Mark, Jerome A. (1987). "Technological change and employment: some results from BLS research." *Monthly Labor Review*, U.S. Department of Labor, Bureau of Labor Statistics, Vol. 110, No. 4, pp. 26-29.

McElroy, Michael P. and Michael B. Hazzard (1994). "Occupational Staffing Patterns at the Four-Digit SIC Level." *Monthly Labor Review*, U.S. Department of Labor, Bureau of Labor Statistics, Vol. 117, No. 2., February, 1994.

Melchionno, Rick, and Michael Sean Steinman (1998). "The 1996-2006 Job Outlook in Brief." *Occupational Outlook Quarterly*, U.S. Department of Labor, Bureau of Labor Statistics, Spring 1998, pp. 2-39.

Mincer, Jacob (1958). "Investments in Human Capital and Personal Income Distribution." *Journal of Political Economy*, Vol. 66, No. 4, pp. 281-302.

_____. (1974). *Schooling, Experience and Earnings*. New York: Columbia University Press.

Mishel, Lawrence, Jared Bernstein, and John Schmitt. (1997). "Did Technology Have Any Effect on the Growth of Wage Inequality in the 1980s and 1990s?" Mimeo/Preliminary Draft. Economic Policy Institute.

Murphy, Kevin M. and Finis Welch. (1992). "The Structure of Wages." *Quarterly Journal of Economics*, Vol. 107, No. 1, pp. 215-326.

_____. (1993). "Occupational Change and the Demand For Skill, 1940-1990." *American Economic Association Papers and Proceedings*, Vol. 83. No. 2. (May 1993).

National Center for Education Statistics (1998). *The Condition of Education, 1998*. Washington, D.C.

Neal, Derek A. and William R. Johnson (1996). "The Role of Premarket Factors in Black-White Wage Differences." *Journal of Political Economy*, Vol. 104, No. 5, pp. 869-895.

Neumark, David (1998). "Youth Labor Markets in the U.S.: Shopping Around vs. Staying Put." NBER Working Paper No. 6581.

Newman, Katherine (1999). *No Shame in My Game: Working Poor in the Inner City*. New York: Knopf and Russell Sage.

Occupational Compensation Survey: National Summary, 1996. Bulletin 2497, U.S. Department of Labor, Bureau of Labor Statistics, March 1998.

Occupational Outlook Handbook, 1966-67 Edition. Bulletin 1450, U.S. Department of Labor, Bureau of Labor Statistics, 1968.

Occupational Outlook Handbook, 1998-99 Edition. Bulletin 2500, U.S. Department of Labor, Bureau of Labor Statistics, January, 1998.

O'Mahony, Mary A. (1998). "Anglo-German Productivity Differences: The Role of Broad Capital." *Bulletin of Economic Research*. Vol. 50 (1), pp. 19-36.

Pencavel, John (1972). "Wages, Specific Training, and Labor Turnover in U.S. Manufacturing Industries." *International Economic Review*. Vol. 13, No. 1, pp. 53-64.

Plunkert, Lois (1981). *Job Openings Pilot Program: Final Report*. Washington: U.S. Department of Labor, Bureau of Labor Statistics.

Revenga, Ana, Michelle Riboud and Hong Tan (1994). "The Impact of Mexico's Retraining Program on Employment and Wages." *The World Bank Economic Review*, Vol. 8, No. 2, pp. 247-277.

Rosen, Sherwin (1974). "Hedonic Prices and Implicit Markets: Product Differentiation in Pure Competition." *Journal of Political Economy*. Vol. 82, No. 1, pp. 34-55.

Ruggles, Nancy and Richard Ruggles (1977). "The Anatomy of Earnings Behavior." In *The Distribution of Economic Well-Being*. New York: NBER, pp. 115-158.

Schultz, Theodore W. (1963). *The Economic Value of Education*. New York: Columbia University Press.

Scott, Elizabeth D., K.C. O'Shaughnessy and Peter Cappelli (1996). "Management Jobs in the Insurance Industry: Organizational Deskilling and Rising Pay Inequality." In *Broken Ladders: Managerial Careers in the New Economy*, Osterman, ed. New York: Oxford University Press, pp. 126-154.

Seike, Atsushi and Hong W. Tan (1994). "Labor Fixity and Labor Market Adjustments in Japan and the United States." In *Troubled Industries in the United States and Japan*, Tan and Shimada, eds. New York: St. Martin's Press, pp. 211-233.

Silvestri, George T., "Occupational Employment Projections to 2006," *Monthly Labor Review*, November 1997, pp. 58-83.

Survey of Current Business (1997). "Selected NIPA Series," July, p. D-49.

Tan, Hong W. and Christine Peterson (1993). "Postschool Training of British and American Youth." In *Something Borrowed, Something Learned?*, pp. 73-95.

Teece, D. J. (1977). "Technology Transfer by Multinational Firms: The Resource Cost of Transferring Technological Know-How." *Economic Journal*. Vol. 87, pp. 242-261.

Topel, Robert (1991). "Specific Capital, Mobility and Wages: Wages Rise with Job Seniority." *Journal of Political Economy*. Vol. 99, pp. 145-176.

Trutko, John W., Burt S. Barnow, Amy B. Chasanov, and Abhay Pande. *Labor Shortage Case Studies*. Washington: U.S. Department of Labor, Employment and Training Administration, Research and Evaluation Report Series 93-E, 1993.

Veneri, Carolyn M. (1999). "Can Occupational Labor Shortages Be Identified Using Available Data?" *Monthly Labor Review*. March, pp. 15-21.

Wash, Darrel Patrick. "A New Way to Classify Occupations by Education and Training." *Occupational Outlook Quarterly*. Winter 1995-96, pp. 28-40.

Weinstein, Harriet. "Overview of the NCS: Summer 1998." *Compensation and Working Conditions*. Summer 1998.

Zuboff, Shoshona. (1988). *In the Age of the Smart Machine: The Future of Work and Power*. N.Y.: Basic Books.

Endnotes

[1] BLS Bulletin 2426 (1993), *Labor Composition and U.S. Productivity Growth, 1948-90*, Washington: U.S. Department of Labor, Bureau of Labor Statistics; *Survey of Current Business* (1997), "Selected NIPA Series," July issue, p. D-49; Mary A. O'Mahony, (1998), "Anglo-German Productivity Differences: The Role of Broad Capital," *Bulletin of Economic Research*, 50 (1), pp. 19-36

[2] Bureau of Labor Statistics, Occupational Employment Statistics survey historical files database, 1989-95.

[3] Jerome A. Mark (1987), "Technological Change and Employment: Some Results from BLS Research," *Monthly Labor Review*, Vol. 110, No. 4, pp. 26-29.

[4] Claudia Golden and Lawrence F. Katz (1998), "The Origin of Technology-skill Complementarity," Quarterly Journal of Economics, pp. 693-732; Stephen N. Broadberry (1993), "Manufacturing and the Convergence Hypothesis: What the Long-Run Data Show," *Journal of Economic History*, Vol. 53, pp. 772-795; Claudia Golden and Robert A. Margo (1992), "The Great Compression: The Wage Structure in the United States in Mid-Century," *Quarterly Journal of Economics*, Vol. 107, pp. 1-34, especially section II.E.

[5] Dave Finegold (1994), "The Changing International Economy," in *Something Borrowed, Something Learned? The Transatlantic Market in Education and Training Reform*, Feingold, McFarland, and Richardson, eds., Washington: Brookings Institution, pp. 47-75; Robert C. Feenstra and Gordon H. Hanson (1997), "Direct Foreign Investment and Relative Wages: Evidence from Mexico's Maquiladoras," *Journal of International Economics*, Vol. 42, pp. 371-393.

[6] Andrew B. Bernard and J. Bradford Jensen (1997), "Exporters, Skill Upgrading, and the Wage Gap," *Journal of International Economics*, Vol. 42, pp. 3-31.

[7] D. J. Teece (1977), "Technology Transfer by Multinational Firms: The Resource Cost of Transferring Technological Know-How," *Economic Journal*, 87, pp. 242-261.

[8] David H. Autor, Lawrence Katz, and Alan B. Krueger (1997), "Computing Inequality: Have Computers Changed the Labor Market?" National Bureau of Economic Research, Working Paper No. 5986; John E. DiNardo and Jorn-Steffan Pischke (1997), "The Returns to Computer Use Revisited: Have Pencils Changed the Wage Structure Too?" *Quarterly Journal of Economics*, pp. 291-303. Ernst R. Berndt and Catherine J. Morrison (1995), "High-Tech Capital Formation and Economic Performance in U.S. Manufacturing Industries: An Exploratory Analysis," *Journal of Econometrics*, Vol. 65, pp. 9-43. Berndt, Morrison and Larry S. Rosenblum (1992), "High-Tech Capital Formation and Labor Composition in U.S. Manufacturing Industries: An Exploratory Analysis," NBER Working Paper No. 4010.

[9] Alan B. Krueger (1997), "Labor Market Shifts and the Price Puzzle Revisited," Princeton University Industrial Relations Section, Working Paper No.375; Feenstra and Hanson, cited above.

[10] David Card (1998), "Falling Union Membership and Rising Wage Inequality: What's the Connection?" NBER Working Paper No. 6520; Card (1996), "The Effect of Unions on the Structure of Wages: A Longitudinal Analysis," *Econometrica*, Vol. 64, No. 4, pp. 957-979.

[11] Goldin and Margo, "The Great Compression..." pp. 1-34, especially section II.E.

[12] See the discussion in section IV below, and in BLS Bulletin 2426 (1993), *Labor Composition*, cited above, pp. 9-11.

[13] Thomas J. Kane (1994), "College Entry by Blacks Since 1970: The Role of College Costs, Family Background, and the Returns to Education," *Journal of Political Economy*, Vol. 102, No.5, pp. 878-911. Derek A. Neal and William R. Johnson (1996), "The Role of Premarket Factors in Black-White Wage Differences," *Journal of Political Economy*, Vol. 104, No. 5, pp. 869-895.

[14] National Center for Education Statistics (1998), *The Condition of Education 1998*, Washington, D.C., Indicator 21; survey data were collected in the fall of 1994.

[15] Harley J. Frazis, Diane E. Herz, and Michael W. Horrigan (1995), "Employer-provided Training: Results from a New Survey," *Monthly Labor Review*, Vol. 118, No. 5, pp. 3-17.

[16] John M. Barron, Dan A. Black, and Mark A. Loewenstein (1989), "Job Matching and On-the-Job Training," *Journal of Labor Economics*, Vol. 7, pp. 1-19.

[17] Hong W. Tan and Christine Peterson (1993), "Postschool Training of British and American Youth," in *Something Borrowed, Something Learned? The Transatlantic Market in Education and Training Reform*, Finegold, McFarland and Richardson, eds. Washington: Brookings Institution, pp. 73-95.

[18] David Neumark (1998), "Youth Labor Markets in the U.S.: Shopping Around vs. Staying Put," NBER Working Paper No. 6581; Robert Topel (1991), "Specific Capital, Mobility and Wages: Wages Rise with Job Seniority," *Journal of Political Economy*, Vol. 99, pp. 145-176.

[19] Rachel Connelly and Peter Gottschalk (1995), "The Effect of Cohort Composition on Human Capital Accumulation Across Generations," *Journal of Labor Economics*, Vol. 13, No. 1, pp. 155-176.

[20] George J. Borjas, Richard B. Freeman and Lawrence F. Katz (1997), "How Much Do Immigration and Trade Affect Labor Market Outcomes?" *Brookings Papers on Economic Activity*, Vol. 1, 1997, pp. 1-90.

[21] Katherine Newman (1999), *No Shame in My Game: Working Poor in the Inner City*, New York: Knopf and Russell Sage; Randall K. Filer (1992), "The Effect of Immigrant Arrivals on Migratory Patterns of National Workers," in *Immigration and the Work Force: Economic Consequences for the United States and Source Areas*, Borjas and Freeman, eds., Chicago: University of Chicago Press, pp. 245-269.

[22] Tables A-1 and A-2, *Employment and Earnings*, 46 (1), Washington: U.S. Department of Labor, Bureau of Labor Statistics.

[23] Division of Productivity Research, Office of Productivity and Technology of the Bureau of Labor Statistics.

[24] Lee Lillard and Hong Tan (1986), "Private Sector Training: Who Gets It and What Are Its Effects," Rand Corporation monograph R-3331-DOL/RC. Lisa M. Lynch and Sandra E. Black (1998), "Beyond the Incidence of Employer-Provided Training," *Industrial and Labor Relations Review*, Vol. 52, No. 1, pp. 64-81. Ana Revenga, Michelle Riboud, and Hong Tan (1994), "The Impact of Mexico's Retraining Program on Employment and Wages," *The World Bank Economic Review*, Vol. 8, No. 2, pp. 247-277. Wiji Arulampalam and Alison L. Booth (1997),"Who Gets Over the Training Hurdle? A Study of the Training Experiences of Young Men and Women in Britain," *Journal of Population Economics*, Vol. 10, pp. 197-217.

[25] Harley Frazis, Maury Gittleman, Michael Horrigan and Mary Joyce, "Results from the 1995 Survey of Employer-Provided Training," *Monthly Labor Review*, June 1998, pp. 3-13 describe the survey and report the results summarized here.

[26] Yoram Ben-Porath, "The Production of Human Capital and the Life Cycle of Earnings," *Journal of Political Economy*, August 1967, pp. 352-365.

[27] Nancy Ruggles and Richard Ruggles (1977), "The Anatomy of Earnings Behavior," *The Distribution of Economic Well-Being*, New York: NBER, pp. 115-158.

[28] More specifically, OPT measures changes in the skill-composition of the work force between years t and $t-1$ with the following formula:

$$\Delta \ln C_t \equiv \Delta \ln L_t - \Delta \ln H_t, \text{ where}$$

$$\Delta \ln L_t \equiv \tilde{\alpha}_{1,t} \Delta \ln H_{1,t} + \tilde{\alpha}_{2,t} \Delta \ln H_{2,t} + \cdots + \tilde{\alpha}_{L,t} \Delta \ln H_{L,t}.$$

In the second equation above, the rate of growth of hours worked by persons with the set of characteristics l at time t is $\Delta \ln H_{lt} = \ln H_{l,t} - \ln H_{l,t-1}$. The rate of growth of hours worked by all persons is $\Delta \ln H_t$.

The labor cost share weight $\tilde{\alpha}_{l,t}$ for persons with characteristics l at time t is calculated with the following formula:

$$\tilde{\alpha}_{l,t} = \frac{1}{2}\left[\left(\hat{w}_{l,t} H_{l,t} \Big/ \sum_{\forall m,t} \hat{w}_{m,t} H_{m,t}\right) + \left(\hat{w}_{l,t-1} H_{l,t-1} \Big/ \sum_{\forall m,t-1} \hat{w}_{m,t-1} H_{m,t-1}\right)\right], \quad l = 1 \ldots m.$$

A conventional human capital wage equation is used to estimate conditional mean wage rates $\hat{w}_{l,t}$. That is, $\hat{w}_{l,t} = \hat{\beta}_o + \hat{\beta}_{s,t} s_{l,t} + \hat{\beta}_{e,t} e_{l,t} + \hat{\beta}_{d,t} d_{l,t}$. The number of years of school completed in year t by persons with characteristics l is represented by $s_{l,t}$, and $e_{l,t}$ is an estimate of the number of years of actual work experience. Demographic and geographic variables are represented by $d_{l,t}$, including categorical variables for the nine Census regions, and additional categorical variables for ever-married status, Black or Hispanic ethnicity, veteran status and residence within a central city. The equations are estimated separately for males and females.

Rearranging terms, $\Delta \ln C_t \equiv \tilde{\alpha}_{,1}(\Delta \ln H_{1,t} - \Delta \ln H_t) + \cdots + \tilde{\alpha}_{L,t}(\Delta \ln H_{L,t} - \Delta \ln H_t)$. Thus, an increase in the labor composition index reflects a faster rate of growth of hours worked by high-skilled workers, longer hours worked by high skilled workers, on average, and/or an increase in the wage rate differential between high-skilled and low-skilled workers.

[29] Production is assumed to exhibit constant returns to scale. That is, doubling all inputs produces exactly twice as much output. Although not required for productivity measurement, meaningful and unambiguous measures of labor composition require that capital is separable from labor (the combination of hours and labor composition) and, in turn, that hours are separable from labor composition. While tests for separability can be made only when production is explicitly modeled, separability exists when one input can

be measured independently of the prices and quantities of other inputs.

[30] Krueger and Summers have provided influential time series estimates of occupational and industrial wage differentials. See Alan B. Krueger and Lawrence H. Summers (1988), "Efficiency Wages and the Inter-Industry Wage Structure," *Econometrica*, Vol. 56, pp. 259-293.

[31] Some sources of wage differentials include unobserved differences in the characteristics or training of workers, compensating differentials for job risks or amenities, rent sharing of monopoly profits of firms, imbalances between the supply and demand for workers, or restrictions in the supply of workers such as unions or licensing requirements.

[32] This theoretical argument is advanced in John Pencavel (1972), "Wages, Specific Training, and Labor Turnover in U.S. Manufacturing Industries," *International Economic Review*, Vol. 13, No. 1, pp. 53-64. Empirical results that are consistent with the theoretical argument are presented in Atsushi Seike and Hong W. Tan (1994), "Labor Fixity and Labor Market Adjustments in Japan and the United States," in *Troubled Industries in the United States and Japan*, Tan and Shimada, Eds., New York: St. Martin's Press, pp. 211-233.

[33] Steven Allen (1984), "Unionized Construction Workers are More Productive," *Quarterly Journal of Economics*, Vol. 99, pp. 251-274.

[34] For sources of skill change in the 1970s and 1980s, see David R. Howell and Edward N. Wolff. (1991). "Trends in the Growth and Distribution of Skills in the U.S. Workplace, 1960-1984." *Industrial and Labor Relations Review*, Vol. 44, No. 3, April 1991.

[35] The Occupational Employment Statistics (OES) survey is an annual mail survey measuring occupational employment and occupational wage rates for wage and salary workers in nonfarm establishments, by industry. The survey samples approximately 400,000 establishments per year, taking 3 years to fully collect the sample of 1.2 million establishments. These annual surveys are part of a Federal-State cooperative program. BLS provides the procedures and technical support, while the State Employment Security Agencies (SESAs) collect the data. The SESAs produce estimates for local areas and the States. BLS produces estimates for the Nation. The OES survey sample is stratified by area, industry, and size class. States' Unemployment Insurance (UI) files provide the universe from which the OES survey draws its sample. The employment benchmarks are obtained from reports submitted by employers to the UI program. In some nonmanufacturing industries, supplemental sources are used for establishments not reporting to the UI program.

The OES survey produces data on employment, average (mean) wage, and median wage for over 750 detailed occupations in 378 detailed industry categories (at the 3-digit level of the Standard Industrial Classification). The survey also covers Federal, State, and local government establishments. The OES classification system uses seven occupational divisions to categorize workers in detailed occupations. The seven divisions are: 1) Managerial and administrative, 2) professional, paraprofessional, and technical, 3) sales and related, 4) clerical and administrative support, 5) service, 6) agriculture, forestry, fishing, and related, and 7) production, construction, operating, maintenance, and material handling.

[36] For a discussion of the conceptual framework underlying this demand measure, see Lawrence F. Katz and Kevin M. Murphy. (1992). "Changes in Relative Wages, 1963-1987: Supply and Demand Factors." *Quarterly Journal of Economics*, Vol. 107, No. 1, February, 1992.

[37] For a similar measure, see Kevin M. Murphy and Finis Welch. (1993). "Occupational Change and the Demand for Skill, 1940-1990." *American Economic Association Papers and Proceedings*, Vol. 83, No. 2, May, 1993.

[38] This decomposition is accomplished by creating a third skill index which measures skill changes for 1-digit occupational codes within detailed industries. The difference between the growth rate of this index and the alternative index (column 2) measures the skill change within broad occupational groups.

[39] The Office of Employment Projections has developed industry-occupation matrices presenting the distribution of occupational employment by industry since the mid-1960s. A time series based on these matrices was not developed until 1994, because of concerns about the comparability of matrix data over time. Because many users of occupational employment data by industry require historical employment data for a variety of analyses, a national industry-occupation matrix time series was developed that covered the 1983-95 time period. In 1996, the time series was updated to cover the 1983-96 period. In 1998, an analysis of this time series was completed to identify trends in educational requirements. The study focused on the 1986-96 period in order to be consistent with the 10-year time frame of the Bureau's most recent employment projections, 1996-2006.

[40] CPS data are used to develop occupational distribution patterns for workers in agriculture and private households, as well as to develop economy-wide estimates of self-employed and unpaid family workers by occupation. Occupational distribution patterns for the Federal Government are developed from data compiled by the Office of Personnel Management.

[41] For an explanation of the rationale underlying the development of the education and training categories, see Darrel Patrick Wash, "A New Way to Classify Occupations by Education and Training," *Occupational Outlook Quarterly*, Winter 1996-97, pp. 28-40.

[42] The OES measure of skill change for the 1989-1997 period generally confirms the OEP findings of rising skill levels in the service sector. Where there are differences in the findings they are due to the fact that the OES measure uses wage-weighted employment, while the OEP data are based on unweighted employment counts.

[43] Of the 456 detailed occupations in the historical matrix, earnings were not available for two: government chief executives and legislators and producers, directors, actors, and entertainers.

[44] The following are the 16 occupations: All other managers and administrators; all other sales and related workers; cashiers; teachers, preschool through college, except special and adult education; general office clerks; computer engineers, scientists, and systems analysts; registered nurses; janitors and cleaners, including maids and housekeeping cleaners; truckdrivers light and heavy; salespersons, retail; all other service workers; all other agriculture, forestry, fishing, and related workers; hand packers and packagers; clerical supervisors and managers; receptionists and information clerks; all other management support workers.

[45] Classic early studies of the human capital model include Jacob Mincer (1958), "Investments in Human Capital and Personal Income Distribution, *Journal of Political Economy*, Vol. 66, No. 4, pp. 281-302; Theodore W. Schultz (1963), *The Economic Value of Education*, New York: Columbia University Press; Gary Becker (1964) Human Capital, 1st edition, New York: Columbia University Press; and Jacob Mincer (1974), *Schooling, Experience and Earnings*, New York: Columbia University Press. Early contributions to related work on hedonic price indexes can be found in Zvi Griliches (Ed., 1971), *Price Indexes and Quality Changes*, Cambridge, Massachusetts: Harvard University Press; and Sherwin Rosen (1974), "Hedonic Prices and Implicit Markets: Product Differentiation in Pure Competition," *Journal of Political Economy*, Vol. 82, No. 1, pp. 34-55.

[46] The procedures followed to develop these estimates are described in BLS Bulletin 2426, *Labor Composition*, cited above, chapter 2.

[47] Chinhui Juhn, Kevin M. Murphy and Brooks Pierce (1993), "Wage Inequality and the Rise in Returns to Skill," *Journal of Political Economy*, Vol. 101, No. 3, pp. 410-442.

[48] John T. Dunlop, "The Task of Contemporary Wage Theory," in *New Concepts in Wage Determination*, G.W. Taylor and F.C. Pierson, eds., New York: McGraw-Hill, 1957.

[49] There are several skill-based pay schemes that have been widely discussed in the press; but they are rather uncommon in practice, and rarely include all workers in the establishment in those firms with such plans. These compensation schemes have various different names, such as "pay for knowledge," "skill-based pay." They set wages based on a repertoire of jobs that workers can perform; that is, their knowledge and mastery of different jobs in the organization.

[50] For a discussion of point-factor pay setting schemes, see, for example, Richard Henderson, *Compensation Management and Rewarding Performance*, Reston, VA: Reston Publishing Co., 1979.

[51] For a complete description of occupations and level characteristics see appendix B in *Occupational Compensation Survey: National Summary, 1996*, Bulletin 2497 (U.S. Department of Labor, Bureau of Labor Statistics), March 1998.

[52] For a description of the National Compensation Survey see, Harriet Weinstein, "Overview of the NCS: Summer 1998," *Compensation and Working Conditions*, Summer 1998.

[53] Supervisory duties is an experimental factor, and has not been used to determine work levels in NCS data published to date.

[54] For a more detailed description of the "generic factors" see *Evaluating Your Firm's Jobs and Pay*, (U.S. Department of Labor, Bureau of Labor Statistics). Brochure

[55] The modal value is that value occurring most frequently.

[56] Table 7 can be viewed as looking at knowledge differentials, for given occupational categories. The regression methodology can be viewed as looking at knowledge differentials for given occupational categories and other control variables. In the regression the natural logarithm of the hourly wage rate is regressed on controls for the generic leveling factors, detailed industry and occupation, survey area, full-time status, incen-

tive pay, union coverage, private or public sector employment, and establishment size.

[57] More precisely, 1.187/1.095=1.084 implies an 8.4 percent differential.

[58] Studies of specific occupations may yield different results. For example, physical risk may be important for police officers.

[59] See Carolyn Veneri (1999), "Can Occupational Labor Shortages Be Identified Using Available Data?" *Monthly Labor Review*, March, pp.15-21.

[60] Rick Melchionno and Michael Steinman, "The 1996-2006 Job Outlook in Brief," *Occupational Outlook Quarterly*, Spring 1998, p. 3.

[61] 1996-2006 employment projections were released in November 1997-see the November 1997 *Monthly Labor Review*. 1998-2008 projections will be released in November 1999.

[62] Job vacancy data by occupation would be an obvious input to analyses of occupational shortages. However, comprehensive occupational vacancy data do not exist. Although trade associations sometimes sponsor surveys of job vacancies, national data are not currently collected by any government agency. The Bureau of Labor Statistics has conducted pilot studies on occupational job vacancies and is reinstituting a Job Openings Labor Turnover Survey that will provide a broad measure of job vacancies, but not by occupation. It is important to keep in mind, however, that the simple fact that employers have vacancies does not mean a shortage exists. Trends in vacancy data would need to be evaluated along with other labor market indicators in order to understand the labor market for a particular occupation. See Lois Plunkert. Job Openings Pilot Program: Final Report, Washington: U.S. Department of Labor, Bureau of Labor Statistics, 1981. Also see Employee Turnover and Job Openings Survey: *Results of a Pilot Study on the Feasibility of Collecting Measures of Imbalances of Supply and Demand for Labor in an Establishment Survey* (1991), Washington: U.S. Department of Labor, Bureau of Labor Statistics.

[63] Studies used data in this way include Cohen and Trutko, Barnow, Chasanov, and Pande.

[64] *America's New Deficit: The Shortage of Information Technology Workers* (U.S. Department of Commerce, Office of Technology Policy), p.3.

[65] "Labor Woes: You Know How Bad It Is," Rural Builder, May 1998, p.26.

[66] George T. Silvestri (1997), "Employment Outlook: 1996-2006, Occupational Employment Projections to 2006," *Monthly Labor Review*, November, p. 62.

Chapter 3

Hours of Work

Jobs are important in the lives of most American adults. Just how important appears to be in dispute. Some researchers claim, for example, that Americans are too busy and overworked. Juliet Schor states in *The Overworked American (1991)*, "in the last twenty years the amount of time Americans have spent at their jobs has risen steadily." Although the study was criticized by some in the academic community for lack of data replicability (Hedges, 1992; Stafford, 1992; and Kniesner, 1993), it was well-received by the popular press (Kuttner, 1992 and Segal, 1992). More recently, Arlie Hochschild (1997) argued in *The Time Bind: When Work Becomes Home and Home Becomes Work,* that more people are opting to work long hours on the job to avoid responsibilities at home. The notion that Americans are working more has become so ingrained in the media that a recent article in *Training Magazine* states "It's become almost banal to comment on how busy and overworked people are today."[1]

Subsequent empirical research, however, has been much less definitive. Using data from decennial censuses and the Bureau of Labor Statistics' (BLS) Current Population Surveys (CPS)[2], Coleman and Pencavel (1993a, 1993b) found little change in the average number of hours men worked between 1940 and 1988. They also found a slight decrease in the number of hours worked by less-educated women and a slight increase in hours worked by well-educated women. Rones, Ilg, and Gardner (1997), using CPS data, also found little change in the average hours worked each week over the period 1976-93 but they did find a slight increase in the percent of persons working long workweeks. Researchers using data on annual hours worked from the Panel Study of Income Dynamics found a small upward trend in annual work hours from 1967-89 for workers age 25 to 54 years (Bluestone and Rose, 1998). In contrast, researchers using data from time-use surveys found a general decline in the time people spend doing paid work over the past three decades (Robinson and Bostrom, 1994). Data from the BLS Current Employment Statistics Survey (CES) also show a decline in the average length of the workweek over time.

Empirical evidence generally does not support rapid growth in the hours that Americans are spending on their jobs. Why then do more people report feeling rushed and under time-pressure? (Robinson and Godbey, 1997) And why do books, such as Schor's and Hochschild's, claiming that Americans are overworked and in a "time-bind" continue to make the best seller's list?

Several possibilities exist for the apparent contradiction between the empirical evidence and the popular perception. One possibility is that some people are working more while others are working less so that trends in average hours have been relatively constant. If this is the case, there may be a portion of the population that is indeed "overworked." Laura Leete and Juliet Schor (1994) found a 7.7-percent increase in annual hours worked among the "fully employed" but only a 3-percent increase for the labor force as a whole.[3] Another possibility is that American workers, on average, are not spending significantly more time at work but that the increase in labor force participation by women and the prevalence of both parents working has placed more constraints on nonwork time, resulting in more people feeling stressed or pressed for time.

Chapter organization

In this chapter, we examine work time using data from BLS surveys and supplementary sources. For the economy as a whole, we review the long-term trends in hours at work and hours paid for by the employer. We then examine the trends among various subgroups of the population. Because the labor force participation patterns of various population groups can change over time, the total working hours for members of these groups depend on both how many people are working and how many hours they work. For example, if a group (such as women) increases its labor force participation, the share of time devoted to work for the group as a whole increases, even if each employed person's workweek does not change. Examining trends in average hours at work among all working-age individuals in the population (rather than just those employed) is one way of measuring work time to capture trends in participation and trends in work hours for those working.

Over the past three decades, there have been some important changes in the structure of families and labor force participation patterns that have had profound effects on the way American families lead their daily lives. Undoubtedly, the most important changes—and the ones that have stirred the most debate—have been the increase in the number of families maintained by a single female and the very rapid increase in the proportion of women in the labor force.[4] This chapter also looks at the trends in working hours among individuals in various types of families and among individuals with and without children. In addition, we examine the trends in combined hours of work among married-couple families, as well as the correlation in the work hours of husbands and wives.

In the last section of the chapter, we shift the focus towards employers, starting with an examination of the prevalence of work arrangements that are aimed at helping workers handle the demands of both work and family. We then turn to a discussion of time off provided by employers and the relationship between the hours employees work and hours of leave (for vacation, sickness, or holidays) that are paid for by the employer. This is followed by a discussion of the types of paid time off benefits available to workers and the amounts of time off they receive.

Time Spent at Work

Overall trends in hours worked

The Bureau of Labor Statistics has a number of data series related to hours worked. The Current Employment Statistics (CES) Survey provides data on the average paid hours for production workers in goods-producing industries and nonsupervisory workers in service-producing industries. This information is collected from employers and is based on payroll records. The survey is limited to the private, nonagricultural sector. The CPS, a monthly household survey, provides data on several different concepts of hours worked. Each month, all survey respondents are asked about the total hours worked at all jobs during the survey reference week; a quarter of the sample respondents each month are asked about the usual hours worked per week on the primary job; and, each year in a supplement to the CPS conducted in March, all survey respondents are asked about the usual hours worked per week during the last year. Chart 3-1 shows the trend in each of these series from 1960 to 1998. Note that because some labor force participants are multiple jobholders, the trend line for the quarter sample series lies below the other CPS measures of hours worked because it measures only hours worked on the worker's main job. Because the CPS was re-designed in 1994, data after this point are not strictly comparable to the earlier data. (The March supplement did not undergo a major revision.) However, the overall averages in the monthly CPS and the quarter sample do not appear to be much affected. (See box.)

CES weekly hours indicate a sharp downward trend from about 1966 to 1998.[5] Between those years, average weekly hours paid to production or nonsupervisory workers fell from 38.6 to 34.6 hours, a reduction of 10.4 percent. In contrast, weekly hours from the monthly CPS declined by

Changes in the Current Population Survey

Current Population Survey (CPS) data for January 1994 and forward are not strictly comparable with data for earlier years because of the introduction of a major redesign of the questionnaire and collection methodology. Among the questionnaire changes were alterations intended to identify all persons who worked for pay during the reference week and to help respondents recall the exact number of hours they worked during the week.

The annual averages on weekly hours worked were little changed from 1993 to 1994, declining from 39.3 to 39.1. This decline is likely because the redesigned survey makes extra efforts to include marginal workers who, by definition, have low weekly hours. Although the redesign did not have a notable impact on the overall average, a comparison of pre- and post-1994 data suggests that the implicit recall strategy associated with the new questionnaire does provide more accurate data on actual hours. For instance, the proportion of persons who reported working exactly 40 hours per week—a common, almost reflex, response—declined substantially between 1993 and 1994. In fact, this decrease was greater than the cumulative effect of the long-term downward trend between 1973 and 1993. In addition, during the 1973-93 period, the share of survey respondents reporting they worked between 35 and 39 hours or 41 and 48 hours decreased. In 1994, with the revised questions, this trend was reversed, indicating that respondents are now giving different, and apparently more precise, answers to the questions on hours actually worked.

2 percent from 40.0 to 39.2 hours. The other two CPS series on usual weekly hours are similarly flat. (Hours from the CPS March supplement rose by 1.5 percent between 1976 and 1997, and the quarter sample hours rose from 38.1 to 38.6 hours between 1973 and 1997.)

Weekly hours fell in both the CES and CPS during the sixties and seventies (more steeply in the CES than the CPS). However, the trends diverge in the mid-eighties, with hours increasing slightly in the CPS series and continuing to fall in the CES, although less sharply than in the previous period.

Given that the CES captures only the hours paid to production or nonsupervisory workers, whereas the CPS refers to all nonagricultural workers, the levels of the two series can differ. However, what is behind the divergence in the trends is not known. One possible explanation is that the share of employment in production and nonsupervisory positions fell enough that the trends in hours among these workers had a decreasing impact on the overall average, and that hours among workers not covered in the CES rose. Although the production and nonsupervisory share of employment has fallen over the entire period, it has been a fairly constant 81 percent of employment since 1980 [6] In addition, Abraham, Spletzer, and Stewart (1998) attempted to identify non-CES individuals in the CPS to see if their hours had risen relative to the hours of workers covered by the CES. They found that between 1973 and 1993, the average weekly hours of workers in the CPS who would potentially be covered in the CES declined by 0.7 hour, while the weekly hours of potentially exempt workers rose by 0.9 hour. Despite the qualitative differences between these two groups of workers, they conclude that the differences are not sufficiently large to account for the divergence of trends between the two surveys.

Another source of difference between the CES and CPS is that the former reflects employers' reports on the hours they paid their employees and the latter captures the reports by workers on the hours that they actually worked. Even assuming no measurement error in either series, the two will differ if workers are paid for a set number of hours but tend to work more hours. Mellow and Sider (1983) examined data on hours reported by individuals and employers. They found that for managers and professionals, hours reported by workers exceed those reported by employers by nearly 11 percent. This finding might be the key to understanding the extent of the gap between CES hours and CPS hours, but it does not explain why the trends of the two measures have diverged. One possible explanation is that workers have been receiving fewer hours of paid leave. However, as will be discussed later, a BLS survey of hours worked (the Hours at Work Survey) indicates there has been no change in the relationship between paid leave and hours worked for production or nonsupervisory workers since 1981.

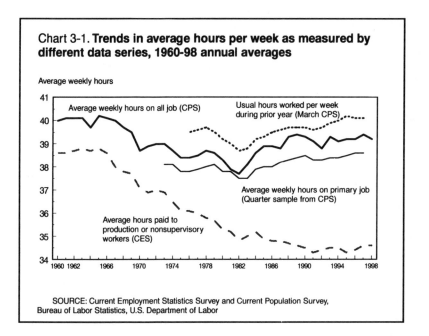

Chart 3-1. **Trends in average hours per week as measured by different data series, 1960-98 annual averages**

Average weekly hours

Average weekly hours on all job (CPS)

Usual hours worked per week during prior year (March CPS)

Average weekly hours on primary job (Quarter sample from CPS)

Average hours paid to production or nonsupervisory workers (CES)

SOURCE: Current Employment Statistics Survey and Current Population Survey, Bureau of Labor Statistics, U.S. Department of Labor

Another possibility for the trend divergence is that workers are over-reporting the hours that they work in the CPS. Research using time-use diaries that require respondents to report the start and stop times of all their activities during a 24-hour period provide some evidence for this hypothesis. Hamermesh (1990) and Robinson and Bostrom (1994) both compared synthetic workweeks, constructed from time-use diaries, to the weekly hours reported in CPS-style questions. They find that people tended to overestimate their hours worked, particularly those who work longer workweeks, and that the overestimate increased over time. However, Jacobs (1998), using data from the 1992 National Survey of the Changing Workforce, finds that CPS-style measures of the workweek correlate well with a new work time measure derived from questions that ask for work departure and return times (less commuting time). Jacobs also argues that the discrepancy between the time-use diaries and CPS estimates of the length of the workweek may be a statistical artifact resulting from random measurement error in both series.

If, in fact, overreporting has worsened over time in the CPS, the question remains as to why. One possibility is that workers now have more flexibility in their hours, thus making it harder for them to remember the exact number of hours that they work in a week.[7] Increased flexibility may also result in workers having more opportu-

nities to run errands or conduct personal business during work hours. These hours would be excluded from estimates of work time captured in time-use diaries but may get included by respondents as work time in the CPS.

Although there are measurement error problems associated with the CPS questions on hours worked, these data have a number of advantages. First, the CPS contains a wealth of information on the demographic characteristics of workers as well as their family situation. This allows trends to be studied separately for various subgroups of interest. Second, because the same question pertaining to weekly hours worked has been asked in the CPS for many years, long-term trends can be examined.[8] Therefore, for the remainder of this chapter we primarily focus on the hours at work obtained from the monthly CPS question, "How many hours did you work last week at all jobs?"[9]

The trends in average weekly work hours discussed to this point pertain only to employed individuals. If participation rates have changed over this period, these trends may not truly reflect whether or not we as a society are working more. For example, if workers start retiring earlier, then the total amount of time spent working by society as a whole will decline. However, this will not be reflected in the trends of average weekly work hours of employed individuals. Charts 3-2 and 3-3 show trends since 1967 in the average number of hours worked per week using annual average data from the monthly CPS. Chart 3-2 shows the trends in average weekly hours worked for all persons age 16 or older in the civilian nonagricultural population. Nonworkers, therefore, are included when computing this average, even though their hours are zero. Chart 3-3 shows the trends in average weekly hours worked for persons age 16 or older in nonagricultural industries (nonworkers are excluded from this average). For all persons age 16 years and older, the average weekly work hours rose from 21.2 to 23.8 hours between 1967 and 1998. This upward trend reflects an increase in overall participation (primarily among women) rather than an increase in the number of hours worked per week as seen in chart 3-3. Between 1967 and 1998, the average workweek for those at work fell from 40.0 to 39.2 hours. The increase in the female labor force participation rate is likely to have exerted downward pressure on the average hours among those at work because women tend to work fewer hours than their male counterparts.

Trends in hours worked by demographic group

As has already been discussed, data from the CPS show that over the last three decades, there has been little change in overall average weekly hours for nonagricultural workers. In this section, we examine the trends for various subgroups of workers to see if their trends differ from the overall average. Using selected annual averages from the monthly CPS during the 1976-98 period, we examine trends in weekly hours worked for men, women, and various age groups.[10] We then examine the trends by education using data from the CPS March supplement.[11]

Sex. Chart 3-4 shows the trends in weekly hours for the entire civilian nonagricultural population age 16 years or older; and chart 3-5 shows the trends for their counterparts who are working. For men, the trends in both series are relatively flat, but show some fluctuation with the business cycle as represented by the unemployment rate. For all women, working or not, average weekly hours have steadily risen over the period, from 13.6 hours per week in 1976 to 19.3 in 1998 (an increase of nearly 42 percent). This has been primarily the result of increased participation; weekly hours for those at work only increased by 5 percent over the same period. (See chart 3-5.)

Charts 3-6 and 3-7 show the proportion of workers age 25 to 54 who reported working less than 40 hours per week, exactly 40 hours, and

more than 40 hours. The proportion of both male and female workers who reported working, on average, more than 40 hours per week has been increasing since the early eighties. From 1983 to 1993, the proportion rose from 32.4 percent to 38.4 percent for men and from 14.1 to 19.9 percent for women. The same trend also is evident among those who worked 60 or more hours. Among men for instance, the proportion employed in nonagricultural industries who were at work 60 or more hours a week increased from 9.4 percent in 1979 to about 11.4 percent in 1989, and 11.9 percent in 1998. The percent of women who reported working 60 or more hours a week almost doubled over the same period, from 2.4 percent in 1979 to 4.4 percent in 1998. (See table 3-1.)

Age. Charts 3-8 through 3-11 show the average weekly hours among all civilian men and women age 16 to 19 and 65 and older. Average weekly hours for both men and women age 16 to 19 showed a slight downward trend. By comparison, the trends for those 65 and over were relatively flat.

Charts 3–12 through 3-15 show similar trends in hours for three age groups; 20 to 24, 25 to 44, and 45 to 64 years. Again, the hours of younger workers (those age 20 to 24) seem to be more sensitive than those of older workers to movements in the business cycle. Weekly hours worked for these younger workers have declined slightly since 1976. This is likely due to the increase in college enrollment for this age group.[12] Charts 3-14 and 3-15 also show that women age 25 to 44 and 45 to 64 are working more today than in 1976, with corresponding increases in their labor force participation rate and average weekly hours.

Perhaps surprisingly, given the trend towards earlier retirement among men, there has not been a substantial decline in average weekly hours worked among males age 45 to 64 during the 1976-98 period.[13] Although the trend for average weekly hours has been relatively flat for male workers age 25 to 54, there has been an increase in the proportion working extended workweeks.[14] (See table 3-1.) For example, the proportion of men who worked 41 or more hours a week increased from 39.9 to 44.9 percent between 1979 and 1998. For women in the same age group, the proportion increased from 15.1 to 24.2 percent over the same period. (Although the changes in the questionnaire may have had some effect on these increases, much of the gains took place among people who worked 49 or more hours a week.) The evidence also shows that workers age 55 and over continue to participate in extended workweeks, but to a lesser extent. Overall, 23.3 percent of these older workers worked 41 or more hours a week in 1979, compared with 27.1 percent in 1998.

In contrast, there was practically no change in the proportion of young workers age 16 to 24 employed 41 or more hours a week. There was, however, a marked rise (from 35.2 percent in 1979 to 46.9 percent in 1998) in the proportion who worked part-time (1 to 34 hours a week). Again, this increase in part-time work among 16 to 24-year-olds partly reflects changes in school enrollment.

Students. Using data from the CPS October supplements, we can directly examine the labor force participation rates and weekly hours worked for students age 16 to 24 enrolled full time in either high school or college. Charts 3-16 and 3-17 show the trends in both participation rates and weekly hours between 1980 and 1997 for high school students and charts 3-18 and 3-19 show comparable trends for college students.

Labor force participation rates for high school students have changed very little over the past several decades. Between October 1980 and October 1997, the participation rate for high school students age 16 to 24 ranged from a high of 44.2 percent in October 1989 to a low of 36.7 percent in October 1983. As can be seen in chart 3-16, the peaks and troughs of the high school students' labor force participation rates appear to be affected by the business cycle as represented by the unemployment rate. Both the participation rates and the trends in the rates were similar for male and female students.

Among high school students, the trend in median weekly hours worked was virtually flat over the period, with the sole exception of a spike for men in 1988. Overall, their median weekly hours worked at all jobs ranged from a low of 14.9 in October 1982 (during a period of very high unemployment) to a high of 16.0 in October 1995. It has remained at about that level since.

In contrast to high school students, participation rates for full-time undergraduate college students have risen. (See chart 3-18.) In October 1980, their participation rate was 44.6 percent. By October 1991, it had reached 52.6 percent. Since then, it has fluctuated in the low 50-percent range without exhibiting any definite trend up or down. The slowdown in the early-1990s occurred largely among men. In contrast, the

women's rate continued to increase, reaching 55.4 percent in October 1997 (compared with 47.5 percent for men). This increase in labor force participation rates might be related to the rapid rise in college tuition costs.

The median weekly hours at work trend for full-time undergraduate college students is unclear. (See chart 3-19.) Through the early-1990s, median hours worked for these students trended up, peaking at 19.8 hours in October 1992. Since then, however, they have been at or below that figure and the changes in the median appear to have no particular trend. Median weekly hours at work for female full-time college undergraduates rose during the 1980s, then leveled off for a number of years before edging down during the mid-1990s. (See chart 3-19.)

In conclusion, students (with the possible exception of college students) do not appear to be working more than they used to. In fact, there has been little change over the past two decades in the relative size of the student labor force, and the number of hours worked.

Education. So far, we have found no large increases in the average weekly hours worked among those employed (although women as a group are clearly working more now than in the past). The focus now shifts to weekly hours by education to further investigate whether there are some groups for which hours worked have increased. Table 3-2 shows the average weekly hours worked for the total civilian population age 25 to 54 and for civilian workers of the same age by educational attainment.[15]

Average weekly hours worked for the male population fell for all education levels. The largest decline was among men with less than a high school diploma. These declines for men appear to be the result of a dropoff in employment rates because the trends in weekly hours among male workers have been relatively flat within all education groups. For women in the overall population, average weekly hours worked have increased at all education levels; women with the least education show the smallest increase. The trends for women primarily reflect increases in participation, but weekly hours worked also increased, most notably for women with at least some college.

For both men and women, weekly hours in the general population tend to increase with education levels. This reflects the fact that both employment rates and weekly hours worked among the employed are positively related to education.

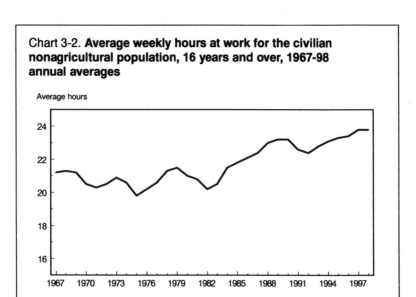

Chart 3-2. **Average weekly hours at work for the civilian nonagricultural population, 16 years and over, 1967-98 annual averages**

Average hours

SOURCE: Current Population Survey, Bureau of Labor Statistics, U.S. Department of Labor

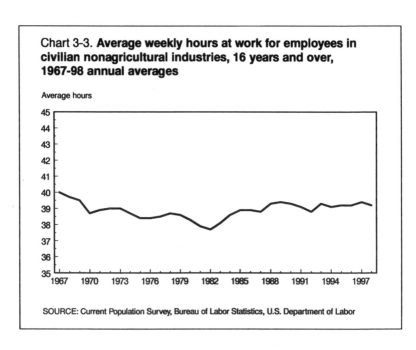

Chart 3-3. **Average weekly hours at work for employees in civilian nonagricultural industries, 16 years and over, 1967-98 annual averages**

Average hours

SOURCE: Current Population Survey, Bureau of Labor Statistics, U.S. Department of Labor

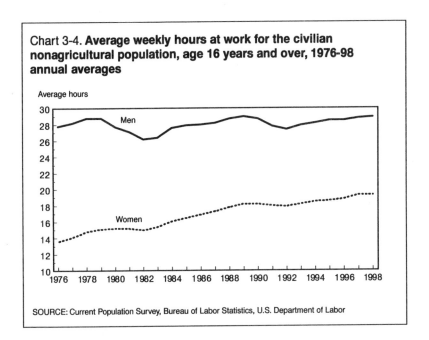

Chart 3-4. **Average weekly hours at work for the civilian nonagricultural population, age 16 years and over, 1976-98 annual averages**

Average hours

SOURCE: Current Population Survey, Bureau of Labor Statistics, U.S. Department of Labor

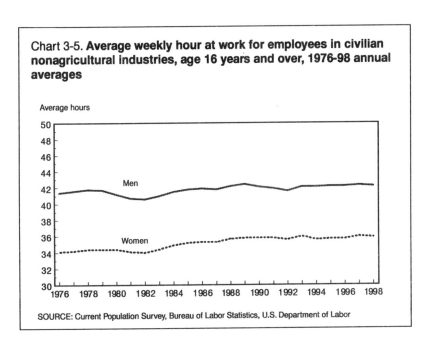

Chart 3-5. **Average weekly hour at work for employees in civilian nonagricultural industries, age 16 years and over, 1976-98 annual averages**

Average hours

SOURCE: Current Population Survey, Bureau of Labor Statistics, U.S. Department of Labor

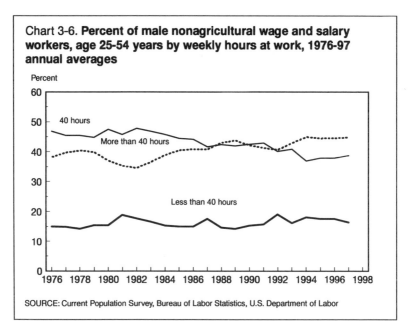

Chart 3-6. **Percent of male nonagricultural wage and salary workers, age 25-54 years by weekly hours at work, 1976-97 annual averages**

Percent

40 hours

More than 40 hours

Less than 40 hours

SOURCE: Current Population Survey, Bureau of Labor Statistics, U.S. Department of Labor

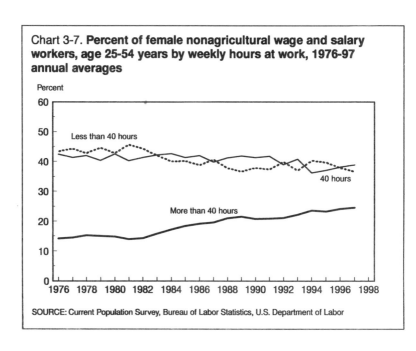

Chart 3-7. **Percent of female nonagricultural wage and salary workers, age 25-54 years by weekly hours at work, 1976-97 annual averages**

Percent

Less than 40 hours

40 hours

More than 40 hours

SOURCE: Current Population Survey, Bureau of Labor Statistics, U.S. Department of Labor

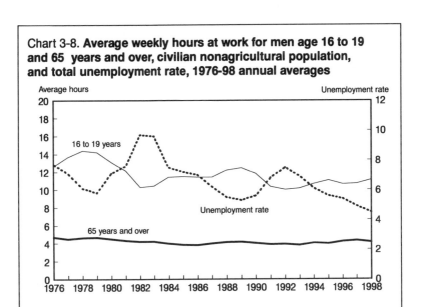

Chart 3-8. **Average weekly hours at work for men age 16 to 19 and 65 years and over, civilian nonagricultural population, and total unemployment rate, 1976-98 annual averages**

Average hours

Unemployment rate

16 to 19 years

Unemployment rate

65 years and over

SOURCE: Current Population Survey, Bureau of Labor Statistics, U.S. Department of Labor

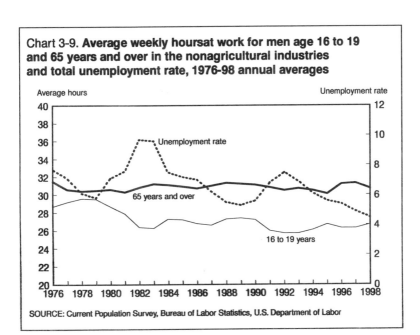

Chart 3-9. **Average weekly hoursat work for men age 16 to 19 and 65 years and over in the nonagricultural industries and total unemployment rate, 1976-98 annual averages**

Average hours

Unemployment rate

Unemployment rate

65 years and over

16 to 19 years

SOURCE: Current Population Survey, Bureau of Labor Statistics, U.S. Department of Labor

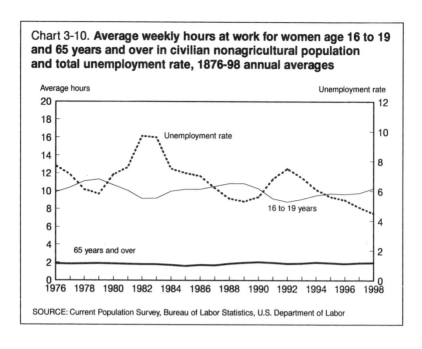

Chart 3-10. **Average weekly hours at work for women age 16 to 19 and 65 years and over in civilian nonagricultural population and total unemployment rate, 1876-98 annual averages**

SOURCE: Current Population Survey, Bureau of Labor Statistics, U.S. Department of Labor

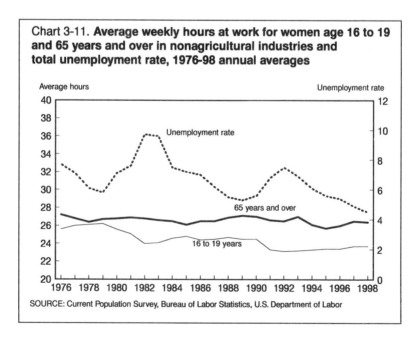

Chart 3-11. **Average weekly hours at work for women age 16 to 19 and 65 years and over in nonagricultural industries and total unemployment rate, 1976-98 annual averages**

SOURCE: Current Population Survey, Bureau of Labor Statistics, U.S. Department of Labor

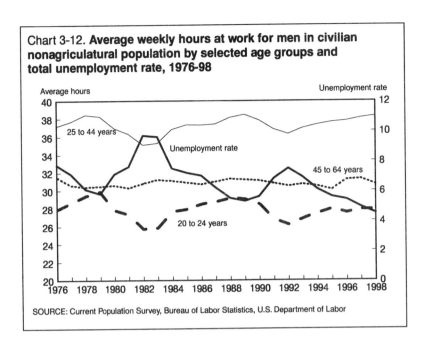

Chart 3-12. **Average weekly hours at work for men in civilian nonagriculatural population by selected age groups and total unemployment rate, 1976-98**

SOURCE: Current Population Survey, Bureau of Labor Statistics, U.S. Department of Labor

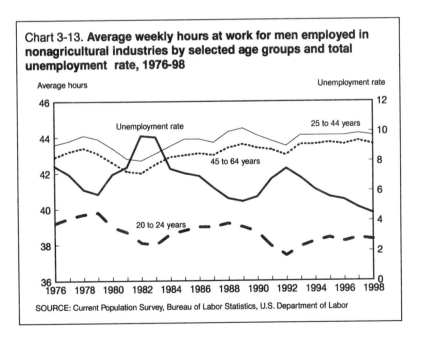

Chart 3-13. **Average weekly hours at work for men employed in nonagricultural industries by selected age groups and total unemployment rate, 1976-98**

SOURCE: Current Population Survey, Bureau of Labor Statistics, U.S. Department of Labor

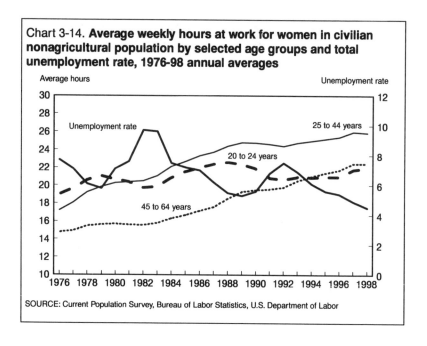

Chart 3-14. **Average weekly hours at work for women in civilian nonagricultural population by selected age groups and total unemployment rate, 1976-98 annual averages**

Average hours

Unemployment rate

SOURCE: Current Population Survey, Bureau of Labor Statistics, U.S. Department of Labor

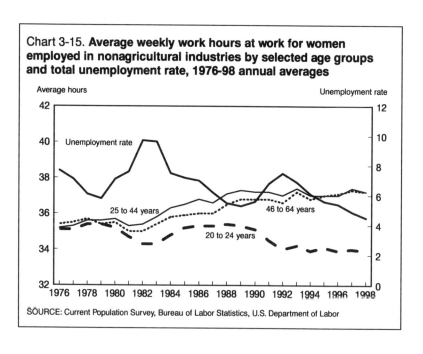

Chart 3-15. **Average weekly work hours at work for women employed in nonagricultural industries by selected age groups and total unemployment rate, 1976-98 annual averages**

Average hours

Unemployment rate

SOURCE: Current Population Survey, Bureau of Labor Statistics, U.S. Department of Labor

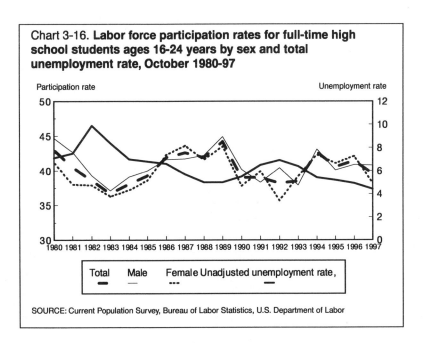

Chart 3-16. **Labor force participation rates for full-time high school students ages 16-24 years by sex and total unemployment rate, October 1980-97**

Participation rate

Unemployment rate

Total	Male	Female	Unadjusted unemployment rate,

SOURCE: Current Population Survey, Bureau of Labor Statistics, U.S. Department of Labor

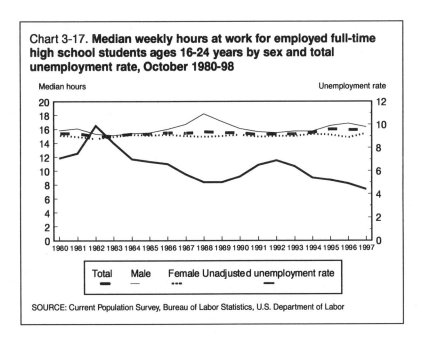

Chart 3-17. **Median weekly hours at work for employed full-time high school students ages 16-24 years by sex and total unemployment rate, October 1980-98**

Median hours

Unemployment rate

Total	Male	Female	Unadjusted unemployment rate

SOURCE: Current Population Survey, Bureau of Labor Statistics, U.S. Department of Labor

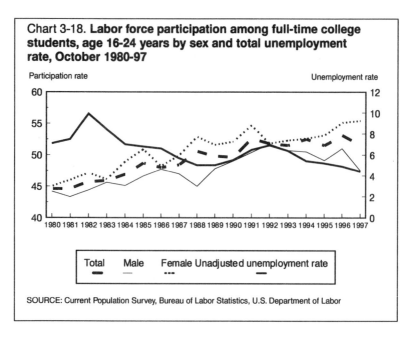

Chart 3-18. **Labor force participation among full-time college students, age 16-24 years by sex and total unemployment rate, October 1980-97**

Participation rate   Unemployment rate

Total   Male   Female Unadjusted unemployment rate

SOURCE: Current Population Survey, Bureau of Labor Statistics, U.S. Department of Labor

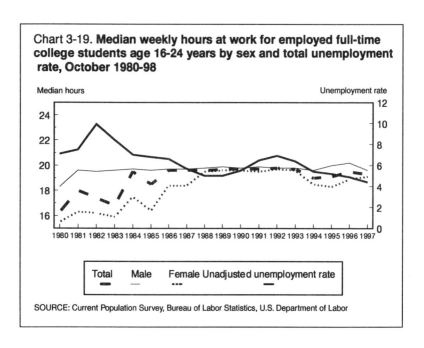

Chart 3-19. **Median weekly hours at work for employed full-time college students age 16-24 years by sex and total unemployment rate, October 1980-98**

Median hours   Unemployment rate

Total   Male   Female Unadjusted unemployment rate

SOURCE: Current Population Survey, Bureau of Labor Statistics, U.S. Department of Labor

94

The hours gap between education levels has widened significantly between 1969 and 1998. In 1969, the population of males with less than a high school diploma worked about 6 fewer hours per week than their college-educated counterparts. By 1998, this gap had increased to about 13 hours. A similar trend is observed for women.

Trends in full-time year round work

Up to this point, we have been examining trends in weekly work time, specifically during the survey reference week. These data, therefore, do not tell us how much individuals work over a longer period of time. (See box for a long-term perspective on working hours using data from the Bureau's *National Longitudinal Survey of Youth, 1979*.) Studying the increases or decreases in long-term hours of work patterns can be helpful in determining whether people are working more now than they did in the past.

One measure of long-term hours worked is derived from questions in the CPS March supplement. Every March, respondents to the CPS are asked additional questions on how much time they spent working during the previous calendar year. This information is used to determine what proportion of the population was employed full-time year round. That is, they worked 50 to 52 weeks a year, and usually worked 35 hours or more in most of the weeks.

Trends in the proportion of the civilian population age 16 or older working full-time year round are given in table 3-4. Like the trends in average weekly hours for this group, we find that while some worker groups spend more time on the job now than they did 30 years ago, others spend less, and, for some, there has been virtually no change at all. For instance, the proportion of youth age 16 to 24 who worked full-time year round increased somewhat during the seventies, was unchanged during the eighties, and declined slightly during the nineties. Workers age 55 and over show a decline between 1969 and 1997 with the majority of the decline taking place between 1969 and 1979. In contrast, workers age 25 to 54 show an increase in the proportion who worked full-time year round, from 53 percent in 1969 to 63 percent in 1997.

Cumulative Hours Worked Between the Ages of 18 and 32

A long-term perspective of working hours can be gained by examining the cumulative hours spent working from age 18 to 32. To construct such a measure, data on the same individuals over time are needed. The *National Longitudinal Survey of Youth, 1979* collects such data. The survey is comprised of a sample of 9,964 men and women age 14 to 22 when first interviewed in 1979 and age 31 to 39 when interviewed in 1996. One of the unique features of the survey is that it collects information on all the jobs held by the respondents and the usual weekly hours that they worked at each job. Therefore, a longitudinal history of each respondent's work experiences can be constructed.

Table 3-3 provides the percent of total available hours spent working (a 40-hour workweek is 24 percent of the 168 total available hours in a week). The findings indicate that persons age 18 to 32 spent 18 percent of their time working. This percentage increased from 13.7 percent for those age 18 to 22 to 20 percent for those age 28 to 32.

On average, young men age 18 to 32 spent roughly 21 percent of their time working compared to 15 percent for their female counterparts. Those who eventually obtained a college degree spent considerably less time working when they were age 18 to 22 (presumably the age they were when attending college) than did their counterparts who ended their formal education earlier. However, between the ages of 28 and 32, males with a college degree spent the most amount of time working, roughly 26 percent of total available hours compared with 24 percent for male high school graduates. The difference is even larger for female college graduates age 28 to 32, who spent 19 percent of their time working, compared with 15 percent for their counterparts with a high school diploma.

Differences in cumulative work time are also apparent between and within race and ethnic groups. Between the ages of 18 and 32, whites spent nearly 19 percent of their time working, compared with 15 percent for blacks, and 17 percent for Hispanics. Among blacks, the time spent working increased dramatically by education level. Between the ages of 28 and 32, black college graduates spent twice as much time working as did blacks without a high school diploma.

95

All of the gain in the proportion of full-time year round workers age 25 to 54 was among women. In 1969, 27 percent of women age 25 to 54 worked full-time year round; by 1997, their proportion had risen to 50 percent. By contrast, the participation rate for men declined from 81 percent to 75 percent over the same period. This general decline for men is also observed within the four education levels. However, the decline is particularly striking for men age 25 to 54 with less than a high school diploma. For these men, the proportion who worked full-time year round went from 72 percent in 1969 to 57 percent in 1997. For women age 25 to 54 with a high school diploma or higher level of education, the proportion of full-time year round workers rose between 20 and 25 percentage points from 1969 to 1997. In contrast, the proportion of women without a high school diploma who worked full-time year round showed a 6-percentage point gain. By1997, the proportion of women without a high school diploma who worked full-time year round was about half that of the other women. (See table 3-4.)

Changes in hours worked by position in the earnings distribution

Another potentially interesting dimension on which to compare hours worked is to examine the hours worked by people in different parts of the earnings distribution. It is well known from the inequality literature (Levy and Murnane, 1992) that the distribution of wages has widened over the last few decades, so that those at the bottom of the earnings scale now earn less in both relative and absolute terms. Are these presumably less-skilled workers working more now in an effort to overcome the loss in their earnings capacity? Conversely, are those with relatively high wages working more now to take advantage of their higher earnings power?

Charts 3-20 and 3-21 show for both men and women age 25 to 54, respectively, the percentage change between 1979 and 1997 in average weekly hours worked for each decile of the weekly earnings distribution. The pattern for men indicates that those in the lower deciles of the earnings distribution were working fewer hours in 1997 than in 1979 and that the percentage decrease in weekly hours was the largest for those at the lowest decile. Conversely, men in the upper deciles of the earnings distribution were working more. These changes mirror the changes in male earnings inequality, in other words, those with lower earnings experienced declines in real earnings while

those with higher earnings experienced gains in real earnings. Viewing the changes in hours and real earnings together shows that men at the bottom of the earnings distribution are working less and earning considerably less today than they did 20 years ago. In contrast, men at the middle of the distribution are working slightly more and making less and men at the upper end are working more and making more.[16]

The pattern is quite different for women. Women in all deciles of the weekly earnings distribution were working more in 1997 than in 1979, with the largest increases occurring among women at the lower deciles. The large increases in hours worked at the low end of the distribution are not surprising given that these women generally work the fewest hours and therefore have the most room to increase their hours. (For example, the 14.6-percent increase in hours among women in the 10th percentile represents an increase in hours from 20.5 hours per week to 23.5 hours.) In general, women were working more and earning more in 1997 than they did in 1979.

Trends in hours worked by family relationship and presence of children

The previous section documented the increase over the last 30 years in the amount of time women spent in the paid labor force. Over this same period, there has been a significant increase in the number of families maintained by a single adult. Both trends affect the amount of time parents, particularly mothers, spend with their children and the level of stress in people's lives. This section discusses the trends in the participation rates and the hours worked for groups of individuals in various types of families and by the presence and age of children.[17]

Charts 3-22 and 3-23 illustrate the dramatic increase in the labor force participation rates of wives and mothers age 25 to 54. In 1969, roughly 43 percent of wives were working or looking for work. By 1998, the percentage had skyrocketed to about 74 percent. Similarly, 23 percent of women with children under the age of 3 were labor force participants in 1969. Today, the majority (63 percent) of women with children under 3 is in the labor force .

In contrast, the participation rates for husbands and fathers have drifted downward over the same period, even among those age 25 to 54. (See charts 3-24 and 3-25.) The labor force participation rate of husbands age 25 to 54 fell from 97 percent in 1969 to 95 percent in 1998. Participation rates for men in the same age group without

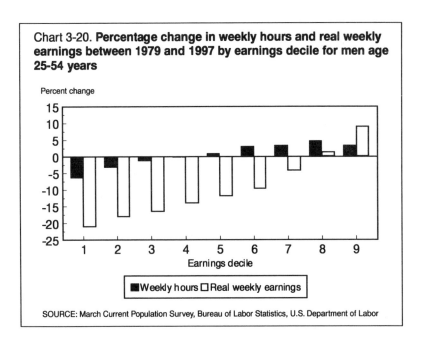

Chart 3-20. **Percentage change in weekly hours and real weekly earnings between 1979 and 1997 by earnings decile for men age 25-54 years**

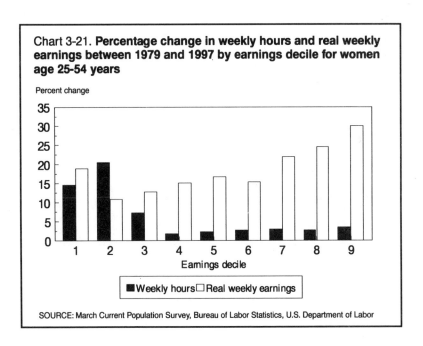

Chart 3-21. **Percentage change in weekly hours and real weekly earnings between 1979 and 1997 by earnings decile for women age 25-54 years**

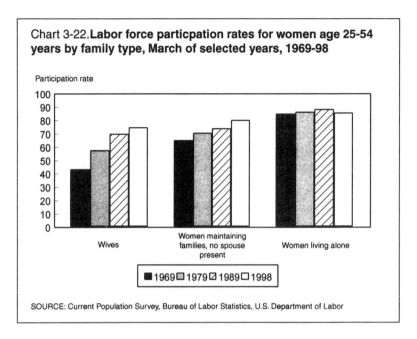

Chart 3-22.**Labor force particpation rates for women age 25-54 years by family type, March of selected years, 1969-98**

Participation rate

SOURCE: Current Population Survey, Bureau of Labor Statistics, U.S. Department of Labor

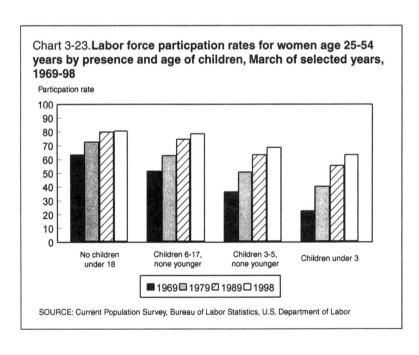

Chart 3-23.**Labor force particpation rates for women age 25-54 years by presence and age of children, March of selected years, 1969-98**

Particpation rate

SOURCE: Current Population Survey, Bureau of Labor Statistics, U.S. Department of Labor

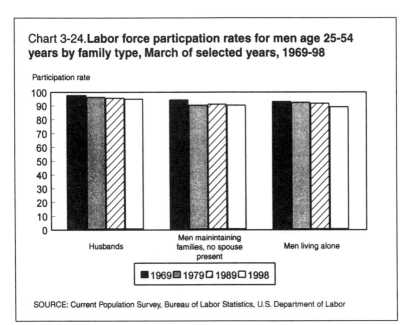

Chart 3-24.**Labor force particpation rates for men age 25-54 years by family type, March of selected years, 1969-98**

Participation rate

SOURCE: Current Population Survey, Bureau of Labor Statistics, U.S. Department of Labor

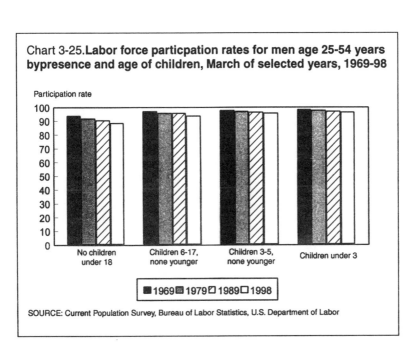

Chart 3-25.**Labor force particpation rates for men age 25-54 years bypresence and age of children, March of selected years, 1969-98**

Participation rate

SOURCE: Current Population Survey, Bureau of Labor Statistics, U.S. Department of Labor

children under 18 fell from 93 percent in 1969 to 89 percent in 1998. Because men in this age group without children are likely to be older than their counterparts with children, the fall in the participation rate among men age 25 to 54 partially reflects the move towards earlier retirement.

Table 3-5 shows the average weekly hours worked by workers age 25 to 54 by family relationship and presence and age of children. It also shows the percent working full-time year round.

Again the most striking trends are for women. While the average weekly hours among married women age 25 to 54 who are employed hovered around 33 per week from 1969 to 1998, the percent of married women working full-time year round doubled (increasing from 23 percent to 46 percent). Similar trends occurred among women in the same age group with children under the age of 3. In 1969, 7 percent of women with children under 3 worked full-time year round; in 1998, 32 percent did so.

Work hours among married couples

As shown earlier, more married women are employed and they are working more hours today than they did 30 years ago. In addition, there has been an increase in the number of men and women working extended workweeks. In this section, we focus on the hours worked by husbands and wives in married-couple families. How much more combined time are married couples devoting to work? Are the men who are working long hours usually married to women who do not work or work fewer hours? Has there been a rise in the number of dual-earner couples who both work longer workweeks?

Using data from the CPS March supplements, we examine the trends in combined average weekly hours worked and combined average annual hours worked by husbands and wives.[18] As shown in table 3-6, married couples spent, on average, 14 more hours working per week in 1998 then they did in 1969 and 717 more hours working per year in 1997 then they did in 1969. This increase in combined work effort occurred for both married couples with and without children under age 18. In fact, married couples with children under 6 experienced the largest increase, as their combined hours rose from 52.3 per week in 1969 to 68.3 in 1998 (an increase of 16 hours per week).

Tables 3-7 and 3-8 show how the distribution of wives' weekly work hours—classified by their husbands' weekly work hours—changed over time. Table 3-7 shows these trends for all married couples age 25 to 54 whereas table 3-8 presents

corresponding data for married couples with children under 6. The results show a marked increase between 1969 and 1998 in the percentage of married couples with both the husband and wife working 35 or more hours per week. In 1969, 24 percent of married couples had both spouses working full-time compared with 43 percent in 1998. The increase is even more striking for married-couple families with children under age 6. In 1998, 31 percent of these couples had both spouses working full-time, up from 13 percent in 1969.

These data also show a decrease in the number of married couples where the husband works full-time (35 or more hours per week) and the wife does not work at all. The decline is apparent for all married couples as well as those with children under age 6. In 1969, two-thirds of married-couple families with children under age 6 had a father who worked 35 or more hours each week and a mother who did not work. By 1998, only 32 percent of these families had this traditional work arrangement, less than half the 1969 level.

Conversely, the number of nontraditional families where the wife works at paid employment 35 or more hours per week and the husband works no hours is small but on the rise. Such arrangements may include situations where the husband is retired, a student, or at home to care for children. Among all married couples, the percent of families with such nontraditional work arrangements increased from 1.3 to 3.6 percent between 1969 and 1998 and from 0.6 to 2.6 percent for married-couple families with children under age 6. Lastly, there has been a steady increase in the number of married-couple families where both the husband and the wife work more than 40 hours per week.[19] (See chart 3-26.)

Changes in married couples hours by position in the income distribution

Have the increases in combined work hours among married couples been evenly distributed across the distribution of family incomes? In other words, have women from across the income spectrum increased the amount of time that they devote to paid employment?

Charts 3-27 and 3-28 show the percentage change between 1979 and 1997 in combined weekly hours worked and combined annual hours worked among married couples in each decile of the family income distribution. Married couples in the lowest 10 percent worked less in 1997 then they did in 1979. Married couples in the middle of the distribution (the 40th through 60th percen-

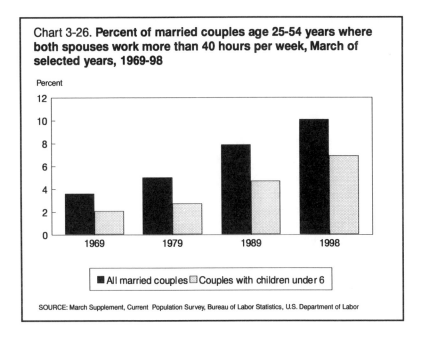

Chart 3-26. **Percent of married couples age 25-54 years where both spouses work more than 40 hours per week, March of selected years, 1969-98**

Percent

■ All married couples ☐ Couples with children under 6

SOURCE: March Supplement, Current Population Survey, Bureau of Labor Statistics, U.S. Department of Labor

tiles) had the largest increases in combined work hours, corresponding to about a 12-percent increase in combined weekly hours and a 16-percent increase in annual hours. Viewing these changes together with the changes in family incomes at each decile indicates that married-couple families in the middle of the income distribution, who have increased their work efforts the most, have not experienced the largest changes in income. Family incomes have grown fastest at the top of the distribution and have actually declined in real terms for married-couple families at the bottom of the distribution.

Employment Arrangements and Time Off

Given the reality that most women are now working in the paid labor market, policy makers at both the State and local level have drafted legislation aimed at helping workers with some of their nonwork responsibilities. Although employment arrangements that assist workers in meeting their family obligations are largely negotiated on an individual or employee group basis, some government mandates do exist.

The most prominent Federal initiative in the area of helping employees coordinate work and family obligations is the Family and Medical

Leave Act of 1993. This law requires that employers grant their workers time off for certain personal or family medical reasons such as caring for a sick child or parent without jeopardizing their jobs.[20] The Family and Medical Leave Act (FMLA) was ground-breaking in the sense that it marked the first Federal legislation mandating time off from work for family reasons. However, prior to its passage in 1993 many individual States had already enacted similar legislation. For example, a 1988 Maine law required private sector employers and local governments with 25 or more employees to grant up to 8 weeks of unpaid leave for births or adoptions, or for the serious illness of the worker, child, parent, or spouse. A similar law was enacted in Wisconsin. In both States, reinstatement in the same, or similar, job was guaranteed.[21] In 1990, New Jersey and the District of Columbia passed comprehensive family leave laws.[22]

With the passage of the FMLA, State legislative activity in this area diminished. Some of the legislation enacted after the FMLA was designed to bring States into compliance with Federal law. Other legislation extended family leave provisions into new areas. In 1994, the District of Columbia required employers to grant time for parents to participate in their children's school related activities.[23] And, in 1997, an extant California law mandating parental leave to attend school functions was extended.[24]

101

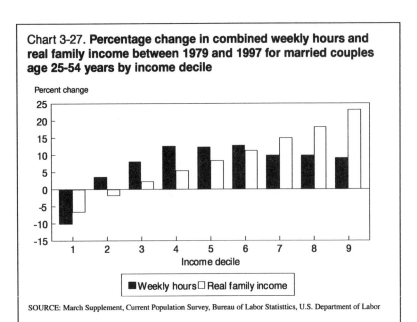

Chart 3-27. Percentage change in combined weekly hours and real family income between 1979 and 1997 for married couples age 25-54 years by income decile

Percent change

SOURCE: March Supplement, Current Population Survey, Bureau of Labor Statisttics, U.S. Department of Labor

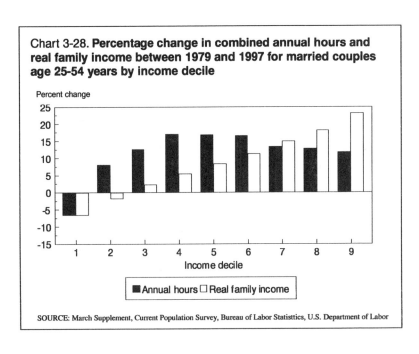

Chart 3-28. Percentage change in combined annual hours and real family income between 1979 and 1997 for married couples age 25-54 years by income decile

Percent change

SOURCE: March Supplement, Current Population Survey, Bureau of Labor Statisttics, U.S. Department of Labor

Flexible work schedules and work at home

The data discussed so far show a fairly consistent picture of the expanding role that paid work is playing in family life. Women are tending to work more paid hours a week; in married-couple families, especially those with children, both spouses are increasingly likely to be labor force participants; both spouses are full-time year round workers in a significant, and growing proportion of families. Meeting work requirements and family responsibilities is a problem for a growing proportion of families. There are two practices that are considered important in helping employees manage personal and work time effectively: Flexible work schedules and work at home.

Flexible work schedules, or "flexitime," have long been viewed as a means by which employees can combine work and family life in a more efficient, less stressful way than is possible if workers adhere to a rigid schedule. There are several types of formal flexible work arrangements. One type is a "gliding schedule" that requires a specified number of hours of work each day but allows employees to vary the time of their arrival and departure, usually around an established set of mandatory "core hours." Other types of flexible work arrangements include variable-day and variable-week schedules that usually require a specified number of hours per pay period. Employees, under these plans, are permitted to choose the number of hours they wish to work each day, or the number of days they want to work each week. Credit or compensatory time arrangements allow employees who accumulate overtime hours to apply those hours to future time off from work, rather than receiving the overtime pay rate for those hours. The presence of one or more of these arrangements in the workplace does not necessarily exclude the others; many can be used in conjunction with other flexible work arrangements.[25]

Flexitime has been in the workplace for many years, but some observers have noted problems that may have retarded its spread. One is the difficulty that management can have in adapting to widespread use of flexitime. Managers often fear that discipline and productivity may slip if they are not present when their employees are on the job (an impossibility with flexitime). On the other hand, employees may be reluctant to use such a benefit for fear of being perceived by management as less important to the organization's operations.[26] Thus, studies indicate limited use of existing flexitime programs.[27]

The proportion of wage and salary workers who vary their beginning and ending hours increased significantly during the 1990s. In May 1997 (the most recent year for which these data are available),[28] 27.6 percent of all wage and salary workers were able to vary their work hours somewhat. (See table 3-9.) Six years earlier, in 1991, the proportion was 15.1 percent. These gains were spread across most demographic groups and most occupational categories. It is likely, though, that a great many of the workers who report being able to vary their beginning and ending times do so under informal arrangements with their employers or supervisors. Data from the Bureau's 1997 Employee Benefits Survey, a survey of employers, indicate that less than 6 percent of employees have formal flexible work schedule arrangements.[29]

Although flexitime is often considered a "family-friendly" benefit, it is by no means only available to parents. In May 1997, the proportion of wage and salary workers with children under age 18 who were able to vary the hours they worked (28.9 percent), was only a little greater than the proportion for those who had no children under age 18 (26.8 percent). Among the parents, the incidence of flexitime was greater among those with children under age 6 (30.2 percent) than among those whose youngest child was age 6 to 17 (27.9 percent). Fathers were more likely to have flexible work schedules than mothers. Generally, only one parent had a flexible hours arrangement. Only in 5 percent of two-parent families in which both the mother and father were wage and salary workers did both parents have some sort of flexible hours arrangement.

Ultimately, however, the family situation is probably not the primary factor in determining whether a worker can elect to vary his or her beginning and ending hours. The data clearly show that the availability of flexitime depends a great deal on the type of job a worker holds. Generally, the jobs with the higher frequencies of flexible hours are those where work can be conducted efficiently regardless of the times that individual workers start and end work. For instance, flexible work hours are most common among workers in executive, administrative, and managerial occupations, and sales occupations, and least common among workers with jobs that must adhere to rigid schedules, such as nursing, teaching, law enforcement, and firefighting.

To a lesser degree, the prevalence of flexible work schedules also varied by industry and was more common in the private sector than the public sector (in 1997, 28.8 percent versus 21.7 percent, respectively). The public sector proportion

103

How Much Time is Spent Commuting to Work in the United States?

The nonwork time use that is most closely related to employment is travel time to work ("commuting time"). Data on commuting times of all workers in the United States are available from the 1980 and 1990 population census. The average one way commuting time for workers changed very little between 1980 and 1990, increasing by less than a minute one way each day. Thus, the 1990 commuting data may provide a good indication of current commuting times.

In 1990, the average one way commuting time for all U.S. workers was about 22 minutes per day. About one-half of all U.S. workers (including those who did not commute) had commuting times of less than 20 minutes per day and about 31 percent spent a half-hour or more on commuting each way. In general, average travel times were less in rural areas than in urban areas (in part because many workers on ranches and farms do not commute at all). For example, average one way commuting times were less than 15 minutes per day for workers in Montana, North Dakota, and South Dakota. However, average commuting times in metropolitan areas were only about a minute longer than the average for all workers. In only one metropolitan area in the United States—New York City along with its adjacent suburban areas in New Jersey and Long Island—did the average one way commute exceed a half-hour a day.

The Bureau of the Census Internet site, *http://www.census.gov*, contains additional information and geographical detail on census data.

is low due to the rate for local government workers—13 percent. Over half of those employed in local governments are in education, where only 7.6 percent of the workers have the ability to vary the hours at which they begin and end work. Within private industry, the proportion of workers with flexible schedules was higher in service producing industries (31.7 percent) than in goods-producing industries (23.3 percent), reflecting the rigidity of work hours in manufacturing, construction, and mining.[30]

Working at home also is viewed as a way to help reconcile the demands of work and family. One obvious advantage of working at home is the savings in commuting time. Working exclusively at home would save the average worker roughly 44 minutes a day. Bureau of the Census data indicate that in 1990 the average journey to work took about 22 minutes each way. (See box.) Table 3-10 shows that overall, about 17.7 percent of nonagricultural employees did some work at home for their primary job in May 1997. (This includes individuals who bring work home from the office, those who have "flexiplace"[31] arrangements, and those who are self-employed and do part of their work out of their own homes.) Of the total who work at home, some 5.2 million, or a little less than one-fourth, do so to coordinate their work schedule with family and personal life.

About one-fifth of married parents who were nonagricultural employees worked at home for 1 hour or more a week on their primary job. Married mothers are somewhat more likely than fathers to work at home. Work at home, however, has not grown a great deal during the 1990s, although there are more mothers in the labor force now than at the beginning of the decade.

Time off from work

Alternative work time and work place arrangements are just some of the means employers have used to accommodate family obligations. In this section, we review BLS data on time off from work—primarily time off from work for which the worker continues to be paid by the employer (paid leave). These data can provide insight into trends in the overall extent of paid leave, the availability of specific types of time off, amounts of time off available, and variations in these data among workers, types of jobs, and types of employers.

The 1976 *Report of the Task Force on Hours Worked* noted the possibility that the work week might be declining more rapidly then hours worked indicates because the amount of paid leave per worker appeared to be increasing. (Periodic Employer Expenditures for Employee Compensation Surveys appear to confirm that paid leave per worker grew during the 1960s and 1970s.) As a result of the 1976 *Report*, the BLS Hours at Work Survey began surveying establishments in 1981 to collect data on both hours at work and hours paid for production and nonsupervisory workers. The survey measures paid leave as vacation, holiday, sick leave, and jury and military

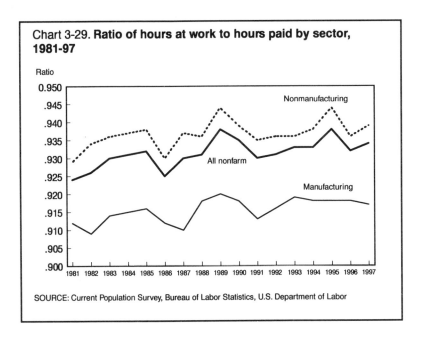

Chart 3-29. **Ratio of hours at work to hours paid by sector, 1981-97**

Ratio

SOURCE: Current Population Survey, Bureau of Labor Statistics, U.S. Department of Labor

leave. Machine down time and other "nonproductive" time are beyond the scope of the survey.

The Hours at Work Survey indicates that hours worked as a proportion of hours paid (for production or nonsupervisory workers) have fluctuated in a narrow range between 92 and 94 percent (with the corresponding paid leave percentage varying from 6 to 8 percent) between 1981 and 1997. (See chart 3-29.) The survey includes full- and part-time, year round, part-year, and seasonal workers (who usually earn much less, if any, paid leave than full-time workers), and excludes most managers (who may earn more leave than production or supervisory employees). The hours worked to hours paid ratios usually fall during recessions and then rise with economic recovery. One explanation for this cyclical behavior focuses on the fact that, during recessions, employers tend to lay off their least senior workers and rehire them when conditions improve; workers with the least job tenure also tend to earn the least leave. Another explanation could be that jobs destroyed during recessions have fewer benefits in general, regardless of tenure, than do jobs that are maintained through the business cycle. For example, construction jobs tend to be highly sensitive to business conditions. For many workers in construction, no paid leave is offered and, on average, paid leave provides only 2.9 percent of hours paid.[32] Chart 3-29 also indicates that more paid leave has been provided, on average, in manu-

facturing industries than in other industries and that this differential in the provision of paid leave has persisted over the 1981-97 period.

The ratio of hours worked to hours paid over time depends on how many jobs provide paid leave as well as how much paid leave is provided in jobs having this benefit. A study of the underlying data used to construct the BLS Employment Cost Index indicates that the percentage of employment in all jobs that do not provide any paid leave is small but has been increasing steadily since the early-1980s.[33] This study indicates that in the 1981-83 period, 7.8 percent of total civilian nonagricultural employment outside the Federal Government was in jobs not offering any paid leave, but that by the 1995-97 period, such jobs were held by 13.9 percent of this group's workers. These research results suggest that the apparent stability of the overall hours worked to hours paid ratio over time reflects both a growth in paid time off in jobs with this benefit and a decline in the share of employment in jobs offering paid time off.

The Hours at Work Survey also indicates substantial differences in paid leave for production and nonsupervisory jobs between industries. (Table 3-11 displays ratios of hours at work to hours paid for selected industries). In construction, production and nonsupervisory workers earn substantially less paid leave, with paid leave comprising 2.9 percent of hours paid (an at-work ratio of 97.1 percent). Retail trade (95.9 percent), lumber and wood products (94.0 percent), and apparel manufacture (94.6 percent) also offer relatively little paid leave. At the other end of the spectrum, communications industries offered the most paid leave, as nonsupervisory employees work 88.2 percent of hours paid. Transportation equipment manufacturers (89.2 percent), electric, gas, and sanitary services (89.6 percent), petroleum and coal products (89.6 percent), and electrical equipment manufacturers (89.8 percent) also allow employees to work less than 90 percent of their paid hours.

The relative amount of paid leave provided tends to be larger in establishments with greater employment. For example, in 1997, employees in establishments with more than 2,500 employees worked just 87 percent of hours paid. In contrast, employees of establishments with less than 50 employees worked more than 95 percent of hours paid. Thus, the paid leave rate for employees of large establishments is more than 2½ times the rate for employees in small establishments.

While hours at work data indicate the ratio of hours worked to hours paid, data from another BLS survey, the Employee Benefits Survey, provide additional detail on the types of paid time off benefits available to employees and the amount of time off these benefits provide. For most workers, paid time off is provided through a series of specific-purpose benefits, such as vacations, holidays, sick leave, and funeral leave. A small percentage of workers receive time off through a consolidated arrangement, where employees are provided a single amount of time off to be used for all purposes. The availability and duration of time off benefits can vary by several factors, including industry, occupation, full- and part-time status, and the size of the establishment. (See tables 3-12 and 3-13.)

Paid vacations are the most prevalent type of time off benefit, available to about 76 percent of all workers. While such benefits are generally widespread among full-time workers, those in larger establishments are provided paid vacations more frequently than those in smaller establishments. Eighty-seven percent of full-time employees receive paid vacations, compared with 34 percent of their part-time counterparts. Workers typically have to have been on the job for some amount of time, such as 1 year, before vacation time is available. The number of vacation days available generally increases with length of service, ranging from about 10 days after 1 year of service to 20 or more days after 20 years of service. Work-

ers in certain industries, notably construction, are less likely to have formal leave arrangements. Such workers are only paid for time worked.

While paid vacations are provided for workers to take leisure time, more specific time-off plans are also common. Paid holidays are widespread; as with paid vacations, full-time workers and those in larger establishments are more likely to receive such benefits. In addition, paid holidays are more prevalent in goods-producing industries than in service-producing industries. This may be due in part to the growing tendency of certain service-producing establishments to be open for business on holidays. For certain enterprises, such as hospitals, hotels, and restaurants, this has always been the case. In more recent years, retail trade and personal service establishments have also followed the trend toward work on holidays. When employees receive paid holidays but work for an establishment that is open on the holiday, those that work either receive another day off in lieu of the holiday or receive extra pay to account for both the holiday and the work day.

Other widespread time off plans pay for time away from work to attend funerals or to fulfill jury duty service. In the case of jury duty leave, employers typically pay the difference between the employee's jury duty pay and their full pay. Employees who receive paid military leave, a less prevalent benefit, generally have a similar payment arrangement.

Paid sick leave is less prevalent than vacation or holiday leave. (Such benefits continue an individual's salary when they are unable to work due to sickness or injury.) Overall, 50 percent of all workers receive paid sick leave, including 75 percent of professional workers. Other white-collar workers may have informal sick leave arrangements. Replacement of lost income during temporary illness or injury for blue-collar workers is generally provided through an insurance plan, which provides less than full wages. Because such payments are not part of earnings, they would not be included in the ratio of hours worked to hours paid.

Another benefit that will generally not be included in the ratio of hours worked to hours paid is unpaid family leave, which is widespread among large employers. Such benefits are provided to fulfill the requirements of the Family and Medical Leave Act, which guarantees certain workers up to 12 weeks of unpaid leave to care for newborns, newly adopted children, or sick relatives, or for personal illness. Such benefits are less widespread among small establishments, because the law generally applies only to those establishments employing 50 or more workers.

A small number of workers receive time off benefits through a consolidated leave plan, which is sometimes referred to as a leave bank. Under such arrangements, employees are given a single amount of time off for a year, such as 30 or 40 days. This is to be used to schedule vacations as well as to cover sick time and other personal matters. Because such plans are generally established in hospitals and other facilities that never close, holidays are not specifically designated. Individuals apply for time off, which may include holidays, often based on seniority.

In contrast to the Employee Benefits Survey, the Bureau's National Longitudinal Survey of Youth, 1979 (NLSY79) looks at the subject of paid time off benefits from an employee, rather than an employer, perspective. That is, the NLSY79 indicates what benefits individuals receive, and variations by demographic group. Among those workers age 32 to 40, 3 out of 4 were eligible for paid vacations while just under two-thirds were eligible for paid sick leave and family leave. (See table 3-14.) Women age 32 to 40 are more likely than men to have jobs that offer maternity and paternity leave, but less likely to be in jobs that have paid vacations. Workers in certain industries, notably construction and retail trade, were less likely to have time off benefits available. Similarly, professional workers and managers tended to be eligible for time off benefits more often than those in other occupations. The benefits were much more prevalent among full-time than among part-time workers and the availability of time off generally increased the longer an individual worked for an employer. These data tend to support the variations found in the hours paid/hours worked data.

For those who had paid vacations and paid sick leave, there was less variation in the number of days available by industry and occupation. (See table 3-15.) Construction and retail trade workers again lagged behind those in other industries, although generally by a day or two. The average number of days of vacation and sick leave rose steadily with job tenure, reflecting the design of many of these plans. Among full- and part-time workers, there was not much difference in the average number of days of paid vacation and sick leave available. However, part-time workers generally receive days off in proportion of their hours worked. So, someone working five 4-hour days may receive an average of 9.4 paid sick leave days, but each paid day off is 4 hours.

Trends in nonwork time

What do Americans do with their nonwork time? To answer this question, one needs detailed individual time-use data. One method of collecting such data is through a time-use survey. In this type of survey, respondents are asked to report sequentially every activity performed during a 24-hour day. Start and stop times are collected for each activity, thus allowing the duration of various types of activities to be calculated. This measurement approach has been used extensively (Szalai, 1972) and is generally viewed as a reliable way to estimate the amount of time spent in various activities such as working, watching television, and performing household chores. (See box for more information on other applications of time-use data.)

A number of national time-use surveys have been conducted in the United States. (None of these surveys have been conducted by the Federal Government.[34]) To examine the ways in which Americans spend their nonworking time, researchers using these data usually group all unpaid activities into the following categories (a) personal care, (b) education, (c) domestic and family care, (d) shopping, (e) volunteer work, (f) social and community activities, and (g) recreation and leisure. Using this data researchers have found small but noticeable changes in the distribution of activities that fill the daily lives of the American worker.

Due to increased labor force participation by women, lower marriage rates, and lower birth rates, the time spent on domestic activities has changed both in its quantity and social pattern since the 1960s (Robinson and Godbey, 1997). Men are spending more time doing housework while women are spending less time at these activities. Table 3-16, taken from John Robinson and Geoffrey Godbey's book, *Time for Life: The Surprising Ways Americans Use Their Time*, shows that women spent nearly 27 hours per week doing housework in 1965, compared with 19 hours per week in 1985. Men, on the other hand, increased their hours of housework from 5 to 9 hours per week between 1965 and 1985. Although the division of housework is not yet evenly split between the sexes, the fact that the trends for men and women are in opposite directions suggests that there is a social thrust toward parity.

Other time-use survey categories show only minimal changes across the decades. One noticeable exception was the increase in the amount of time spent on free-time activities, the majority of which is spent viewing television. This increase

Potential Applications for National Time-use Survey Data

A time-use survey is one approach to collecting information on the hours that people spend working or doing other activities. In addition to providing data on hours spent working that could be used to verify data that are currently collected in the CPS and other surveys, time-use survey data could also provide a wealth of information on how Americans spend their time. Data are obtained on time spent in productive nonmarket activities such as child care; housework and home repairs; leisure activities such as reading, watching television, and socializing; and nonproductive, nonleisure activities such as waiting and commuting. Given the wide range of information collected, national level time-use survey data could have numerous potential applications. Potential uses include:

International comparisons. In addition to comparing measures of material-well-being, such as gross domestic product (GDP), analysts could also study how the United States compares with other countries on nonmaterial dimensions such as hours of free time. Furthermore, time-use data, in conjunction with wage rates, could be used to enhance our measures of aggregate production by incorporating the value of nonmarket production. Because many of the goods and services that households enjoy—particularly child care, meal preparation, and household maintenance—are not purchased in the market but "produced" at home through the direct efforts of family members, GDP comparisons do not provide a comprehensive picture of aggregate output. This may be particularly important for comparisons with less-developed countries, where household production often includes food production which is a large contribution to family well being.

Quality of life measures. Usually, analysts use quantifiable measures, such as real income or earnings, to assess changes in the quality of life over time. Collecting information on time-use would permit a more complete assessment of changes in the quality of life. For example, stories in the mass media report on individuals quitting high salary jobs that require long working hours to take lower paying jobs with fewer hours. While such people consider themselves "better off," any objective measure of income or earnings would indicate that these individuals are "worse off." Data from a time-use survey would permit analysts to account for the increase in nonmarket production and leisure time in assessing changes to the quality of life.

Marketing applications. Marketers could use time-use data to determine how activities (such as TV viewing, radio listening, shopping, and eating out) differ by demographic characteristics and income.

Legal applications. For the judicial system, time-use data might be useful for estimating the economic damages in personal injury and wrongful death cases. Currently, economic damages primarily include only lost earnings. Time-use data might provide a more complete picture.

---

in hours of TV viewing was particularly large for women. (See table 3-17.)

Summary and Conclusions

This chapter discussed what empirical data indicate about the hours worked in the labor force and the provisions for time off that are provided by employers. The major labor force survey, the CPS, indicates that average weekly hours of work among those employed have been fairly stable

since 1960, fluctuating in a narrow range between 38 and 40 hours per week. However, the stability of this economy-wide average conceals a number of interesting changes that have occurred within certain subpopulations and within the distribution of weekly hours.

First, the proportion of women employed has increased substantially, as wives and mothers have joined the labor force in very large numbers. This increase in participation has been coupled with a small upward trend in the average number of hours worked among employed women, so women are

108

clearly working more now than they did 30 years ago. Second, although the trends in the average weekly hours worked among employed men have been flat, there has been an increase in the proportion of men who are working extended workweeks (more than 40 hours per week). Third, data on married-couple families indicates that couples, particularly those with small children, are spending considerably more combined hours at work. The number of couples where both spouses work long hours has also increased. These trends, combined with an increase in the number of single parents, have likely resulted in a "time-bind" for some individuals.

However, some people are working less today than in the past. For example, the average weekly hours worked among the population of men age 25 to 54 with less than a high school education fell from 38.3 hours per week in 1969 to 29.7 hours per week in 1998. Male workers in the lower end of the earnings distribution were also working less in 1998 than in 1979.

The overall stability of work hours since 1960 also masks certain changes that have occurred in the basic structure of work time; traditional work hours and time off benefits are changing. BLS labor force data show the proportion of wage and salary workers indicating they had some flexibility in their work schedules increased from 16 per-

cent in 1991 to 30 percent in 1997.

Finally, the data indicate that the availability of paid time off has declined slightly over time. Traditional time off benefits, such as paid vacations and paid holidays, are still prevalent, but may not always meet the needs of today's workers. Those in part-time jobs are substantially less likely to be offered paid time off benefits and, even if offered, are likely to receive less generous benefits than their full-time counterparts. Likewise, the trend away from traditional work hours, such as retailers remaining open on Sundays and holidays, may require less traditional time off benefits. There is evidence from the Employee Benefits Survey that employers may be beginning to address this need through flexible time off arrangements.

With the passage of the Family and Medical Leave Act in 1993 both employers and employees entered a new era. While work hours and overtime provisions have been regulated for much of the 20th century, this Act imposed upon employers, for the first time, a mandate to provide leave benefits. Since that time, policy makers have continued to debate this topic, with regular calls to expand these benefits. A better understanding of work-family conflicts that could come from more comprehensive time-use data could aid in this debate.

Table 3-1. **Percent distribution of employed persons by weekly hours at work, age, and sex, annual averages, selected years 1979-98**

Age and sex	Total	1 to 34 hours					35 or more hours			41 or more hours			
		Total	1-4	5-14	15-29	30-34	Total	35-39	40	Total	41-48	49-59	60 or more
16 years and over													
1979	100.0	25.0	0.8	4.3	11.9	8.0	75.0	7.1	41.7	26.2	10.7	9.16	.5
1989	100.0	23.3	.7	3.9	11.7	7.0	76.7	6.7	40.1	30.0	10.8	11.3	7.9
1998	100.0	26.3	1.1	3.9	12.3	9.0	73.7	6.9	35.1	31.6	11.6	11.5	8.5
Men													
1979	100.0	17.1	.5	2.7	7.6	6.3	82.9	4.4	43.3	35.1	13.0	12.7	9.4
1989	100.0	15.8	.4	2.6	7.7	5.1	84.2	4.4	40.8	39.0	12.5	15.1	11.4
1998	100.0	18.9	.8	2.6	8.4	7.2	81.1	5.1	35.7	40.2	13.1	15.1	11.9
Women													
1979	100.0	35.8	1.2	6.6	17.7	10.3	64.2	10.7	39.5	14.0	7.5	4.1	2.4
1989	100.0	32.2	1.0	5.5	16.5	9.2	67.8	9.4	39.2	19.2	8.8	6.7	3.7
1998	100.0	35.1	1.4	5.5	17.0	11.2	64.9	9.2	34.3	21.6	9.8	7.3	4.4
16 to 24 years													
1979	100.0	35.2	1.4	8.7	19.6	5.5	64.8	7.4	39.0	18.4	9.5	5.7	3.2
1989	100.0	40.7	1.3	8.8	23.1	7.5	59.3	7.0	34.4	17.9	8.1	6.3	3.5
1998	100.0	46.9	1.5	9.5	25.6	10.3	53.1	7.6	28.7	16.8	7.6	5.6	3.5
Men													
1979	100.0	32.3	1.1	7.0	16.7	7.5	67.7	4.9	38.8	24.0	11.4	7.9	4.7
1989	100.0	35.4	1.1	7.6	20.9	5.9	64.6	5.7	36.0	22.8	9.4	8.4	5.0
1998	100.0	40.9	1.3	8.1	22.2	9.4	59.1	6.6	31.2	21.4	9.1	7.3	4.9
Women													
1979	100.0	38.6	1.7	10.6	23.1	3.2	61.4	10.3	39.3	11.7	7.3	3.1	1.3
1989	100.0	46.2	1.4	10.1	25.4	9.2	53.8	8.4	32.6	12.8	6.7	4.1	2.0
1998	100.0	53.6	1.7	11.2	29.3	11.4	46.4	8.6	26.1	11.7	6.1	3.7	1.9
25 to 54 years													
1979	100.0	20.5	.5	2.5	8.7	8.9	79.5	6.9	43.0	29.6	11.3	10.5	7.7
1989	100.0	17.8	.4	2.3	8.3	6.8	82.2	6.4	41.9	33.8	11.8	12.9	9.1
1998	100.0	26.7	.8	2.3	8.9	8.7	79.3	6.8	37.0	35.5	12.9	13.0	9.6
Men													
1979	100.0	11.2	.2	1.0	4.1	5.9	88.8	4.2	44.8	39.9	13.9	14.7	11.2
1989	100.0	10.2	.2	1.1	4.1	4.8	89.8	4.0	42.0	43.8	13.6	17.1	13.1
1998	100.0	13.1	.5	1.1	4.9	6.6	86.9	4.8	37.2	44.9	14.4	17.0	13.5
Women													
1979	100.0	33.7	.9	4.6	15.1	13.1	66.3	10.8	40.4	15.1	7.7	4.6	2.7
1989	100.0	27.2	.8	3.8	13.5	9.1	72.8	9.4	41.9	21.5	9.7	7.6	4.2
1998	100.0	29.9	1.1	3.8	13.7	11.2	76.1	9.2	36.7	24.2	11.0	8.3	4.9
55 years and over													
1979	100.0	29.1	1.3	6.0	13.9	7.9	70.9	7.3	40.3	23.3	9.5	7.7	6.1
1989	100.0	30.9	1.5	6.3	15.7	7.4	69.1	7.5	37.1	24.5	8.6	9.0	7.0
1998	100.0	34.1	2.1	6.4	16.2	9.4	65.9	6.9	31.9	27.1	9.0	9.9	8.2
Men													
1979	100.0	21.4	.9	4.3	9.7	6.5	78.6	4.8	43.5	30.4	11.7	10.6	8.1
1989	100.0	23.3	1.1	4.8	11.5	5.9	76.7	4.9	40.0	31.8	10.1	12.1	9.6
1998	100.0	27.5	1.7	4.9	12.9	8.1	72.5	5.6	33.3	34.2	10.1	13.0	11.1
Women													
1979	100.0	40.4	1.9	8.4	20.1	10.0	59.6	11.1	35.7	12.9	6.3	3.6	3.0
1989	100.0	40.6	2.0	8.4	21.0	9.3	59.4	10.9	33.4	15.1	6.6	4.9	3.6
1998	100.0	42.4	2.6	8.2	20.5	11.1	57.6	9.4	30.1	18.1	7.7	5.9	4.5

NOTE: Data for 1998 are not directly comparable with data for earlier years. For additional information, see household data section of Explanatory Notes in *Employment and Earnings*, Bureau of Labor Statistics.

SOURCE: Current Population Survey, Bureau of Labor Statistics, U.S. Department of Labor

110

Table 3-2. **Average weekly hours at work for persons age 25-54 by educational attainment and sex, March of selected years 1969-98**

Education level and sex	1969	1979	1989	1998
Civilian population				
Men	41.3	38.9	38.2	37.9
Less than a high school diploma	38.3	33.4	29.4	29.7
High school diploma	42.8	39.4	37.7	36.4
Some college	42.1	40.1	39.7	38.4
College degree or higher	44.0	42.6	43.0	42.8
Women	16.2	20.3	25.0	26.6
Less than a high school diploma	14.6	14.9	15.7	16.7
High school diploma	16.6	20.3	24.8	25.5
Some college	15.7	22.1	26.7	27.6
College degree or higher	20.2	25.9	30.1	31.1
Civilian employed				
Men	43.7	43.0	43.1	43.2
Less than a high school diploma	42.0	40.6	39.1	39.9
High school diploma	44.3	42.9	42.7	42.5
Some college	44.2	43.5	43.4	43.0
College degree or higher	45.5	44.6	45.4	45.2
Women	34.3	34.3	35.6	36.1
Less than a high school diploma	34.3	33.6	33.8	34.2
High school diploma	34.3	34.1	35.3	35.6
Some college	33.3	34.2	35.5	35.7
College degree or higher	35.1	35.5	36.9	37.4

NOTE: Data for 1998 are not directly comparable with data for earlier years. In 1998, information on educational levels reflects highest degree or diploma attained; in prior years, data reflect years of school completed. For additional information on other comparability issues, see household data section of Explanatory Notes in *Employment and Earnings*, Bureau of Labor Statistics.

SOURCE: Current Population Survey, March supplement, Bureau of Labor Statistics, U.S. Department of Labor

Table 3-3. **Percent of total available hours[1] spent working for persons age 18-32, by sex, educational attainment, race, and Hispanic origin, 1978-95**

Characteristic	Percent			
	Total	Age[2]		
		18-22	23-27	28-32
Total	18.0	13.7	18.8	20.0
Men	20.8	15.2	21.6	23.8
Less than a high school diploma	19.7	16.0	20.5	20.7
High school diploma	21.8	17.6	22.0	23.9
Some college	21.1	15.8	22.0	23.5
College graduates	19.6	9.7	21.3	25.9
Women	15.0	12.0	15.8	16.1
Less than a high school diploma	10.0	7.7	8.7	10.9
High school diploma	14.7	13.6	14.7	15.1
Some college	16.1	13.3	17.4	17.2
College graduates	16.9	10.1	19.8	19.3
White	18.7	14.4	19.5	20.7
Less than a high school diploma	17.1	13.8	16.9	17.9
High school diploma	19.3	16.9	19.2	20.3
Some college	19.0	15.3	20.1	20.5
College graduates	18.3	10.1	20.6	22.5
Black	14.7	10.1	15.8	17.1
Less than a high school diploma	11.0	8.0	11.6	12.2
High school diploma	14.6	10.9	15.6	16.8
Some college	15.8	10.5	16.8	17.9
College graduates	18.1	8.7	20.7	24.4
Hispanic origin	16.7	13.2	16.9	18.5
Less than a high school diploma	15.0	12.5	14.1	15.4
High school diploma	16.7	14.0	17.2	18.6
Some college	18.4	14.1	18.6	19.6
College graduates	18.2	9.2	18.5	22.7

[1] Total available hours equal 168 per week.

[2] Data for a group of individuals was collected over a period of years (1979-95). In 1978 the participating individuals were age 14-22. In 1995 these same individuals were age 31-38.

SOURCE: National Longitudinal Survey of Youth, 1979, Bureau of Labor Statistics, U.S. Department of Labor

Table 3-4. **Percent of persons age 16 and over working full-time year round, by age, educational attainment, and sex, selected years 1969-97**

Age, educational attainment, and sex	1969	1979	1989	1997
Age				
16-24	19.1	23.3	23.7	21.4
25-54	53.0	54.8	59.9	62.6
55 and over	27.4	22.2	19.3	21.1
Educational attainment				
Men age 25-54	80.6	75.5	74.6	75.4
Less than a high school diploma..	72.0	62.3	55.1	57.4
High school diploma	84.6	76.6	74.2	74.1
Some college	85.0	77.2	78.1	77.3
College degree or higher	86.7	84.1	83.7	83.5
Women age 25-54	27.5	35.4	45.8	50.2
Less than a high school diploma..	22.3	23.3	27.0	28.9
High school diploma	28.7	36.4	45.0	48.6
Some college	27.9	39.5	49.5	52.9
College degree or higher	39.5	44.4	55.9	58.4

NOTE: Data for 1997 are not directly comparable with data for earlier years. In 1998, information on educational levels reflects highest degree or diploma attained; in prior years data reflect years of school completed. For additional information on other comparability issues, see household data section or Explanatory Notes in Employment and Earnings, Bureau of Labor Statistics.

SOURCE: Current Population Survey, March supplement, Bureau of Labor Statistics, U.S. Department of Labor

Table 3-5. Average weekly hours at work and percent of workers working full-time year-round for workers age 25-54 by family relationship, presence and age of youngest child, and sex, selected years

Family relationship and presence and age of youngest child[1]	Average weekly hours March—				Percent working full-time year round			
	1969	1979	1989	1998[2]	1969	1979	1989	1997
Family relationship								
Men								
Married, spouse present	44.2	43.6	44.1	44.2	83.7	80.7	80.9	82.5
Maintaining a family no spouse present	41.6	42.4	41.2	41.5	74.5	68.2	68.3	71.0
Living alone	41.7	41.7	42.3	42.3	68.3	64.3	68.1	68.8
Women								
Married, spouse present.............	33.2	32.8	34.3	34.9	22.5	29.8	41.1	46.1
Maintaining a family, no spouse present	36.0	36.6	37.3	36.9	39.5	44.2	48.4	52.6
Living alone.............................	38.5	38.5	39.4	39.6	62.2	60.7	65.6	64.0
Presence and age of youngest child								
Men								
No children under 18.................	41.9	41.9	42.2	42.3	72.8	68.6	69.7	69.7
Children 6-17...........................	44.5	43.7	43.9	44.4	84.9	81.0	80.2	82.1
Children 3-5.............................	44.6	43.9	44.1	44.3	84.8	81.4	79.6	83.3
Children under 3.......................	44.4	43.9	44.3	43.6	83.4	79.9	79.7	81.5
Women								
No children under 18.................	36.7	36.5	37.6	38.0	44.6	47.8	57.2	58.8
Children 6-17...........................	33.1	33.5	35.0	35.6	25.8	33.7	43.3	48.6
Children 3-5............................	32.0	31.5	33.2	33.4	15.4	23.6	32.8	39.0
Children under 3.....................	30.3	28.9	30.4	30.9	6.7	14.8	25.0	31.8

[1] Children may be biological, adopted, or stepchildren. Not included are nieces, nephews, grandchildren, other related children, and unrelated children.

[2] Data for 1998 are not directly comparable with data for earlier years. For additional information, see household data section of Explanatory Notes in *Employment and Earnings*, Bureau of Labor Statistics.

SOURCE: Current Population Survey, March supplement, Bureau of Labor Statistics, U.S. Department of Labor

Table 3-6. Average combined weekly hours at work and average combined annual hours at work for married couples by presence and age of youngest child, March of selected years 1969-98

Year	All married couples	Presence and age of youngest child[1]			
		No children under 18	Children 6 to 17	Children 3 to 5	Children under 3
Combined weekly hours					
1969	57.5	62.2	56.3	59.6	52.3
1979	66.2	70.5	64.7	66.4	62.2
1989	70.4	74.1	68.7	70.5	66.7
1998	71.8	74.8	70.4	72.2	68.3
Combined annual hours					
1969	2,804.8	3,047.5	2,739.8	2,906.5	2,537.4
1979	3,135.2	3,380.3	3,050.8	3,164.2	2,884.9
1989	3,401.2	3,632.4	3,293.3	3,406.9	3,164.6
1997	3,521.4	3,686.6	3,442.7	3,545.0	3,316.5

[1] Children may be biological, adopted, or stepchildren. Not included are nieces, nephews, grandchildren, other related children, and unrelated children.

SOURCE: Current Population Survey, March supplement, Bureau of Labor Statistics, U.S. Department of Labor

Table 3-7. **Percent distribution of wives' weekly hours worked by husbands' weekly hours worked, both spouses age 25-54, March of selected years 1969-98**

Wives' hours	Percent					
	Total	Husbands' hours				
		0	1-19	20-34	35-40	41 or more
1969						
Total	100.0	3.9	1.7	5.2	43.2	45.9
0	59.2	2.2	1.1	3.1	25.1	27.7
1-19	5.5	0.2	0.1	0.3	2.3	2.7
20-34	8.7	.3	.1	.7	3.8	3.9
35-40	20.8	1.1	.3	1.0	10.4	8.1
41 or more	5.8	.2	.1	.3	1.6	3.6
1979						
Total	100.0	6.6	1.6	5.3	43.9	42.6
0	44.7	3.4	.8	2.6	19.5	18.4
1-19	7.9	.3	.2	.4	2.9	4.1
20-34	12.8	.7	.1	.8	5.6	5.6
35-40	26.7	1.7	.3	1.2	14.0	9.5
41 or more	7.8	.5	.1	.2	2.0	5.0
1989						
Total	100.0	7.4	1.5	5.3	41.8	44.0
0	31.8	3.1	.5	1.8	12.7	13.8
1-19	7.0	.3	.2	.5	2.5	3.5
20-34	14.7	.9	.2	1.2	5.9	6.5
35-40	33.8	2.3	.4	1.4	17.4	12.2
41 or more	12.7	.8	.2	.4	3.3	7.9
1998						
Total	100.0	6.9	1.9	6.5	38.1	45.6
0	28.2	3.1	.6	1.9	10.1	12.6
1-19	7.3	.4	.3	.7	2.2	3.8
20-34	15.1	.9	.3	1.3	5.5	7.2
35-40	33.1	2.5	.5	1.8	16.4	12.0
41 or more	15.3	.1	.3	.9	4.0	10.1

SOURCE: Current Population Survey, Bureau of Labor Statistics, U.S. Department of Labor

Table 3-8. **Percent distribution of wives' weekly hours worked by husbands' weekly hours worked, both spouses age 25–54 with children[1] under 6, March of selected years 1969-98**

Wives' hours	Percent					
	Total	Husbands' hours				
		0	1-19	20-34	35-40	41 or more
1969						
Total	100.0	3.4	1.9	5.8	41.4	47.6
0	74.5	2.4	1.4	4.1	31.1	35.5
1-19	5.5	0.2	0.2	0.3	2.1	2.8
20-34	5.7	.2	.1	.7	2.3	2.5
35-40	10.9	.5	.1	.6	4.9	4.7
41 or more	3.5	.1	.1	.1	1.0	2.1
1979						
Total	100.0	5.5	1.4	4.8	43.3	45.1
0	59.4	3.7	.9	2.9	25.5	26.5
1-19	9.6	.2	.2	.4	3.5	5.3
20-34	9.5	.4	.1	.5	4.0	4.4
35-40	17.3	1.0	.2	.8	9.3	6.0
41 or more	4.1	.3	.0	.1	1.0	2.7
1989						
Total	100.0	6.1	1.7	5.3	39.7	47.2
0	43.8	3.3	.8	2.3	16.6	20.8
1-19	8.9	.3	.1	.6	2.8	5.0
20-34	14.4	.6	.2	1.1	5.7	6.8
35-40	25.2	1.3	.4	1.1	12.5	9.9
41 or more	7.7	.6	.1	.2	2.1	4.7
1998						
Total	100.0	6.0	2.2	7.2	37.4	47.2
0	38.8	2.5	1.0	2.9	14.2	18.2
1-19	9.1	.3	.2	.8	2.8	4.9
20-34	15.6	.6	.3	1.4	5.7	7.8
35-40	25.2	1.8	.5	1.4	12.1	9.4
41 or more	11.3	.8	.3	.7	2.6	6.9

[1] Children may be biological, adopted, or stepchildren. Not included are nieces, nephews, grandchildren, other related children, and unrelated children.

SOURCE: Current Population Survey, Bureau of Labor Statistics, U.S. Department of Labor

Table 3-9 **Percent of full-time wage and salary workers with flexible schedules on their principal job by marital status, presence and age of youngest child, and sex, May of 1991 and 1997**

Marital status	Total	With no children[1] under age 18	With children[1] under age 18		
			Total	6-17, none younger	Under 6
May 1991					
Total	15.1	15.1	14.9	15.0	14.8
Married, spouse present	14.7	14.5	14.7	14.6	14.9
Other marital status	15.7	15.6	16.2	17.5	13.7
Men	15.5	15.4	15.6	15.8	15.4
Married, spouse present	15.7	15.8	15.8	16.0	15.6
Other marital status	15.0	15.2	11.0	12.1	9.3
Women	14.5	14.8	14.0	14.1	13.7
Married, spouse present	12.9	13.1	12.7	12.2	13.4
Other marital status	16.4	16.1	17.5	18.5	15.0
May 1997					
Total	27.6	26.8	28.9	27.9	30.2
Married, spouse present	28.8	28.3	29.2	28.0	30.7
Other marital status	26.0	25.8	27.4	27.8	26.8
Men	28.7	27.5	30.5	29.7	31.5
Married, spouse present	30.8	30.9	30.7	29.8	31.6
Other marital status	25.2	25.0	28.8	28.0	29.9
Women	26.2	26.0	26.6	25.8	27.8
Married, spouse present	25.6	24.8	26.4	25.1	28.6
Other marital status	24.1	26.8	27.0	27.7	25.6

[1] Children may be biological, adopted, or stepchildren. Not included are nieces, nephews, grandchildren, other related children, and unrelated children.

SOURCE: Current Population Survey, May supplement, Bureau of Labor Statistics, U.S. Department of Labor

Table 3-10 **Percent of nonagricultural workers who worked at home on their principal job by marital status, presence and age of youngest child, and sex, May of 1991 and 1997**

Marital status	Total	With no children[1] under age 18	With children[1] under age 18		
			Total	6-17, none younger	Under 6
May 1991					
Total	18.3	16.5	21.2	22.0	20.2
Married, spouse present	21.7	21.4	21.9	22.9	20.9
Other marital status	13.1	12.7	15.6	17.1	12.8
Men	18.3	16.3	21.4	22.9	19.8
Married, spouse present	21.7	21.7	21.7	23.2	20.1
Other marital status	12.0	11.9	14.6	17.2	11.0
Women	18.4	16.8	20.9	21.1	20.7
Married, spouse present	21.7	21.0	22.3	22.4	22.1
Other marital status	14.0	13.6	15.9	17.1	13.3
May 1997					
Total	17.7	16.0	20.4	21.0	19.6
Married, spouse present	21.5	21.6	21.5	21.9	21.0
Other marital status	12.3	12.1	13.9	16.3	9.8
Men	17.2	15.4	20.4	22.0	18.7
Married, spouse present	21.0	21.4	20.7	22.1	19.2
Other marital status	11.1	10.8	16.1	20.9	8.6
Women	18.2	16.9	20.3	20.1	20.7
Married, spouse present	22.2	21.7	22.6	21.7	23.8
Other marital status	13.5	13.6	13.3	15.1	10.2

[1] Children may be biological, adopted, or stepchildren. Not included are nieces, nephews, grandchildren, other related children, and unrelated children.

SOURCE: Current Population Survey, May supplement, Bureau of Labor Statistics, U.S. Department of Labor

117

Table 3-11. **Ratio of hours worked to hours paid for nonfarm production or nonsupervisory workers, selected industries, 1997**

Industry	Ratio
Nonfarm establishments	0.934
Manufacturing	.917
Lumber and wood products	.940
Primary metals	.916
Fabricated metals	.924
Machinery (except electrical	.917
Electrical equipment	.898
Transportation equipment	.892
Instruments	.905
Food and kindred products	.926
Textile mill products	.939
Apparel and other textiles	.946
Paper and allied products	.901
Printing and publishing	.927
Chemicals	.888
Petroleum and coal products	.896
Nonmanufacturing Industries	.939
Mining	.932
Construction	.971
Transportation	.912
Communications	.882
Electric, gas and sanitary services	.896
Wholesale trade	.923
Retail trade	.959
Finance, insurance and real estate	.930
Services	.932

SOURCE: 1997 Hours at Work Survey, Bureau of Labor Statistics, U.S. Department of Labor

Table 3-12. **Percent of full-time year round workers participating in selected time-off programs by establishment, selected years**

Time-off program	Establishments						
	Private						Government
	Large	All	All	Large	Small	All
	1979	1989	1994-97	1996-97	1997	1996	1994
All workers							
Paid							
Vacation	-	-	76	79	87	72	60
Holidays	-	-	72	73	81	66	68
Sick leave	-	-	50	44	50	40	87
Funeral leave	-	-	56	56	73	42	58
Military leave	-	-	32	27	41	14	69
Jury duty leave ..	-	-	66	63	79	50	88
Family leave	-	-	2	2	2	2	4
Unpaid							
Family leave	-	-	66	62	87	42	89
Full-time workers							
Paid							
Vacation	100	97	87	91	95	86	66
Holidays	99	97	83	85	89	80	73
Sick leave	56	68	59	53	56	50	93
Funeral leave	-	84	65	66	81	51	62
Military leave	-	53	38	32	47	18	75
Jury duty leave ..	-	90	76	73	87	59	94
Family leave	-	3	2	2	2	2	4
Unpaid							
Family leave	-	-	73	70	93	48	93
Part-time workers							
Paid							
Vacation	-	-	34	35	44	30	22
Holidays	-	-	29	29	40	24	30
Sick leave	-	-	15	13	18	10	42
Funeral leave	-	-	23	22	34	16	30
Military leave	-	-	9	7	9	5	32
Jury duty leave ..	-	-	30	28	37	23	51
Family leave	-	-	1	1	1	1	1
Unpaid							
Family leave	-	-	37	35	54	25	62

NOTE: Dash indicates less than 0.5 percent.

SOURCE: Employee Benefits Survey, Bureau of Labor Statistics, U.S. Department of Labor

119

Table 3-13. **Average paid leave days available to full-time year round workers by establishment, selected years**

Time-off program	Establishments					
	Private					Government
	Large	All		Large	Small	All
	1989	1994-96	1995-96	1995	1996	1994
All full-time workers						
Paid						
Vacation after—						
1 year	9.1	9.2	8.8	9.6	8.1	12.3
10 years	16.5	15.7	15.3	16.9	13.9	18.3
20 years	20.4	18.3	17.8	20.4	15.4	21.9
Holidays	9.2	8.7	8.3	9.1	7.6	11.5
Funeral leave	-	3.3	3.2	3.3	3.0	3.7
Personal leave	3.1	3.1	3.2	3.3	3.0	3.0

NOTE: Dash indicates less than 0.5 percent.

SOURCE: Employee Benefits Survey, Bureau of Labor Statistics, U.S. Department of Labor

Table 3-14. **Percent of workers age 31–39 eligible for benefits at their current job by selected characteristics, 1996**

Characteristic	Paid leave		Maternity/paternity leave
	Vacation	Sick	
Total	77.5	63.6	65.8
Men	80.1	62.0	58.4
Women	74.5	65.5	74.2
Race and Hispanic origin			
White	77.2	62.9	66.0
Black	78.1	65.6	64.5
Hispanic	80.5	67.2	65.3
Education			
Less than a high school diploma	66.2	41.2	44.3
High school diploma	77.2	55.6	62.9
Some college	78.3	69.9	70.9
College degree or higher	82.2	81.5	75.1
Industry			
Mining	-	-	-
Construction	49.8	30.3	31.4
Manufacturing	91.5	57.9	73.0
Transportation, communication, and public utilities	84.4	74.9	71.7
Wholesale trade	87.5	66.2	61.9
Retail trade	70.2	47.9	56.0
Finance, insurance, and real estate	83.3	81.6	74.5
Services	73.3	69.0	67.0
Public administration	91.6	92.7	84.3
Occupation			
Professional, technical, kindred	81.1	79.6	78.8
Manager, officials, proprietors	86.6	77.9	71.0
Sales workers	74.9	61.0	63.1
Clerical and kindred	81.8	70.9	73.6
Craftsman, foreman, kindred	75.5	47.3	50.0
Operatives and kindred	80.8	46.9	60.2
Laborers	63.6	44.6	49.0
Service workers	62.4	51.1	58.2
Hours			
Part-time [1]	40.2	34.6	45.5
Full-time [2]	84.6	69.5	70.5
Years of tenure			
Less than 1	59.3	47.8	47.8
1-2	74.0	58.8	60.7
3-5	80.9	67.7	68.9
6-9	6.4	74.1	77.0
10 or more	91.7	74.1	78.2
Class of worker			
Government	83.2	90.2	83.2
Private for profit	77.7	58.1	63.0
Private non-profit	77.5	77.0	71.0

[1] Less than 35 hours per week.
[2] 35 or more hours per week.

NOTE: Dash indicates data not available.

SOURCE: National Longitudinal Survey of Youth, 1979, Bureau of Labor Statistics, U.S. Department of Labor

121

Table 3-15. **Number of paid vacation and sick leave days entitled to workers age 31–39 at their current job by selected characteristics, 1996**

Characteristic	Paid leave	
	Vacation	Sick
Total	13.2	9.8
Men	13.5	9.7
Women	12.9	10.0
Race and Hispanic origin		
White	13.3	9.7
Black	12.8	10.2
Hispanic	12.9	9.9
Education		
Less than a high school diploma...	10.7	8.8
High school diploma	12.5	9.5
Some college	13.2	9.5
College degree or higher	15.5	10.9
Industry		
Mining	-	-
Construction	9.7	8.5
Manufacturing	12.7	7.9
Transportation, communication, and public utilities	13.6	11.0
Wholesale trade	11.2	7.2
Retail trade	11.1	9.0
Finance, insurance, and real estate	14.0	9.5
Services	13.8	10.0
Public administration	17.2	13.2
Occupation		
Professional, technical, kindred	15.3	10.7
Manager, officials, proprietors	14.0	9.9
Sales workers	12.9	9.4
Clerical and kindred	12.9	9.8
Craftsman, foreman, kindred	11.9	8.7
Operatives and kindred	11.4	7.7
Laborers	12.1	9.9
Service workers	12.3	10.9
Hours		
Part-time[1]	10.5	9.4
Full-time[2]	13.5	9.8
Years of tenure		
Less than 1	9.2	8.0
1-2	10.5	8.5
3-5	12.9	9.8
6-9	15.2	11.2
10 or more	17.2	11.3
Class of worker		
Government	17.3	12.5
Private for profit	12.4	8.8
Private non-profit	14.8	11.0

[1] Less than 35 hours per week.
[2] 35 or more hours per week.

NOTE: Dash indicates data not available.

SOURCE: National Longitudinal Survey of Youth, 1979, Bureau of Labor Statistics, U.S. Department of Labor

Table 3-16. **Average weekly hours persons age 18-64 spent in selected family-care activities by employment status and sex, selected years 1965-65**

Family-care activity	1965	1975	1985	Change in hours 1965-85
Total family care	27.3	23.6	24.0	-3.3
Women	40.2	32.9	30.9	-9.3
Employed	26.1	23.7	25.6	-0.5
Nonemployed	51.5	42.0	39.0	-12.5
Men	11.5	12.2	15.7	4.2
Employed	11.1	10.7	14.5	3.4
Nonemployed	15.2	16.1	20.3	5.1
Core housework				
Women	26.9	21.3	18.7	-8.2
Employed	17.9	15.2	15.3	-2.6
Nonemployed	34.2	27.5	23.8	-10.4
Men	4.7	6.5	9.4	4.7
Employed	4.4	5.8	8.4	.4
Nonemployed	8.3	10.2	13.2	4.9
Child care				
Women	6.4	5.1	4.9	-1.5
Employed	2.7	3.2	3.6	.9
Nonemployed	9.3	6.8	7.0	-2.3
Men	1.7	1.6	1.4	-.3
Employed	1.8	1.7	1.6	-.2
Nonemployed	1.2	1.5	1.0	-.2
Shopping				
Women	7.0	6.5	7.3	.3
Employed	5.7	5.3	6.7	1.0
Nonemployed	7.9	7.7	8.2	.3
Men	5.1	4.2	4.9	-.2
Employed	4.9	4.2	4.5	-.4
Nonemployed	5.7	4.4	6.1	.4

SOURCE: John P. Robinson and Geoffrey Godbey, *Time for Life: The Surprising Ways Americans Use Their Time*, Pennsylvania State University Press, 1997

Table 3-17. **Change in average weekly hours persons age 18-64 spent in free-time activities by employment status and sex, 1965-85**

Employment status	Total	TV viewing	Reading	Radio/ recordings
Total	4.8	4.7	-0.8	-0.2
Women	4.9	5.2	-.3	-.2
Employed	6.8	4.8	-.1	-.4
Nonemployed	7.0	7.2	-.2	.2
Men	4.7	3.9	-1.4	-.2
Employed	3.3	3.1	-1.6	-.3
Nonemployed	-5.5	4.7	-1.0	.2

SOURCE: John P. Robinson and Geoffrey Godbey, *Time for Life: The Surprising Ways Americans Use Their Time*, Pennsylvania State University Press, 1997

References

Abraham, Katharine, James Spletzer, and Jay Stewart, "Divergent Trends in Alternative Wage Series," in *Labor Statistics Measurement Issues*, John Haltiwanger, Marilyn Manser, and Robert Topel, eds., NBER/University of Chicago Press, 1998, pp. 293-323.

Bluestone, Barry and Stephen Rose, "The Unmeasured Labor Force: The Growth in Work Hours," Public Policy Brief no. 39, The Jerome Levy Economics Institute of Bard College, 1998.

Bluestone, Barry and Stephen Rose, "Overworked and Underemployed: Unraveling an Economic Enigma," *American Prospect*, March-April 1997.

Capowski, Genevieve, "The Joy of Flex," *American Management Association*, March 1996, pp. 12-18.

Coleman, Mary T. and John Pencavel, "Changes in Work Hours of Male Employees Since 1940," *Industrial and Labor Relations Review*, 1993a, vol. 46(2), pp. 262-283.

Coleman, Mary T. and John Pencavel, "Trends in Marked Work Behavior of Women Since 1940," *Industrial and Labor Relations Review*, 1993b, vol. 46(4), pp. 653-676.

Frazis, Harley, Michelle Harrison Ports, and Jay Stewart, "Comparing Measures of Educational Attainment in the CPS," *Monthly Labor Review*, 1995, vol. 118(9), pp. 40-44.

Freeman, Richard, "The Facts about Rising Economic Disparity," *The Inequality Paradox: Growth of Income Disparity*, James Auerbach and Richard Belous, eds., National Policy Association, Washington, DC, 1998, pp. 19-33.

Hamermesh, Daniel, "Shirking or Productive Schmoozing: Wages and Allocation of Time at Work," *Industrial Labor Relations Review*, 1990, vol. 43, no. 3, pp. 121S-133S.

Hayghe, Howard, "Developments in Women's Labor Force Participation," *Monthly Labor Review*, 1997, vol. 120(9), pp. 41-46.

Hecker, Daniel, "How Hours of Work Affect Occupational Earnings," *Monthly Labor Review*, 1998, vol. 121(10), pp. 8-18.

Hedges, Janice Neipert, "Review of the *Overworked American*" by Juliet Schor, *Monthly Labor Review*, 1992, vol. 115(5), pp. 53-54.

Hochschild, Arlie R. *The Time Bind: When Work Becomes Home and Home Becomes Work*, New York, Metropolitan Books.

Jacobs, Jerry, "Measuring Time at Work: Are Self-Reports Accurate?" *Monthly Labor Review*, 1998, vol. 121(12), pp. 42-53.

Kniesner, Thomas, "Review Essay: The Overworked American," *Journal of Human Resources*, 1993, vol. 28(3), pp. 681-688.

Kuttner, Robert, "Review of *The Overworked American*, by Juliet B. Schor," *New York Times*, February 2, 1999, p. 1 (Section7).

Leete, Laura and Juliet Schor, "Assessing the Time-Squeeze Hypothesis: Hours Worked in the United States, 1969-89," *Industrial and Labor Relations Review*, 1994, vol. 3, no. 1, pp. 25-43.

Levy, F. and R. J. Murnane, "U.S. Earnings Levels and Earnings Inequality: A Review of Recent Trends and Proposed Explanations," *Journal of Economic Literature*, 1992, vol. 30(3), pp. 1333-1381.

Mellow, Wesley and Hal Sider, "Accuracy of Response in Labor Market Surveys: Evidence and Implications," *Journal of Labor Economics*, vol.1, no. 4, pp. 331-334.

Robinson, John and Ann Bostrom, "The Overestimated Workweek? What Time Diary Measures Suggest," *Monthly Labor Review*, 1994, vol. 117(8), pp. 11-23.

Robinson, John and Geoffrey Godbey, *Time for Life: The Surprising Ways Americans Use Their Time*, Pennsylvania State University Press, 1997.

Rones, Philip, Randy Ilg, and Jennifer Gardner, "Trends in the Hours of Work Since the Mid 1970s," *Monthly Labor Review*, 1997, vol. 120(4), pp. 3-14.

Schor, Juliet, *The Overworked American*, New York, Basic Books, 1991.

Segal, Troy, "Review of the *Overworked American*, by Juliet Schor," *Business Week*, February 17, 1999, pp. 21-23.

Stafford, Frank P. "Review of the *Overworked American*, by Juliet Schor," *Journal of Economic Literature*, 1992, vol. 30(3), pp. 1528-1529.

Szalai, A., ed., *The Use of Time: Daily Activities in Urban and Suburban Populations in Twelve Countries*, The Hague: Mouton, 1972.

Endnotes

[1] "The Busyness Trap," by Barbara Moses, *Training Magazine*, November 1998.

[2] The CPS is a monthly survey of about 50,000 households, conducted by the Bureau of the Census for the Bureau of Labor Statistics. For additional information about the Survey, see the "Explanatory Notes and Estimates of Errors," in *Employment and Earnings*, May 1999.

[3] Leete and Schor examine the changes between 1969 and 1989. A fully-employed person was defined as someone who worked full-time year round and did not report that additional work was desired but not available.

[4] See chapter 2, p. 62 of the 1995 *Report on the American Workforce*, U.S. Department of Labor, for a discussion of the rise in female-headed families. See also Hayghe, 1997.

[5] Much of the discussion of chart 3-1 follows that of Abraham, Spletzer, and Stewart, 1998.

[6] See Abraham, Spletzer, and Stewart, 1998.

[7] The implicit assumption is that workers, on average, error on the side of over rather than underreporting their hours.

[8] The 1994 redesign represents the most serious break in these series.

[9] The CPS relies on the accuracy and completeness of respondents'—or proxy respondents'—recall about hours worked during the reference week. Proxy respondents particularly may not have full knowledge of the actual work hours of other household members. Consequently, small amounts of leave taken during the reference week or changes in work schedules may be ignored and some commuting time may be inadvertently included. If these types of reporting errors have increased over time then this reduces the consistency of the series although the actual wording of the question has not changed.

[10] Published data on annual average weekly hours worked are only available from 1976 forward for these subpopulations.

[11] These data represent hours worked per week during the reporting week in March; they do not represent the average over all reporting weeks during the year.

[12] See Hayghe, 1997, p. 42.

[13] Part of the reason that we don't observe a sizable decline in average hours worked for men age 45-64 is because the decline in participation rates was more heavily concentrated among those age 55-64. Furthermore, the size of the 45- to 54-year-old group grew relative to the size of the 55- to 54-year old group, so that changes for the younger group tend to predominate when both age groups are considered together. (In 1976, there were 11,243,000 men age 45-54, compared with 9,444,000 age 55-64. In 1998, these numbers were 16,773,000 and 10,649,000, respectively).

[14] Hecker, 1998, found that the proportion of workers who work extended workweeks varies considerably by occupation with executives, officials, and managers being the most likely to have extended workweeks.

[15] The 1994 redesign of the CPS changed the question on educational attainment so that the 1998 numbers are not strictly comparable to previous years. See Frazis, Ports, and Stewart, 1995, for a comparison of the new and old CPS education questions.

[16] Freeman, 1998, finds a similar pattern using data on changes in annual hours worked from the 1970 and 1990 Census of Population public use files.

[17] Children are defined as "own" children and include sons, daughters, adopted, and stepchildren. Not included are nieces, nephews, grandchildren, other related children, and unrelated children.

[18] For this analysis, we examine the trends in usual weekly hours worked during the last year rather than hours worked during the reference week in March. Annual hours are calculated by multiplying usual hours worked per week by weeks worked in the last year. Note that the usual weekly hours question was not asked in 1969 so the variable for hours worked during the reference week was used instead with weekly hours being imputed for those who said they usually worked full time but were not at work that week.

[19] Some of the rise in 1998 is likely due to the CPS redesign.

[20] The FMLA excludes any employee who is employed at a worksite at which the employer employs fewer than 50 employees or if the total number of employees employed by that employer within 75 miles of that worksite is also fewer than 50.

[21] Nelson, Richard R., "State Labor Legislation Enacted in 1988," *Monthly Labor Review*, January 1989, vol. 112(1), p. 41.

[22] Nelson, Richard R., "State Labor Legislation Enacted in 1990," *Monthly Labor Review*, January 1991, vol. 114(1), p. 41.

[23] Nelson, Richard R., "State Labor Legislation Enacted in 1994," *Monthly Labor Review*, January 1995, vol. 118(1), p. 41.

[24] Nelson, Richard R., "State Labor Legislation Enacted in 1997," *Monthly Labor Review*, January 1998, vol. 120(1), p. 4.

[25] McCampbell, Atefah Sadri, "Benefits Achieved Through Alternative Work Schedules," *Human Resource Planning*, 1996, vol. 19, p. 3.

[26] See Elizabeth Sheley, "Work Options Beyond 9 to 5," *HRMagazine*, February 1996.

[27] See Genevieve Capowski, "The Joys of Flex," *American Management Association*, March 1996.

[28] The source of the data used here is the CPS May 1997 supplement.

[29] Employee Benefits Survey, Bureau of Labor Statistics, Bulletins 2475, 2477, 2496, 1994-1995. This is an establishment-based survey that asks employers questions about the formal kinds of benefits they offer their employees, and what proportion of their employees are eligible for these benefits. The data from the CPS, in comparison, are based on a question that asks individual workers whether they are able to vary their beginning and ending hours on the job. This can be done either through formal arrangements specified in workers' contracts or union contracts, or through an informal agreement between worker and employer.

[30] Forthcoming article in the *Monthly Labor Review,* by Thomas Beers.

[31] "Flexiplace" is a term used to describe an arrangement with an employer whereby the employee can perform work somewhere other than at the employer's place of business or job site. Flexiplace arrangements may involve the use of electronic equipment such as personal computers or fax machines, and may require the worker to report periodically to the employer's place of business for assignments or reviews.

[32] For an example of leave benefits available to workers in the construction industry, see *Jacksonville, FL Wages and Benefits in the Construction Industry*, Bureau of Labor Statistics, Bulletin 2510-1, October 1998.

[33] Brooks Pierce, "Compensation Inequality," unpublished, Bureau of Labor Statistics, September 1998.

[34] National time-use studies were conducted in 1965-66, 1975-76, and 1981 by the Survey Research Center at the University of Michigan. The Survey Research Center at the University of Maryland conducted studies in 1985 and 1992-94. This latter survey was sponsored by the Environmental Protection Agency.

APPENDIX

Statistical Tables

The tables in this appendix to the *Report on the American Workforce* are organized along thematic lines, rather than by the program office responsible for collecting them. This extends the ideas suggested in Background Paper No. 22, National Commission on Employment and Unemployment Statistics, "Improving the Presentation of Employment and Unemployment Statistics." Unless noted otherwise, data are from the Bureau of Labor Statistics, U.S. Department of Labor. Technical descriptions of their sources, methods, and limitations are found in *BLS Handbook of Methods*, Bulletin 2490 (1997).

Section

127

Section 1. General conditions in the labor market

The labor market improves and declines in swings that are conditioned by, similar to, and part of the general business cycle. The tables in this section contain indicators of the current condition of the labor market; the State of labor market-related processes that are more highly sensitive to cyclical swings and, therefore, tend to reach turning points somewhat earlier; and the complete cycle of processes that take longer to unfold and thus reach their turning points somewhat later.

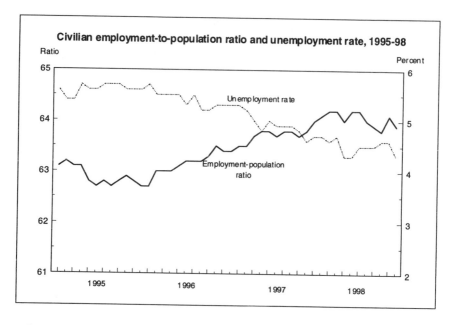

Table

1. Selected labor market indicators: Current conditions, annual averages, 1948-98

2. Selected labor market indicators: Cyclically sensitive conditions, annual averages, 1948-98

3. Selected labor market indicators: Processes requiring additional time to complete the cycle, annual averages, 1948-98

Section 2. Employment and the labor force

The number of working people, their characteristics, and the types of jobs they hold are shown in the tables in this section.

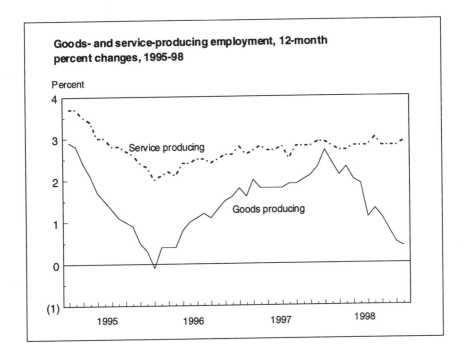

Goods- and service-producing employment, 12-month percent changes, 1995-98

4. Civilian labor force for selected demographic groups, annual averages, 1948-98

5. Civilian labor force participation rates for selected demographic groups, annual averages, 1948-98

6. Labor force participation rates of women by presence and age of children, March 1980-98

7. Percent distribution of the labor force of women by presence and age of children, March 1980-98

8. Employment for selected demographic groups, annual averages 1948-98

9. Employment-population ratios for selected demographic groups, annual averages, 1948-98

10. Employed persons by major occupation, annual averages, 1985-98

11. Employed persons by usual full- or part-time status and sex, annual averages, 1970-98

12. Employees on nonfarm payrolls by major industry division, annual averages, 1947-98

Section 3. Wages and productivity

How much workers are paid per unit of time (usually per hour), how productively that time is used, and how much each unit of production costs in terms of labor input is the focus of the following tables.

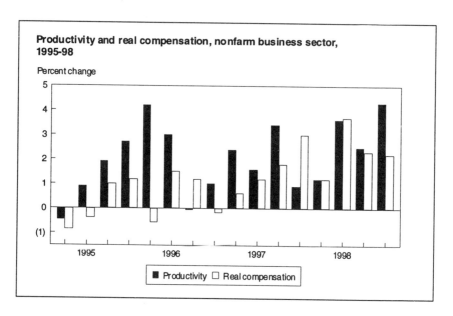

Productivity and real compensation, nonfarm business sector, 1995-98

Section 4. Earnings, prices, and expenditures

This section is concerned with standards of living: The weekly pay packet, the price of goods and services, and the patterns of consumer expenditures.

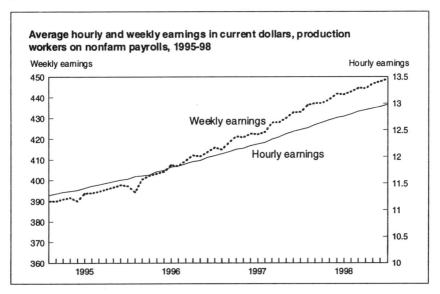

Average hourly and weekly earnings in current dollars, production workers on nonfarm payrolls, 1995-98

34. Producer price indexes for major commodity groups, 1947-98

35. Producer price indexes by stage of processing, special groups, 1947-98

36. Consumer Price Index for All Urban Consumers (CPI-U), 1960-98

37. Average annual expenditures and percent distribution of all consumer units, selected periods, 1935-36 to 1996-97

38. Shares of average annual expenditures and characteristics of all consumer units classified by quintiles of income before taxes, Consumer Expenditure Survey, 1987 and 1997

39. Shares of average annual expenditures and characteristics of all consumer units classified by age of the reference person, Consumer Ependiture Survey, 1987 and 1997

40. Shares of average annual expenditures and characteristics of all consumer units classified by composition of the consumer unit, Consumer Expenditure Survey, 1987 and 1997

41. Shares of average annual expenditures and characteristics of all consumer units classified by region of residence, Consumer Expenditure Survey, 1987 and 1997

42. Shares of average annual expenditures of all consumer units classified by origin of the reference person, Consumer Expenditure Survey, 1987 and 1997

43. Number of earners in families by type of family, selected years, 1990-98

Section 5. Benefits and working conditions

Information on what compensation beyond cash wages workers receive and how safe and healthy their workplaces are is shown in the following tables.

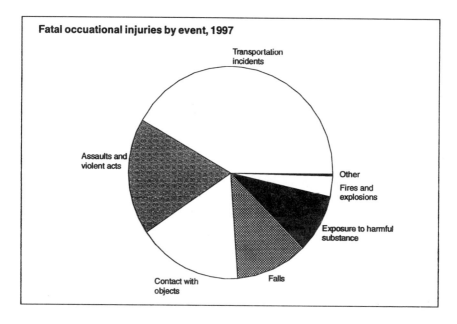

132

Section 6. Unemployment

The number of people looking for work, their characteristics, and the duration of, and reason for unemployment are shown in the tables in this section.

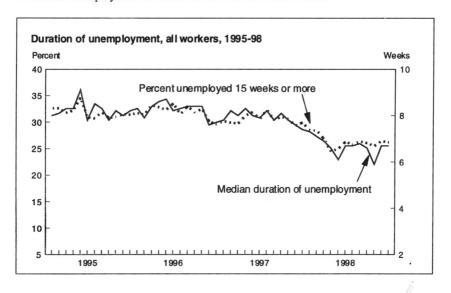

Duration of unemployment, all workers, 1995-98

133

Section 7. International comparisons

Key indicators of unemployment, inflation, and productivity across international boundaries are compared in this section.

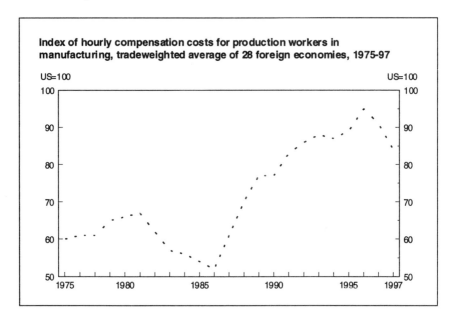

Index of hourly compensation costs for production workers in manufacturing, tradeweighted average of 28 foreign economies, 1975-97

Table 1. **Selected labor market indicators: Current conditions, annual averages, 1948-98**

Year	Employment (thousands)[1]	Employment population ratio[1]	Nonfarm payroll employment (thousands)	Aggregate hours index, private nonfarm (1982=100)	Total hours of nonfarm wage and salary workers (millions)	Goods-producing employment (thousands)	Employment Cost Index, compensation, private nonfarm[2] (June 1989=100)	Unemployment rate[1]	Insured unemployment as percent of covered employment[3]
1948	58,343	56.6	44,866	–	92,470	18,774	–	3.8	3.0
1949	57,651	55.4	43,754	–	88,958	17,565	–	5.9	6.2
1950	58,918	56.1	45,197	–	92,514	18,506	–	5.3	4.5
1951	59,961	57.3	47,819	–	98,277	19,959	–	3.3	2.7
1952	60,250	57.3	48,793	–	99,972	20,198	–	3.0	2.8
1953	61,179	57.1	50,202	–	102,361	21,074	–	2.9	2.7
1954	60,109	55.5	48,990	–	98,885	19,751	–	5.5	5.2
1955	62,170	56.7	50,641	–	103,133	20,513	–	4.4	3.4
1956	63,799	57.5	52,369	–	106,031	21,104	–	4.1	3.1
1957	64,071	57.1	52,855	–	105,893	20,967	–	4.3	3.6
1958	63,036	55.4	51,322	–	101,997	19,513	–	6.8	6.5
1959	64,630	56.0	53,270	–	106,774	20,411	–	5.5	4.2
1960	65,778	56.1	54,189	–	108,050	20,434	–	5.5	4.7
1961	65,746	55.4	53,999	–	107,440	19,857	–	6.7	5.7
1962	66,702	55.5	55,549	–	110,966	20,451	–	5.5	4.3
1963	67,762	55.4	56,653	–	113,135	20,640	–	5.7	4.2
1964	69,305	55.7	58,283	75.8	116,153	21,005	–	5.2	3.7
1965	71,088	56.2	60,763	79.1	121,433	21,926	–	4.5	2.9
1966	72,895	56.9	63,901	82.5	127,289	23,158	–	3.8	2.2
1967	74,372	57.3	65,803	82.9	129,558	23,308	–	3.8	2.4
1968	75,920	57.5	67,897	84.9	132,921	23,737	–	3.6	2.2
1969	77,902	58.0	70,384	87.7	137,340	24,361	–	3.5	2.1
1970	78,678	57.4	70,880	86.3	136,445	23,578	–	4.9	3.4
1971	79,367	56.6	71,211	85.8	136,179	22,935	–	5.9	4.1
1972	82,153	57.0	73,675	89.2	141,269	23,668	–	5.6	3.0
1973	85,064	57.8	76,790	93.2	147,051	24,893	–	4.9	2.5
1974	86,794	57.8	78,265	93.2	148,423	24,794	–	5.6	3.4
1975	85,846	56.1	76,945	88.8	144,255	22,600	–	8.5	6.1
1976	88,752	56.8	79,382	92.3	149,040	23,352	–	7.7	4.4
1977	92,017	57.9	82,471	96.0	154,517	24,346	–	7.1	3.7
1978	96,048	59.3	86,697	100.7	162,169	25,585	–	6.1	2.8
1979	98,824	59.9	89,823	104.0	167,092	26,461	59.1	5.8	2.8
1980	99,303	59.2	90,406	102.8	166,885	25,658	64.8	7.1	3.9
1981	100,397	59.0	91,152	104.1	167,547	25,497	71.2	7.6	3.5
1982	99,526	57.8	89,544	100.0	163,573	23,812	75.8	9.7	4.7
1983	100,834	57.9	90,152	101.5	165,612	23,330	80.1	9.6	3.9
1984	105,005	59.5	94,408	107.7	174,500	24,718	84.0	7.5	2.7
1985	107,150	60.1	97,387	110.5	179,096	24,842	87.3	7.2	2.8
1986	109,597	60.7	99,344	112.3	182,067	24,533	90.1	7.0	2.8
1987	112,440	61.5	101,958	115.6	186,664	24,674	93.1	6.2	2.3
1988	114,968	62.3	105,209	119.3	193,304	25,125	97.6	5.5	2.0
1989	117,342	63.0	107,884	122.1	197,110	25,254	102.3	5.3	2.1
1990	118,793	62.8	109,403	123.0	199,214	24,905	107.0	5.6	2.4
1991	117,718	61.7	108,249	120.4	196,437	23,745	111.7	6.8	3.2
1992	118,492	61.5	108,601	121.2	197,614	23,231	115.6	7.5	3.1
1993	120,259	61.7	110,713	124.6	202,304	23,352	119.8	6.9	2.6
1994	123,060	62.5	114,163	130.0	208,843	23,908	123.5	6.1	2.4
1995	124,900	62.9	117,191	133.5	213,704	24,265	126.7	5.6	2.3
1996	126,708	63.2	119,608	136.7	218,156	24,493	130.6	5.4	–
1997	129,558	63.8	122,690	141.5	224,886	24,962	135.1	4.9	1.9
1998	131,463	64.1	125,826	145.1	230,796	25,347	139.8	4.5	1.8

[1] The comparability of historical labor force data has been affected at various times by methodological and conceptual changes. For an explanation, see the Explanatory Notes and Estimates of Error section of *Employment and Earnings*, a monthly periodical published by the Bureau of Labor Statistics.
[2] December.
[3] Data from Employment and Training Administration, U.S. Department of Labor.

Dash indicates data not available.

Table 2. **Selected labor market indicators: Cyclically sensitive conditions, annual averages, 1948-98**

Year	Producer Price Index for crude non-food materials, less energy (1982=100)	Manufacturing		Unemployed[1]		Nonagricultural workers on part-time schedules for economic reasons, slack work[1] or business conditions (in thousands)
		Average workweek	Average overtime hours	Less than 5 weeks (in thousands)	Job losers on temporary layoff as percent of civilian labor force	
1948	–	40.0	–	1,300	–	–
1949	–	39.1	–	1,756	–	–
1950	–	40.5	–	1,450	–	–
1951	–	40.6	–	1,177	–	–
1952	–	40.7	–	1,135	–	–
1953	–	40.5	–	1,142	–	–
1954	–	39.6	–	1,605	–	–
1955	–	40.7	–	1,335	–	905
1956	–	40.4	2.8	1,412	–	1,013
1957	–	39.8	2.3	1,408	–	1,180
1958	–	39.2	2.0	1,753	–	1,695
1959	–	40.3	2.7	1,585	–	1,078
1960	–	39.7	2.5	1,719	–	1,300
1961	–	39.8	2.4	1,806	–	1,429
1962	–	40.4	2.8	1,663	–	1,077
1963	–	40.5	2.8	1,751	–	1,060
1964	–	40.7	3.1	1,697	–	972
1965	–	41.2	3.6	1,628	–	868
1966	–	41.4	3.9	1,573	–	727
1967	–	40.6	3.4	1,634	0.5	979
1968	–	40.7	3.6	1,594	.4	794
1969	–	40.6	3.6	1,629	.4	838
1970	–	39.8	3.0	2,139	.8	1,126
1971	–	39.9	2.9	2,245	.9	1,245
1972	–	40.5	3.5	2,242	.7	1,079
1973	70.8	40.7	3.8	2,224	.5	1,067
1974	83.3	40.0	3.3	2,604	.8	1,339
1975	69.3	39.5	2.6	2,940	1.8	1,925
1976	80.2	40.1	3.1	2,844	1.1	1,550
1977	79.8	40.3	3.5	2,919	.9	1,472
1978	87.8	40.4	3.6	2,865	.7	1,391
1979	106.2	40.2	3.3	2,950	.8	1,518
1980	113.1	39.7	2.8	3,295	1.4	2,093
1981	111.7	39.8	2.8	3,449	1.3	2,251
1982	100.0	38.9	2.3	3,883	1.9	3,050
1983	105.3	40.1	3.0	3,570	1.6	2,684
1984	111.7	40.7	3.4	3,350	1.0	2,291
1985	104.9	40.5	3.3	3,498	1.0	2,273
1986	103.1	40.7	3.4	3,448	.9	2,305
1987	115.7	41.0	3.7	3,246	.8	2,201
1988	133.0	41.1	3.9	3,084	.7	2,199
1989	137.9	41.0	3.8	3,174	.7	2,143
1990	136.3	40.8	3.6	3,265	.8	2,409
1991	128.2	40.7	3.6	3,480	1.0	3,059
1992	128.4	41.0	3.8	3,376	1.0	3,094
1993	140.2	41.4	4.1	3,262	.9	3,033
1994	156.2	42.0	4.7	2,728	.7	2,311
1995	173.6	41.6	4.4	2,700	.8	2,346
1996	155.8	41.6	4.5	2,633	.8	2,263
1997	156.5	42.0	4.8	2,538	.7	2,167
1998	142.1	41.7	4.6	2,622	.6	1,997

[1] The comparability of historical labor force data has been affected at various times by methodological and conceptual changes. For an explanation, see the Explanatory Notes and Estimates of Error section of *Employment and Earnings*, a monthly periodical published by the Bureau of Labor Statistics.

Dash indicates data not available.

Table 3. **Selected labor market indicators: Processes requiring additional time to complete the cycle, annual averages, 1948-98**

Year	Consumer Price Index (CPI-U) for services (1982-84=100)	Unit labor costs business sector (1992=100)	Duration of unemployment[1]	
			Mean	Median
1948	15.6	21.0	8.6	–
1949	16.4	20.8	10.0	–
1950	16.9	20.6	12.1	–
1951	17.8	21.9	9.7	–
1952	18.6	22.6	8.4	–
1953	19.4	23.2	8.0	–
1954	20.0	23.5	11.8	–
1955	20.4	23.1	13.0	–
1956	20.9	24.6	11.3	–
1957	21.8	25.5	10.5	–
1958	22.6	25.9	13.9	–
1959	23.3	25.9	14.4	–
1960	24.1	26.6	12.8	–
1961	24.5	26.7	15.6	–
1962	25.0	26.6	14.7	–
1963	25.5	26.6	14.0	–
1964	26.0	26.7	13.3	–
1965	26.6	26.8	11.8	–
1966	27.6	27.5	10.4	–
1967	28.8	28.4	8.7	2.3
1968	30.3	29.7	8.4	4.5
1969	32.4	31.7	7.8	4.4
1970	35.0	33.5	8.6	4.9
1971	37.0	34.2	11.3	6.3
1972	38.4	35.1	12.0	6.2
1973	40.1	37.0	10.0	5.2
1974	43.8	41.3	9.8	5.2
1975	48.0	44.0	14.2	8.4
1976	52.0	46.2	15.8	8.2
1977	56.0	49.0	14.3	7.0
1978	60.8	52.8	11.9	5.9
1979	67.5	58.2	10.8	5.4
1980	77.9	64.7	11.9	6.5
1981	88.1	69.6	13.7	6.9
1982	96.0	75.1	15.6	8.7
1983	99.4	75.8	20.0	10.1
1984	104.6	77.2	18.2	7.9
1985	109.9	79.7	15.6	6.8
1986	115.4	81.7	15.0	6.9
1987	120.2	84.9	14.5	6.5
1988	125.7	88.3	13.5	5.9
1989	131.9	90.0	11.9	4.8
1990	139.2	94.4	12.0	5.3
1991	146.3	98.3	13.7	6.8
1992	152.0	100.0	17.7	8.7
1993	157.9	102.4	18.0	8.3
1994	163.1	103.7	18.8	9.2
1995	168.7	105.8	16.6	8.3
1996	174.1	106.8	16.7	8.3
1997	179.4	109.0	15.8	8.0
1998	184.2	111.1	14.5	6.7

[1] The comparability of historical labor force data has been affected at various times by methodological and conceptual changes. For an explanation, see the Explanatory Notes and Estimates of Error section of *Employment and Earnings*, a monthly periodical published by the Bureau of Labor Statistics.

Dash indicates data not available.

Table 4. **Civilian labor force for selected demographic groups, annual averages, 1948–98**

(In thousands)

Year	Total, 16 years and over	Men, 20 years and over	Women, 20 years and over	Both sexes, 16 to 19 years	White	Black and other	Black	Hispanic origin
1948	60,621	40,687	15,500	4,435	–	–	–	–
1949	61,286	41,022	15,978	4,288	–	–	–	–
1950	62,208	41,316	16,678	4,216	–	–	–	–
1951	62,017	40,655	17,259	4,103	–	–	–	–
1952	62,138	40,558	17,517	4,064	–	–	–	–
1953[1]	63,015	41,315	17,674	4,027	–	–	–	–
1954	63,643	41,669	17,997	3,976	56,816	6,825	–	–
1955	65,023	42,106	18,825	4,092	58,085	6,942	–	–
1956	66,552	42,658	19,599	4,296	59,428	7,125	–	–
1957	66,929	42,780	19,873	4,275	59,754	7,174	–	–
1958	67,639	43,092	20,285	4,260	60,293	7,346	–	–
1959	68,369	43,289	20,587	4,492	60,952	7,416	–	–
1960[1]	69,628	43,603	21,185	4,841	61,915	7,716	–	–
1961	70,459	43,860	21,664	4,936	62,656	7,804	–	–
1962[1]	70,614	43,831	21,868	4,916	62,750	7,864	–	–
1963	71,833	44,222	22,473	5,139	63,830	8,003	–	–
1964	73,091	44,604	23,098	5,388	64,921	8,170	–	–
1965	74,455	44,857	23,686	5,910	66,137	8,321	–	–
1966	75,770	44,788	24,431	6,558	67,276	8,499	–	–
1967	77,347	45,354	25,475	6,521	68,699	8,649	–	–
1968	78,737	45,852	26,266	6,619	69,976	8,759	–	–
1969	80,734	46,351	27,413	6,970	71,778	8,955	–	–
1970	82,771	47,220	28,301	7,249	73,556	9,218	–	–
1971	84,382	48,009	28,904	7,470	74,963	9,418	–	–
1972[1]	87,034	49,079	29,901	8,054	77,275	9,761	8,707	–
1973[1]	89,429	49,932	30,991	8,507	79,151	10,280	8,976	–
1974	91,949	50,879	32,201	8,871	81,281	10,668	9,167	–
1975	93,775	51,494	33,410	8,870	82,831	10,942	9,263	–
1976	96,158	52,288	34,814	9,056	84,767	11,391	9,561	–
1977	99,009	53,348	36,310	9,351	87,141	11,867	9,932	–
1978[1]	102,251	54,471	38,128	9,652	89,634	12,617	10,432	–
1979	104,962	55,615	39,708	9,638	91,923	13,038	10,678	–
1980	106,940	56,455	41,106	9,378	93,600	13,340	10,865	6,146
1981	108,670	57,197	42,485	8,988	95,052	13,618	11,086	6,492
1982	110,204	57,980	43,699	8,526	96,143	14,061	11,331	6,734
1983	111,550	58,744	44,636	8,171	97,021	14,529	11,647	7,033
1984	113,544	59,701	45,900	7,943	98,492	15,052	12,033	7,451
1985	115,461	60,277	47,283	7,901	99,926	15,535	12,364	7,698
1986[1]	117,834	61,320	48,589	7,926	101,801	16,034	12,654	8,076
1987	119,865	62,095	49,783	7,988	103,290	16,576	12,993	8,541
1988	121,669	62,768	50,870	8,031	104,756	16,913	13,205	8,982
1989	123,869	63,704	52,212	7,954	106,355	17,514	13,497	9,323
1990[1]	125,840	64,916	53,131	7,792	107,447	18,393	13,740	10,720
1991	126,346	65,374	53,708	7,265	107,743	18,604	13,797	10,920
1992	128,105	66,213	54,796	7,096	108,837	19,268	14,162	11,338
1993	129,200	66,642	55,388	7,170	109,700	19,500	14,225	11,610
1994[1]	131,056	66,921	56,655	7,481	111,082	19,974	14,502	11,975
1995	132,304	67,324	57,215	7,765	111,950	20,354	14,817	12,267
1996	133,943	68,044	58,094	7,806	113,108	20,835	15,134	12,774
1997[1]	136,297	69,166	59,198	7,932	114,693	21,604	15,529	13,796
1998[1]	137,673	69,715	59,702	8,256	115,415	22,259	15,982	14,317

[1] The comparability of historical labor force data has been affected at various times by methodological and conceptual changes. For an explanation, see the Explanatory Notes and Estimates of Error section of *Employment and Earnings*, a monthly periodical published by the Bureau of Labor Statistics.

NOTE: Detail for the above race and Hispanic-origin groups will not sum to totals because data for the "other races" group are not presented and Hispanics are included in both the white and black population groups. Dash indicates data are not available.

Table 5. **Civilian labor force participation rates for selected demographic groups, annual averages, 1948-98**

(Percent)

Year	Total, 16 years and over	Men, 20 years and over	Women, 20 years and over	Both sexes, 16 to 19 years	White	Black and other	Black	Hispanic origin
1948	58.8	88.6	31.8	52.5	–	–	–	–
1949	58.9	88.5	32.3	52.2	–	–	–	–
1950	59.2	88.4	33.3	51.8	–	–	–	–
1951	59.2	88.2	34.0	52.2	–	–	–	–
1952	59.0	88.3	34.1	51.3	–	–	–	–
1953[1]	58.9	88.0	33.9	50.2	–	–	–	–
1954	58.8	87.8	34.2	48.3	58.2	64.0	–	–
1955	59.3	87.6	35.4	48.9	58.7	64.2	–	–
1956	60.0	87.6	36.4	50.9	59.4	64.9	–	–
1957	59.6	86.9	36.5	49.6	59.1	64.4	–	–
1958	59.5	86.6	36.9	47.4	58.9	64.8	–	–
1959	59.3	86.3	37.1	46.7	58.7	64.3	–	–
1960[1]	59.4	86.0	37.6	47.5	58.8	64.5	–	–
1961	59.3	85.7	38.0	46.9	58.8	64.1	–	–
1962[1]	58.8	84.8	37.8	46.1	58.3	63.2	–	–
1963	58.7	84.4	38.3	45.2	58.2	63.0	–	–
1964	58.7	84.2	38.9	44.5	58.2	63.1	–	–
1965	58.9	83.9	39.4	45.7	58.4	62.9	–	–
1966	59.2	83.6	40.1	48.2	58.7	63.0	–	–
1967	59.6	83.4	41.1	48.4	59.2	62.8	–	–
1968	59.6	83.1	41.6	48.3	59.3	62.2	–	–
1969	60.1	82.8	42.7	49.4	59.9	62.1	–	–
1970	60.4	82.6	43.3	49.9	60.2	61.8	–	–
1971	60.2	82.1	43.3	49.7	60.1	60.9	–	–
1972[1]	60.4	81.6	43.7	51.9	60.4	60.2	59.9	–
1973[1]	60.8	81.3	44.4	53.7	60.8	60.5	60.2	–
1974	61.3	81.0	45.3	54.8	61.4	60.3	59.8	–
1975	61.2	80.3	46.0	54.0	61.5	59.6	58.8	–
1976	61.6	79.8	47.0	54.5	61.8	59.8	59.0	–
1977	62.3	79.7	48.1	56.0	62.5	60.4	59.8	–
1978[1]	63.2	79.8	49.6	57.8	63.3	62.2	61.5	–
1979	63.7	79.8	50.6	57.9	63.9	62.2	61.4	–
1980	63.8	79.4	51.3	56.7	64.1	61.7	61.0	64.0
1981	63.9	79.0	52.1	55.4	64.3	61.3	60.8	64.1
1982	64.0	78.7	52.7	54.1	64.3	61.6	61.0	63.6
1983	64.0	78.5	53.1	53.5	64.3	62.1	61.5	63.8
1984	64.4	78.3	53.7	53.9	64.6	62.6	62.2	64.9
1985	64.8	78.1	54.7	54.5	65.0	63.3	62.9	64.6
1986[1]	65.3	78.1	55.5	54.7	65.5	63.7	63.3	65.4
1987	65.6	78.0	56.2	54.7	65.8	64.3	63.8	66.4
1988	65.9	77.9	56.8	55.3	66.2	64.0	63.8	67.4
1989	66.5	78.1	57.7	55.9	66.7	64.7	64.2	67.6
1990[1]	66.5	78.2	58.0	53.7	66.9	64.4	64.0	67.4
1991	66.2	77.7	57.9	51.6	66.6	63.8	63.3	66.5
1992	66.4	77.7	58.5	51.3	66.8	64.6	63.9	66.8
1993	66.3	77.3	58.5	51.5	66.8	63.8	63.2	66.2
1994[1]	66.6	76.8	59.3	52.7	67.1	63.9	63.4	66.1
1995	66.6	76.7	59.4	53.5	67.1	64.3	63.7	65.8
1996	66.8	76.8	59.9	52.3	67.2	64.6	64.1	66.5
1997[1]	67.1	77.0	60.5	51.6	67.5	65.2	64.7	67.9
1998[1]	67.1	76.8	60.4	52.8	67.3	66.0	65.6	67.9

[1] The comparability of historical labor force data has been affected at various times by methodological and conceptual changes. For an explanation, see the Explanatory Notes and Estimates of Error section of *Employment and Earnings*, a monthly periodical published by the Bureau of Labor Statistics.

Dash indicates data not available.

139

Table 6. **Labor force participation rates of women by presence and age of children, March 1980-98**

(Percent)

Year	Total women	With no children under 18	With children under 18		With children under 6		
			Total	6 to 17 years	Total	3 to 5 years	Under 3 years
1980	51.1	48.1	56.6	64.3	46.8	54.5	41.9
1981	52.0	48.7	58.1	65.5	48.9	56.1	44.3
1982	52.1	48.6	58.5	65.8	49.9	56.5	45.6
1983	52.3	48.7	58.9	66.3	50.5	57.7	46.0
1984	53.1	49.3	60.5	68.1	52.1	58.8	47.6
1985	54.1	50.4	62.1	69.9	53.5	59.5	49.5
1986	54.7	50.5	62.8	70.4	54.4	59.9	50.8
1987	55.4	50.5	64.7	72.0	56.7	62.4	52 9
1988	56.0	51.2	65.1	73.3	56.1	61.5	52.4
1989	56.7	51.9	65.7	74.2	56.7	63.1	52.4
1990	57.2	52.3	66.7	74.7	58.2	65.3	53.6
1991	57.0	52.0	66.6	74.4	58.4	64.4	54.5
1992	57.4	52.3	67.2	75.9	58.0	63.3	54.5
1993	57.2	52.1	66.9	75.4	57.9	63.7	53.9
1994[1]	58.4	53.1	68.4	76.0	60.3	64.9	57.1
1995	58.7	52.9	69.7	76.4	62.3	67.1	58.7
1996	58.8	53.0	70.2	77.2	62.3	66.9	59.0
1997[1]	59.8	53.6	72.1	78.1	65.0	69.3	61.8
1998[1]	60.2	54.1	72.3	78.4	65.2	69.3	62.2

[1] The comparability of historical labor force data has been affected at various times by methodological and conceptual changes. For an explanation, see the Explanatory Notes and Estimates of Error section of *Employment and Earnings*, a monthly periodical published by the Bureau of Labor Statistics.

NOTE: Data refer to single, married, spouse present, and widowed, divorced, and separated women.

Table 7. **Percent distribution of the labor force of women by presence and age of children, March 1980-98**

(Percent)

Year	Total women	With no children under 18	With children under 18		With children under 6		
			Total	6 to 17 years	Total	3 to 5 years	Under 3 years
1980	100.0	60.4	39.6	25.0	14.6	6.6	7.9
1981	100.0	60.3	39.7	24.8	14.9	6.7	8.2
1982	100.0	60.2	39.8	24.2	15.6	6.9	8.8
1983	100.0	60.4	39.6	23.7	15.9	7.0	8.9
1984	100.0	60.3	39.7	23.4	16.3	7.3	8.9
1985	100.0	60.6	39.4	23.2	16.1	7.1	9.0
1986	100.0	60.1	39.9	23.3	16.5	7.3	9.3
1987	100.0	59.6	40.4	23.5	17.0	7.4	9.6
1988	100.0	60.1	39.9	23.5	16.4	7.2	9.2
1989	100.0	60.3	39.7	23.2	16.6	7.4	9.2
1990	100.0	60.5	39.5	22.8	16.7	7.4	9.3
1991	100.0	60.4	39.6	22.5	17.1	7.5	9.6
1992	100.0	60.2	39.8	23.0	16.7	7.4	9.3
1993	100.0	59.9	40.1	23.4	16.7	7.4	9.3
1994[1]	100.0	59.4	40.6	23.2	17.3	7.7	9.6
1995	100.0	59.2	40.8	23.6	17.2	7.8	9.3
1996	100.0	59.6	40.4	23.6	16.8	7.6	9.2
1997[1]	100.0	59.3	40.7	23.8	16.9	7.6	9.3
1998[1]	100.0	59.9	40.1	23.5	16.6	7.4	9.2

[1] The comparability of historical labor force data has been affected at various times by methodological and conceptual changes. For an explanation, see the Explanatory Notes and Estimates of Error section of *Employment and Earnings*, a monthly periodical published by the Bureau of Labor Statistics.

NOTE: Data refer to single, married, spouse present, and widowed, divorced, and separated women.

Table 8. **Employment for selected demographic groups, annual averages, 1948-98**

(In thousands)

Year	Total, 16 years and over	Men, 20 years and over	Women, 20 years and over	Both sexes, 16 to 19 years	White	Black and other	Black	Hispanic origin
1948	58,343	39,382	14,936	4,026	–	–	–	–
1949	57,651	38,803	15,137	3,712	–	–	–	–
1950	58,918	39,394	15,824	3,703	–	–	–	–
1951	59,961	39,626	16,570	3,767	–	–	–	–
1952	60,250	39,578	16,958	3,719	–	–	–	–
1953[1]	61,179	40,296	17,164	3,720	–	–	–	–
1954	60,109	39,634	17,000	3,475	53,957	6,152	–	–
1955	62,170	40,526	18,002	3,642	55,833	6,341	–	–
1956	63,799	41,216	18,767	3,818	57,269	6,534	–	–
1957	64,071	41,239	19,052	3,778	57,465	6,604	–	–
1958	63,036	40,411	19,043	3,582	56,613	6,423	–	–
1959	64,630	41,267	19,524	3,838	58,006	6,623	–	–
1960[1]	65,778	41,543	20,105	4,129	58,850	6,928	–	–
1961	65,746	41,342	20,296	4,108	58,913	6,833	–	–
1962[1]	66,702	41,815	20,693	4,195	59,698	7,003	–	–
1963	67,762	42,251	21,257	4,255	60,622	7,140	–	–
1964	69,305	42,886	21,903	4,516	61,922	7,383	–	–
1965	71,088	43,422	22,630	5,036	63,446	7,643	–	–
1966	72,895	43,668	23,510	5,721	65,021	7,877	–	–
1967	74,372	44,294	24,397	5,682	66,361	8,011	–	–
1968	75,920	44,859	25,281	5,781	67,750	8,169	–	–
1969	77,902	45,388	26,397	6,117	69,518	8,384	–	–
1970	78,678	45,581	26,952	6,144	70,217	8,464	–	–
1971	79,367	45,912	27,246	6,208	70,878	8,488	–	–
1972[1]	82,153	47,130	28,276	6,746	73,370	8,783	7,802	–
1973[1]	85,064	48,310	29,484	7,271	75,708	9,356	8,128	–
1974	86,794	48,922	30,424	7,448	77,184	9,610	8,203	–
1975	85,846	48,018	30,726	7,104	76,411	9,435	7,894	–
1976	88,752	49,190	32,226	7,336	78,853	9,899	8,227	–
1977	92,017	50,555	33,775	7,688	81,700	10,317	8,540	–
1978[1]	96,048	52,143	35,836	8,070	84,936	11,112	9,102	–
1979	98,824	53,308	37,434	8,083	87,259	11,565	9,359	–
1980	99,303	53,101	38,492	7,710	87,715	11,588	9,313	5,527
1981	100,397	53,582	39,590	7,225	88,709	11,688	9,355	5,813
1982	99,526	52,891	40,086	6,549	87,903	11,624	9,189	5,805
1983	100,834	53,487	41,004	6,342	88,893	11,941	9,375	6,072
1984	105,005	55,769	42,793	6,444	92,120	12,885	10,119	6,651
1985	107,150	56,562	44,154	6,434	93,736	13,414	10,501	6,888
1986[1]	109,597	57,569	45,556	6,472	95,660	13,937	10,814	7,219
1987	112,440	58,726	47,074	6,640	97,789	14,652	11,309	7,790
1988	114,968	59,781	48,383	6,805	99,812	15,156	11,658	8,250
1989	117,342	60,837	49,745	6,759	101,584	15,757	11,953	8,573
1990[1]	118,793	61,678	50,535	6,581	102,261	16,533	12,175	9,845
1991	117,718	61,178	50,634	5,906	101,182	16,536	12,074	9,828
1992	118,492	61,496	51,328	5,669	101,669	16,823	12,151	10,027
1993	120,259	62,355	52,099	5,805	103,045	17,214	12,382	10,361
1994[1]	123,060	63,294	53,606	6,161	105,190	17,870	12,835	10,788
1995	124,900	64,085	54,396	6,419	106,490	18,409	13,279	11,127
1996	126,708	64,897	55,311	6,500	107,808	18,900	13,542	11,642
1997[1]	129,558	66,284	56,613	6,661	109,856	19,702	13,969	12,726
1998[1]	131,463	67,135	57,278	7,051	110,931	20,532	14,556	13,291

[1] The comparability of historical labor force data has been affected at various times by methodological and conceptual changes. For an explanation, see the Explanatory Notes and Estimates of Error section of *Employment and Earnings*, a monthly periodical published by the Bureau of Labor Statistics.

NOTE: Detail for the above race and Hispanic-origin groups will not sum to totals because data for the "other races" group are not presented and Hispanics are included in both the white and black population groups. Dash indicates data are not available.

Table 9. **Employment -population ratios for selected demographic groups, annual averages, 1948-98**

(Percent)

Year	Total, 16 years and over	Men, 20 years and over	Women, 20 years and over	Both sexes, 16 to 19 years	White	Black and other	Black	Hispanic origin
1948	56.6	85.8	30.7	47.7	–	–	–	–
1949	55.4	83.7	30.6	45.2	–	–	–	–
1950	56.1	84.2	31.6	45.5	–	–	–	–
1951	57.3	86.1	32.6	47.9	–	–	–	–
1952	57.3	86.2	33.0	46.9	–	–	–	–
1953[1]	57.1	85.9	32.9	46.4	–	–	–	–
1954	55.5	83.5	32.3	42.3	55.2	58.0	–	–
1955	56.7	84.3	33.8	43.5	56.5	58.7	–	–
1956	57.5	84.6	34.9	45.3	57.3	59.5	–	–
1957	57.1	83.8	35.0	43.9	56.8	59.3	–	–
1958	55.4	81.2	34.6	39.9	55.3	56.7	–	–
1959	56.0	82.3	35.1	39.9	55.9	57.5	–	–
1960[1]	56.1	81.9	35.7	40.5	55.9	57.9	–	–
1961	55.4	80.8	35.6	39.1	55.3	56.2	–	–
1962[1]	55.5	80.9	35.8	39.4	55.4	56.3	–	–
1963	55.4	80.6	36.3	37.4	55.3	56.2	–	–
1964	55.7	80.9	36.9	37.3	55.5	57.0	–	–
1965	56.2	81.2	37.6	38.9	56.0	57.8	–	–
1966	56.9	81.5	38.6	42.1	56.8	58.4	–	–
1967	57.3	81.5	39.3	42.2	57.2	58.2	–	–
1968	57.5	81.3	40.0	42.2	57.4	58.0	–	–
1969	58.0	81.1	41.1	43.4	58.0	58.1	–	–
1970	57.4	79.7	41.2	42.3	57.5	56.8	–	–
1971	56.6	78.5	40.9	41.3	56.8	54.9	–	–
1972[1]	57.0	78.4	41.3	43.5	57.4	54.1	53.7	–
1973[1]	57.8	78.6	42.2	45.9	58.2	55.0	54.5	–
1974	57.8	77.9	42.8	46.0	58.3	54.3	53.5	–
1975	56.1	74.8	42.3	43.3	56.7	51.4	50.1	–
1976	56.8	75.1	43.5	44.2	57.5	52.0	50.8	–
1977	57.9	75.6	44.8	46.1	58.6	52.5	51.4	–
1978[1]	59.3	76.4	46.6	48.3	60.0	54.7	53.6	–
1979	59.9	76.5	47.7	48.5	60.6	55.2	53.8	–
1980	59.2	74.6	48.1	46.6	60.0	53.6	52.3	57.6
1981	59.0	74.0	48.6	44.6	60.0	52.6	51.3	57.4
1982	57.8	71.8	48.4	41.5	58.8	50.9	49.4	54.9
1983	57.9	71.4	48.8	41.5	58.9	51.0	49.5	55.1
1984	59.5	73.2	50.1	43.7	60.5	53.6	52.3	57.9
1985	60.1	73.3	51.0	44.4	61.0	54.7	53.4	57.8
1986[1]	60.7	73.3	52.0	44.6	61.5	55.4	54.1	58.5
1987	61.5	73.8	53.1	45.5	62.3	56.8	55.6	60.5
1988	62.3	74.2	54.0	46.8	63.1	57.4	56.3	61.9
1989	63.0	74.5	54.9	47.5	63.8	58.2	56.9	62.2
1990[1]	62.8	74.3	55.2	45.3	63.7	57.9	56.7	61.9
1991	61.7	72.7	54.6	42.0	62.6	56.7	55.4	59.8
1992	61.5	72.1	54.8	41.0	62.4	56.4	54.9	59.1
1993	61.7	72.3	55.0	41.7	62.7	56.3	55.0	59.1
1994[1]	62.5	72.6	56.2	43.4	63.5	57.2	56.1	59.5
1995	62.9	73.0	56.5	44.2	63.8	58.1	57.1	59.7
1996	63.2	73.2	57.0	43.5	64.1	58.6	57.4	60.6
1997[1]	63.8	73.7	57.8	43.4	64.6	59.4	58.2	62.6
1998[1]	64.1	73.9	58.0	45.1	64.7	60.9	59.7	63.1

[1] The comparability of historical labor force data has been affected at various times by methodological and conceptual changes. For an explanation, see the Explanatory Notes and Estimates of Error section of *Employment and Earnings,* a monthly periodical published by the Bureau of Labor Statistics.

Dash indicates data not available.

Table 10. Employed persons by major occupation, annual averages, 1985-98

(In thousands)

Occupation	1985	1986[1]	1987	1988	1989	1990[1]	1991
Total	107,150	109,597	112,440	114,968	117,342	118,793	117,718
Managerial and professional specialty	25,851	26,554	27,742	29,190	30,398	30,602	30,934
Executive, administrative, and managerial	12,221	12,642	13,316	14,216	14,848	14,802	14,904
Professional specialty	13,630	13,911	14,426	14,974	15,550	15,800	16,030
Technical, sales, and administrative support ...	33,231	34,354	35,082	35,532	36,127	36,913	36,318
Technicians and related support	3,255	3,364	3,346	3,521	3,645	3,866	3,814
Sales	12,667	13,245	13,480	13,747	14,065	14,285	14,052
Administrative support, including clerical	17,309	17,745	18,256	18,264	18,416	18,762	18,452
Service occupations	14,441	14,680	15,054	15,332	15,556	16,012	16,254
Private household	1,006	981	934	909	872	792	799
Protective service	1,718	1,787	1,907	1,944	1,960	2,000	2,083
Service, except private household and protective ...	11,718	11,913	12,213	12,479	12,724	13,220	13,372
Precision production, craft, and repair	13,340	13,405	13,568	13,664	13,818	13,745	13,250
Mechanics and repairers	4,475	4,374	4,445	4,454	4,550	4,470	4,445
Construction trades	4,745	4,924	5,011	5,098	5,142	5,199	4,852
Other precision production, craft, and repair ...	4,120	4,108	4,112	4,112	4,126	4,076	3,953
Operators, fabricators, and laborers	16,816	17,160	17,486	17,814	18,022	18,071	17,456
Machine operators, assemblers, and inspectors ...	7,840	7,911	7,994	8,117	8,248	8,200	7,820
Transportation and material moving occupations ...	4,535	4,564	4,712	4,831	4,886	4,886	4,913
Handlers, equipment cleaners, helpers, and laborers ...	4,441	4,685	4,779	4,866	4,888	4,985	4,723
Farming, forestry, and fishing	3,470	3,444	3,507	3,437	3,421	3,450	3,506

Occupation	1992	1993	1994[1]	1995	1996	1997[1]	1998[1]
Total	118,492	120,259	123,060	124,900	126,708	129,558	131,463
Managerial and professional specialty	31,085	32,231	33,847	35,318	36,497	37,686	38,937
Executive, administrative, and managerial	14,722	15,338	16,312	17,186	17,746	18,440	19,054
Professional specialty	16,363	16,893	17,536	18,132	18,752	19,245	19,883
Technical, sales, and administrative support ...	37,048	37,058	37,306	37,417	37,683	38,309	38,521
Technicians and related support	4,277	4,039	3,869	3,909	3,926	4,214	4,261
Sales	14,014	14,342	14,817	15,119	15,404	15,734	15,850
Administrative support, including clerical	18,757	18,677	18,620	18,389	18,353	18,361	18,410
Service occupations	16,377	16,821	16,912	16,930	17,177	17,537	17,836
Private household	891	928	817	821	804	795	847
Protective service	2,114	2,165	2,249	2,237	2,187	2,300	2,417
Service, except private household and protective ...	13,373	13,727	13,847	13,872	14,186	14,442	14,572
Precision production, craft, and repair	13,225	13,429	13,489	13,524	13,587	14,124	14,411
Mechanics and repairers	4,466	4,442	4,419	4,423	4,521	4,675	4,786
Construction trades	4,827	5,048	5,008	5,098	5,108	5,378	5,594
Other precision production, craft, and repair ...	3,931	3,939	4,062	4,004	3,959	4,071	4,031
Operators, fabricators, and laborers	17,247	17,341	17,876	18,068	18,197	18,399	18,256
Machine operators, assemblers, and inspectors ...	7,658	7,553	7,754	7,907	7,874	7,962	7,791
Transportation and material moving occupations ...	4,908	5,036	5,136	5,171	5,302	5,389	5,363
Handlers, equipment cleaners, helpers, and laborers ...	4,682	4,753	4,986	4,990	5,021	5,048	5,102
Farming, forestry, and fishing	3,510	3,379	3,629	3,642	3,566	3,503	3,502

[1] The comparability of historical labor force data has been affected at various times by methodological and conceptual changes. For an explanation, see the Explanatory Notes and Estimates of Error section of *Employment and Earnings*, a monthly periodical published by the Bureau of Labor Statistics.

Table 11. **Employed persons by usual full- or part-time status and sex, annual averages, 1970-98**

(In thousands)

Year	Total employed	Full time	Part time	Economic part time[1]
TOTAL				
1970	78,678	66,753	11,925	2,446
1971	79,367	66,973	12,393	2,688
1972[2]	82,153	69,214	12,939	2,648
1973[2]	85,064	71,803	13,262	2,554
1974	86,794	73,093	13,701	2,988
1975	85,846	71,586	14,260	3,804
1976	88,752	73,964	14,788	3,607
1977	92,017	76,625	15,391	3,608
1978[2]	96,048	80,193	15,855	3,516
1979	98,824	82,654	16,171	3,577
1980	99,303	82,562	16,740	4,321
1981	100,397	83,243	17,154	4,768
1982	99,526	81,421	18,106	6,170
1983	100,834	82,322	18,511	6,266
1984	105,005	86,544	18,462	5,744
1985	107,150	88,534	18,615	5,590
1986[2]	109,597	90,529	19,069	5,588
1987	112,440	92,957	19,483	5,401
1988	114,968	95,214	19,754	5,206
1989	117,342	97,369	19,973	4,894
1990[2]	118,793	98,666	20,128	5,204
1991	117,718	97,190	20,528	6,161
1992	118,492	97,664	20,828	6,520
1993	120,259	99,114	21,145	6,481
1994[2]	123,060	99,772	23,288	4,625
1995	124,900	101,679	23,220	4,473
1996	126,708	103,537	23,170	4,315
1997[2]	129,558	106,334	23,224	4,068
1998[2]	131,463	108,202	23,261	3,665
Men				
1970	48,990	44,825	4,166	1,298
1971	49,390	45,023	4,367	1,395
1972[2]	50,896	46,373	4,523	1,347
1973[2]	52,349	47,843	4,507	1,279
1974	53,024	48,378	4,646	1,519
1975	51,857	46,988	4,870	1,973
1976	53,138	48,150	4,988	1,825
1977	54,728	49,551	5,178	1,749
1978[2]	56,479	51,281	5,198	1,638
1979	57,607	52,427	5,180	1,645
1980	57,186	51,717	5,471	2,107
1981	57,397	51,906	5,492	2,285
1982	56,271	50,334	5,937	3,030
1983	56,787	50,643	6,145	2,966
1984	59,091	53,070	6,020	2,651
1985	59,891	53,862	6,028	2,572
1986[2]	60,892	54,685	6,207	2,590
1987	62,107	55,746	6,360	2,513
1988	63,273	56,816	6,457	2,474
1989	64,315	57,885	6,430	2,287
1990[2]	65,104	58,501	6,604	2,519
1991	64,223	57,407	6,815	3,104
1992	64,440	57,363	7,077	3,230
1993	65,349	58,123	7,226	3,124
1994[2]	66,450	58,832	7,617	2,299
1995	67,377	59,936	7,441	2,210
1996	68,207	60,762	7,445	2,106
1997[2]	69,685	62,258	7,427	1,988
1998[2]	70,693	63,189	7,504	1,796

See footnotes at end of table.

Table 11. **Employed persons by usual full- and part-time status and sex, annual averages, 1970-98—Continued**

(In thousands)

Year	Total employed	Full time	Part time	Economic part time[1]
Women				
1970	29,688	21,929	7,758	1,148
1971	29,976	21,950	8,026	1,293
1972[2]	31,257	22,842	8,416	1,300
1973[2]	32,715	23,960	8,756	1,274
1974	33,769	24,714	9,055	1,468
1975	33,989	24,598	9,391	1,832
1976	35,615	25,814	9,799	1,782
1977	37,289	27,076	10,213	1,859
1978[2]	39,569	28,912	10,658	1,879
1979	41,217	30,227	10,990	1,932
1980	42,117	30,845	11,270	2,215
1981	43,000	31,337	11,664	2,484
1982	43,256	31,086	12,170	3,140
1983	44,047	31,679	12,367	3,300
1984	45,915	33,473	12,441	3,091
1985	47,259	34,672	12,587	3,018
1986[2]	48,706	35,845	12,862	2,999
1987	50,334	37,210	13,124	2,889
1988	51,696	38,398	13,298	2,733
1989	53,027	39,484	13,544	2,607
1990[2]	53,689	40,165	13,524	2,685
1991	53,496	39,783	13,713	3,057
1992	54,052	40,301	13,751	3,290
1993	54,910	40,991	13,919	3,357
1994[2]	56,610	40,940	15,670	2,325
1995	57,523	41,743	15,779	2,263
1996	58,501	42,776	15,725	2,209
1997[2]	59,873	44,076	15,797	2,080
1998[2]	60,771	45,014	15,757	1,869

[1] Includes some persons who usually work full time.
[2] The comparability of historical labor force data has been affected at various times by methodological and conceptual changes. For an explanation, see the Explanatory Notes and Estimates of Error section of *Employment and Earnings*, a monthly periodical published by the Bureau of Labor Statistics.

Table 12. Employees on nonfarm payrolls by major industry division, annual averages, 1947-98

(In thousands)

Year	Total	Total private	Mining	Construction	Manufacturing	Transportation and public utilities	Wholesale trade	Retail trade	Finance, insurance and, real estate	Services	Government
1947	43,857	38,382	955	2,009	15,545	4,166	2,478	6,477	1,728	5,025	5,474
1948	44,866	39,216	994	2,198	15,582	4,189	2,612	6,659	1,800	5,181	5,650
1949	43,754	37,897	930	2,194	14,441	4,001	2,610	6,654	1,828	5,239	5,856
1950	45,197	39,170	901	2,364	15,241	4,034	2,643	6,743	1,888	5,356	6,026
1951	47,819	41,430	929	2,637	16,393	4,226	2,735	7,007	1,956	5,547	6,389
1952	48,793	42,185	898	2,668	16,632	4,248	2,821	7,184	2,035	5,699	6,609
1953	50,202	43,556	866	2,659	17,549	4,290	2,862	7,385	2,111	5,835	6,645
1954	48,990	42,238	791	2,646	16,314	4,084	2,875	7,360	2,200	5,969	6,751
1955	50,641	43,727	792	2,839	16,882	4,141	2,934	7,601	2,298	6,240	6,914
1956	52,369	45,091	822	3,039	17,243	4,244	3,027	7,831	2,389	6,497	7,278
1957	52,855	45,239	828	2,962	17,176	4,241	3,037	7,848	2,438	6,708	7,616
1958	51,322	43,483	751	2,817	15,945	3,976	2,989	7,761	2,481	6,765	7,839
1959	53,270	45,186	732	3,004	16,675	4,011	3,092	8,035	2,549	7,087	8,083
1960	54,189	45,836	712	2,926	16,796	4,004	3,153	8,238	2,628	7,378	8,353
1961	53,999	45,404	672	2,859	16,326	3,903	3,142	8,195	2,688	7,619	8,594
1962	55,549	46,660	650	2,948	16,853	3,906	3,207	8,359	2,754	7,982	8,890
1963	56,653	47,429	635	3,010	16,995	3,903	3,258	8,520	2,830	8,277	9,225
1964	58,283	48,686	634	3,097	17,274	3,951	3,347	8,812	2,911	8,660	9,596
1965	60,763	50,689	632	3,232	18,062	4,036	3,477	9,239	2,977	9,036	10,074
1966	63,901	53,116	627	3,317	19,214	4,158	3,608	9,637	3,058	9,498	10,784
1967	65,803	54,413	613	3,248	19,447	4,268	3,700	9,906	3,185	10,045	11,391
1968	67,897	56,058	606	3,350	19,781	4,318	3,791	10,308	3,337	10,567	11,839
1969	70,384	58,189	619	3,575	20,167	4,442	3,919	10,785	3,512	11,169	12,195
1970	70,880	58,325	623	3,588	19,367	4,515	4,006	11,034	3,645	11,548	12,554
1971	71,211	58,331	609	3,704	18,623	4,476	4,014	11,338	3,772	11,797	12,881
1972	73,675	60,341	628	3,889	19,151	4,541	4,127	11,822	3,908	12,276	13,334
1973	76,790	63,058	642	4,097	20,154	4,656	4,291	12,315	4,046	12,857	13,732
1974	78,265	64,095	697	4,020	20,077	4,725	4,447	12,539	4,148	13,441	14,170
1975	76,945	62,259	752	3,525	18,323	4,542	4,430	12,630	4,165	13,892	14,686
1976	79,382	64,511	779	3,576	18,997	4,582	4,562	13,193	4,271	14,551	14,871
1977	82,471	67,344	813	3,851	19,682	4,713	4,723	13,792	4,467	15,302	15,127
1978	86,697	71,026	851	4,229	20,505	4,923	4,985	14,556	4,724	16,252	15,672
1979	89,823	73,876	958	4,463	21,040	5,136	5,221	14,972	4,975	17,112	15,947
1980	90,406	74,166	1,027	4,346	20,285	5,146	5,292	15,018	5,160	17,890	16,241
1981	91,152	75,121	1,139	4,188	20,170	5,165	5,375	15,171	5,298	18,615	16,031
1982	89,544	73,707	1,128	3,904	18,780	5,081	5,295	15,158	5,340	19,021	15,837
1983	90,152	74,282	952	3,946	18,432	4,952	5,283	15,587	5,466	19,664	15,869
1984	94,408	78,384	966	4,380	19,372	5,156	5,568	16,512	5,684	20,746	16,024
1985	97,387	80,992	927	4,668	19,248	5,233	5,727	17,315	5,948	21,927	16,394
1986	99,344	82,651	777	4,810	18,947	5,247	5,761	17,880	6,273	22,957	16,693
1987	101,958	84,948	717	4,958	18,999	5,362	5,848	18,422	6,533	24,110	17,010
1988	105,209	87,823	713	5,098	19,314	5,512	6,030	19,023	6,630	25,504	17,386
1989	107,884	90,105	692	5,171	19,391	5,614	6,187	19,475	6,668	26,907	17,779
1990	109,403	91,098	709	5,120	19,076	5,777	6,173	19,601	6,709	27,934	18,304
1991	108,249	89,847	689	4,650	18,406	5,755	6,081	19,284	6,646	28,336	18,402
1992	108,601	89,956	635	4,492	18,104	5,718	5,997	19,356	6,602	29,052	18,645
1993	110,713	91,872	610	4,668	18,075	5,811	5,981	19,773	6,757	30,197	18,841
1994	114,163	95,036	601	4,986	18,321	5,984	6,162	20,507	6,896	31,579	19,128
1995	117,191	97,885	581	5,160	18,524	6,132	6,378	21,187	6,806	33,117	19,305
1996	119,608	100,189	580	5,418	18,495	6,253	6,482	21,597	6,911	34,454	19,419
1997	122,690	103,133	596	5,691	18,675	6,408	6,648	21,966	7,109	36,040	19,557
1998	125,826	106,007	590	5,985	18,772	6,600	6,831	22,296	7,407	37,526	19,819

NOTE: Current estimates are projected from March 1996 benchmark levels.

Table 13. **Employees on nonfarm payrolls by industry, annual averages, 1990-98**

(In thousands)

Industry	1990	1991	1992	1993	1994	1995	1996	1997	1998
Total nonfarm	109,403	108,249	108,601	110,713	114,163	117,191	119,608	122,690	125,826
Total private	91,098	89,847	89,956	91,872	95,036	97,885	100,189	103,133	106,007
Goods-producing	24,905	23,745	23,231	23,352	23,908	24,265	24,493	24,962	25,347
Mining	709	689	635	610	601	581	508	596	590
Metal mining	58	56	53	50	49	51	54	54	50
Coal mining	147	136	127	109	112	104	98	96	92
Oil and gas extraction	395	393	353	350	337	320	322	339	339
Nonmetallic minerals, except fuels	110	105	102	102	104	105	106	108	109
Construction	5,120	4,650	4,492	4,668	4,986	5,160	5,418	5,691	5,985
General building contractors	1,298	1,140	1,077	1,120	1,188	1,207	1,257	1,310	1,372
Heavy construction, except building	770	727	711	713	740	752	777	799	838
Special trade contractors ...	3,051	2,783	2,704	2,836	3,058	3,201	3,384	3,582	3,774
Manufacturing	19,076	18,406	18,104	18,075	18,321	18,524	18,495	18,675	18,772
Durable goods	11,109	10,569	10,277	10,221	10,448	10,683	10,789	11,010	11,170
Lumber and wood products	733	675	680	709	754	769	778	796	813
Furniture and fixtures	506	475	478	487	505	510	504	512	530
Stone, clay, and glass products	556	522	513	517	532	540	544	552	563
Primary metal industries	756	723	695	683	698	712	711	711	712
Blast furnaces and basic steel products ..	276	263	250	240	239	242	240	235	232
Fabricated metal products	1,419	1,355	1,329	1,339	1,388	1,437	1,449	1,479	1,501
Industrial machinery and equipment	2,095	2,000	1,929	1,931	1,990	2,067	2,115	2,168	2,203
Computer and office equipment	438	415	391	363	354	352	362	376	379
Electronic and other electrical equipment .	1,673	1,591	1,528	1,526	1,571	1,625	1,661	1,689	1,704
Electronic components and accessories	582	555	527	528	544	581	617	650	660
Transportation equipment	1,989	1,890	1,830	1,756	1,761	1,790	1,785	1,845	1,884
Motor vehicles and equipment	812	789	813	837	909	971	967	986	990
Aircraft and parts	712	669	612	542	482	451	458	501	524
Instruments and related products	1,006	974	929	896	861	843	855	866	868
Miscellaneous manufacturing industries	375	366	368	378	389	390	388	392	393
Nondurable goods	7,968	7,837	7,827	7,854	7,873	7,841	7,706	7,665	7,602
Food and kindred products	1,661	1,667	1,663	1,680	1,678	1,692	1,692	1,685	1,686
Tobacco products	49	49	48	44	43	42	41	41	41
Textile mill products	691	670	674	675	676	663	627	616	598
Apparel and other textile products	1,036	1,006	1,007	989	974	936	868	824	763
Paper and allied products	697	688	690	692	692	693	684	683	675
Printing and publishing ..	1,569	1,536	1,507	1,517	1,537	1,546	1,540	1,552	1,565
Chemicals and allied products	1,086	1,076	1,084	1,081	1,057	1,038	1,034	1,036	1,043
Petroleum and coal products	157	160	158	152	149	145	142	141	140
Rubber and miscellaneous plastics products	888	862	878	909	953	980	983	996	1,009
Leather and leather products	133	124	120	117	113	106	96	91	83

See note at end of table.

147

Table 13. **Employees on nonfarm payrolls by industry, annual averages, 1990-98—Continued**

(In thousands)

Industry	1990	1991	1992	1993	1994	1995	1996	1997	1998
Service-producing	84,497	84,504	85,370	87,361	90,256	92,925	95,115	97,727	100,480
Transportation and public utilities	5,777	5,755	5,718	5,811	5,984	6,132	6,253	6,408	6,600
Transportation	3,511	3,495	3,495	3,598	3,761	3,904	4,019	4,123	4,276
Railroad transportation	279	262	254	248	241	238	231	227	231
Local and interurban passenger transit..............	338	354	361	379	404	419	437	452	468
Trucking and warehousing .	1,395	1,378	1,385	1,444	1,526	1,587	1,637	1,677	1,745
Water transportation	177	184	173	168	172	175	174	179	180
Transportation by air	968	962	964	988	1,023	1,068	1,107	1,134	1,183
Pipelines, except natural gas	19	19	19	18	17	15	15	14	14
Transportation services	336	336	338	352	378	401	418	441	455
Communications and public utilities	2,266	2,260	2,223	2,214	2,223	2,229	2,234	2,285	2,324
Communications	1,309	1,299	1,269	1,269	1,295	1,318	1,351	1,419	1,469
Electric, gas, and sanitary services............................	957	961	954	944	928	911	884	866	855
Wholesale trade	6,173	6,081	5,997	5,981	6,162	6,378	6,482	6,648	6,831
Durable goods	3,614	3,531	3,446	3,433	3,559	3,715	3,805	3,927	4,042
Nondurable goods	2,559	2,550	2,552	2,549	2,604	2,663	2,677	2,721	2,789
Retail trade.............................	19,601	19,284	19,356	19,773	20,507	21,187	21,597	21,966	22,296
Building materials and garden supplies	771	747	758	779	833	868	894	929	948
General merchandise stores	2,540	2,453	2,451	2,488	2,583	2,681	2,702	2,701	2,730
Department stores	2,150	2,074	2,080	2,140	2,246	2,346	2,367	2,380	2,425
Food stores	3,215	3,204	3,180	3,224	3,291	3,366	3,436	3,478	3,482
Automotive dealers and service stations	2,063	1,984	1,966	2,014	2,116	2,190	2,267	2,311	2,341
New and used car dealers ...	924	879	875	908	963	996	1,031	1,046	1,048
Apparel and accessory stores	1,183	1,151	1,131	1,144	1,144	1,125	1,098	1,109	1,143
Furniture and home furnishings stores	820	801	800	828	889	946	975	999	1,026
Eating and drinking places	6,509	6,476	6,609	6,821	7,078	7,354	7,517	7,646	7,760
Miscellaneous retail establishments	2,499	2,468	2,461	2,476	2,573	2,658	2,709	2,794	2,867
Finance, insurance, and real estate	6,709	6,646	6,602	6,757	6,896	6,806	6,911	7,109	7,407
Finance	3,268	3,187	3,160	3,238	3,299	3,231	3,303	3,424	3,593
Depository institutions ...	2,251	2,164	2,096	2,089	2,066	2,025	2,019	2,027	2,042
Commercial banks	1,564	1,529	1,490	1,497	1,484	1,466	1,458	1,463	1,468
Savings institutions	438	382	346	324	305	276	266	260	258
Nondepository institutions	373	379	406	455	491	463	522	577	658
Mortgage bankers and brokers	152	152	180	225	249	205	233	263	328
Security and commodity brokers	424	420	440	472	516	525	553	596	645
Holding and other investment offices	221	224	219	223	227	217	210	223	248
Insurance	2,126	2,161	2,152	2,197	2,236	2,225	2,226	2,264	2,344
Insurance carriers...........	1,462	1,495	1,496	1,529	1,552	1,529	1,517	1,539	1,598
Insurance agents, brokers, and service	663	666	657	668	684	696	709	725	746
Real estate	1,315	1,299	1,290	1,322	1,361	1,351	1,382	1,421	1,471
Services	27,934	28,336	29,052	30,197	31,579	33,117	34,454	36,040	37,526
Agricultural services	490	487	490	519	564	582	627	678	706
Hotels and other lodging places...............................	1,631	1,589	1,576	1,596	1,631	1,668	1,715	1,746	1,776
Personal services..............	1,104	1,112	1,116	1,137	1,140	1,163	1,180	1,186	1,195
Business services	5,139	5,086	5,315	5,735	6,281	6,812	7,293	7,988	8,584
Services to buildings	807	796	805	823	857	882	907	930	950
Personnel supply services	1,535	1,485	1,629	1,906	2,272	2,476	2,654	2,985	3,230
Help supply services ..	1,288	1,268	1,411	1,669	2,017	2,189	2,352	2,656	2,872
Computer and data processing services	772	797	836	893	959	1,090	1,228	1,409	1,599

See note at end of table.

Table 13. **Employees on nonfarm payrolls by industry, annual averages, 1990-98—Continued**

(In thousands)

Industry	1990	1991	1992	1993	1994	1995	1996	1997	1998
Services—Continued									
Auto repair, services, and parking	914	882	881	925	968	1,020	1,080	1,120	1,144
Miscellaneous repair services	374	341	347	349	338	359	372	374	382
Motion pictures	408	411	401	412	441	488	525	550	573
Amusement and recreation services	1,076	1,122	1,188	1,258	1,334	1,417	1,476	1,552	1,601
Health services	7,814	8,183	8,490	8,756	8,992	9,230	9,478	9,703	9,846
Offices and clinics of medical doctors	1,338	1,405	1,463	1,506	1,545	1,609	1,678	1,739	1,803
Nursing and personal care facilities	1,415	1,493	1,533	1,585	1,649	1,691	1,730	1,756	1,762
Hospitals	3,549	3,655	3,750	3,779	3,763	3,772	3,812	3,860	3,926
Home health care services	291	345	398	469	559	629	675	710	672
Legal services	908	912	914	924	924	921	928	944	973
Educational services	1,661	1,710	1,678	1,711	1,850	1,965	2,030	2,104	2,177
Social services	1,734	1,845	1,959	2,070	2,200	2,336	2,413	2,518	2,644
Child day care services .	391	417	451	473	515	563	565	576	605
Residential care	461	501	534	567	604	643	677	716	747
Museums, botanical and zoological gardens	66	69	73	76	79	80	85	90	93
Membership organizations	1,946	1,982	1,973	2,035	2,082	2,146	2,201	2,277	2,361
Engineering and management services	2,478	2,433	2,471	2,521	2,579	2,731	2,844	2,988	3,185
Engineering and architectural services	786	750	742	757	778	815	836	865	905
Management and public relations	610	617	655	688	719	805	870	939	1,034
Government	18,304	18,402	18,645	18,841	19,128	19,305	19,419	19,557	19,819
Federal	3,085	2,966	2,969	2,915	2,870	2,822	2,757	2,699	2,686
Federal, except Postal Service	2,267	2,159	2,177	2,128	2,053	1,978	1,901	1,842	1,819
State government	4,305	4,355	4,408	4,488	4,576	4,635	4,606	4,582	4,612
State government, except education	2,574	2,587	2,610	2,654	2,694	2,715	2,695	2,678	2,695
State government education	1,730	1,768	1,799	1,834	1,882	1,919	1,911	1,904	1,916
Local government	10,914	11,081	11,267	11,438	11,682	11,849	12,056	12,276	12,521
Local government, except education	4,873	4,945	5,048	5,085	5,203	5,243	5,308	5,357	5,440
Local government education	6,042	6,136	6,220	6,353	6,479	6,606	6,748	6,918	7,082

NOTE: Current estimates are projected from March 1998 benchmark levels.

149

Table 14. **Average weekly hours of production workers on private nonfarm payrolls by major industry division, annual averages, 1947-98**

Year	Total private	Mining	Construc-tion	Manu-facturing	Trans-porta-tion and public utilities	Wholesale trade	Retail trade	Finance, insur-ance, and real estate	Services
1947	40.3	40.8	38.2	40.4	–	41.1	40.3	37.9	–
1948	40.0	39.4	38.1	40.0	–	41.0	40.2	37.9	–
1949	39.4	36.3	37.7	39.1	–	40.8	40.4	37.8	–
1950	39.8	37.9	37.4	40.5	–	40.7	40.4	37.7	–
1951	39.9	38.4	38.1	40.6	–	40.8	40.4	37.7	–
1952	39.9	38.6	38.9	40.7	–	40.7	39.8	37.8	–
1953	39.6	38.8	37.9	40.5	–	40.6	39.1	37.7	–
1954	39.1	38.6	37.2	39.6	–	40.5	39.2	37.6	–
1955	39.6	40.7	37.1	40.7	–	40.7	39.0	37.6	–
1956	39.3	40.8	37.5	40.4	–	40.5	38.6	36.9	–
1957	38.8	40.1	37.0	39.8	–	40.3	38.1	36.7	–
1958	38.5	38.9	36.8	39.2	–	40.2	38.1	37.1	–
1959	39.0	40.5	37.0	40.3	–	40.6	38.2	37.3	–
1960	38.6	40.4	36.7	39.7	–	40.5	38.0	37.2	–
1961	38.6	40.5	36.9	39.8	–	40.5	37.6	36.9	–
1962	38.7	41.0	37.0	40.4	–	40.6	37.4	37.3	–
1963	38.8	41.6	37.3	40.5	–	40.6	37.3	37.5	–
1964	38.7	41.9	37.2	40.7	41.1	40.7	37.0	37.3	36.1
1965	38.8	42.3	37.4	41.2	41.3	40.8	36.6	37.2	35.9
1966	38.6	42.7	37.6	41.4	41.2	40.7	35.9	37.3	35.5
1967	38.0	42.6	37.7	40.6	40.5	40.3	35.3	37.1	35.1
1968	37.8	42.6	37.3	40.7	40.6	40.1	34.7	37.0	34.7
1969	37.7	43.0	37.9	40.6	40.7	40.2	34.2	37.1	34.7
1970	37.1	42.7	37.3	39.8	40.5	39.9	33.8	36.7	34.4
1971	36.9	42.4	37.2	39.9	40.1	39.4	33.7	36.6	33.9
1972	37.0	42.6	36.5	40.5	40.4	39.4	33.4	36.6	33.9
1973	36.9	42.4	36.8	40.7	40.5	39.2	33.1	36.6	33.8
1974	36.5	41.9	36.6	40.0	40.2	38.8	32.7	36.5	33.6
1975	36.1	41.9	36.4	39.5	39.7	38.6	32.4	36.5	33.5
1976	36.1	42.4	36.8	40.1	39.8	38.7	32.1	36.4	33.3
1977	36.0	43.4	36.5	40.3	39.9	38.8	31.6	36.4	33.0
1978	35.8	43.4	36.8	40.4	40.0	38.8	31.0	36.4	32.8
1979	35.7	43.0	37.0	40.2	39.9	38.8	30.6	36.2	32.7
1980	35.3	43.3	37.0	39.7	39.6	38.4	30.2	36.2	32.6
1981	35.2	43.7	36.9	39.8	39.4	38.5	30.1	36.3	32.6
1982	34.8	42.7	36.7	38.9	39.0	38.3	29.9	36.2	32.6
1983	35.0	42.5	37.1	40.1	39.0	38.5	29.8	36.2	32.7
1984	35.2	43.3	37.8	40.7	39.4	38.5	29.8	36.5	32.6
1985	34.9	43.4	37.7	40.5	39.5	38.4	29.4	36.4	32.5
1986	34.8	42.2	37.4	40.7	39.2	38.3	29.2	36.4	32.5
1987	34.8	42.4	37.8	41.0	39.2	38.1	29.2	36.3	32.5
1988	34.7	42.3	37.9	41.1	38.2	38.1	29.1	35.9	32.6
1989	34.6	43.0	37.9	41.0	38.3	38.0	28.9	35.8	32.6
1990	34.5	44.1	38.2	40.8	38.4	38.1	28.8	35.8	32.5
1991	34.3	44.4	38.1	40.7	38.1	38.1	28.6	35.7	32.4
1992	34.4	43.9	38.0	41.0	38.3	38.2	28.8	35.8	32.5
1993	34.5	44.3	38.5	41.4	39.3	38.2	28.8	35.8	32.5
1994	34.7	44.8	38.9	42.0	39.7	38.4	28.9	35.8	32.5
1995	34.5	44.7	38.9	41.6	39.4	38.3	28.8	35.9	32.4
1996	34.4	45.3	39.0	41.6	39.6	38.3	28.8	35.9	32.4
1997	34.6	45.4	39.0	42.0	39.7	38.4	28.9	36.1	32.6
1998	34.6	43.9	38.8	41.7	39.5	38.4	29.0	36.4	32.6

Dash indicates data not available.

NOTE: Current estimates are projected from March 1998 benchmark levels.

150

Table 15. **Indexes of aggregate weekly hours of production workers on private nonfarm payrolls by major industry division, annual averages, 1947-98**

(1982=100)

Year	Total private	Mining	Construc- tion	Manu- facturing	Trans- porta- tion and public utilities	Wholesale trade	Retail trade	Finance, insur- ance, and real estate	Services
1947	–	101.4	62.0	105.8	–	56.8	–	–	–
1948	–	101.9	67.6	104.2	–	59.5	–	–	–
1949	–	86.8	66.7	93.0	–	59.0	–	–	–
1950	–	88.3	71.3	102.2	–	59.7	–	–	–
1951	–	91.9	81.0	109.6	–	61.7	–	–	–
1952	–	88.2	83.3	109.6	–	63.3	–	–	–
1953	–	84.8	80.5	114.8	–	63.7	–	–	–
1954	–	75.5	78.2	102.4	–	63.1	–	–	–
1955	–	78.9	83.4	109.0	–	64.4	–	–	–
1956	–	81.5	90.2	109.5	–	65.9	–	–	–
1957	–	79.6	86.6	105.9	–	65.4	–	–	–
1958	–	67.9	80.8	94.8	–	63.6	–	–	–
1959	–	68.1	86.7	102.3	–	66.4	–	–	–
1960	–	65.7	83.2	100.7	–	67.3	–	–	–
1961	–	61.5	81.4	97.0	–	66.8	–	–	–
1962	–	59.8	83.9	101.6	–	68.1	–	–	–
1963	–	59.1	86.8	102.4	–	68.8	–	–	–
1964	75.8	59.4	89.1	104.9	87.7	70.6	73.2	60.4	51.9
1965	79.1	59.6	93.4	111.5	89.9	73.3	75.9	61.4	54.0
1966	82.5	59.3	96.3	119.2	91.7	75.7	77.6	62.8	56.4
1967	82.9	57.0	93.8	117.1	92.1	76.5	78.3	64.8	58.9
1968	84.9	56.0	95.6	119.2	93.4	77.7	80.1	67.8	61.3
1969	87.7	57.9	103.6	121.0	96.3	80.6	82.6	71.6	64.2
1970	86.3	57.6	101.3	112.8	96.9	81.7	83.4	73.0	65.3
1971	85.8	54.9	103.6	108.8	95.1	80.4	85.3	74.3	65.6
1972	89.2	57.8	107.9	114.8	97.3	82.5	88.2	76.5	68.0
1973	93.2	58.8	113.7	121.7	99.9	85.6	90.9	78.9	71.3
1974	93.2	63.4	109.5	118.1	100.4	87.6	91.0	79.8	73.9
1975	88.8	68.3	92.7	103.8	94.6	86.4	90.6	79.9	76.0
1976	92.3	71.5	94.0	110.3	95.5	89.1	93.9	81.5	78.8
1977	96.0	76.5	100.2	115.0	97.9	92.5	96.5	85.4	82.0
1978	100.7	79.0	112.2	120.1	101.3	97.7	100.0	90.3	86.3
1979	104.0	88.2	119.9	122.1	104.9	102.0	101.5	94.4	90.2
1980	102.8	94.1	115.1	113.8	104.1	101.9	100.1	97.8	94.3
1981	104.1	104.8	109.3	112.5	103.3	103.3	100.6	105.5	98.2
1982	100.0	100.0	100.0	100.0	100.0	100.0	100.0	100.0	100.0
1983	101.5	81.5	102.2	101.4	97.3	99.9	102.7	101.6	103.6
1984	107.7	84.9	116.8	109.0	102.8	105.3	108.2	106.4	108.2
1985	110.5	81.4	125.3	106.9	104.6	108.4	111.7	110.9	114.0
1986	112.3	65.7	128.2	105.7	104.0	108.5	114.3	116.7	119.2
1987	115.6	61.8	132.7	107.0	106.5	109.4	117.9	120.1	124.9
1988	119.3	61.7	136.9	109.3	108.2	113.3	121.0	119.2	132.2
1989	122.1	60.5	138.9	109.3	111.1	116.1	122.9	119.5	139.3
1990	123.0	63.9	138.0	106.4	114.5	115.7	123.0	120.2	144.2
1991	120.4	62.0	122.8	102.1	113.4	113.7	119.5	118.3	145.3
1992	121.2	56.2	118.4	101.7	113.6	112.8	120.6	118.1	149.3
1993	124.6	54.3	125.4	103.1	118.2	112.8	123.4	121.2	155.4
1994	130.0	54.6	136.3	107.0	121.8	116.9	128.6	124.0	163.1
1995	133.5	54.1	140.9	107.5	123.9	121.1	132.2	122.9	120.7
1996	136.7	55.6	148.7	107.2	127.5	122.9	134.6	125.0	177.4
1997	141.5	58.3	156.2	109.4	130.5	126.1	137.7	129.6	186.6
1998	145.1	56.1	163.7	108.8	132.1	128.8	140.0	136.6	194.3

Dash indicates data not available.

NOTE: Current estimates are projected from March 1998 benchmark levels.

Table 16. **Percent distribution of all hours worked by women in the private business sector by years of completed schooling, 1948-97**

Year	Years of completed schooling						
	0-4	5-8	9-11	12	13-15	16	17+
1948	4.8	29.5	18.8	36.3	6.8	2.5	1.3
1949	4.5	25.4	20.5	35.5	9.2	3.2	1.6
1950	4.5	25.4	20.3	35.7	9.2	3.2	1.6
1951	4.6	25.8	20.1	36.4	8.4	3.2	1.6
1952	4.6	26.2	19.8	37.0	7.6	3.2	1.6
1953	4.3	25.5	19.9	37.9	7.7	3.2	1.6
1954	4.1	24.7	19.8	38.8	7.8	3.3	1.6
1955	3.7	24.1	19.8	39.6	7.8	3.3	1.6
1956	3.4	23.4	19.9	40.4	7.9	3.4	1.6
1957	3.1	22.5	19.8	41.3	8.0	3.5	1.7
1958	3.0	22.3	20.6	40.2	8.8	3.4	1.6
1959	2.9	22.5	21.7	38.7	9.5	3.2	1.5
1960	2.7	21.7	22.2	38.0	10.6	3.3	1.5
1961	2.5	20.5	20.8	40.3	10.5	4.1	1.2
1962	2.3	18.9	19.4	43.0	10.6	4.8	1.0
1963	2.2	18.5	19.4	44.2	10.1	4.4	1.2
1964	2.1	18.2	19.4	45.2	9.7	4.0	1.4
1965	2.0	17.4	19.2	45.9	9.7	4.2	1.6
1966	1.6	16.7	19.1	47.4	10.3	3.5	1.5
1967	1.3	15.2	18.9	48.0	12.0	3.5	1.1
1968	1.4	13.5	18.6	50.1	11.7	3.3	1.3
1969	1.1	12.4	17.7	50.6	12.3	4.1	1.7
1970	1.1	11.7	17.2	50.3	13.2	4.4	2.1
1971	1.2	10.5	16.9	51.3	13.6	4.8	1.6
1972	1.1	9.5	16.0	52.5	14.2	4.8	1.8
1973	1.0	8.9	15.5	50.8	15.9	5.6	2.2
1974	.8	8.3	14.9	50.8	16.1	6.3	2.8
1975	.8	7.7	15.1	50.3	16.4	6.9	2.8
1976	.9	7.3	14.9	50.4	16.8	7.1	2.7
1977	.8	6.9	14.4	50.1	17.6	7.3	2.8
1978	.8	6.0	13.2	50.4	18.5	7.7	3.4
1979	.7	5.7	12.4	50.2	18.8	8.6	3.6
1980	.6	5.2	11.9	50.0	19.7	8.9	3.6
1981	.7	4.9	11.3	49.8	19.7	9.3	4.4
1982	.6	4.4	10.4	48.7	20.6	10.4	4.9
1983	.6	3.9	9.9	48.5	21.0	11.0	5.2
1984	.6	3.7	9.7	47.3	22.0	11.7	5.1
1985	.5	3.4	9.1	47.0	22.6	12.2	5.2
1986	.4	3.3	8.9	46.8	22.7	12.3	5.5
1987	.7	3.0	9.3	46.0	23.0	12.5	5.5
1988	.7	2.8	9.0	45.6	22.8	13.2	5.9
1989	.6	2.7	8.5	45.0	23.3	13.5	6.3
1990	.6	2.7	8.4	44.4	23.4	14.1	6.3
1991[1]	.5	2.2	6.6	41.1	29.5	15.2	4.9
1992[2]	.5	2.1	6.2	39.8	30.4	15.7	5.2
1993[2]	.5	2.2	6.6	37.4	32.2	15.8	5.2
1994	.5	2.2	6.6	36.5	32.4	16.2	5.6
1995	.5	2.2	6.8	36.1	31.8	16.9	5.7
1996	.4	2.1	6.5	36.7	31.2	17.4	5.7
1997	.5	2.1	6.3	35.8	31.5	17.6	6.2

[1] March 1992 Current Population Survey used in measuring 1991 data revised questions on educational attainment. Data prior to 1991 are not strictly comparable.
[2] May not be strictly comparable before 1993 data due to comprehensive revisions in the CPS questionnaire.

NOTE: Rows may not sum to 100.0 due to rounding.

Table 17. **Percent distribution of all hours worked by men in the private business sector by years of completed schooling, 1948-97**

Year	Years of completed schooling						
	0-4	5-8	9-11	12	13-15	16	17+
1948	8.3	35.6	20.5	23.1	6.5	3.6	2.4
1949	9.3	36.0	19.5	21.4	7.1	4.0	2.7
1950	9.1	35.9	19.5	21.5	7.2	4.1	2.7
1951	8.8	35.1	19.1	22.4	7.4	4.3	2.9
1952	8.5	34.4	18.8	23.3	7.6	4.4	3.0
1953	8.1	33.4	19.0	24.0	7.7	4.7	3.2
1954	7.6	32.4	19.1	24.7	7.7	4.9	3.4
1955	7.1	31.3	19.4	25.7	7.8	5.1	3.6
1956	6.7	30.3	19.6	26.5	7.9	5.3	3.7
1957	6.2	29.3	19.8	27.3	7.9	5.5	3.9
1958	5.9	28.9	20.2	26.8	8.6	5.5	4.0
1959	5.5	28.4	20.7	26.4	9.3	5.5	4.0
1960	5.2	27.8	21.1	26.1	10.1	5.6	4.1
1961	4.8	25.8	20.4	28.2	10.2	6.5	4.2
1962	4.5	23.8	19.6	30.2	10.2	7.3	4.3
1963	4.1	22.9	19.6	31.5	10.2	7.2	4.5
1964	3.7	22.0	19.6	32.8	10.2	7.0	4.7
1965	3.8	21.1	19.3	33.8	10.1	7.5	4.5
1966	3.4	20.4	19.5	34.4	10.2	7.8	4.4
1967	2.9	18.6	18.8	35.3	11.9	7.6	5.1
1968	2.7	17.9	18.7	35.8	12.2	7.7	5.0
1969	2.5	17.0	17.7	36.4	12.8	8.2	5.4
1970	2.4	15.7	16.9	37.2	13.5	8.6	5.7
1971	2.3	14.8	17.2	37.2	13.8	8.8	5.8
1972	2.3	12.9	16.3	38.8	14.6	9.1	6.0
1973	2.1	12.4	15.7	38.6	15.2	9.5	6.5
1974	1.7	10.7	14.9	38.7	16.0	10.9	7.2
1975	1.8	10.8	14.9	38.9	15.9	10.7	7.0
1976	1.7	10.1	15.0	38.5	16.4	10.9	7.3
1977	1.7	9.7	14.5	38.4	17.4	10.9	7.5
1978	1.5	8.9	13.6	39.0	18.1	11.1	7.8
1979	1.4	8.5	13.7	39.0	17.8	11.5	8.1
1980	1.4	7.8	13.1	39.5	17.8	12.1	8.3
1981	1.3	7.3	12.5	39.6	17.6	12.5	9.2
1982	1.3	6.5	11.7	38.6	18.0	13.8	10.2
1983	1.0	6.4	10.9	39.2	18.4	13.9	10.1
1984	1.1	6.2	11.0	39.2	18.7	14.1	9.8
1985	1.1	5.8	10.5	39.4	19.4	14.5	9.5
1986	1.0	5.6	10.7	39.0	39.0	14.5	9.9
1987	1.1	5.2	10.7	39.2	18.8	14.8	10.1
1988	1.2	5.1	10.2	38.8	19.5	14.7	10.6
1989	1.3	4.9	10.0	38.8	20.0	15.2	10.1
1990	1.2	4.5	9.7	39.2	20.2	15.1	10.0
1991 [1]	1.0	3.9	8.2	37.1	24.4	17.0	8.4
1992 [2]	1.0	3.7	7.8	36.2	25.0	17.2	9.1
1993 [2]	1.0	3.8	7.7	35.2	26.0	17.4	8.9
1994	1.0	3.7	7.6	34.7	26.1	18.0	8.9
1995	1.0	3.7	8.0	34.5	26.3	17.6	8.9
1996	1.0	3.7	8.1	34.3	26.0	18.0	8.8
1997	1.0	3.4	7.8	34.8	26.0	18.2	8.9

[1] March 1992 Current Population Survey used in measuring 1991 data contained revised questions on educational attainment. Data prior to 1991 are not strictly comparable.
[2] May not be strictly comparable before 1993 data due to comprehensive revisions in the CPS questionnaire.

NOTE: Rows may not sum to 100.0 due to rounding.

Table 18. Employment Cost Index for wages and salaries, annual averages,[1] 1976-98

Year	Civilian workers	State and local government workers	Private industry workers						
			All private industry workers	White-collar workers	Blue-collar workers	Goods-producing workers	Service-producing workers	Manufac-turing workers	Nonman-ufacturing workers
1976	–	–	47.9	46.8	49.5	49.0	47.1	48.3	47.7
1977	–	–	51.3	49.8	53.3	52.8	50.1	52.1	50.8
1978	–	–	55.2	53.5	57.5	57.0	53.9	56.2	54.7
1979	–	–	59.6	57.5	62.4	61.6	58.1	60.9	59.0
1980	–	–	65.1	62.7	68.4	67.5	63.4	66.8	64.2
1981	–	–	71.0	68.5	74.6	73.5	69.2	72.8	70.2
1982	75.1	71.0	76.0	73.6	79.4	78.6	74.2	77.7	75.2
1983	79.1	75.0	80.0	77.9	83.0	82.0	78.5	81.2	79.4
1984	82.8	79.3	83.5	81.7	86.0	85.2	82.5	84.7	83.1
1985	86.5	83.8	87.2	85.7	89.2	88.6	86.3	88.3	86.7
1986	89.9	88.3	90.2	89.2	91.7	91.5	89.4	91.3	89.7
1987	92.9	92.4	93.1	92.4	94.0	93.9	92.5	93.9	92.8
1988	96.6	96.7	96.5	96.1	97.1	97.2	96.1	97.1	96.3
1989	100.8	101.6	100.6	100.7	100.4	100.5	100.7	100.5	100.7
1990	105.3	107.2	104.8	105.3	104.1	104.6	105.0	104.9	104.8
1991	109.4	111.9	108.8	109.5	107.6	108.4	109.0	108.9	108.7
1992	112.6	115.1	111.9	112.7	110.7	111.8	112.0	112.6	111.6
1993	115.8	118.4	115.2	116.1	113.7	114.9	115.3	116.0	114.8
1994	119.2	121.8	118.5	119.7	116.9	118.4	118.6	119.5	118.1
1995	122.6	125.7	121.9	123.1	120.3	121.7	122.0	123.2	121.3
1996	126.6	129.2	126.0	127.4	123.9	125.5	126.2	127.0	125.4
1997	130.9	132.7	130.4	132.1	127.7	129.2	130.9	130.7	130.1
1998	135.9	136.7	135.7	137.9	131.8	133.7	136.5	135.3	135.5

Dash indicates data not available.
[1] The annual average is the average for four quarters of a year.

Table 19. Employer compensation costs per employee hours worked, all private industry, 1986-98

Measure	Total compen- sation	Wage and salaries	Total benefits	Paid leave	Supple- mental pay	Insurance	Retire- ment and savings	Legally required benefits	Other benefits
Cost per hour worked									
1986	$13.25	$9.67	$3.58	$0.93	$0.30	$0.73	$0.50	$1.11	$0.02
1987	13.42	9.83	3.60	0.93	0.32	.72	.48	1.13	.02
1988	13.79	10.02	3.77	.97	.33	.78	.45	1.22	.02
1989	14.28	10.38	3.90	1.00	.34	.85	.42	1.27	.02
1990	14.96	10.84	4.13	1.03	.37	.92	.45	1.35	(¹)
1991	15.40	11.14	4.27	1.05	.36	1.01	.44	1.40	(¹)
1992	16.14	11.58	4.55	1.09	.39	1.12	.46	1.47	.02
1993	16.70	11.90	4.80	1.11	.42	1.19	.48	1.55	.04
1994	17.08	12.14	4.94	1.11	.44	1.23	.52	1.60	.04
1995	17.10	12.25	4.85	1.09	.47	1.15	.52	1.59	.03
1996	17.49	12.58	4.91	1.12	.49	1.14	.55	1.59	.03
1997	17.97	13.04	4.94	1.14	.51	1.09	.55	1.62	.03
1998	18.50	13.47	5.02	1.16	.56	1.10	.55	1.63	.03
Percent of total compensation									
1996	100.0	73.0	27.0	7.0	2.3	5.5	3.8	8.4	.1
1987	100.0	73.2	26.8	6.9	2.4	5.4	3.6	8.4	.1
1988	100.0	72.7	27.3	7.0	2.4	5.6	3.3	8.8	.2
1989	100.0	72.7	27.3	7.0	2.4	6.0	2.9	8.9	.1
1990	100.0	72.4	27.6	6.9	2.5	6.1	3.0	9.0	(¹)
1991	100.0	72.3	27.7	6.8	2.3	6.5	2.9	9.1	(¹)
1992	100.0	71.8	28.2	6.8	2.4	6.9	2.9	9.1	.1
1993	100.0	71.3	28.7	6.6	2.5	7.2	2.9	9.3	.2
1994	100.0	71.1	28.9	6.5	2.6	7.2	3.0	9.4	.2
1995	100.0	71.6	28.4	6.4	2.8	6.7	3.0	9.3	.2
1996	100.0	71.9	28.1	6.4	2.8	6.5	3.1	9.1	.2
1997	100.0	72.5	27.5	6.3	2.9	6.1	3.0	9.0	.1
1998	100.0	72.8	27.1	6.3	3.0	5.9	3.0	8.8	.2

¹ Cost per hour worked is $0.01 or less.

NOTE: The Employment Cost Index (ECI) sample—source of these data—systematically replaced industry by industry over about a 4 ¹/₂ year period, and with processing time, individual establishments may remain in the ECI sample for as long as 6 years. Changes over time in Employer Costs for Employee Compensation are, therefore, affected both by changes in the costs for the establishments in industry samples continuing from previous periods, and by changes in the samples of establishments for industries that have been resurveyed. The updating of industry samples periodically (rather than on an ongoing basis) may have a significant impact on cost changes estimated over short time intervals. Consequently, the Bureau advises caution in interpreting short-term comparisons of costs per hour worked.

Table 20. **Mean hourly earnings[1] for selected occupations, all workers, all industries, selected areas,[2] 1998**

Occupation[3]	Columbus, OH	Denver-Boulder-Greeley, CO	Detroit-Ann Arbor-Flint, MI	San Francisco-Oakland-San Jose, CA
ALL	$15.42	$16.99	$18.55	$20.72
All excluding sales	15.67	17.12	18.69	21.06
WHITE COLLAR	17.57	19.58	21.89	24.51
White collar excluding sales	18.24	20.19	22.58	25.48
Professional specialty and technical	21.70	24.70	26.02	29.95
Professional specialty	23.87	26.27	28.23	31.70
Engineers, architects, and surveyors	27.36	29.63	29.10	33.44
Civil engineers	23.76	30.91	–	35.69
Electrical and electronic engineers	28.40	29.14	–	33.84
Industrial engineers	–	21.91	27.69	30.58
Mechanical engineers	22.58	30.00	27.48	30.64
Engineers, n.e.c.	31.12	30.98	30.39	33.35
Mathematical and computer scientists	23.53	27.27	26.00	35.94
Computer systems analysts and scientists	23.72	29.13	25.63	35.89
Operations and systems researchers and analysts	23.06	18.05	26.86	–
Natural scientists	22.99	34.93	20.15	29.19
Chemists, except biochemists	26.65	–	–	–
Geologists and geodesists	–	36.23	–	–
Physical scientists, n.e.c.	–	–	–	29.54
Biological and life scientists	–	37.66	–	–
Health related	19.33	20.96	22.92	27.76
Physicians	–	–	29.08	26.82
Registered nurses	19.33	19.27	21.84	28.57
Pharmacists	26.18	27.02	27.74	–
Dietitians	–	–	15.73	18.89
Respiratory therapists	–	17.43	–	–
Physical therapists	–	–	26.84	–
Teachers, college and university	29.23	34.23	37.84	36.79
Psychology teachers	–	–	–	27.75
Engineering teachers	–	–	63.03	–
Health specialities teachers	–	–	32.82	–
Business, commerce and marketing teachers	–	–	–	36.89
English teachers	–	–	–	36.75
Teachers, post secondary, subject not specified	–	–	46.76	–
Teachers, post secondary, n.e.c.	–	–	28.07	31.79
Teachers, except college and university	27.77	23.51	34.20	31.95
Prekindergarten and kindergarten	–	–	33.93	18.22
Elementary school teachers	28.69	25.95	35.18	34.45
Secondary school teachers	29.50	25.89	36.90	32.43
Teachers, special education	26.39	–	38.78	36.21
Teachers, n.e.c.	26.45	22.34	33.36	34.64
Substitute teachers	–	9.94	10.92	12.65
Vocational and educational counselors	–	17.60	21.52	25.01
Librarians, archivists, and curators	20.39	–	23.93	24.25
Librarians	20.39	–	23.93	24.25
Social scientists and urban planners	19.82	17.53	17.94	27.34
Economists	17.29	18.43	–	29.10
Psychologists	–	14.16	–	24.90
Social, recreation, and religious workers	22.53	15.47	22.04	19.37
Social workers	22.59	16.25	22.23	22.18
Recreation workers	–	13.36	–	–
Lawyers and judges	–	43.89	45.80	46.70
Lawyers	–	–	45.64	46.70
Writers, authors, entertainers, athletes, and professionals, n.e.c.	22.04	25.80	30.97	27.03
Designers	–	–	–	26.07
Editors and reporters	25.41	27.53	–	–
Public relations specialists	–	19.47	–	–
Professional, n.e.c.	26.46	26.16	–	26.35
Technical	15.36	19.21	19.19	23.09
Clinical laboratory technologists and technicians	9.93	18.46	15.50	22.58

See footnotes at end of table.

Table 20. **Mean hourly earnings[1] for selected occupations, all workers, all industries, selected areas,[2] 1998**—Continued

Occupation[3]	Columbus, OH	Denver-Boulder-Greeley, CO	Detroit-Ann Arbor-Flint, MI	San Francisco-Oakland-San Jose, CA
WHITE COLLAR–Continued				
Professional specialty and technical–Continued				
Technical–Continued				
Health record technologists and technicians	–	–	$14.04	$15.62
Radiological technicians	–	$16.47	17.30	23.51
Licensed practical nurses	$14.02	13.22	14.63	17.50
Health technologists and technicians, n.e.c.	10.89	10.87	12.97	17.94
Electrical and electronic technicians	–	18.29	20.21	20.75
Mechanical engineering technicians	–	–	22.19	–
Engineering technicians, n.e.c.	–	20.50	–	20.46
Drafters	–	21.58	21.28	28.34
Biological technicians	–	15.02	–	–
Chemical technicians	–	15.93	18.68	–
Airplane pilots and navigators	–	–	–	121.54
Computer programmers	–	26.86	28.21	29.58
Legal assistants	–	–	–	20.25
Technical and related, n.e.c.	19.21	17.92	19.28	19.72
Executive, administrative, and managerial	26.54	26.57	28.75	33.47
Executives, administrators, and managers	31.74	30.44	34.14	39.67
Administrators and officials, public administration	20.43	28.56	29.84	31.00
Financial managers	32.03	24.69	37.95	36.45
Personnel and labor relations managers	–	27.93	–	33.37
Managers, marketing, advertising and public relations	33.44	27.98	40.38	41.16
Administrators, education and related fields	33.74	33.35	36.90	33.80
Managers, medicine and health	30.19	–	28.20	33.91
Managers, food servicing and lodging establishments	20.44	–	–	–
Managers, service organizations, n.e.c.	19.88	25.34	–	21.94
Managers and administrators, n.e.c.	34.41	34.24	36.43	45.22
Management related	21.31	20.64	23.26	25.37
Accountants and auditors	20.88	19.45	21.37	23.99
Underwriters	–	23.05	–	–
Other financial officers	22.11	23.35	31.03	26.50
Management analysts	–	27.83	–	29.67
Personnel, training, and labor relations specialists	19.60	19.26	24.07	30.49
Purchasing agents and buyers, n.e.c.	22.11	23.94	26.76	26.37
Construction inspectors	–	–	21.35	27.62
Inspectors and compliance officers, except construction	–	15.61	–	22.64
Management related, n.e.c.	25.24	20.37	24.08	23.74
Sales	11.91	15.68	16.28	15.42
Supervisors, sales	14.08	24.35	18.56	20.03
Real estate sales	–	19.73	–	–
Securities and financial services sales	–	–	–	16.55
Advertising and related sales	26.05	–	21.17	26.35
Sales, other business services	–	16.24	21.23	15.00
Sales representatives, mining, manufacturing, and wholesale	30.05	20.87	23.84	31.19
Sales workers, motor vehicles and boats	–	–	25.76	–
Sales workers, apparel	7.41	–	–	9.89
Sales workers, furniture & home furnishings	–	6.87	13.23	9.08
Sales workers, other commodities	8.36	–	10.98	10.28
Sales counter clerks	–	–	8.51	–
Cashiers	6.69	8.89	8.06	10.59
Sales support, n.e.c.	–	10.67	–	16.46
Administrative support, including clerical	11.74	12.05	13.07	14.65
Supervisors, general office	14.36	15.73	18.08	19.98

See footnotes at end of table.

Occupation[3]	Columbus, OH	Denver- Boulder- Greeley, CO	Detroit- Ann Arbor- Flint, MI	San Francisco- Oakland- San Jose, CA
WHITE COLLAR–Continued				
Administrative support, including clerical–Continued				
Supervisors, financial records processing	–	$17.24	$18.34	$23.62
Supervisors, distribution, scheduling, and adjusting clerks	–	–	–	19.05
Computer operators	–	15.75	15.95	18.20
Secretaries	$14.02	13.69	14.43	17.06
Stenographers	–	–	13.16	19.51
Typists	12.33	11.93	9.71	14.23
Interviewers	–	11.08	10.21	–
Hotel clerks	–	–	–	10.11
Transportation ticket and reservation agents	–	–	–	14.25
Receptionists	8.34	9.28	9.19	10.66
Information clerks, n.e.c.	9.28	10.39	–	10.66
Correspondence clerks	–	11.48	–	14.88
Order clerks	11.98	11.38	12.16	13.52
Personnel clerks except payroll & timekeeping	–	11.52	14.01	18.46
Library clerks	10.60	10.61	10.99	13.95
File clerks	–	9.48	–	10.49
Records clerks, n.e.c.	12.26	11.98	10.82	13.07
Bookkeepers, accounting and auditing clerks	12.07	12.09	11.47	14.96
Payroll and timekeeping clerks	–	–	12.43	–
Billing clerks	9.95	–	10.92	15.06
Cost and rate clerks	–	12.52	–	–
Telephone operators	–	–	11.28	–
Dispatchers	–	–	–	18.56
Production coordinators	13.26	14.08	19.28	15.72
Traffic, shipping and receiving clerks	10.39	10.13	11.99	14.31
Stock and inventory clerks	10.11	12.75	10.64	12.31
Expeditors	–	11.12	–	–
Material recording, scheduling, and distribution clerks, n.e.c.	11.33	10.16	14.25	16.76
Insurance adjusters, examiners, & investigators	13.86	14.23	13.63	15.99
Investigators and adjusters except insurance	–	12.73	13.88	14.17
Eligibility clerks, social welfare	–	–	–	18.00
Bill and account collectors	10.71	–	12.14	15.61
General office clerks	10.08	11.47	11.98	13.81
Bank tellers	–	–	9.81	9.52
Data entry keyers	9.03	8.92	8.59	12.34
Teachers' aides	9.16	8.18	10.80	11.99
Administrative support, n.e.c.	11.53	10.76	13.88	15.24
BLUE COLLAR	12.77	13.19	16.35	15.19
Precision production, craft, and repair	15.52	15.99	20.41	18.72
Supervisors, mechanics and repairers	–	20.25	22.22	24.55
Automobile mechanics	–	–	18.54	22.22
Bus, truck, and stationary engine mechanics	–	16.03	15.65	19.22
Heavy equipment mechanics	–	–	20.32	–
Industrial machinery repairers	16.97	17.85	20.28	20.91
Machinery maintenance	–	14.66	–	–
Electronic repairers, communications and industrial equipment	16.00	–	–	17.53
Millwrights	–	–	22.77	–
Mechanics and repairers, n.e.c.	16.99	14.81	19.86	20.01
Supervisors, construction trades, n.e.c.	15.90	–	24.95	–
Carpenters	14.83	–	21.65	–
Electricians	–	19.23	23.14	23.87
Plumbers, pipefitters and steamfitters	–	–	23.65	–
Construction trades, n.e.c.	17.53	–	15.69	19.15
Supervisors, production	18.85	14.77	20.06	22.65
Tool and die makers	–	–	22.57	–

See footnotes at end of table.

Table 20. **Mean hourly earnings[1] for selected occupations, all workers, all industries, selected areas,[2] 1998**—Continued

Occupation[3]	Columbus, OH	Denver-Boulder-Greeley, CO	Detroit-Ann Arbor-Flint, MI	San Francisco-Oakland-San Jose, CA
BLUE COLLAR—Continued				
Precision production, craft, and repair—Continued				
Tool and die maker apprentices	–	–	$15.85	–
Machinists	–	$16.99	20.38	$21.78
Precision grinders, filers, and tool sharpeners	–	–	21.75	–
Patternmakers, layout workers, and cutters	–	–	24.30	–
Electrical and electronic equipment assemblers ..	–	9.91	–	10.07
Butchers and meat cutters	–	11.24	14.66	–
Inspectors, testers, and graders	–	16.73	19.88	15.18
Stationary engineers	–	–	19.36	24.68
Machine operators, assemblers, and inspectors	$12.08	10.93	15.33	12.28
Lathe and turning machine operators	–	–	14.72	–
Punching and stamping press operators	12.56	–	16.04	–
Grinding, abrading, buffing, and polishing machine operators	–	–	11.90	–
Fabricating machine operators, n.e.c.	12.34	–	20.27	–
Printing press operators	–	16.59	–	–
Textile sewing machine operators	–	–	11.86	–
Laundering and dry cleaning machine operators ..	–	–	7.63	–
Packaging and filling machine operators	12.33	–	10.62	–
Mixing and blending machine operators	–	14.04	–	–
Miscellaneous machine operators, n.e.c.	12.93	10.31	12.35	12.17
Welders and cutters	12.58	12.72	16.13	–
Assemblers	10.66	8.83	16.48	11.53
Production inspectors, checkers and examiners ..	10.74	11.73	15.18	11.20
Transportation and material moving	13.45	13.99	15.36	15.79
Truck drivers	11.76	15.09	14.44	15.63
Bus drivers	14.72	11.90	12.17	14.94
Motor transportation, n.e.c.	–	6.35	–	–
Crane and tower operators	–	–	15.28	–
Industrial truck and tractor equipment operators ..	12.63	11.88	15.56	15.56
Miscellaneous material moving equipment operators, n.e.c.	–	14.79	–	–
Handlers, equipment cleaners, helpers, and laborers	10.11	10.38	10.57	10.85
Groundskeepers and gardeners except farm	–	12.45	12.90	15.74
Construction laborers	13.19	10.91	–	–
Production helpers	11.40	9.37	–	–
Stock handlers and baggers	9.46	8.94	9.32	9.27
Freight, stock, and material handlers, n.e.c.	11.40	12.59	11.19	13.07
Vehicle washers and equipment cleaners	–	9.39	10.30	6.64
Hand packers and packagers	–	9.21	9.70	7.83
Laborers except construction, n.e.c.	9.31	9.58	12.68	14.30
SERVICE	9.79	10.10	9.81	12.66
Protective service	14.47	19.81	13.27	16.96
Supervisors, guards	–	–	–	14.70
Firefighting	–	–	15.96	22.49
Police and detectives, public service	–	22.33	19.01	27.92
Sheriffs, bailiffs, and other law enforcement officers	–	–	–	21.99
Correctional institution officers	–	–	15.65	20.58
Crossing guards	–	–	6.85	–
Guards and police except public service	7.39	12.82	7.28	8.85
Protective service, n.e.c.	–	–	14.87	–
Food service	5.84	7.03	6.84	8.73
Supervisors, food preparation and service	–	15.26	–	11.94
Bartenders	5.24	5.07	7.57	–
Waiters and waitresses	2.61	3.59	4.00	6.39

See footnotes at end of table.

Table 20. **Mean hourly earnings[1] for selected occupations, all workers, all industries, selected areas,[2] 1998**—Continued

Occupation[3]	Columbus, OH	Denver-Boulder-Greeley, CO	Detroit-Ann Arbor-Flint, MI	San Francisco-Oakland-San Jose, CA
SERVICE–Continued				
Food service–Continued				
Cooks	$8.52	$8.30	$9.00	$13.72
Food counter, fountain, and related	–	–	5.72	–
Kitchen workers, food preparation	8.81	8.94	–	8.55
Waiters'/Waitresses' assistants	5.19	3.76	–	8.32
Food preparation, n.e.c.	7.47	6.40	6.36	7.57
Health service	8.46	9.19	8.71	11.69
Health aides, except nursing	9.21	9.34	10.48	14.08
Nursing aides, orderlies and attendants	8.37	8.96	8.28	10.84
Cleaning and building service	9.51	8.80	11.27	11.38
Supervisors, cleaning & building service workers	–	11.99	11.81	23.86
Maids and housemen	–	6.78	6.91	9.61
Janitors and cleaners	9.62	8.79	11.82	11.22
Personal service	8.47	9.29	8.20	12.58
Attendants, amusement and recreation facilities ..	–	–	–	8.70
Baggage porters and bellhops	–	–	–	8.03
Welfare service aides	–	–	–	6.52
Early childhood teachers' assistants	–	6.68	7.47	9.71
Child care workers, n.e.c.	9.78	7.09	9.34	12.96
Service, n.e.c.	7.18	8.57	8.51	10.54

[1] Earnings are the straight-time hourly wages or salaries paid to employees. They include incentive pay, cost-of-living adjustments, hazard pay, deferred income payments, and deadhead pay. Excluded are shift differentials, premium pay for overtime, vacations, and holidays, non-production bonuses, uniform and tool allowances, room and board, third party payments, on-call pay, and tips. The mean is computed by totaling the pay of all workers weighted by hours and dividing by the number of workers.
[2] The average payroll month for Columbus, OH, was March 1998; Denver-Boulder-Greeley, CO, was May 1998;

Detroit-Ann Arbor-Flint, MI, was March 1998, and San Francisco-Oakland-San Jose, CA, was June 1998.
[3] A classification system including about 480 individual occupations is used to cover all workers in the civilian economy. Individual occupations are classified into one of nine major occupational groups.

NOTE: Dashes indicate that no data were reported or that data did not meet publication criteria. Overall occupational groups may include data for categories not shown separately. n.e.c. means "not elsewhere classified."

Table 21. **Average weekly pay,[1] executive, administrative, and professional specialty occupations, United States, June 1996**

Occupation and level [2]	All industries[3]	Industry		Region[4]			
		Private	State and local government	Northeast	South	Midwest	West
Accountants							
1	$523	$520	$535	$539	$504	$510	$573
2	626	627	621	639	600	624	659
3	811	819	774	815	792	794	848
4	1,041	1,055	968	1,067	1,027	1,024	1,053
5	1,375	1,396	1,183	1,418	1,374	1,362	1,349
6	1,734	1,763	-	1,679	1,764	1,819	1,624
Engineers							
1	675	677	658	671	649	691	702
2	805	808	785	794	793	808	826
3	959	960	957	960	940	952	995
4	1,167	1,173	1,107	1,161	1,162	1,160	1,183
5	1,411	1,420	1,276	1,387	1,408	1,410	1,434
6	1,659	1,676	1,367	1,635	1,686	1,609	1,676
7	1,962	1,970	-	1,963	1,873	1,967	2,020
8	2,343	2,346	-	2,253	-	-	2,303
Personnel specialists							
1	515	540	530	535	497	510	588
2	611	608	630	631	592	611	631
3	804	801	819	815	775	794	845
4	1,045	1,052	1,003	1,071	1,015	1,039	1,072
5	1,362	1,378	1,183	1,384	1,299	1,382	1,389
6	1,784	1,787	-	-	-	1,822	-
Systems Analysts							
1	779	784	755	773	732	799	806
2	940	945	921	954	906	948	962
3	1,111	1,120	1,026	1,115	1,080	1,119	1,143
4	1,321	1,325	-	1,329	1,303	1,325	1,340
5	1,527	1,527	-	-	-	-	-

[1] Excludes premium pay for overtime and for work on weekends, holidays, and late shifts. Also excluded are performance bonuses and lump-sum payments of the type in the automobile manufacturing and aerospace industries, as well as profit-sharing payments, attendance bonuses, Christmas or yearend bonuses, and other nonproduction bonuses. Pay increases, but not bonuses, under cost-of-living clauses, and incentive payments, however, are included.

[2] See *Occupational Compensation Survey, National Summary, 1996* (Bureau of Labor Statistics, Bulletin 2497, March 1998), for occupational definitions and survey methods. These bulletins are available from the bookstores of the U.S. Government Printing Office and the Bureau of Labor Statistics, Publication Sales Center, P.O. Box 2145, Chicago, IL 60690-2145.

[3] All industries estimates may include data for industries not shown separately.

[4] The regions are defined as follows: **Northeast**—Connecticut, Maine, Massachusetts, New Hampshire, New Jersey, New York, Pennsylvania, Rhode Island, and Vermont; **South**—Alabama, Arkansas, Delaware, District of Columbia, Florida, Georgia, Kentucky, Louisiana, Maryland, Mississippi, North Carolina, Oklahoma, South Carolina, Tennessee, Texas, Virginia, and West Virginia; **Midwest**—Illinois, Indiana, Iowa, Kansas, Michigan, Minnesota, Missouri, Nebraska, North Dakota, Ohio, South Dakota, and Wisconsin; **West**—Arizona, California, Colorado, Idaho, Montana, Nevada, New Mexico, Oregon, Utah, Washington, and Wyoming.

NOTE: Dashes indicate that no data were reported or that data did not meet publication criteria.

Table 22. **Average weekly pay,[1] technical and administrative support occupations, United States, June 1996**

Occupation and level [2]	All industries[3]	Industry		Region[4]			
		Private	State and local government	Northeast	South	Midwest	West
Computer programmers							
1	$543	$548	$509	$549	$553	$534	$525
2	639	644	608	657	626	637	656
3	788	793	760	832	769	770	812
4	945	945	940	939	944	918	1,000
5	1,095	1,096	-	-	-	-	-
Secretaries							
1	385	395	371	416	371	399	389
2	476	487	459	500	440	471	529
3	557	564	536	584	522	555	580
4	665	674	631	691	621	643	680
5	809	815	751	825	754	821	812

[1] Excludes premium pay for overtime and for work on weekends, holidays, and late shifts. Also excluded are performance bonuses and lump-sum payments of the type in the automobile manufacturing and aerospace industries, as well as profit-sharing payments, attendance bonuses, Christmas or yearend bonuses, and other nonproduction bonuses. Pay increases, but not bonuses, under cost-of-living clauses, and incentive payments, however, are included.
[2] See *Occupational Compensation Survey, National Summary, 1996* (Bureau of Labor Statistics, Bulletin 2497, March 1998), for occupational definitions and survey methods. These bulletins are available from the bookstores of the U.S. Government Printing Office and the Bureau of Labor Statistics, Publication Sales Center, P.O. Box 2145, Chicago, IL 60690-2145.
[3] All industries estimates may include data for industries not shown separately.
[4] The regions are defined as follows: **Northeast**—Connecticut, Maine, Massachusetts, New Hampshire, New Jersey, New York, Pennsylvania, Rhode Island, and Vermont; **South**—Alabama, Arkansas, Delaware, District of Columbia, Florida, Georgia, Kentucky, Louisiana, Maryland, Mississippi, North Carolina, Oklahoma, South Carolina, Tennessee, Texas, Virginia, and West Virginia; **Midwest**—Illinois, Indiana, Iowa, Kansas, Michigan, Minnesota, Missouri, Nebraska, North Dakota, Ohio, South Dakota, and Wisconsin; **West**—Arizona, California, Colorado, Idaho, Montana, Nevada, New Mexico, Oregon, Utah, Washington, and Wyoming.

NOTE: Dashes indicate that no data were reported or that data did not meet publication criteria.

Table 23. **Average hourly pay,[1] service, maintenance, transportation, and material movement occupations, United States, June 1996**

Occupation and level [2]	All industries[3]	Industry		Region[4]			
		Private	State and local government	Northeast	South	Midwest	West
Guards							
1	$7.11	$6.99	$10.02	$7.79	$6.78	$6.99	$6.99
2	12.14	12.04	12.67	13.73	11.67	11.54	12.44
Janitors	7.97	7.30	9.65	9.88	6.43	8.25	8.03
Maintenance electricians	18.74	18.79	18.44	19.01	16.63	19.84	19.36
Maintenance motor vehicle mechanics	15.91	16.07	15.60	16.61	14.14	16.26	17.72
Material handling laborers	8.85	8.85	8.65	10.22	7.52	10.81	7.67
Truckdrivers							
Light truck	8.53	8.44	9.89	10.66	7.92	8.82	7.86
Medium truck	14.81	14.93	12.15	15.75	13.36	15.72	14.77
Heavy truck	13.38	13.29	13.94	15.36	10.78	13.55	14.30
Tractor trailor	14.24	14.22	16.84	15.54	12.28	15.07	15.16

[1] Excludes premium pay for overtime and for work on weekends, holidays, and late shifts. Also excluded are performance bonuses and lump-sum payments of the type in the automobile manufacturing and aerospace industries, as well as profit-sharing payments, attendance bonuses, Christmas or yearend bonuses, and other nonproduction bonuses. Pay increases, but not bonuses, under cost-of-living clauses, and incentive payments, however, are included.

[2] See *Occupational Compensation Survey, National Summary, 1996* (Bureau of Labor Statistics, Bulletin 2497, March 1998), for occupational definitions and survey methods. These bulletins are available from the bookstores of the U.S. Government Printing Office and the Bureau of Labor Statistics, Publication Sales Center, P.O. Box 2145, Chicago, IL 60690-2145.

[3] All industries estimates may include data for industries not shown separately.

[4] The regions are defined as follows: **Northeast**—Connecticut, Maine, Massachusetts, New Hampshire, New Jersey, New York, Pennsylvania, Rhode Island, and Vermont; **South**—Alabama, Arkansas, Delaware, District of Columbia, Florida, Georgia, Kentucky, Louisiana, Maryland, Mississippi, North Carolina, Oklahoma, South Carolina, Tennessee, Texas, Virginia, and West Virginia; **Midwest**—Illinois, Indiana, Iowa, Kansas, Michigan, Minnesota, Missouri, Nebraska, North Dakota, Ohio, South Dakota, and Wisconsin; **West**—Arizona, California, Colorado, Idaho, Montana, Nevada, New Mexico, Oregon, Utah, Washington, and Wyoming.

NOTE: Dashes indicate that no data were reported or that data did not meet publication criteria.

Table 24. **Average hourly earnings of production workers on private nonfarm payrolls by major industry division, annual averages, 1947-98**

(In current dollars)

Year	Total private	Mining	Construc- tion	Manu- facturing	Trans- porta- tion and public utilities	Wholesale trade	Retail trade	Finance, insur- ance and real estate	Servces
1947	$1.13	$1.46	$1.54	$1.21	–	$1.21	$0.83	$1.14	–
1948	1.22	1.66	1.71	1.32	–	1.30	.90	1.20	–
1949	1.27	1.71	1.79	1.37	–	1.35	.95	1.26	–
1950	1.33	1.77	1.86	1.43	–	1.35	.98	1.26	–
1951	1.45	1.93	2.02	1.56	–	1.52	1.06	1.45	–
1952	1.52	2.01	2.13	1.64	–	1.61	1.09	1.51	–
1953	1.61	2.14	2.28	1.74	–	1.69	1.16	1.58	–
1954	1.65	2.14	2.38	1.78	–	1.76	1.20	1.65	–
1955	1.71	2.20	2.45	1.85	–	1.83	1.25	1.70	–
1956	1.80	2.33	2.57	1.95	–	1.93	1.30	1.78	–
1957	1.89	2.45	2.71	2.04	–	2.02	1.37	1.84	–
1958	1.95	2.47	2.82	2.10	–	2.09	1.42	1.89	–
1959	2.02	2.56	2.93	2.19	–	2.18	1.47	1.95	–
1960	2.09	2.60	3.07	2.26	–	2.24	1.52	2.02	–
1961	2.14	2.64	3.20	2.32	–	2.31	1.56	2.09	–
1962	2.22	2.70	3.31	2.39	–	2.37	1.63	2.17	–
1963	2.28	2.75	3.41	2.45	–	2.45	1.68	2.25	–
1964	2.36	2.81	3.55	2.53	$2.89	2.52	1.75	2.30	$1.94
1965	2.46	2.92	3.70	2.61	3.03	2.60	1.82	2.39	2.05
1966	2.56	3.05	3.89	2.71	3.11	2.73	1.91	2.47	2.17
1967	2.68	3.19	4.11	2.82	3.23	2.87	2.01	2.58	2.29
1968	2.85	3.35	4.41	3.01	3.42	3.04	2.16	2.75	2.42
1969	3.04	3.60	4.79	3.19	3.63	3.23	2.30	2.93	2.61
1970	3.23	3.85	5.24	3.35	3.85	3.43	2.44	3.07	2.81
1971	3.45	4.06	5.69	3.57	4.21	3.64	2.60	3.22	3.04
1972	3.70	4.44	6.06	3.82	4.65	3.85	2.75	3.36	3.27
1973	3.94	4.75	6.41	4.09	5.02	4.07	2.91	3.53	3.47
1974	4.24	5.23	6.81	4.42	5.41	4.38	3.14	3.77	3.75
1975	4.53	5.95	7.31	4.83	5.88	4.72	3.36	4.06	4.02
1976	4.86	6.46	7.71	5.22	6.45	5.02	3.57	4.27	4.31
1977	5.25	6.94	8.10	5.68	6.99	5.39	3.85	4.54	4.65
1978	5.69	7.67	8.66	6.17	7.57	5.88	4.20	4.89	4.99
1979	6.16	8.49	9.27	6.70	8.16	6.39	4.53	5.27	5.36
1980	6.66	9.17	9.94	7.27	8.87	6.95	4.88	5.79	5.85
1981	7.25	10.04	10.82	7.99	9.70	7.55	5.25	6.31	6.41
1982	7.68	10.77	11.63	8.49	10.32	8.08	5.48	6.78	6.92
1983	8.02	11.28	11.94	8.83	10.79	8.54	5.74	7.29	7.31
1984	8.32	11.63	12.13	9.19	11.12	8.88	5.85	7.63	7.59
1985	8.57	11.98	12.32	9.54	11.40	9.15	5.94	7.94	7.90
1986	8.76	12.46	12.48	9.73	11.70	9.34	6.03	8.36	8.18
1987	8.98	12.54	12.71	9.91	12.03	9.59	6.12	8.73	8.49
1988	9.28	12.80	13.08	10.19	12.24	9.98	6.31	9.06	8.88
1989	9.66	13.26	13.54	10.48	12.57	10.39	6.53	9.53	9.38
1990	10.01	13.68	13.77	10.83	12.92	10.79	6.75	9.97	9.83
1991	10.32	14.19	14.00	11.18	13.20	11.15	6.94	10.39	10.23
1992	10.57	14.54	14.15	11.46	13.43	11.39	7.12	10.82	10.54
1993	10.83	14.60	14.38	11.74	13.55	11.74	7.29	11.35	10.78
1994	11.12	14.88	14.73	12.07	13.78	12.06	7.49	11.83	11.04
1995	11.43	15.30	15.09	12.37	14.13	12.43	7.69	12.32	11.39
1996	11.82	15.62	15.47	12.77	14.45	12.87	7.99	12.80	11.79
1997	12.28	16.15	16.04	13.17	14.92	13.45	8.33	13.34	12.28
1998	12.78	16.90	16.59	13.49	15.31	14.06	8.73	14.06	12.85

Dash indicates data not available.

NOTE: Current estimates are projected from March 1998 benchmark levels.

Table 25. **Productivity and related data, business and nonfarm business sectors, 1947-98**
(Index, 1992=100)

Year	Output per hour of all persons		Output[1]		Hours of all persons[2]		Compensation per hour[3]		Real compensation per hour[4]		Unit labor costs		Implicit price deflator[5]	
	Business sector	Nonfarm business sector	Business sector	Nonfarm business sector	Business sector	Nonfarm business sector	Business sector	Nonfarm business sector	Business sector	Nonfarm business sector	Business sector	Nonfarm business sector	Business sector	Nonfarm business sector
1947..	33.7	39.0	21.9	21.5	65.0	55.3	6.8	7.3	42.8	45.9	20.2	18.7	19.6	18.3
1948..	35.2	39.9	23.1	22.5	65.5	56.2	7.4	7.9	43.0	46.1	21.0	19.8	20.8	19.6
1949..	36.0	41.3	22.8	22.3	63.4	54.0	7.5	8.2	44.2	48.1	20.8	19.8	20.6	19.7
1950..	39.1	44.2	25.1	24.6	64.1	55.6	8.0	8.7	46.8	50.5	20.6	19.6	20.8	20.0
1951..	40.3	45.3	26.7	26.4	66.2	58.3	8.8	9.4	47.5	50.8	21.9	20.8	22.4	21.3
1952..	41.4	46.1	27.5	27.2	66.3	58.9	9.4	9.9	49.6	52.7	22.6	21.6	22.7	21.7
1953..	43.0	47.2	28.8	28.4	67.0	60.3	10.0	10.5	52.4	55.3	23.2	22.3	22.9	22.1
1954..	43.9	48.1	28.4	28.0	64.7	58.2	10.3	10.9	53.8	56.7	23.5	22.6	23.1	22.4
1955..	45.8	50.1	30.7	30.3	67.1	60.5	10.6	11.3	55.4	59.0	23.1	22.5	23.4	22.8
1956..	45.8	49.7	31.2	30.8	68.1	62.0	11.3	12.0	58.2	61.7	24.6	24.1	24.1	23.6
1957..	47.2	50.9	31.7	31.4	67.1	61.6	12.0	12.7	60.0	63.2	25.5	24.9	24.9	24.4
1958..	48.5	52.0	31.0	30.7	64.0	59.0	12.6	13.2	61.0	63.9	25.9	25.3	25.4	24.8
1959..	50.5	54.2	33.7	33.5	66.7	61.7	13.1	13.7	63.1	66.0	25.9	25.3	25.6	25.0
1960..	51.4	54.8	34.3	34.0	66.7	62.0	13.7	14.3	64.7	67.8	26.6	26.1	25.8	25.3
1961..	53.2	56.6	34.9	34.7	65.6	61.3	14.2	14.8	66.6	69.4	26.7	26.1	26.1	25.6
1962..	55.7	59.2	37.2	37.0	66.8	62.6	14.8	15.4	68.9	71.5	26.6	26.0	26.3	25.8
1963..	57.9	61.2	38.9	38.7	67.2	63.3	15.4	15.9	70.6	73.0	26.6	26.0	26.5	26.0
1964..	60.6	63.8	41.4	41.3	68.3	64.8	16.2	16.7	73.3	75.4	26.7	26.1	26.8	26.3
1965..	62.7	65.8	44.2	44.2	70.6	67.3	16.8	17.2	74.8	76.7	26.8	26.2	27.2	26.7
1966..	65.2	68.0	47.2	47.4	72.5	69.7	17.9	18.2	77.6	78.9	27.5	26.8	27.9	27.3
1967..	66.6	69.2	48.1	48.2	72.3	69.7	18.9	19.3	79.5	81.0	28.4	27.8	28.7	28.2
1968..	68.8	71.6	50.5	50.7	73.3	70.9	20.5	20.8	82.5	83.8	29.7	29.0	29.8	29.3
1969..	69.2	71.7	52.0	52.3	75.2	72.9	21.9	22.2	83.8	84.9	31.7	31.0	31.1	30.5
1970..	70.6	72.7	52.0	52.1	73.6	71.8	23.6	23.8	85.4	86.1	33.5	32.8	32.4	31.9
1971..	73.6	75.7	54.0	54.1	73.3	71.5	25.1	25.4	87.1	87.9	34.2	33.5	33.9	33.3
1972..	76.0	78.3	57.6	57.8	75.7	73.9	26.7	27.0	89.6	90.6	35.1	34.5	35.0	34.3
1973..	78.4	80.7	61.6	62.0	78.5	76.9	29.0	29.2	91.6	92.3	37.0	36.2	36.8	35.5
1974..	77.1	79.4	60.6	61.1	78.6	76.9	31.8	32.1	90.6	91.3	41.3	40.4	40.3	39.1
1975..	79.8	81.6	60.0	60.0	75.2	73.6	35.1	35.3	91.5	92.2	44.0	43.3	44.2	43.2
1976..	82.5	84.5	64.0	64.3	77.5	76.1	38.2	38.4	94.1	94.7	46.2	45.4	46.5	45.6
1977..	84.0	85.8	67.6	67.9	80.6	79.1	41.2	41.5	95.3	96.0	49.0	48.3	49.4	48.6
1978..	84.9	87.0	71.7	72.3	84.5	83.1	44.9	45.2	96.5	97.3	52.8	52.0	53.0	51.9
1979..	84.5	86.3	73.9	74.3	87.4	86.1	49.2	49.5	95.0	95.7	58.2	57.4	57.6	56.4
1980..	84.2	86.0	73.0	73.4	86.6	85.4	54.5	54.8	92.8	93.4	64.7	63.8	62.8	61.9
1981..	85.8	87.0	74.8	74.8	87.2	86.0	59.6	60.2	92.1	92.8	69.6	69.2	68.7	67.9
1982..	85.3	86.3	72.5	72.4	85.0	83.9	64.1	64.6	93.2	93.9	75.1	74.8	72.7	72.2
1983..	88.0	89.9	76.1	76.8	86.4	85.4	66.8	67.3	94.0	94.8	75.8	74.9	75.4	74.7
1984..	90.2	91.4	82.5	82.8	91.5	90.6	69.7	70.2	94.1	94.8	77.2	76.8	77.7	77.0
1985..	91.7	92.3	85.7	85.8	93.5	92.9	73.1	73.4	95.3	95.7	79.7	79.5	80.0	79.6
1986..	94.1	94.7	88.5	88.7	94.1	93.6	76.8	77.2	98.4	98.8	81.7	81.5	81.7	81.4
1987..	94.0	94.5	91.1	91.3	96.9	96.6	79.8	80.1	98.6	98.9	84.9	84.7	83.8	83.6
1988..	94.7	95.3	94.6	95.1	99.9	99.8	83.6	83.7	99.1	99.3	88.3	87.8	86.8	86.4
1989..	95.5	95.8	97.8	98.1	102.4	102.4	85.9	86.0	97.2	97.3	90.0	89.7	90.4	90.0
1990..	96.1	96.3	98.6	98.8	102.6	102.6	90.8	90.7	97.4	97.3	94.4	94.2	94.1	93.8
1991..	96.7	97.0	96.9	97.1	100.2	100.1	95.1	95.1	98.0	98.0	98.3	98.1	97.7	97.6
1992..	100.0	100.0	100.0	100.0	100.0	100.0	100.0	100.0	100.0	100.0	100.0	100.0	100.0	100.0
1993..	100.1	100.1	102.7	103.0	102.6	102.9	102.5	102.2	99.5	99.3	102.4	102.2	102.5	102.5
1994..	100.7	100.6	107.0	107.0	106.2	106.3	104.4	104.2	98.8	98.7	103.7	103.6	104.8	104.9
1995..	101.0	101.2	109.9	110.2	108.8	108.9	106.8	106.7	98.4	98.2	105.8	105.4	106.9	107.0
1996..	103.7	103.7	114.5	114.8	110.4	110.7	110.7	110.4	99.0	98.7	106.8	106.5	108.6	108.5
1997..	105.2	104.9	119.8	119.9	113.8	114.3	114.7	114.3	100.3	99.9	109.0	108.9	110.4	110.6
1998..	107.7	107.2	125.3	125.5	116.3	117.0	119.7	119.1	103.0	102.5	111.1	111.1	111.0	111.4

[1]Output is an annual-weighted index of real gross domestic product of the sector.
[2]Hours at work of all persons engaged in the sector, including hours of proprietors and unpaid family workers. Estimates based primarily on establishment data.
[3]Wages and salaries of employees plus employers' contributions for social insurance and private benefit plans. Also includes an estimate of wages, salaries, and supplemental payments for the self-employed.
[4]Hourly compensation divided by the Consumer Price Index for All Urban Consumers.
[5]Current dollar gross domestic product divided by the index of real gross domestic product.

165

Table 26. **Changes in productivity and related data, business and nonfarm business sectors, 1948-98**

(Percent change from previous year)

Year	Output per hour of all persons		Output[1]		Hours of all persons[2]		Compensation per hour[3]		Real compensation per hour[4]		Unit labor cost		Implicit price deflator[5]	
	Business sector	Non-farm business sector	Business sector	Non-farm business sector	Business sector	Non-farm business sector	Business sector	Non-farm business sector	Business sector	Non-farm business sector	Business sector	Non-farm business sector	Business sector	Non-farm business sector
1948..	4.4	2.5	5.3	4.2	0.8	1.7	8.5	8.6	0.4	0.5	3.9	6.0	6.2	6.9
1949..	2.1	3.4	-1.2	-0.7	-3.3	-4.0	1.5	3.0	2.8	4.3	-0.6	-0.3	-0.7	0.8
1950..	8.7	7.0	10.0	10.3	1.2	3.1	7.3	6.2	6.0	4.8	-1.3	-0.8	1.0	1.1
1951..	3.1	2.4	6.4	7.3	3.2	4.8	9.6	8.7	1.6	0.7	6.3	6.1	7.6	6.6
1952..	2.8	1.9	3.0	2.9	0.1	1.0	6.3	5.6	4.3	3.6	3.3	3.7	1.2	2.0
1953..	3.7	2.3	4.9	4.8	1.1	2.4	6.6	5.7	5.8	4.9	2.7	3.3	0.8	2.1
1954..	2.2	2.0	-1.3	-1.6	-3.5	-3.5	3.3	3.3	2.6	2.6	1.1	1.3	0.7	1.1
1955..	4.2	4.1	8.0	8.3	3.7	4.0	2.6	3.8	3.0	4.1	-1.5	-0.4	1.2	1.8
1956..	0.1	-0.8	1.6	1.7	1.5	2.5	6.6	6.1	5.1	4.5	6.6	6.9	3.3	3.6
1957..	3.0	2.4	1.5	1.8	-1.4	-0.6	6.5	5.8	3.1	2.4	3.4	3.3	3.2	3.2
1958..	2.8	2.2	-1.9	-2.2	-4.6	-4.3	4.5	4.0	1.7	1.2	1.7	1.8	2.0	1.7
1959..	4.2	4.2	8.5	9.0	4.1	4.6	4.2	4.0	3.5	3.2	0.0	-0.2	0.6	1.1
1960..	1.7	1.2	1.8	1.6	0.1	0.5	4.3	4.4	2.6	2.7	2.5	3.2	1.1	1.1
1961..	3.5	3.1	1.9	1.9	-1.6	-1.2	4.0	3.4	2.9	2.4	0.4	0.3	0.9	0.9
1962..	4.7	4.6	6.5	6.9	1.7	2.1	4.5	4.1	3.5	3.0	-0.2	-0.5	0.9	0.8
1963..	3.9	3.4	4.5	4.5	0.6	1.1	3.7	3.5	2.3	2.2	-0.2	0.1	0.7	0.8
1964..	4.6	4.3	6.4	6.8	1.7	2.4	5.2	4.6	3.8	3.3	0.5	0.3	1.0	1.2
1965..	3.5	3.0	7.0	7.0	3.4	3.9	3.7	3.3	2.1	1.7	0.2	0.3	1.7	1.5
1966..	4.0	3.5	6.7	7.1	2.6	3.6	6.7	5.8	3.7	2.8	2.6	2.3	2.5	2.3
1967..	2.2	1.7	1.9	1.7	-0.3	0.0	5.7	5.8	2.5	2.7	3.4	4.0	2.9	3.3
1968..	3.4	3.4	4.9	5.2	1.4	1.7	8.2	7.9	3.8	3.5	4.6	4.3	3.9	3.9
1969..	0.4	0.1	3.0	3.0	2.5	2.9	7.0	6.8	1.5	1.3	6.6	6.7	4.3	4.2
1970..	2.0	1.4	-0.1	-0.2	-2.0	-1.6	7.8	7.2	1.9	1.4	5.7	5.7	4.4	4.5
1971..	4.3	4.1	3.8	3.8	-0.4	-0.3	6.4	6.5	1.9	2.0	2.0	2.3	4.5	4.5
1972..	3.3	3.4	6.7	6.9	3.3	3.4	6.3	6.4	3.0	3.1	2.9	2.9	3.3	2.9
1973..	3.2	3.1	7.0	7.3	3.7	4.0	8.6	8.2	2.2	1.9	5.2	4.9	5.2	3.6
1974..	-1.7	-1.6	-1.5	-1.5	0.1	0.1	9.7	9.9	-1.2	-1.1	11.6	11.6	9.4	10.0
1975..	3.5	2.7	-1.0	-1.7	-4.3	-4.3	10.3	10.1	1.0	0.9	6.6	7.2	9.5	10.6
1976..	3.4	3.6	6.7	7.1	3.1	3.4	8.8	8.6	2.9	2.7	5.2	4.9	5.4	5.6
1977..	1.7	1.6	5.7	5.7	3.9	4.0	7.9	8.0	1.3	1.4	6.0	6.3	6.1	6.4
1978..	1.1	1.3	6.1	6.4	4.9	5.0	8.9	9.1	1.3	1.4	7.7	7.6	7.3	6.9
1979..	-0.4	-0.8	2.9	2.8	3.4	3.6	9.7	9.5	-1.5	-1.7	10.1	10.3	8.6	8.6
1980..	-0.3	-0.4	-1.2	-1.2	-0.9	-0.8	10.8	10.8	-2.4	-2.4	11.1	11.2	9.1	9.8
1981..	1.8	1.1	2.5	1.9	0.7	0.7	9.5	9.7	-0.8	-0.6	7.6	8.5	9.3	9.6
1982..	-0.5	-0.8	-3.1	-3.2	-2.5	-2.5	7.5	7.4	1.2	1.1	8.0	8.2	5.9	6.4
1983..	3.2	4.2	4.9	6.1	1.7	1.9	4.2	4.2	0.9	1.0	0.9	0.1	3.7	3.4
1984..	2.5	1.7	8.5	7.9	5.8	6.0	4.4	4.2	0.0	-0.1	1.8	2.5	3.0	3.1
1985..	1.6	1.0	3.9	3.6	2.2	2.5	4.9	4.6	1.3	1.0	3.2	3.6	3.0	3.4
1986..	2.6	2.6	3.3	3.4	0.7	0.8	5.2	5.2	3.3	3.2	2.5	2.5	2.1	2.2
1987..	-0.1	-0.2	2.9	3.0	3.0	3.2	3.9	3.8	0.2	0.1	3.9	4.0	2.6	2.6
1988..	0.7	0.8	3.8	4.1	3.1	3.3	4.7	4.5	0.6	0.4	4.0	3.7	3.5	3.4
1989..	0.8	0.6	3.4	3.2	2.5	2.6	2.8	2.7	-1.9	-2.0	1.9	2.1	4.2	4.2
1990..	0.7	0.5	0.8	0.7	0.2	0.3	5.7	5.5	0.3	0.1	5.0	5.0	4.0	4.2
1991..	0.6	0.7	-1.7	-1.8	-2.3	-2.4	4.8	4.9	0.5	0.7	4.1	4.2	3.8	4.1
1992..	3.4	3.1	3.2	3.0	-0.2	-0.1	5.2	5.1	2.1	2.1	1.7	1.9	2.4	2.4
1993..	0.1	0.1	2.7	3.0	2.6	2.9	2.5	2.2	-0.5	-0.7	2.4	2.2	2.5	2.5
1994..	0.6	0.5	4.1	3.9	3.5	3.3	1.8	1.9	-0.7	-0.6	1.2	1.4	2.2	2.3
1995..	0.3	0.6	2.7	3.0	2.4	2.4	2.3	2.4	-0.5	-0.5	2.0	1.8	2.0	2.0
1996..	2.7	2.4	4.2	4.1	1.5	1.6	3.6	3.5	0.7	0.6	0.9	1.1	1.6	1.4
1997..	1.5	1.2	4.6	4.5	3.1	3.2	3.6	3.5	1.2	1.2	2.1	2.3	1.7	1.9
1998..	2.4	2.2	4.6	4.6	2.2	2.4	4.4	4.2	2.8	2.6	2.0	2.0	0.6	0.7

[1]Output is an annual-weighted index of real gross domestic product of the sector.
[2]Hours at work of all persons engaged in the sector, including hours of proprietors and unpaid family workers. Estimates based primarily on establishment data.
[3]Wages and salaries of employees plus employers' contributions for social insurance and private benefit plans. Also includes an estimate of wages, salaries, and supplemental payments for the self-employed.
[4]Hourly compensation divided by the Consumer Price Index for All Urban Consumers.
[5]Current dollar gross domestic product divided by the index of real gross domestic product.

NOTE: Percent changes are based on original data and therefore may differ slightly from percent changes based on indexes.

Table 27. Private business sector: Productivity and related measures, 1948-97[1]

(Indexes 1992=100)

Year	Productivity			Output[3]	Inputs			Capital per hour of all persons
	Output per hour of all persons	Output per unit of capital	Multifactor productivity[2]		Labor input[4]	Capital services[5]	Combined units of labor and capital inputs[6]	
1948	34.7	114.6	55.9	23.0	57.3	20.1	41.1	30.3
1949	35.9	111.6	56.6	23.0	55.4	20.6	40.6	32.2
1950	39.0	117.7	60.6	25.3	56.5	21.5	41.7	33.2
1955	45.6	121.6	67.1	30.8	60.2	25.3	45.9	37.5
1956	45.8	119.6	66.8	31.4	61.2	26.2	47.0	38.2
1957	47.2	118.1	67.8	31.9	60.5	27.0	47.0	40.0
1958	48.6	113.5	68.1	31.2	57.9	27.5	45.9	42.8
1959	50.0	118.7	70.3	33.4	60.3	28.2	47.5	42.1
1960	50.8	117.3	70.7	34.0	60.6	29.0	48.1	43.3
1961	52.7	116.9	72.1	34.7	60.0	29.7	48.1	45.0
1962	55.2	121.0	74.7	36.9	61.6	30.5	49.4	45.6
1963	57.3	122.3	76.8	38.6	62.1	31.6	50.2	46.9
1964	60.0	125.4	79.8	41.1	63.1	32.7	51.4	47.8
1965	62.1	128.1	82.3	43.9	65.2	34.3	53.4	48.5
1966	64.6	129.5	84.8	46.9	66.9	36.2	55.3	49.9
1967	66.0	124.7	85.0	47.8	66.8	38.3	56.2	53.0
1968	68.4	124.9	87.2	50.2	67.6	40.2	57.6	54.7
1969	68.7	122.6	86.7	51.7	69.5	42.2	59.6	56.0
1970	70.1	117.1	86.5	51.6	68.3	44.1	59.7	59.9
1971	73.1	116.7	89.2	53.6	67.8	45.9	60.1	62.7
1972	75.6	119.4	91.9	57.3	70.1	47.9	62.3	63.3
1973	78.0	121.2	94.5	61.3	72.6	50.6	64.9	64.4
1974	76.7	113.4	91.1	60.3	73.1	53.2	66.2	67.7
1975	79.4	108.4	92.0	59.7	69.9	55.1	64.9	73.3
1976	82.2	112.4	95.4	63.7	71.9	56.7	66.8	73.2
1977	83.6	114.6	97.1	67.4	74.8	58.8	69.4	72.9
1978	84.5	116.5	98.3	71.5	78.6	61.3	72.7	72.5
1979	84.1	114.1	97.5	73.6	81.0	64.4	75.4	73.7
1980	83.8	107.3	95.3	72.6	80.5	67.7	76.2	78.1
1981	85.4	104.9	95.3	74.5	81.6	71.0	78.1	81.4
1982	85.1	97.8	92.4	72.2	80.3	73.9	78.2	87.0
1983	87.7	99.8	94.7	75.8	82.1	76.0	80.1	87.9
1984	90.0	103.8	97.5	82.4	87.0	79.3	84.5	86.7
1985	91.6	103.3	98.3	85.6	89.1	82.9	87.1	88.7
1986	94.0	102.5	99.5	88.4	90.1	86.3	88.9	91.7
1987	94.0	102.3	99.3	91.1	93.0	89.1	91.8	91.9
1988	94.7	103.2	99.5	94.6	96.7	91.7	95.1	91.7
1989	95.5	103.8	100.0	97.8	99.6	94.2	97.8	92.0
1990	96.1	102.1	99.6	98.6	100.2	96.5	99.0	94.1
1991	96.7	98.6	98.1	96.9	99.0	98.3	98.7	98.1
1992	100.0	100.0	100.0	100.0	100.0	100.0	100.0	100.0
1993	100.1	100.7	100.1	102.7	102.9	102.0	102.6	99.4
1994	100.6	102.3	100.6	107.0	107.1	104.6	106.3	98.3
1995	101.0	101.9	100.7	110.0	109.8	108.0	109.3	99.2
1996	103.7	102.3	102.4	114.7	112.0	112.2	112.1	101.4
1997	105.2	102.6	103.1	120.1	116.2	117.1	116.5	102.6

[1] The private business sector includes all of gross domestic product except the output of general government, government enterprises, non-profit institutions, the rental value of owner-occupied real estate and the output of paid employees of private households.
[2] Output per unit of combined labor and capital inputs.
[3] Gross domestic product originating in the sector, superlative chained index.
[4] Index of the hours at work of all persons including employees, proprietors, and unpaid family workers classified by education, work experience and gender. This superlative chain index is computed by combining changes in the hours of each education, experience and gender group weighted by its share of labor compensation.
[5] A measure of the flow of capital services used in the sector.
[6] Labor input combined with capital input, using labor's and capital's shares of costs as weights to form a superlative chain index.

Source: Output data are from the Bureau of Economic Analysis (BEA), U.S. Department of Commerce, and modified by the Bureau of Labor Statistics (BLS), U.S. Department of Labor. Compensation and hours data are from the BLS. Capital measures are based on data supplied by BEA and the U.S. Department of Agriculture.

Table 28. **Productivity and related data, nonfinancial corporate sector, 1958-98**

(Index, 1992=100, and percent change from previous year)

Year	Output per all-employee hour		Output[1]		Employee hours[2]		Compensation per hour[3]		Real compensation per hour[4]		Unit labor costs		Implicit price deflator[5]	
	Index	Change from previous year	Index	Change from previous year	Index	Change from previous year	Index	Change from previous year	Index	Change from previous year	Index	Change from previous year	Index	Change from previous year
1958...	50.9	—	25.0	—	49.2	—	14.4	—	70.1	—	28.4	—	29.2	—
1959...	53.5	5.1	27.9	11.5	52.1	6.1	15.0	3.8	72.2	3.1	28.0	-1.3	29.4	0.7
1960...	54.5	1.8	28.8	3.3	52.9	1.5	15.6	4.1	73.9	2.4	28.6	2.3	29.6	0.6
1961...	56.2	3.1	29.4	2.1	52.4	-1.0	16.1	3.3	75.6	2.3	28.7	0.2	29.7	0.5
1962...	58.6	4.3	31.9	8.4	54.4	3.9	16.7	3.9	77.8	2.9	28.6	-0.4	29.9	0.7
1963...	60.6	3.4	33.7	5.7	55.7	2.2	17.3	3.2	79.2	1.8	28.5	-0.2	30.1	0.7
1964...	63.1	4.1	36.1	7.0	57.2	2.9	18.0	4.4	81.6	3.1	28.6	0.4	30.4	0.9
1965...	64.6	2.3	39.1	8.2	60.5	5.8	18.5	2.8	82.6	1.2	28.7	0.5	30.9	1.5
1966...	65.5	1.4	41.8	7.0	63.9	5.5	19.5	5.4	84.6	2.5	29.8	3.9	31.6	2.4
1967...	66.4	1.4	42.9	2.5	64.5	1.1	20.6	5.5	86.6	2.4	31.0	4.0	32.4	2.6
1968...	68.7	3.4	45.6	6.3	66.4	2.8	22.2	7.5	89.4	3.2	32.3	4.0	33.6	3.8
1969...	68.7	0.0	47.4	4.0	69.0	4.0	23.7	6.8	90.6	1.3	34.5	6.8	35.1	4.4
1970...	69.1	0.5	47.0	-0.9	68.0	-1.5	25.4	7.1	91.7	1.3	36.7	6.5	36.6	4.3
1971...	72.0	4.2	48.9	4.0	67.9	-0.1	27.0	6.3	93.4	1.9	37.5	2.1	38.0	3.8
1972...	73.9	2.6	52.7	7.9	71.4	5.1	28.5	5.8	95.8	2.5	38.6	3.1	39.2	2.9
1973...	74.5	0.8	55.8	5.8	74.9	5.0	30.8	7.8	97.2	1.5	41.3	6.9	41.5	5.9
1974...	72.7	-2.3	54.8	-1.8	75.3	0.5	33.7	9.5	95.9	-1.4	46.3	12.1	45.6	10.0
1975...	75.6	3.9	53.9	-1.5	71.3	-5.3	37.1	10.0	96.6	0.8	49.0	5.9	50.1	9.9
1976...	78.2	3.4	58.3	8.1	74.6	4.5	40.2	8.4	99.0	2.5	51.4	4.8	52.4	4.5
1977...	80.1	2.5	62.6	7.4	78.1	4.8	43.3	7.8	100.3	1.2	54.0	5.2	55.1	5.3
1978...	80.8	0.8	66.7	6.6	82.6	5.7	47.0	8.6	101.2	1.0	58.2	7.7	59.0	7.0
1979...	79.4	-1.7	68.2	2.2	85.8	3.9	51.4	9.2	99.3	-1.9	64.7	11.1	64.3	9.0
1980...	80.4	1.1	68.3	0.3	85.1	-0.9	56.7	10.3	96.5	-2.8	70.5	9.1	69.7	8.4
1981...	82.9	3.1	71.5	4.6	86.2	1.4	61.9	9.2	95.5	-1.1	74.7	5.8	75.8	8.8
1982...	84.2	1.6	70.5	-1.4	83.7	-3.0	66.3	7.1	96.3	0.9	78.7	5.4	79.3	4.7
1983...	86.9	3.2	73.7	4.6	84.9	1.4	68.7	3.7	96.8	0.5	79.1	0.6	81.1	2.2
1984...	89.6	3.1	81.0	9.8	90.3	6.5	71.7	4.3	96.8	0.0	80.0	1.1	82.8	2.1
1985...	91.1	1.6	84.2	4.0	92.5	2.3	75.0	4.6	97.8	1.0	82.3	2.9	84.4	1.9
1986...	93.7	2.9	86.9	3.2	92.7	0.3	78.8	5.1	100.8	3.1	84.0	2.1	85.2	0.9
1987...	95.2	1.5	91.1	4.9	95.8	3.3	81.6	3.6	100.8	-0.1	85.7	2.0	87.1	2.2
1988...	96.9	1.8	95.9	5.3	99.1	3.4	84.9	4.1	100.7	-0.1	87.7	2.3	89.6	2.9
1989...	95.5	-1.4	97.5	1.6	102.0	3.0	87.1	2.5	98.5	-2.2	91.1	3.9	92.8	3.5
1990...	96.1	0.6	98.4	1.0	102.4	0.3	91.5	5.1	98.2	-0.3	95.2	4.4	96.1	3.5
1991...	97.6	1.5	97.1	-1.3	99.6	-2.7	95.7	4.5	98.5	0.3	98.0	3.0	98.8	2.9
1992...	100.0	2.5	100.0	3.0	100.0	0.5	100.0	4.5	100.0	1.5	100.0	2.0	100.0	1.2
1993...	101.1	1.1	103.4	3.4	102.3	2.3	102.0	2.0	99.1	-0.9	100.9	0.9	101.7	1.7
1994...	103.5	2.3	109.9	6.3	106.2	3.9	104.1	2.0	98.5	-0.6	100.6	-0.3	103.4	1.8
1995...	104.7	1.2	114.8	4.4	109.6	3.2	106.2	2.1	97.8	-0.8	101.4	0.9	104.7	1.2
1996...	107.6	2.8	120.0	4.5	111.5	1.7	109.5	3.1	97.9	0.2	101.7	0.3	105.6	0.9
1997...	110.3	2.5	127.3	6.1	115.4	3.6	113.3	3.5	99.0	1.1	102.7	1.0	106.3	0.6
1998...	113.6	3.0	134.5	5.6	118.4	2.6	118.0	4.1	101.6	2.5	103.8	1.1	106.1	-0.1

[1]Output is an annual-weighted index of real gross domestic product originating in the sector.
[2]Hours at work of all employees engaged in the sector. Estimates based primarily on establishment data.
[3]Wages and salaries of employees plus employers' contributions for social insurance and private benefit plans.
[4]Hourly compensation divided by the Consumer Price Index for All Urban Consumers.
[5]Current dollar gross domestic product divided by the index of real gross domestic product.

NOTE: Percent changes are based on original data and therefore may differ slightly from percent changes based on indexes.

Dash indicates data not available.

168

Table 29. **Productivity and related data, manufacturing sector, 1949-98**

(Index, 1992=100, and percent change from previous year)

Year	Output per hour of all persons		Output[1]		Hours of all persons[2]		Compensation per hour[3]		Real compensation per hour[4]		Unit labor costs		Implicit price deflator[5]	
	Index	Change from previous year	Index	Change from previous year	Index	Change from previous year	Index	Change from previous year	Index	Change from previous year	Index	Change from previous year	Index	Change from previous year
1949....	33.7	—	26.7	—	79.1	—	8.3	—	48.9	—	24.6	—	23.9	—
1950....	34.3	1.5	29.3	9.7	85.5	8.1	8.7	5.1	50.7	3.7	25.4	3.5	24.4	2.3
1951....	34.0	-0.7	31.3	7.0	92.1	7.7	9.6	10.1	51.7	2.0	28.2	10.8	26.6	9.2
1952....	35.5	4.2	33.1	5.6	93.3	1.3	10.2	6.6	54.1	4.6	28.8	2.3	26.5	-0.4
1953....	36.6	3.2	35.9	8.5	98.1	5.1	10.8	5.5	56.6	4.7	29.4	2.2	26.5	-0.3
1954....	37.5	2.6	33.7	-6.3	89.6	-8.6	11.3	4.6	58.8	3.8	30.0	1.9	26.8	1.4
1955....	39.1	4.0	36.9	9.7	94.6	5.5	11.7	3.9	61.3	4.3	30.0	-0.1	27.0	0.8
1956....	38.9	-0.4	37.3	1.0	96.0	1.5	12.5	6.4	64.2	4.9	32.0	6.9	28.0	3.5
1957....	39.7	2.0	37.5	0.4	94.5	-1.6	13.2	6.0	65.9	2.6	33.3	3.9	29.0	3.6
1958....	40.3	1.6	34.9	-6.8	86.6	-8.3	13.8	4.6	67.0	1.7	34.3	3.0	29.7	2.5
1959....	41.2	2.2	38.1	9.0	92.5	6.7	14.3	3.7	69.0	3.0	34.8	1.5	30.1	1.3
1960....	42.1	2.1	38.7	1.8	92.1	-0.4	14.9	4.2	70.7	2.4	35.5	2.0	30.1	-0.1
1961....	43.1	2.4	38.7	-0.2	89.7	-2.6	15.4	2.9	72.1	1.9	35.6	0.5	30.1	0.2
1962....	44.5	3.2	41.5	7.5	93.4	4.1	15.9	3.8	74.1	2.8	35.9	0.6	30.2	0.1
1963....	46.0	3.4	43.4	4.5	94.4	1.0	16.4	3.0	75.3	1.7	35.7	-0.4	30.1	-0.1
1964....	47.7	3.7	46.0	5.9	96.4	2.1	17.1	4.2	77.4	2.8	35.9	0.4	30.2	0.2
1965....	48.8	2.3	49.8	8.3	102.0	5.8	17.5	2.1	77.8	0.5	35.8	-0.2	30.5	1.1
1966....	49.3	1.0	53.6	7.6	108.6	6.5	18.3	4.5	79.1	1.6	37.1	3.5	31.4	2.9
1967....	51.1	3.6	55.2	3.0	108.0	-0.6	19.3	5.4	80.9	2.3	37.7	1.7	31.9	1.5
1968....	52.9	3.5	57.9	5.0	109.6	1.5	20.7	7.6	83.5	3.3	39.2	4.0	32.7	2.5
1969....	53.8	1.7	59.6	3.0	110.9	1.2	22.2 ·	7.4	85.1	1.8	41.4	5.6	33.7	3.3
1970....	54.4	1.1	56.8	-4.8	104.4	-5.9	23.8	7.1	86.2	1.3	43.8	5.9	34.9	3.5
1971....	58.2	6.9	58.5	3.0	100.5	-3.7	25.3	6.1	87.6	1.6	43.5	-0.8	36.1	3.5
1972....	60.7	4.3	63.7	9.0	105.1	4.5	26.6	5.2	89.3	1.9	43.9	0.9	37.3	3.1
1973....	61.9	2.0	68.3	7.2	110.4	5.1	28.7	7.7	90.6	1.4	46.3	5.6	40.1	7.7
1974....	61.6	-0.4	66.5	-2.6	107.9	-2.2	31.8	11.1	90.6	0.1	51.7	11.5	47.1	17.3
1975....	64.7	5.0	62.9	-5.5	97.2	-9.9	35.7	12.1	93.1	2.7	55.2	6.8	52.7	11.9
1976....	67.4	4.1	68.6	9.1	101.9	4.8	38.7	8.4	95.3	2.4	57.4	4.1	55.0	4.3
1977....	70.1	4.0	74.3	8.3	106.1	4.2	42.0	8.7	97.3	2.1	60.0	4.5	58.4	6.2
1978....	70.7	1.0	78.2	5.2	110.6	4.2	45.4	8.0	97.7	0.4	64.2	7.0	62.4	6.9
1979....	70.2	-0.7	79.1	1.2	112.7	2.0	49.9	9.8	96.4	-1.4	71.0	10.6	69.6	11.4
1980....	70.4	0.3	75.7	-4.3	107.5	-4.6	55.8	11.9	95.0	-1.4	79.3	11.6	79.5	14.3
1981....	71.1	0.9	76.0	0.4	107.0	-0.5	61.3	9.9	94.7	-0.4	86.3	8.9	86.7	9.1
1982....	74.7	5.1	73.1	-3.8	97.9	-8.4	67.3	9.7	97.8	3.3	90.1	4.3	89.2	2.8
1983....	77.1	3.2	76.3	4.3	98.9	1.0	69.1	2.7	97.4	-0.5	89.6	-0.5	89.6	0.5
1984....	79.8	3.4	84.0	10.1	105.3	6.5	71.5	3.4	96.5	-0.9	89.6	0.0	91.1	1.7
1985....	82.8	3.8	86.6	3.0	104.6	-0.7	75.3	5.4	98.2	1.8	91.0	1.6	90.5	-0.7
1986....	86.5	4.5	89.1	2.9	103.0	-1.5	78.7	4.5	100.7	2.6	91.0	0.0	87.0	-3.9
1987....	88.8	2.6	92.1	3.4	103.8	0.8	80.9	2.8	99.9	-0.8	91.2	0.2	88.7	2.0
1988....	90.5	2.0	96.5	4.7	106.6	2.7	84.2	4.1	99.9	-0.1	93.0	2.1	91.4	3.0
1989....	90.7	0.2	97.1	0.7	107.1	0.5	86.9	3.2	98.3	-1.6	95.8	3.0	95.3	4.4
1990....	93.0	2.5	97.5	0.4	104.8	-2.1	91.0	4.7	97.7	-0.6	97.9	2.2	98.8	3.6
1991....	95.1	2.3	95.5	-2.0	100.4	-4.2	95.8	5.3	98.7	1.1	100.7	2.9	99.5	0.7
1992....	100.0	5.1	100.0	4.7	100.0	-0.4	100.0	4.3	100.0	1.3	100.0	-0.7	100.0	0.5
1993....	102.2	2.2	103.6	3.6	101.4	1.4	102.9	2.9	99.9	-0.1	100.7	0.7	100.9	0.9
1994....	105.3	3.0	109.1	5.3	103.6	2.2	105.8	2.8	100.1	0.2	100.5	-0.3	101.9	1.0
1995....	109.4	3.9	113.8	4.3	104.0	0.4	108.3	2.4	99.7	-0.4	99.0	-1.4	103.9	1.9
1996....	113.8	4.1	118.0	3.7	103.7	-0.4	110.7	2.2	99.0	-0.8	97.2	-1.8	104.7	0.8
1997....	119.4	4.9	125.7	6.5	105.3	1.6	115.3	4.2	100.8	1.8	96.6	-0.7	—	—
1998....	124.4	4.2	130.9	4.2	105.2	-0.1	120.4	4.5	103.7	2.9	96.8	0.2	—	—

[1]Output is an annual-weighted index of real gross sectoral product.
[2]Hours at work of all persons engaged in the sector, including hours of proprietors. Estimates based primarily on establishment data.
[3]Wages and salaries of employees plus employers' contributions for social insurance and private benefit plans. Also includes an estimate of wages, salaries, and supplemental payments for the self-employed.
[4]Hourly compensation divided by the Consumer Price Index for All Urban Consumers.
[5]Current dollar sectoral product divided by the index of real sectoral product.

NOTE: Percent changes are based on original data and therefore may differ slightly from percent changes based on indexes.

Dash indicates data not available.

Table 30. **Annual Indexes of output per hour for selected 3-digit SIC Industries, 1991-97**

(Index, 1987=100)

Industry	SIC code[1]	1991	1992	1993	1994	1995	1996	1997	Average annual percent change 1987 to latest year[2]
Mining									
Copper ores	102	100.5	115.2	118.1	126.0	117.2	116.5	118.9	1.7
Gold and silver ores	104	127.4	141.6	159.8	160.8	144.2	138.3	158.0	4.7
Bituminous coal and lignite mining	122	122.4	133.0	141.2	148.1	155.9	168.0	176.8	5.9
Crude petroleum and natural gas	131	97.9	102.1	105.9	112.4	119.4	123.7	126.1	2.3
Crushed and broken stone	142	99.8	105.0	103.6	108.7	105.4	107.2	114.8	1.4
Manufacturing									
Meat products	201	99.7	104.6	104.3	101.2	102.4	97.7	n.a.	-0.3
Dairy products	202	108.4	111.5	109.7	111.9	116.6	115.9	n.a.	1.7
Preserved fruits and vegetables	203	99.2	100.6	106.8	107.6	109.1	109.4	n.a.	1.0
Grain mill products	204	104.9	107.7	109.1	108.4	115.3	107.7	n.a.	0.8
Bakery products	205	90.6	93.8	94.4	96.4	97.3	95.4	n.a.	-0.5
Sugar and confectionery products	206	101.3	99.1	103.9	105.4	107.5	112.7	n.a.	1.3
Fats and oils	207	120.1	114.1	112.6	111.8	120.3	111.1	n.a.	1.2
Beverages	208	120.5	127.6	127.0	130.9	134.3	135.7	n.a.	3.4
Miscellaneous food and kindred products	209	101.6	101.6	105.3	101.0	103.1	107.6	n.a.	0.8
Cigarettes	211	107.6	111.6	106.5	126.6	142.9	147.7	n.a.	4.4
Broadwoven fabric mills, cotton	221	111.2	110.3	117.8	122.1	134.0	137.8	n.a.	3.6
Broadwoven fabric mills, manmade	222	116.2	126.2	131.7	142.5	145.2	151.1	n.a.	4.7
Narrow fabric mills	224	99.6	112.9	111.4	120.1	118.9	127.5	n.a.	2.7
Knitting mills	225	114.1	119.5	128.1	134.3	138.6	150.8	n.a.	4.7
Textile finishing, except wool	226	79.9	78.6	79.3	81.2	78.5	79.8	n.a.	-2.5
Carpets and rugs	227	89.2	96.1	97.1	93.3	95.8	101.2	n.a.	0.1
Yarn and thread mills	228	111.4	119.6	126.6	130.7	137.4	146.6	n.a.	4.3
Miscellaneous textile goods	229	104.6	106.5	110.4	118.5	123.7	125.4	n.a.	2.5
Men's and boys' suits and coats	231	90.2	89.0	97.4	97.7	92.5	96.5	n.a.	-0.4
Men's and boys' furnishings	232	108.4	109.1	108.4	111.7	123.4	134.0	n.a.	3.3
Women's and misses' outerwear	233	104.3	109.4	121.8	127.4	135.5	144.2	n.a.	4.2
Women's and children's undergarments	234	113.6	117.4	124.5	138.0	161.3	171.6	n.a.	6.2
Hats, caps, and millinery	235	91.1	93.6	87.2	77.7	84.3	80.9	n.a.	-2.3
Miscellaneous apparel and accessories	238	91.8	91.3	94.0	105.5	116.8	121.3	n.a.	2.2
Miscellaneous fabricated textile products	239	100.7	107.5	108.5	107.8	109.2	106.3	n.a.	0.7
Logging	241	86.0	96.2	88.6	87.8	86.0	86.0	n.a.	-1.7
Sawmills and planing mills	.242	102.6	108.1	101.9	103.3	110.2	114.9	n.a.	1.6
Millwork, plywood, and structural members	243	98.0	99.9	97.0	94.5	92.7	92.2	n.a.	-0.9
Wood containers	244	113.1	109.4	100.1	100.9	106.1	106.5	n.a.	0.7
Wood buildings and mobile homes	245	103.0	103.1	103.8	98.3	97.0	97.0	n.a.	-0.3
Miscellaneous wood products	249	110.5	114.2	115.3	111.8	115.4	114.2	n.a.	1.5
Household furniture	.251	107.1	110.5	110.6	112.5	116.9	122.2	n.a.	2.3
Office furniture	252	94.1	102.5	103.2	100.5	101.1	106.8	n.a.	0.7
Public building and related furniture	253	120.2	140.6	161.0	157.4	173.3	179.9	n.a.	6.7
Partitions and fixtures	254	93.0	102.7	107.4	98.9	101.2	97.3	n.a.	-0.3
Miscellaneous furniture and fixtures	259	102.1	99.5	103.6	104.7	110.0	113.6	n.a.	1.4
Pulp mills	261	128.3	137.3	122.5	128.9	131.9	132.7	n.a.	3.2
Paper mills	262	99.2	103.3	102.4	110.2	119.0	111.9	n.a	1.3
Paperboard mills	263	101.4	104.4	108.4	114.9	119.5	118.7	n.a	1.9
Paperboard containers and boxes	265	103.4	105.2	107.9	108.4	105.1	106.5	n.a	0.7

See note at end of table.

Table 30. **Annual Indexes of output per hour for selected 3-digit SIC Industries, 1991-97—Continued**

(Index, 1987=100)

Industry	SIC code[1]	1991	1992	1993	1994	1995	1996	1997	Average annual percent change 1987 to latest year[2]
Miscellaneous converted paper products	267	105.4	105.5	108.0	110.8	113.4	114.6	n.a.	1.5
Newspapers	271	85.8	81.5	79.4	79.9	79.0	77.1	n.a.	-2.8
Periodicals	272	89.5	92.9	89.6	82.4	88.5	90.9	n.a.	-1.1
Books	273	100.8	97.7	103.5	103.0	101.5	100.5	n.a.	0.1
Miscellaneous publishing	274	95.9	105.8	104.5	97.5	94.8	93.4	n.a.	-0.8
Commercial printing	275	102.0	108.0	106.9	106.5	107.2	108.7	n.a.	0.9
Manifold business forms	276	89.1	94.5	91.1	82.0	76.9	74.5	n.a.	-3.2
Greeting cards	277	92.7	96.7	91.4	89.0	92.5	91.8	n.a.	-0.9
Blankbooks and bookbinding	278	96.1	103.6	98.7	105.4	108.7	115.0	n.a.	1.6
Printing trade services	279	100.6	112.0	115.3	111.0	116.7	126.7	n.a.	2.7
Industrial inorganic chemicals	281	109.6	109.6	105.4	102.0	109.2	110.4	n.a.	1.1
Plastics materials and synthetics	282	100.0	107.5	111.9	125.0	128.7	125.1	n.a.	2.5
Drugs	283	104.7	99.6	100.0	105.5	108.9	112.9	n.a.	1.4
Soaps, cleaners, and toilet goods	284	105.3	104.4	108.7	111.2	118.6	121.4	n.a.	2.2
Paints and allied products	285	104.3	102.9	108.8	116.7	118.0	124.2	n.a.	2.4
Industrial organic chemicals	286	95.8	94.5	92.2	100.0	98.8	98.4	n.a.	-0.2
Agricultural chemicals	287	99.9	99.9	104.3	105.7	109.0	111.4	n.a.	1.2
Miscellaneous chemical products	289	96.1	101.8	107.1	105.7	107.8	110.2	n.a.	1.1
Petroleum refining	291	106.6	111.3	120.1	123.8	132.3	142.0	n.a.	4.0
Asphalt paving and roofing materials	295	94.1	100.4	108.0	104.9	111.2	114.4	n.a.	1.5
Miscellaneous petroleum and coal products	299	90.6	101.5	104.2	96.3	87.4	86.4	n.a.	-1.6
Tires and inner tubes	301	102.4	107.8	116.5	124.1	131.1	138.8	n.a.	3.7
Hose and belting and gaskets and packing	305	92.4	97.8	99.7	102.7	104.6	107.2	n.a.	0.8
Fabricated rubber products, n.e.c.[3]	306	110.1	115.3	123.2	119.2	121.6	120.3	n.a.	2.1
Miscellaneous plastics products, n.e.c.[3]	308	108.1	114.1	116.4	120.4	120.7	124.9	n.a.	2.5
Footwear, except rubber	314	94.4	104.2	105.2	113.0	117.1	125.8	n.a.	2.6
Luggage	316	100.3	90.7	89.5	92.3	90.5	108.5	n.a.	0.9
Handbags and personal leather goods	317	98.7	111.2	97.8	86.8	81.8	83.9	n.a.	-1.9
Flat glass	321	83.6	92.7	97.7	97.6	99.6	104.2	n.a.	0/5
Glass and glassware, pressed or blown	322	102.3	108.9	108.7	112.9	115.7	121.9	n.a.	2.2
Products of purchased glass	323	97.7	101.5	106.2	105.9	106.1	124.5	n.a.	2.5
Cement, hydraulic	324	108.3	115.1	119.9	125.6	124.3	127.9	n.a.	2.8
Structural clay products	325	109.8	111.5	105.8	113.0	111.6	119.5	n.a.	2.0
Pottery and related products	326	95.8	99.5	100.3	108.4	109.3	119.4	n.a.	2.0
Concrete, gypsum, and plaster products	327	101.2	102.5	104.6	101.5	104.5	107.5	n.a.	0.8
Miscellaneous nonmetallic mineral products	329	94.0	104.3	104.5	106.3	107.8	111.3	n.a.	1.2
Blast furnace and basic steel products	331	107.8	117.1	133.5	142.4	142.7	153.6	n.a.	4.9
Iron and steel foundries	332	104.5	107.2	112.1	113.0	112.7	115.7	n.a.	1.6
Primary nonferrous metals	333	110.9	102.0	108.0	105.4	111.1	111.0	n.a.	1.2
Nonferrous rolling and drawing	335	90.9	95.8	98.2	101.1	99.1	103.9	n.a.	0.4
Nonferrous foundries (castings)	336	103.6	103.6	108.5	112.1	117.8	122.6	n.a.	2.3
Miscellaneous primary metal products	339	109.1	114.5	111.3	134.5	152.2	149.6	n.a.	4.6
Metal cans and shipping containers	341	122.9	127.8	132.3	140.9	144.2	155.2	n.a.	5.0
Cutlery, handtools, and hardware	342	96.8	100.1	104.0	109.2	111.3	117.9	n.a.	1.8
Plumbing and heating, except electric	343	102.0	98.4	102.0	109.1	109.2	118.6	n.a.	1.9
Fabricated structural metal products	344	100.0	103.9	104.8	107.7	105.8	106.7	n.a.	0.7
Screw machine products, bolts, etc	345	97.9	102.3	104.4	107.2	109.7	110.4	n.a.	1.1
Metal forgings and stampings	346	92.9	103.7	108.7	108.5	109.3	113.7	n.a.	1.4

See note at end of table.

Table 30. **Annual Indexes of output per hour for selected 3-digit SIC Industries, 1991-97—Continued**

(Index, 1987=100)

Industry	SIC code[1]	1991	1992	1993	1994	1995	1996	1997	Average annual percent change 1987 to latest year[2]
Metal services, n.e.c. [3]	347	99.4	111.6	120.6	123.0	127.7	127.5	n.a.	2.7
Ordnance and accessories, n.e.c. [3]	348	81.5	88.6	84.6	83.6	87.6	87.4	n.a.	-1.5
Miscellaneous fabricated metal products	349	97.3	100.9	101.8	103.0	106.4	108.6	n.a.	0.9
Engines and turbines	351	105.8	103.3	109.2	122.3	122.7	136.9	n.a.	3.6
Farm and garden machinery ...	352	112.9	113.9	118.6	125.0	134.7	136.6	n.a.	3.5
Construction and related machinery	353	99.1	102.0	108.2	117.7	122.1	123.8	n.a.	2.4
Metalworking machinery	354	96.4	104.3	107.4	109.9	114.8	114.7	n.a.	1.5
Special industry machinery	355	108.3	106.0	113.6	121.2	132.3	134.7	n.a.	3.4
General industrial machinery ..	356	101.6	101.6	104.8	106.7	109.0	110.0	n.a.	1.1
Refrigeration and service machinery	358	100.7	104.9	108.6	110.7	112.7	114.4	n.a.	1.5
Industrial machinery, n.e.c. [3] ...	359	109.0	116.9	118.4	127.3	138.8	142.1	n.a.	4.0
Electric distribution equipment	361	106.5	119.6	122.2	131.8	143.0	145.1	n.a.	4.2
Electrical industrial apparatus	362	106.8	116.8	132.5	134.5	150.4	154.1	n.a.	4.9
Household appliances	363	106.5	115.0	123.4	131.4	127.3	126.7	n.a.	2.7
Electric lighting and wiring equipment	364	97.5	105.7	107.8	113.4	113.7	117.4	n.a.	1.8
Communications equipment ...	366	123.8	145.4	149.0	164.8	169.6	189.6	n.a.	7.4
Miscellaneous electrical equipment & supplies	369	98.6	101.3	108.2	110.5	114.1	123.0	n.a.	2.3
Motor vehicles and equipment	371	96.6	104.2	105.3	107.1	104.1	104.1	n.a.	0.4
Aircraft and parts	372	108.1	112.2	115.1	109.5	107.8	112.6	n.a.	1.3
Ship and boat building and repairing	373	96.3	102.7	106.2	103.8	97.9	100.5	n.a.	0.1
Railroad equipment	374	146.9	147.9	151.0	152.5	150.0	146.3	n.a.	4.3
Motorcycles, bicycles, and parts	375	99.8	108.4	130.9	125.1	120.3	123.3	n.a.	2.4
Guided missiles, space vehicles, parts	376	109.8	109.3	120.9	117.5	118.7	127.3	n.a.	2.7
Search and navigation equipment	381	118.9	122.1	129.1	132.1	149.5	141.8	n.a.	4.0
Measuring and controlling devices	382	112.9	119.9	124.0	133.8	146.4	150.4	n.a.	4.6
Medical instruments and supplies	384	118.4	123.3	126.9	126.1	130.9	140.4	n.a.	3.8
Ophthalmic goods	385	125.1	144.5	157.8	160.6	167.2	188.9	n.a.	7.3
Photographic equipment & supplies	386	110.2	116.4	126.9	132.7	129.5	129.0	n.a.	2.9
Jewelry, silverware, and plated ware	391	95.8	96.7	96.7	99.5	100.2	103.2	n.a.	0.4
Musical instruments	393	96.9	96.0	95.6	88.7	86.9	78.9	n.a.	-2.6
Toys and sporting goods	394	109.7	104.9	114.2	109.7	113.6	120.0	n.a.	2.0
Pens, pencils, office, and art supplies	395	117.3	111.7	112.0	130.2	135.4	144.4	n.a.	4.2
Costume jewelry and notions ..	396	106.7	110.8	115.8	129.0	143.7	142.3	n.a.	4.0
Miscellaneous manufactures ..	399	109.9	109.6	107.8	106.2	108.2	113.5	n.a.	1.4
Transportation									
U.S. postal service [4]	431	103.7	104.5	107.1	106.6	106.5	104.7	108.3	0.8
Air transportation [5]	4512,13,22 (pts.)	92.5	96.9	100.2	105.7	108.6	111.1	112.1	1.1
Utilities									
Telephone communications	481	119.8	127.7	135.5	142.2	148.1	159.4	160.2	4.8
Radio and television broadcasting	483	106.1	108.3	106.7	110.1	109.6	105.9	101.3	0.1
Cable and other pay TV services	484	87.5	88.3	85.1	83.3	84.3	81.6	84.1	-1.7
Electric utilities	491,3 (pt.)	113.4	115.2	120.6	126.8	135.0	146.5	150.5	4.2
Gas utilities	492,3 (pt.)	94.0	95.3	107.0	102.2	107.5	116.0	119.9	1.8

See note at end of table.

172

Table 30. **Annual Indexes of output per hour for selected 3-digit SIC Industries, 1991-97—Continued**

(Index, 1987=100)

Industry	SIC code[1]	1991	1992	1993	1994	1995	1996	1997	Average annual percent change 1987 to latest year[2]
Trade									
Lumber and other building materials dealers	521	101.3	105.4	110.3	117.9	117.0	121.5	124	2.2
Paint, glass, and wallpaper stores	523	99.4	106.5	112.1	124.6	126.8	132.1	132.2	2.8
Hardware stores	525	102.5	107.2	106.5	114.2	110.7	115.2	115.8	1.5
Retail nurseries, lawn and garden supply stores	526	88.5	100.4	106.6	116.6	117.1	136.6	119.3	1.8
Department stores	531	98.2	100.9	108.1	111.2	113.4	121.0	125.7	2.3
Variety stores	533	154.2	167.7	185.5	191.8	205.8	232.6	246.1	9.4
Miscellaneous general merchandise stores	539	121.8	136.1	159.7	160.9	164.0	165.1	165.7	5.2
Grocery stores	541	93.7	93.3	93.0	92.9	91.9	90.2	89.1	-1.2
Meat and fish (seafood) markets	542	88.4	95.8	95.8	95.3	95.5	88.8	90.8	-1.0
Retail bakeries	546	94.7	94.0	88.0	90.1	91.2	87.3	97.6	-0.2
New and used car dealers	551	104.1	106.5	107.6	108.7	107.1	108.2	107.3	0.7
Auto and home supply stores .	553	99.0	100.0	100.9	107.0	112.6	113.9	109.7	0.9
Gasoline service stations	554	104.3	109.7	113.3	116.5	120.4	117.2	116.5	1.5
Men's and boys' wear stores ...	561	119.2	118.2	115.6	118.1	117.9	126.3	139.1	3.4
Women's clothing stores	562	103.0	112.2	116.8	115.8	122.8	133.6	134.1	3.0
Family clothing stores	565	106.4	111.7	114.9	121.2	135.2	140.5	143.2	3.7
Shoe stores	566	105.1	111.5	112.4	124.4	131.5	142.6	143.5	3.7
Miscellaneous apparel and accessory stores	569	78.8	89.1	95.2	105.4	131.2	139.9	128	2.5
Furniture and homefurnishings stores	571	101.5	108.4	108.5	110.5	114.7	122.5	125.7	2.3
Household appliance stores ...	572	105.2	113.9	115.0	116.8	131.6	132.0	149.4	4.1
Radio, television, computer, and music stores	573	128.3	137.8	153.4	178.8	200.0	209.3	220.4	8.2
Eating and drinking places	581	103.1	102.5	101.7	98.9	97.6	95.2	93.7	-0.6
Drug and proprietary stores	591	104.7	103.6	104.8	104.5	105.2	107.5	113.8	1.3
Liquor stores	592	105.9	108.4	100.1	98.1	102.0	110.3	107.8	0.8
Used merchandise stores	593	98.6	110.4	110.4	111.6	111.6	121.6	122.1	2.0
Miscellaneous shopping goods stores	594	105.0	102.7	106.2	111.5	117.2	119.5	124.5	2.2
Nonstore retailers	596	109.3	122.1	121.8	130.6	125.7	138.3	148	4.0
Fuel dealers	598	85.3	84.4	92.2	99.7	112.3	113.3	106.5	-1.1
Retail stores, n.e.c. [3]	599	103.2	111.6	115.5	121.3	120.5	130.6	137.8	3.3
Finance and services									
Commercial banks	602	110.1	111.0	118.9	122.3	127.6	130.9	134.1	3.0
Hotels and motels	701	99.1	107.8	106.2	109.6	110.1	109.7	107.9	0.8
Laundry, cleaning, and garment services	721	99.2	98.3	98.9	104.0	105.5	108.7	108.1	0.8
Photographic studios, portrait .	722	92.8	97.7	105.9	117.4	129.3	126.4	135.4	3.1
Beauty shops...........................	723	94.8	99.6	95.7	99.8	103.5	106.3	108.9	0.9
Barber shops	724	94.1	112.1	120.8	117.7	114.6	127.6	153.3	4.4
Funeral services and crematories	726	89.5	103.2	98.2	103.8	99.7	97.1	101.3	0.1
Automotive repair shops	753	98.7	103.3	104.0	112.3	119.5	114.1	115.8	1.5
Motion picture theaters	783	116.0	110.8	109.8	106.5	101.4	100.4	100.8	0.1

[1] 1987 Standard Industrial Classification.
[2] Average annual percent change based on compound rate formula.
[3] N.e.c. means not elsewhere classified.
[4] Refers to output per full-time equivalent employee years on fiscal basis.
[5] Refers to output per employee.

Source: U.S. Bureau of Labor Statistics, Internet site <http://stats.bls.gov/iprhome.htm>

Table 31. **Average weekly earnings of production workers on private nonfarm payrolls by major industry division, annual averages, 1947-98**

(Incurrent dollars)

Year	Total private	Mining	Construction	Manufacturing	Transportation and public utilities	Wholesale trade	Retail trade	Finance, insurance, and real estate	Services
1947	$45.58	$59.89	$58.83	$49.13	–	$50.06	$33.77	$43.21	–
1948	49.00	65.52	65.23	53.08	–	53.59	36.22	45.48	–
1949	50.24	62.33	67.56	53.80	–	55.45	38.42	47.63	–
1950	53.13	67.16	69.68	58.28	–	55.31	39.71	47.50	–
1951	57.86	74.11	76.96	63.34	–	62.02	42.82	54.67	–
1952	60.65	77.59	82.86	66.75	–	65.53	43.38	57.08	–
1953	63.76	83.03	86.41	70.47	–	68.61	45.36	59.57	–
1954	64.52	82.60	88.54	70.49	–	71.28	47.04	62.04	–
1955	67.72	89.54	90.90	75.30	–	74.48	48.75	63.92	–
1956	70.74	95.06	96.38	78.78	–	78.17	50.18	65.68	–
1957	73.33	98.25	100.27	81.19	–	81.41	52.20	67.53	–
1958	75.08	96.08	103.78	82.32	–	84.02	54.10	70.12	–
1959	78.78	103.68	108.41	88.26	–	88.51	56.15	72.74	–
1960	80.67	105.04	112.67	89.72	–	90.72	57.76	75.14	–
1961	82.60	106.92	118.08	92.34	–	93.56	58.66	77.12	–
1962	85.91	110.70	122.47	96.56	–	96.22	60.96	80.94	–
1963	88.46	114.40	127.19	99.23	–	99.47	62.66	84.38	–
1964	91.33	117.74	132.06	102.97	$118.78	102.56	64.75	85.79	$70.03
1965	95.45	123.52	138.38	107.53	125.14	106.08	66.61	88.91	73.60
1966	98.82	130.24	146.26	112.19	128.13	111.11	68.57	92.13	77.04
1967	101.84	135.89	154.95	114.49	130.82	115.66	70.95	95.72	80.38
1968	107.73	142.71	164.49	122.51	138.85	121.90	74.95	101.75	83.97
1969	114.61	154.80	181.54	129.51	147.74	129.85	78.66	108.70	90.57
1970	119.83	164.40	195.45	133.33	155.93	136.86	82.47	112.67	96.66
1971	127.31	172.14	211.67	142.44	168.82	143.42	87.62	117.85	103.06
1972	136.90	189.14	221.19	154.71	187.86	151.69	91.85	122.98	110.85
1973	145.39	201.40	235.89	166.46	203.31	159.54	96.32	129.20	117.29
1974	154.76	219.14	249.25	176.80	217.48	169.94	102.68	137.61	126.00
1975	163.53	249.31	266.08	190.79	233.44	182.19	108.86	148.19	134.67
1976	175.45	273.90	283.73	209.32	256.71	194.27	114.60	155.43	143.52
1977	189.00	301.20	295.65	228.90	278.90	209.13	121.66	165.26	153.45
1978	203.70	332.88	318.69	249.27	302.80	228.14	130.20	178.00	163.67
1979	219.91	365.07	342.99	269.34	325.58	247.93	138.62	190.77	175.27
1980	235.10	397.06	367.78	288.62	351.25	266.88	147.38	209.60	190.71
1981	255.20	438.75	399.26	318.00	382.18	290.68	158.03	229.05	208.97
1982	267.26	459.88	426.82	330.26	402.48	309.46	163.85	245.44	225.59
1983	280.70	479.40	442.97	354.08	420.81	328.79	171.05	263.90	239.04
1984	292.86	503.58	458.51	374.03	438.13	341.88	174.33	278.50	247.43
1985	299.09	519.93	464.46	386.37	450.30	351.36	174.64	289.02	256.75
1986	304.85	525.81	466.75	396.01	458.64	357.72	176.08	304.30	265.85
1987	312.50	531.70	480.44	406.31	471.58	365.38	178.70	316.90	275.93
1988	322.02	541.44	495.73	418.81	467.57	380.24	183.62	325.25	289.49
1989	334.24	570.18	513.17	429.68	481.43	394.82	188.72	341.17	305.79
1990	345.35	603.29	526.01	441.86	496.13	411.10	194.40	356.93	319.48
1991	353.98	630.04	533.40	455.03	502.92	424.82	198.48	370.92	331.45
1992	363.61	638.31	537.70	469.86	514.37	435.10	205.06	387.36	342.55
1993	373.64	646.78	553.63	486.04	532.52	448.47	209.95	406.33	350.35
1994	385.86	666.62	573.00	506.94	547.07	463.10	216.46	423.51	358.80
1995	394.34	683.91	587.00	514.59	556.72	476.07	221.47	442.29	369.04
1996	406.61	707.59	603.33	531.23	572.22	492.92	230.11	459.52	382.00
1997	424.89	733.21	625.56	553.14	592.32	516.48	240.74	481.57	400.33
1998	442.19	741.91	643.69	562.53	604.75	539.90	253.17	511.78	418.91

Dash indicates data not available.

NOTE: Current estimates are projected from March 1998 benchmark levels.

174

Table 32. **Median weekly earnings of full-time wage and salary workers by age, sex, race, and Hispanic origin, annual averages, 1981-98**

(In current dollars)

Characteristic	1981	1982	1983	1984	1985	1986[1]	1987	1988	1989
Total, 16 years and over	$283	$302	$313	$326	$343	$358	$373	$385	$399
16 to 24 years	200	208	210	217	223	231	242	249	259
16 to 19 years	161	164	163	168	173	178	185	195	204
20 to 24 years	213	220	222	230	240	248	258	265	276
25 years and over	308	326	343	361	378	391	403	414	427
25 to 54 years	309	328	344	362	379	391	403	414	429
25 to 34 years	296	311	321	335	349	360	373	383	394
35 to 44 years	325	353	369	389	405	418	435	449	472
45 to 54 years	320	345	366	385	400	415	429	452	472
55 years and over	301	319	337	356	374	389	398	411	420
55 to 64 years	308	325	346	365	380	396	405	419	431
65 years and over	222	253	260	271	296	298	310	323	334
Men	339	364	378	391	406	419	433	449	468
Women	219	238	252	265	277	290	303	315	328
White, both sexes	290	309	319	336	355	370	383	394	409
Men	349	375	387	400	417	433	450	465	482
Women	220	241	254	268	281	294	307	318	334
Black, both sexes	234	245	261	269	277	291	301	314	319
Men	268	278	293	302	304	318	326	347	348
Women	205	217	231	241	252	263	275	288	301
Hispanic origin, both sexes	(2)	(2)	(2)	(2)	(2)	277	284	290	298
Men	(2)	(2)	(2)	(2)	(2)	299	306	307	315
Women	(2)	(2)	(2)	(2)	(2)	241	251	260	269

	1990[1]	1991	1992	1993	1994[1]	1995	1996	1997[1]	1998[1]
Total, 16 years and over	$412	$426	$440	$459	$467	$479	$490	$503	$523
16 to 24 years	269	277	276	282	286	292	298	306	319
16 to 19 years	209	213	212	214	221	231	240	252	268
20 to 24 years	285	291	290	297	300	306	312	321	339
25 years and over	449	467	479	491	500	510	520	540	572
25 to 54 years	450	468	479	492	501	511	521	541	571
25 to 34 years	407	415	422	436	439	451	463	481	502
35 to 44 years	486	498	503	517	537	550	559	579	597
45 to 54 years	489	507	522	542	566	582	594	607	620
55 years and over	440	457	472	483	490	502	518	534	579
55 to 64 years	457	469	483	492	501	514	535	558	592
65 years and over	343	381	378	393	384	389	384	393	405
Men	481	493	501	510	522	538	557	579	598
Women	346	366	380	393	399	406	418	431	456
White, both sexes	424	442	458	475	484	494	506	519	545
Men	494	506	514	524	547	566	580	595	615
Women	353	373	387	401	408	415	428	444	468
Black, both sexes	329	348	357	369	371	383	387	400	426
Men	361	375	380	392	400	411	412	432	468
Women	308	323	335	348	346	355	362	375	400
Hispanic origin, both sexes	304	312	322	331	324	329	339	351	370
Men	318	323	339	346	343	350	356	371	390
Women	278	292	302	313	305	305	316	318	337

[1] The comparability of historical labor force data has been affected at various times by methodological and conceptual changes. For an explanation, see the Explanatory Notes and Estimates of Error section of *Employment and Earnings*, a monthly periodical published by the Bureau of Labor Statistics.
[2] Data not available.

Table 33. **Median weekly earnings of full-time wage and salary workers 25 years and older by sex and educational attainment, annual averages, selected years, 1990-98**

(In current dollars)

Characteristic	1990[1]	1994[1]	1995	1996	1997[1]	1998[1]
TOTAL						
Total, 25 years and over	$449	$500	$510	$520	$540	$572
Less than a high school diploma	303	307	309	317	321	337
High school graduates, no college	386	421	432	443	461	479
Some college or associate degree	476	499	508	518	535	558
College graduates, total	638	733	747	758	779	821
Men						
Total, 25 years and over	512	576	588	599	615	639
Less than a high school diploma	349	342	347	357	365	383
High school graduates, no college	459	496	507	516	535	559
Some college or associate degree	542	587	596	604	621	643
College graduates, total	741	826	845	874	896	939
Women						
Total, 25 years and over	369	421	428	444	462	485
Less than a high school diploma	240	257	262	268	275	283
High school graduates, no college	315	351	356	365	378	396
Some college or associate degree	395	423	427	442	459	476
College graduates, total	535	634	644	657	672	707

[1] Data on educational attainment prior to 1992 reflect years of school completed rather than degrees or diplomas received and are not strictly comparable with data for 1992 and later years. In addition, the comparability of historical labor force data has been affected at various times by methodological and conceptual changes. For an explanation, see the Explanatory Notes and Estimates of Error section of *Employment and Earnings*, a monthly periodical published by the Bureau of Labor Statistics.

Table 34. Producer price indexes for major commodity groups, 1947-98

(1982=100)

Year	Farm products, processed foods and feeds	Farm products	Processed foods and feeds	Industrial commodities	Textile products and apparel	Hides, skins, leather, and products	Fuels and related products and power[1]	Chemicals and allied products[1]	Rubber and plastic products
1947	37.9	45.1	33.0	22.7	50.6	31.7	11.1	32.1	29.2
1948	40.8	48.5	35.3	24.6	52.8	32.1	13.1	32.8	30.2
1949	36.0	41.9	32.1	24.1	48.3	30.4	12.4	30.0	29.2
1950	37.7	44.0	33.2	25.0	50.2	32.9	12.6	30.4	35.6
1951	43.0	51.2	36.9	27.6	56.0	37.7	13.0	34.8	43.7
1952	41.3	48.4	36.4	26.9	50.5	30.5	13.0	33.0	39.6
1953	38.6	43.8	34.8	27.2	49.3	31.0	13.4	33.4	36.9
1954	38.5	43.2	35.4	27.2	48.2	29.5	13.2	33.8	37.5
1955	36.6	40.5	33.8	27.8	48.2	29.4	13.2	33.7	42.4
1956	36.4	40.0	33.8	29.1	48.2	31.2	13.6	33.9	43.0
1957	37.7	41.1	34.8	29.9	48.3	31.2	14.3	34.6	42.8
1958	39.4	42.9	36.5	30.0	47.4	31.6	13.7	34.9	42.8
1959	37.6	40.2	35.6	30.5	48.1	35.9	13.7	34.8	42.6
1960	37.7	40.1	35.6	30.5	48.6	34.6	13.9	34.8	42.7
1961	37.7	39.7	36.2	30.4	47.8	34.9	14.0	34.5	41.1
1962	38.1	40.4	36.5	30.4	48.2	35.3	14.0	33.9	39.9
1963	37.7	39.6	36.8	30.3	48.2	34.3	13.9	33.5	40.1
1964	37.5	39.0	36.7	30.5	48.5	34.4	13.5	33.6	39.6
1965	39.0	40.7	38.0	30.9	48.8	35.9	13.8	33.9	39.7
1966	41.6	43.7	40.2	31.5	48.9	39.4	14.1	34.0	40.5
1967	40.2	41.3	39.8	32.0	48.9	38.1	14.4	34.2	41.4
1968	41.1	42.3	40.6	32.8	50.7	39.3	14.3	34.1	42.8
1969	43.4	45.0	42.7	33.9	51.8	41.5	14.6	34.2	43.6
1970	44.9	45.8	44.6	35.2	52.4	42.0	15.3	35.0	44.9
1971	45.8	46.6	45.5	36.5	53.3	43.4	16.6	35.6	45.2
1972	49.2	51.6	48.0	37.8	55.5	50.0	17.1	35.6	45.3
1973	63.9	72.7	58.9	40.3	60.5	54.5	19.4	37.6	46.6
1974	71.3	77.4	68.0	49.2	68.0	55.2	30.1	50.2	56.4
1975	74.0	77.0	72.6	54.9	67.4	56.5	35.4	62.0	62.2
1976	73.6	78.8	70.8	58.4	72.4	63.9	38.3	64.0	66.0
1977	75.9	79.4	74.0	62.5	75.3	68.3	43.6	65.9	69.4
1978	83.0	87.7	80.6	67.0	78.1	76.1	46.5	68.0	72.4
1979	92.3	99.6	88.5	75.7	82.5	96.1	58.9	76.0	80.5
1980	98.3	102.9	95.9	88.0	89.7	94.7	82.8	89.0	90.1
1981	101.1	105.2	98.9	97.4	97.6	99.3	100.2	98.4	96.4
1982	100.0	100.0	100.0	100.0	100.0	100.0	100.0	100.0	100.0
1983	102.0	102.4	101.8	101.1	100.3	103.2	95.9	100.3	100.8
1984	105.5	105.5	105.4	103.3	102.7	109.0	94.8	102.9	102.3
1985	100.7	95.1	103.5	103.7	102.9	108.9	91.4	103.7	101.9
1986	101.2	92.9	105.4	100.0	103.2	113.0	69.8	102.6	101.9
1987	103.7	95.5	107.9	102.6	105.1	120.4	70.2	106.4	103.0
1988	110.0	104.9	112.7	106.3	109.2	131.4	66.7	116.3	109.3
1989	115.4	110.9	117.8	111.6	112.3	136.3	72.9	123.0	112.6
1990	118.6	112.2	121.9	115.8	115.0	141.7	82.3	123.6	113.6
1991	116.4	105.7	121.9	116.5	116.3	138.9	81.2	125.6	115.1
1992	115.9	103.6	122.1	117.4	117.8	140.4	80.4	125.9	115.1
1993	118.4	107.1	124.0	119.0	118.0	143.7	80.0	128.2	116.0
1994	119.1	106.3	125.5	120.7	118.3	148.5	77.8	132.1	117.6
1995	120.5	107.4	127.0	125.5	120.8	153.7	78.0	142.5	124.3
1996	129.7	122.4	133.3	127.3	122.4	150.5	85.8	142.1	123.8
1997	127.0	112.9	134.0	127.7	122.6	154.2	86.1	143.6	123.2
1998	122.7	104.6	131.6	124.8	122.9	148.0	75.3	143.9	122.6

See footnote at end of table.

177

Table 34. Producer price indexes for major commodity groups, 1947-98—Continued

(1982=100)

Year	Lumber and wood products	Pulp, paper, and allied products	Metals and metal products	Machinery and equipment	Furniture and household durables	Non-metallic mineral products	Transportation and equipment	Motor vehicles and equipment	Miscellaneous products
1947	25.8	25.1	18.2	19.3	37.2	20.7	–	25.5	26.6
1948	29.5	26.2	20.7	20.9	39.4	22.4	–	28.2	27.7
1949	27.3	25.1	20.9	21.9	40.1	23.0	–	30.1	28.2
1950	31.4	25.7	22.0	22.6	40.9	23.5	–	30.0	28.6
1951	34.1	30.5	24.5	25.3	44.4	25.0	–	31.6	30.3
1952	33.2	29.7	24.5	25.3	43.5	25.0	–	33.4	30.2
1953	33.1	29.6	25.3	25.9	44.4	26.0	–	33.3	31.0
1954	32.5	29.6	25.5	26.3	44.9	26.6	–	33.4	31.3
1955	34.1	30.4	27.2	27.2	45.1	27.3	–	34.3	31.3
1956	34.6	32.4	29.6	29.3	46.3	28.5	–	36.3	31.7
1957	32.8	33.0	30.2	31.4	47.5	29.6	–	37.9	32.6
1958	32.5	33.4	30.0	32.1	47.9	29.9	–	39.0	33.3
1959	34.7	33.7	30.6	32.8	48.0	30.3	–	39.9	33.4
1960	33.5	34.0	30.6	33.0	47.8	30.4	–	39.3	33.6
1961	32.0	33.0	30.5	33.0	47.5	30.5	–	39.2	33.7
1962	32.2	33.4	30.2	33.0	47.2	30.5	–	39.2	33.9
1963	32.8	33.1	30.3	33.1	46.9	30.3	–	38.9	34.2
1964	33.5	33.0	31.1	33.3	47.1	30.4	–	39.1	34.4
1965	33.7	33.3	32.0	33.7	46.8	30.4	–	39.2	34.7
1966	35.2	34.2	32.8	34.7	47.4	30.7	–	39.2	35.3
1967	35.1	34.6	33.2	35.9	48.3	31.2	–	39.8	36.2
1968	39.8	35.0	34.0	37.0	49.7	32.4	–	40.9	37.0
1969	44.0	36.0	36.0	38.2	50.7	33.6	40.4	41.7	38.1
1970	39.9	37.5	38.7	40.0	51.9	35.3	41.9	43.3	39.8
1971	44.7	38.1	39.4	41.4	53.1	38.2	44.2	45.7	40.8
1972	50.7	39.3	40.9	42.3	53.8	39.4	45.5	47.0	41.5
1973	62.2	42.3	44.0	43.7	55.7	40.7	46.1	47.4	43.3
1974	64.5	52.5	57.0	50.0	61.8	47.8	50.3	51.4	48.1
1975	62.1	59.0	61.5	57.9	67.5	54.4	56.7	57.6	53.4
1976	72.2	62.1	65.0	61.3	70.3	58.2	60.5	61.2	55.6
1977	83.0	64.6	69.3	65.2	73.2	62.6	64.6	65.2	59.4
1978	96.9	67.7	75.3	70.3	77.5	69.6	69.5	70.0	66.7
1979	105.5	75.9	86.0	76.7	82.8	77.6	75.3	75.8	75.5
1980	101.5	86.3	95.0	86.0	90.7	88.4	82.9	83.1	93.6
1981	102.8	94.8	99.6	94.4	95.9	96.7	94.3	94.6	96.1
1982	100.0	100.0	100.0	100.0	100.0	100.0	100.0	100.0	100.0
1983	107.9	103.3	101.8	102.7	103.4	101.6	102.8	102.2	104.8
1984	108.0	110.3	104.8	105.1	105.7	105.4	105.2	104.1	107.0
1985	106.6	113.3	104.4	107.2	107.1	108.6	107.9	106.4	109.4
1986	107.2	116.1	103.2	108.8	108.2	110.0	110.5	109.1	111.6
1987	112.8	121.8	107.1	110.4	109.9	110.0	112.5	111.7	114.9
1988	118.9	130.4	118.7	113.2	113.1	111.2	114.3	113.1	120.2
1989	126.7	137.8	124.1	117.4	116.9	112.6	117.7	116.2	126.5
1990	129.7	141.2	122.9	120.7	119.2	114.7	121.5	118.2	134.2
1991	132.1	142.9	120.2	123.0	121.2	117.2	126.4	122.1	140.8
1992	146.6	145.2	119.2	123.4	122.2	117.3	130.4	124.9	145.3
1993	174.0	147.3	119.2	124.0	123.7	120.0	133.7	128.0	145.4
1994	180.0	152.5	124.8	125.1	126.1	124.2	137.2	131.4	141.9
1995	178.1	172.2	134.5	126.6	128.2	129.0	139.7	133.0	145.4
1996	176.1	168.7	131.0	126.5	130.4	131.0	141.7	134.1	147 7
1997	183.8	167.9	131.8	125.9	130.8	133.2	141.6	132.7	150.9
1998	179.1	171.7	127.8	124.9	131.3	135.4	141.2	131.4	156.0

[1] Prices for some items in this grouping are lagged and refer to 1 month earlier than the index month.

Table 35. **Producer price indexes by stage of processing, special groups, 1947-98**

(1982=100)

Year	Total finished goods	Finished foods	Finished energy	Finished goods excluding foods and energy	Capital equipment	Consumer goods excluding foods and energy	Total Intermediate	Intermediate foods and feeds[1]	Intermediate energy	Intermediate other	Total crude	Crude foods and feeds	Crude energy	Crude other
1947	26.4	31.9	–	–	19.8	–	23.3	–	–	–	31.7	45.1	–	–
1948	28.5	34.9	–	–	21.6	–	25.2	–	–	–	34.7	48.8	–	–
1949	27.7	32.1	–	–	22.7	–	24.2	–	–	–	30.1	40.5	–	–
1950	28.2	32.7	–	–	23.2	–	25.3	–	–	–	32.7	43.4	–	–
1951	30.8	36.7	–	–	25.5	–	28.4	–	–	–	37.6	50.2	–	–
1952	30.6	36.4	–	–	25.9	–	27.5	–	–	–	34.5	47.3	–	–
1953	30.3	34.5	–	–	26.3	–	27.7	–	–	–	31.9	42.3	–	–
1954	30.4	34.2	–	–	26.7	–	27.9	–	–	–	31.6	42.3	–	–
1955	30.5	33.4	–	–	27.4	–	28.4	–	–	–	30.4	38.4	–	–
1956	31.3	33.3	–	–	29.5	–	29.6	–	–	–	30.6	37.6	–	–
1957	32.5	34.4	–	–	31.3	–	30.3	–	–	–	31.2	39.2	–	–
1958	33.2	36.5	–	–	32.1	–	30.4	–	–	–	31.9	41.6	–	–
1959	33.1	34.8	–	–	32.7	–	30.8	–	–	–	31.1	38.8	–	–
1960	33.4	35.5	–	–	32.8	–	30.8	–	–	–	30.4	38.4	–	–
1961	33.4	35.4	–	–	32.9	–	30.6	–	–	–	30.2	37.9	–	–
1962	33.5	35.7	–	–	33.0	–	30.6	–	–	–	30.5	38.6	–	–
1963	33.4	35.3	–	–	33.1	–	30.7	–	–	–	29.9	37.5	–	–
1964	33.5	35.4	–	–	33.4	–	30.8	–	–	–	29.6	36.6	–	–
1965	34.1	36.8	–	–	33.8	–	31.2	–	–	–	31.1	39.2	–	–
1966	35.2	39.2	–	–	34.6	–	32.0	–	–	–	33.1	42.7	–	–
1967	35.6	38.5	–	–	35.8	–	32.2	41.8	–	–	31.3	40.3	–	–
1968	36.6	40.0	–	–	37.0	–	33.0	41.5	–	–	31.8	40.9	–	–
1969	38.0	42.4	–	–	38.3	–	34.1	42.9	–	–	33.9	44.1	–	–
1970	39.3	43.8	–	–	40.1	–	35.4	45.6	–	–	35.2	45.2	–	–
1971	40.5	44.5	–	–	41.7	–	36.8	46.7	–	–	36.0	46.1	–	–
1972	41.8	46.9	–	–	42.8	–	38.2	49.5	–	–	39.9	51.5	–	–
1973	45.6	56.5	–	48.1	44.2	50.4	42.4	70.3	–	44.3	54.5	72.6	–	70.8
1974	52.6	64.4	26.2	53.6	50.5	55.5	52.5	83.6	33.1	54.0	61.4	76.4	27.8	83.3
1975	58.2	69.8	30.7	59.7	58.2	60.6	58.0	81.6	38.7	60.2	61.6	77.4	33.3	69.3
1976	60.8	69.6	34.3	63.1	62.1	63.7	60.9	77.4	41.5	63.8	63.4	76.8	35.3	80.2
1977	64.7	73.3	39.7	66.9	66.1	67.3	64.9	79.6	46.8	67.6	65.5	77.5	40.4	79.8
1978	69.8	79.9	42.3	71.9	71.3	72.2	69.5	84.8	49.1	72.5	73.4	87.3	45.2	87.8
1979	77.6	87.3	57.1	78.3	77.5	78.8	78.4	94.5	61.1	80.7	85.9	100.0	54.9	106.2
1980	88.0	92.4	85.2	87.1	85.8	87.8	90.3	105.5	84.9	90.3	95.3	104.6	73.1	113.1
1981	96.1	97.8	101.5	94.6	94.6	94.6	98.6	104.6	100.5	97.7	103.0	103.9	97.7	111.7
1982	100.0	100.0	100.0	100.0	100.0	100.0	100.0	100.0	100.0	100.0	100.0	100.0	100.0	100.0
1983	101.6	101.0	95.2	103.0	102.8	103.1	100.6	103.6	95.3	101.6	101.3	101.8	98.7	105.3
1984	103.7	105.4	91.2	105.5	105.2	105.7	103.1	105.7	95.5	104.7	103.5	104.7	98.0	111.7
1985	104.7	104.6	87.6	108.1	107.5	108.4	102.7	97.3	92.6	105.2	95.8	94.8	93.3	104.9
1986	103.2	107.3	63.0	110.6	109.7	111.1	99.1	96.2	72.6	104.9	87.7	93.2	71.8	103.1
1987	105.4	109.5	61.8	113.3	111.7	114.2	101.5	99.2	73.0	107.8	93.7	96.2	75.0	115.7
1988	108.0	112.6	59.8	117.0	114.3	118.5	107.1	109.5	70.9	115.2	96.0	106.1	67.7	133.0
1989	113.6	118.7	65.7	122.1	118.8	124.0	112.0	113.8	76.1	120.2	103.1	111.2	75.9	137.9
1990	119.2	124.4	75.0	126.6	122.9	128.8	114.5	113.3	85.5	120.9	108.9	113.1	85.9	136.3
1991	121.7	124.1	78.1	131.1	126.7	133.7	114.4	111.1	85.1	121.4	101.2	105.5	80.4	128.2
1992	123.2	123.3	77.8	134.2	129.1	137.3	114.7	110.7	84.3	122.0	100.4	105.1	78.8	128.4
1993	124.7	125.7	78.0	135.8	131.4	138.5	116.2	112.7	84.6	123.8	102.4	108.4	76.7	140.2
1994	125.5	126.8	77.0	137.1	134.1	139.0	118.5	114.8	83.0	127.1	101.8	106.5	72.1	156.2
1995	127.9	129.0	78.1	140.0	136.7	141.9	124.9	114.8	84.1	135.2	102.7	105.8	69.4	173.6
1996	131.3	133.6	83.2	142.0	138.3	144.3	125.7	128.1	89.8	134.0	113.8	121.5	85.0	155.8
1997	131.8	134.5	83.4	142.4	138.2	145.1	125.6	125.4	89.0	134.2	111.1	112.2	87.3	156.5
1998	130.7	134.3	75.1	143.7	137.6	147.7	123.0	116.2	80.8	133.5	96.8	103.9	68.6	142.1

[1] Intermediate materials for food manufacturing and feeds .

Dash indicates data not available.

179

Table 36. **Consumer Price Index for All Urban Consumers (CPI-U), 1960-98**

Year	Annual average				December			
	All items	Food	Energy	All items less food and energy	All items	Food	Energy	All items less food and energy
1960	29.6	30.0	22.4	30.6	29.8	30.4	22.7	30.8
1961	29.9	30.4	22.5	31.0	30.0	30.2	22.4	31.2
1962	30.2	30.6	22.6	31.4	30.4	30.6	22.9	31.6
1963	30.6	31.1	22.6	31.8	30.9	31.2	22.7	32.1
1964	31.0	31.5	22.5	32.3	31.2	31.6	22.7	32,5
1965	31.5	32,2	22.9	32.7	31.8	32.7	23.1	33.0
1966	32.4	33.8	23.3	33.5	32.9	34.0	23.5	34.1
1967	33.4	34.1	23.8	34.7	33.9	34.4	23.9	35.4
1968	34.8	35.3	24.2	36.3	35.5	35.9	24.3	37.2
1969	36.7	37.1	24.8	38.4	37.7	38.4	25.0	39.5
1970	38.8	39.2	25.5	40.8	39.8	39.3	26.2	42.1
1971	40.5	40.4	26.5	42.7	41.1	41.0	27.0	43.4
1972	41.8	42.1	27.2	44.0	42.5	42.9	27.7	44.7
1973	44.4	48.2	29.4	45.6	46.2	51.6	32.4	46.8
1974	49.3	55.1	38.1	49.4	51.9	57.8	39.4	52.0
1975	53.8	59.8	42.1	53.9	55.5	61.6	43.9	55.5
1976	56.9	61.6	45.1	57.4	58.2	61.9	47.0	58.9
1977	60.6	65.5	49.4	61.0	62.1	66.9	50.4	62.7
1978	65.2	72.0	52.5	65.5	67.7	74.8	54.4	68.0
1979	72.6	79.9	65.7	71.9	76.7	82.4	74.8	75.7
1980	82.4	86.8	86.0	80.8	86.3	90.8	88.3	84.9
1981	90.9	93.6	97.7	89.2	94.0	94.7	98.8	93.0
1982	96.5	97.4	99.2	95.8	97.6	97.6	100.1	97.2
1983	99.6	99.4	99.9	99.6	101.3	100.2	99.6	101.9
1984	103.9	103.2	100.9	104.6	105.3	104.0	99.8	106.7
1985	107.6	105.6	101.6	109.1	109.3	106.7	101.6	111.3
1986	109.6	109.0	88.2	113.5	110.5	110.8	81.6	115.5
1987	113.6	113.5	88.6	118.2	115.4	114.7	88.3	120.4
1988	118.3	118.2	89.3	123.4	120.5	120.7	88.7	126.0
1989	124.0	125.1	94.3	129.0	126.1	127.4	93.2	131.5
1990	130.7	132.4	102.1	135.5	133.8	134.2	110.1	138.3
1991	136.2	136.3	102.5	142.1	137.9	136.7	101.9	144.4
1992	140.3	137.9	103.0	147.3	141.9	138.7	103.9	149.2
1993	144.5	140.9	104.2	152.2	145.8	142.7	102.4	153.9
1994	148.2	144.3	104.6	156.5	149.7	146.8	104.7	157.9
1995	152.4	148.4	105.2	161.2	153.5	149.9	103.3	162.7
1996	156.9	153.3	110.1	165.6	158.6	156.3	112.2	167.0
1997	160.5	157.3	111.5	169.5	161.3	158.7	108.4	170.7
1998	163.0	160.7	102.9	173.4	163.9	162.3	98.9	174.8

Table 36. **Consumer Price Index for All Urban Consumers (CPI-U), 1960-98—Continued**

Year	Annual average percent change from previous year				Percent change to December from prior December			
	All items	Food	Energy	All items less food and energy	All items	Food	Energy	All items less food and energy
1960	1.7	1.0	2.3	1.3	1.4	3.1	1.3	1.0
1961	1.0	1.3	.4	1.3	.7	-.7	-1.3	1.3
1962	1.0	.7	.4	1.3	1.3	1.3	2.2	1.3
1963	1.3	1.6	.0	1.3	1.6	2.0	-.9	1.6
1964	1.3	1.3	-.4	1.6	1.0	1.3	0	1.2
1965	1.6	2.2	1.8	1.2	1.9	3.5	1.8	1.5
1966	2.9	5.0	1.7	2.4	3.5	4.0	1.7	3.3
1967	3.1	.9	2.1	3.6	3.0	1.2	1.7	3.8
1968	4.2	3.5	1.7	4.6	4.7	4.4	1.7	5.1
1969	5.5	5.1	2.5	5.8	6.2	7.0	2.9	6.2
1970	5.7	5.7	2.8	6.3	5.6	2.3	4.8	6.6
1971	4.4	3.1	3.9	4.7	3.3	4.3	3.1	3.1
1972	3.2	4.2	2.6	3.0	3.4	4.6	2.6	3.0
1973	6.2	14.5	8.1	3.6	8.7	20.3	17.0	4.7
1974	11.0	14.3	29.6	8.3	12.3	12.0	21.6	11.1
1975	9.1	8.5	10.5	9.1	6.9	6.6	11.4	6.7
1976	5.8	3.0	7.1	6.5	4.9	.5	7.1	6.1
1977	6.5	6.3	9.5	6.3	6.7	8.1	7.2	6.5
1978	7.6	9.9	6.3	7.4	9.0	11.8	7.9	8.5
1979	11.3	11.0	25.1	9.8	13.3	10.2	37.5	11.3
1980	13.5	8.6	30.9	12.4	12.5	10.2	18.0	12.2
1981	10.3	7.8	13.6	10.4	8.9	4.3	11.9	9.5
1982	6.2	4.1	1.5	7.4	3.8	3.1	1.3	4.5
1983	3.2	2.1	.7	4.0	3.8	2.7	-.5	4.8
1984	4.3	3.8	1.0	5.0	3.9	3.8	.2	4.7
1985	3.6	2.3	.7	4.3	3.8	2.6	1.8	4.3
1986	1.9	3.2	-13.2	4.0	1.1	3.8	-19.7	3.8
1987	3.6	4.1	.5	4.1	4.4	3.5	8.2	4.2
1988	4.1	4.1	.8	4.4	4.4	5.2	.5	4.7
1989	4.8	5.8	5.6	4.5	4.6	5.6	5.1	4.4
1990	5.4	5.8	8.3	5.0	6.1	5.3	18.1	5.2
1991	4.2	2.9	.4	4.9	3.1	1.9	-7.4	4.4
1992	3.0	1.2	.5	3.7	2.9	1.5	2.0	3.3
1993	3.0	2.2	1.2	3.3	2.7	2.9	-1.4	3.2
1994	2.6	2.4	.4	2.8	2.7	2.9	2.2	2.6
1995	2.8	2.8	.6	3.0	2.5	2.1	-1.3	3.0
1996	3.0	3.3	4.7	2.7	3.3	4.3	8.6	2.6
1997	2.3	2.6	1.3	2.4	1.7	1.5	-3.4	2.2
1998	1.6	2.2	-7.7	2.3	1.6	2.3	-8.8	2.4

Table 37. **Average annual expenditures and percent distribution of all consumer units, selected periods, 1935-36 to 1996-97**

Item	Averages				Percent of current consumption			
	1935-36	1960-61	1972-73	1996-97	1935-36	1960-61	1972-73	1996-97
Characteristics								
Number of consumer units (in thousands) .	39,458	55,306	71,220	104,894				
Income before taxes	$1,502	$6,253	$11,726	$38,983				
Income after taxes	-	5,564	10,174	35,787				
Average consumer unit size	3.2	3.2	2.9	2.5				
Percent homeowner	-	61	58	64				
Expenditures								
Current Consumption	$1,273	$5,056	$7,920	$28,935	100.0	100.0	100.0	100.0
Food	428	1,236	1,679	4,681	33.6	24.4	21.2	16.2
Food at home	-	990	1,303	2,837	-	19.6	16.5	9.8
Food away from home	-	246	376	1,844	-	4.9	4.7	6.4
Alcoholic beverages	-	78	82	292	-	1.5	1.0	1.0
Shelter	241	664	1,395	6,158	18.9	13.1	17.6	21.3
Household operations and utilities	134	538	715	2,834	10.5	10.6	9.0	9.8
Housefurnishings	36	266	378	1,335	2.8	5.3	4.8	4.6
Apparel and services	133	519	647	1,518	10.4	10.3	8.2	5.2
Vehicle purchases [1]	96	299	714	2,755	7.5	5.9	9.0	9.5
Vehicle operations	-	393	935	3,160	-	7.8	11.8	10.9
Public transportation	22	77	96	390	1.7	1.5	1.2	1.3
Health care	56	340	429	1,638	4.4	6.7	5.4	5.7
Insurance	-	90	152	723	-	1.8	1.9	2.5
Services	-	168	216	510	-	3.3	2.7	1.8
Drugs	-	69	47	307	-	1.4	0.6	1.1
Supplies	-	13	14	99	-	0.3	0.2	0.3
Entertainment	42	200	373	1,709	3.3	4.0	4.7	5.9
Personal care	26	145	101	418	2.0	2.9	1.3	1.4
Tobacco	24	91	128	259	1.9	1.8	1.6	0.9
Education	13	54	109	406	1.0	1.1	1.4	1.4
Reading	14	45	48	159	1.1	0.9	0.6	0.5
Other items	8	111	91	1,223	0.6	2.2	1.1	4.2

[1] Vehicle purchases also includes vehicle operations for 1935-36 data.

Dash indicates data not available.

Table 38. **Shares of average annual expenditures and characteristics of all consumer units classified by quintiles of income before taxes, Consumer Expenditure Survey, 1987 and 1997**

Item	All consumer units	Complete reporting of income						Incomplete reporting of income
		Total complete reporting	Lowest 20 percent	Second 20 percent	Third 20 percent	Fourth 20 percent	Highest 20 percent	
1987								
Number of consumer units (in thousands)	94,150	81,070	16,187	16,215	16,215	16,214	16,239	13,080
Consumer unit characteristics:								
Income before taxes [1]	$27,326	$27,326	$4,611	$11,954	$20,943	$33,276	$65,750	([1])
Age of reference person	47.0	47.0	51.7	50.7	44.9	43.0	44.8	47.3
Average number in consumer unit:								
Persons	2.6	2.5	1.8	2.2	2.6	2.9	3.2	2.7
Children under 18	.7	.7	.4	.6	.7	.9	.9	.7
Persons 65 and over	.3	.3	.4	.5	.3	.2	.1	.2
Earners	1.4	1.3	.6	.9	1.4	1.7	2.1	1.5
Vehicles	2.0	2.0	.8	1.5	2.0	2.5	3.0	2.0
Percent homeowner	63	62	40	51	58	73	86	65
Average annual expenditures	$24,414	$24,776	$10,355	$15,686	$21,708	$29,603	$46,470	$22,668
Percent distribution	100.0	100.0	100.0	100.0	100.0	100.0	100.0	100.0
Food	15.0	15.1	18.5	17.7	16.5	14.6	13.3	14.7
Food at home	8.6	8.6	12.8	11.7	9.5	8.2	6.6	8.5
Cereals and bakery products ..	1.2	1.2	1.8	1.7	1.4	1.2	.9	1.2
Meats, poultry, fish, and eggs .	2.3	2.4	3.5	3.2	2.6	2.3	1.8	2.3
Dairy products	1.1	1.1	1.7	1.5	1.3	1.1	.9	1.1
Fruits and vegetables	1.5	1.4	2.3	2.0	1.6	1.3	1.1	1.5
Other food at home	2.3	2.4	3.3	3.1	2.6	2.3	1.8	2.2
Food away from home	6.4	6.5	5.7	6.0	7.0	6.4	6.7	6.2
Alcoholic beverages	1.2	1.2	1.2	1.2	1.5	1.1	1.2	1.0
Housing	30.4	29.6	36.4	32.3	29.5	28.2	28.2	35.2
Shelter	16.4	15.8	19.8	17.3	15.6	14.8	15.1	19.8
Owned dwellings	9.7	9.3	6.6	6.4	7.2	9.6	11.7	12.3
Rented dwellings	5.5	5.4	12.4	10.1	7.7	4.5	1.8	6.0
Other lodging	1.1	1.1	.9	.7	.7	.8	1.6	1.5
Utilities, fuels, and public services	6.8	6.6	10.4	8.7	7.3	6.3	5.0	8.1
Household operations	1.5	1.5	1.2	1.1	1.2	1.4	1.9	1.8
Housekeeping supplies	1.4	1.5	1.8	1.8	1.7	1.5	1.2	1.0
Household furnishings and equipment	4.2	4.2	3.2	3.4	3.6	4.3	4.9	4.5
Apparel and services	5.9	5.9	5.3	6.0	5.6	6.2	5.9	6.3
Transportation	18.8	18.5	15.0	18.6	19.1	20.0	18.1	20.8
Vehicle purchases	8.3	8.1	5.9	7.8	8.3	9.1	8.1	9.1
Gasoline and motor oil	3.6	3.6	3.6	4.1	4.1	3.8	3.0	4.1
Other vehicle expenses	5.8	5.8	4.2	5.7	5.8	6.2	5.8	6.0
Public transportation	1.1	1.0	1.2	1.0	.9	.9	1.2	1.6
Health care	4.6	4.6	7.1	6.8	5.3	4.1	3.3	5.0
Entertainment	4.9	4.9	3.7	3.8	4.9	5.0	5.4	4.9
Personal care products and services	1.4	1.4	1.4	1.6	1.5	1.3	1.3	1.2
Reading	.6	.6	.6	.6	.6	.6	.6	.6
Education	1.4	1.3	2.3	1.1	1.0	.9	1.5	1.9
Tobacco products and smoking supplies	1.0	.9	1.6	1.4	1.1	1.0	.6	1.0
Miscellaneous	2.9	3.0	2.8	2.3	2.9	3.3	3.2	2.2
Cash contributions	3.0	3.1	1.7	2.2	2.5	2.7	4.3	2.3
Personal insurance and pensions	8.9	9.7	2.3	4.6	8.0	10.9	13.2	3.0
Life and other personal insurance	1.2	1.2	1.1	1.0	1.1	1.2	1.3	1.3
Pensions and Social Security	7.7	8.6	1.3	3.6	6.8	9.7	12.0	1.7

See footnotes at end of table.

183

Table 38. Shares of average annual expenditures and characteristics of all consumer units classified by quintiles of income before taxes, Consumer Expenditure Survey, 1987 and 1997—Continued

Item	All consumer units	Complete reporting of income						Incomplete reporting of income
		Total complete reporting	Lowest 20 percent	Second 20 percent	Third 20 percent	Fourth 20 percent	Highest 20 percent	
1997								
Number of consumer units (in thousands)	105,576	84,991	16,975	16,997	16,998	16,996	17,025	20,585
Consumer unit characteristics:								
Income before taxes [1]	$39,926	$39,926	$7,086	$17,246	$30,285	$48,478	$96,397	(¹)
Age of reference person	47.7	47.8	51.4	51.4	46.5	44.3	45.3	47.6
Average number in consumer unit:								
Persons	2.5	2.5	1.8	2.3	2.5	2.9	3.1	2.6
Children under 18	.7	.7	.5	.6	.7	.9	.9	.7
Persons 65 and over	.3	.3	.4	.5	.3	.2	.1	.3
Earners	1.3	1.3	.6	.9	1.4	1.8	2.1	1.3
Vehicles	2.0	2.0	1.0	1.6	2.0	2.5	2.9	1.8
Percent homeowner	64	64	40	56	60	75	86	64
Average annual expenditures	$34,819	$36,146	$16,008	$23,558	$31,447	$42,846	$66,800	$29,557
Percent distribution:	100.0	100.0	100.0	100.0	100.0	100.0	100.0	100.0
Food	13.8	13.6	16.8	15.8	14.3	13.3	11.8	15.0
Food at home	8.3	8.2	11.7	10.9	9.1	7.7	6.3	8.7
Cereals and bakery products	1.3	1.3	1.8	1.7	1.4	1.2	1.0	1.4
Meats, poultry, fish, and eggs	2.1	2.1	3.1	3.0	2.4	1.9	1.5	2.4
Dairy products	.9	.9	1.3	1.2	1.0	.9	.7	.9
Fruits and vegetables	1.4	1.3	2.0	1.8	1.5	1.2	1.1	1.5
Other food at home	2.6	2.6	3.6	3.2	2.9	2.6	2.0	2.6
Food away from home	5.5	5.3	5.0	4.9	5.2	5.5	5.5	6.3
Alcoholic beverages	.9	.9	.9	.8	1.0	.9	.9	.8
Housing	32.4	31.4	37.0	33.1	31.5	30.2	30.2	37.2
Shelter	18.2	17.5	20.3	18.1	17.6	16.8	17.1	21.5
Owned dwellings	11.3	10.9	7.4	7.8	9.0	11.5	13.3	13.3
Rented dwellings	5.7	5.5	12.1	9.6	7.8	4.4	2.0	6.8
Other lodging	1.2	1.2	.8	.7	.8	.9	1.8	1.4
Utilities, fuels, and public services	6.9	6.7	9.8	8.7	7.4	6.4	5.0	8.2
Household operations	1.6	1.6	1.3	1.3	1.2	1.3	2.0	1.7
Housekeeping supplies	1.3	1.3	1.6	1.5	1.3	1.4	1.2	1.2
Household furnishings and equipment	4.3	4.3	4.0	3.5	4.0	4.3	4.8	4.6
Apparel and services	5.0	4.9	4.7	5.1	5.0	4.8	5.0	5.2
Transportation	18.5	18.5	15.1	18.3	19.5	20.3	17.6	18.9
Vehicle purchases (net outlay)	7.9	7.9	5.9	8.0	8.6	9.3	7.1	7.6
Gasoline and motor oil	3.2	3.1	3.3	3.5	3.4	3.3	2.6	3.5
Other vehicle expenses	6.4	6.4	5.0	6.0	6.5	6.8	6.6	6.4
Public transportation	1.1	1.1	1.0	.9	.9	.9	1.4	1.4
Health care	5.3	5.3	7.3	7.7	5.9	4.8	3.9	5.5
Entertainment	5.2	5.2	4.3	4.6	4.5	5.1	5.9	5.4
Personal care products and services	1.5	1.5	1.6	1.7	1.8	1.5	1.4	1.5
Reading	.5	.5	.5	.5	.5	.4	.5	.4
Education	1.6	1.5	2.7	1.2	1.3	1.2	1.6	2.3
Tobacco products and smoking supplies	.8	.7	1.4	1.1	.9	.7	.4	.8
Miscellaneous	2.4	2.5	3.1	2.5	2.6	2.7	2.1	2.3
Cash contributions	2.9	3.0	2.2	3.0	3.0	2.7	3.4	2.2
Personal insurance and pensions	9.3	10.6	2.3	4.6	8.3	11.4	15.3	2.4
Life and other personal insurance	1.1	1.1	.8	.9	1.0	1.0	1.3	1.2
Pensions and Social Security	8.2	9.5	1.5	3.7	7.3	10.4	14.0	1.3

¹ Components of income and taxes are derived from "complete income reporters" only; see glossary.
n.a. Not applicable.

Table 39. **Shares of average annual expenditures and characteristics of all consumer units classified by age of the reference person, Consumer Expenditure Survey, 1987 and 1997**

Item	All consumer units	Under 25	25-34	35-44	45-54	55-64	65 and over	65-74	75 and over
1987									
Number of consumer units (in thousands)	94,150	7,811	21,345	18,747	13,395	13,080	19,772	11,578	8,194
Consumer unit characteristics:									
Income before taxes [1]	$27,326	$12,621	$27,835	$36,240	$36,941	$31,038	$16,242	$18,598	$12,912
Age of reference person	47.0	21.6	29.6	39.1	49.2	59.6	73.7	69.1	80.2
Average number in consumer unit:									
Persons	2.6	1.8	2.8	3.4	2.9	2.3	1.7	1.9	1.5
Children under 18	.7	.4	1.1	1.5	.6	.2	.1	.1	(²)
Persons 65 and over	.3	(²)	(²)	(²)	(²)	.1	1.3	1.3	1.3
Earners	1.4	1.2	1.5	1.8	2.0	1.4	.4	.6	.2
Vehicles	2.0	1.2	1.9	2.4	2.7	2.3	1.3	1.6	.9
Percent homeowner	63	10	45	68	76	82	74	77	69
Average annual expenditures	$24,414	$14,368	$24,177	$31,473	$31,708	$25,707	$16,129	$18,888	$12,230
Percent distribution	100.0	100.0	100.0	100.0	100.0	100.0	100.0	100.0	100.0
Food	15.0	15.3	14.8	14.7	14.6	15.1	16.2	15.7	17.2
Food at home	8.6	7.3	8.2	8.1	8.3	9.0	10.7	10.0	12.2
Cereals and bakery products	1.2	1.0	1.2	1.2	1.1	1.2	1.6	1.5	1.9
Meats, poultry, fish, and eggs	2.3	1.7	2.2	2.2	2.4	2.6	2.9	2.7	3.2
Dairy products	1.1	1.0	1.1	1.1	1.1	1.1	1.4	1.3	1.6
Fruits and vegetables	1.5	1.2	1.3	1.3	1.4	1.6	2.1	1.9	2.5
Other food at home	2.3	2.3	2.4	2.2	2.2	2.3	2.6	2.5	2.9
Food away from home	6.4	8.1	6.5	6.7	6.3	6.1	5.5	5.7	5.0
Alcoholic beverages	1.2	2.2	1.5	1.1	1.1	1.0	.8	.9	.6
Housing	30.4	29.9	33.0	30.5	27.8	27.6	32.6	30.9	36.4
Shelter	16.4	18.7	19.3	16.8	14.7	13.1	15.8	14.8	18.3
Owned dwellings	9.7	2.3	10.1	11.5	9.9	9.0	9.0	8.9	9.0
Rented dwellings	5.5	15.4	8.6	4.2	3.2	2.5	5.6	4.4	8.3
Other lodging	1.1	1.0	.6	1.0	1.6	1.6	1.3	1.4	.9
Utilities, fuels, and public services	6.8	5.7	6.2	6.3	6.5	7.4	9.2	8.5	10.8
Household operations	1.5	.9	1.9	1.7	.9	1.1	2.0	1.7	2.6
Housekeeping supplies	1.4	1.0	1.3	1.2	1.4	1.5	1.9	1.9	1.9
Household furnishings and equipment	4.2	3.6	4.2	4.5	4.3	4.4	3.7	4.2	2.7
Apparel and services	5.9	6.2	6.0	6.4	6.1	5.4	5.2	5.5	4.5
Transportation	18.8	23.7	18.8	18.9	19.6	19.4	15.5	17.3	11.4
Vehicle purchases	8.3	11.7	8.4	8.6	8.7	8.4	5.7	6.7	3.5
Gasoline and motor oil	3.6	4.2	3.7	3.5	3.7	3.8	3.3	3.5	2.7
Other vehicle expenses	5.8	6.4	5.8	5.8	6.2	5.9	5.0	5.5	4.0
Public transportation	1.1	1.3	.9	1.0	1.0	1.3	1.5	1.6	1.2
Health care	4.6	2.4	3.2	3.4	4.0	5.4	10.2	8.9	13.0
Entertainment	4.9	5.2	5.4	5.3	4.6	4.4	4.0	4.6	2.5
Personal care products and services	1.4	1.2	1.3	1.3	1.3	1.5	1.6	1.5	1.8
Reading	.6	.5	.5	.5	.5	.6	.8	.8	.8
Education	1.4	4.3	.9	1.5	2.1	1.0	.3	.4	.1
Tobacco products and smoking supplies	1.0	1.1	.9	.9	1.1	1.0	.9	1.0	.7
Miscellaneous	2.9	1.8	2.9	3.0	2.9	3.1	3.1	3.4	2.5
Cash contributions	3.0	.5	1.6	2.5	3.8	4.1	5.1	4.4	6.5
Personal insurance and pensions	8.9	5.8	9.4	9.9	10.5	10.4	3.8	4.6	2.1
Life and other personal insurance..............................	1.2	.4	.9	1.3	1.3	1.6	1.3	1.4	1.0
Pensions and Social Security ..	7.7	5.4	8.4	8.6	9.2	8.8	2.6	3.2	1.1

See footnotes at end of table.

185

Table 39. **Shares of average annual expenditures and characteristics of all consumer units classified by age of the reference person, Consumer Expenditure Survey, 1987 and 1997—Continued**

Item	All consumer units	Under 25	25-34	35-44	45-54	55-64	65 and over	65-74	75 and over
1997									
Number of consumer units (in thousands)	105,576	7,501	19,918	24,560	19,343	12,316	21,936	12,109	9,827
Consumer unit characteristics:									
Income before taxes [1]	$39,926	$15,666	$40,247	$48,788	$55,260	$41,734	$23,965	$27,492	$19,425
Age of reference person	47.7	21.2	29.7	39.5	49.1	59.3	74.6	69.4	81.1
Average number in consumer unit:									
Persons	2.5	1.8	2.8	3.2	2.7	2.2	1.7	1.9	1.5
Children under 18	.7	.4	1.1	1.3	.6	.2	.1	.1	(²)
Persons 65 and over	.3	(²)	(²)	(²)	(²)	.1	1.3	1.3	1.4
Earners	1.3	1.2	1.5	1.7	1.8	1.4	.4	.6	.2
Vehicles	2.0	1.0	1.8	2.2	2.5	2.3	1.5	1.8	1.2
Percent homeowner	64	9	44	64	77	79	79	81	77
Average annual expenditures	$34,819	$18,450	$34,902	$40,413	$45,239	$35,954	$24,413	$27,792	$20,279
Percent distribution:	100.0	100.0	100.0	100.0	100.0	100.0	100.0	100.0	100.0
Food	13.8	15.4	13.3	14.0	13.3	14.1	14.3	14.6	13.7
Food at home	8.3	8.5	7.9	8.4	7.6	8.7	9.4	9.4	9.5
Cereals and bakery products	1.3	1.3	1.2	1.3	1.2	1.3	1.5	1.4	1.5
Meats, poultry, fish, and eggs	2.1	2.1	2.0	2.1	2.0	2.3	2.4	2.4	2.3
Dairy products	.9	.9	.9	1.0	.8	.9	1.0	1.0	1.0
Fruits and vegetables	1.4	1.3	1.2	1.3	1.2	1.5	1.8	1.7	1.9
Other food at home	2.6	2.8	2.5	2.6	2.3	2.7	2.7	2.8	2.7
Food away from home	5.5	6.9	5.4	5.6	5.7	5.4	4.9	5.3	4.3
Alcoholic beverages	.9	1.4	1.1	.9	.8	.8	.8	1.0	.5
Housing	32.4	31.8	33.7	33.2	30.7	30.8	33.1	31.9	35.0
Shelter	18.2	19.8	20.0	19.5	17.3	16.1	16.4	15.7	17.5
Owned dwellings	11.3	2.1	9.8	13.0	12.3	11.3	10.7	10.9	10.4
Rented dwellings	5.7	16.3	9.4	5.5	3.3	3.2	4.3	3.3	6.0
Other lodging	1.2	1.5	.7	1.0	1.6	1.6	1.4	1.6	1.1
Utilities, fuels, and public services	6.9	5.9	6.4	6.7	6.4	7.4	8.8	8.4	9.6
Household operations	1.6	1.0	1.9	1.8	1.2	1.1	1.9	1.4	2.6
Housekeeping supplies	1.3	.9	1.2	1.3	1.2	1.5	1.7	1.6	1.8
Household furnishings and equipment	4.3	4.1	4.3	4.0	4.6	4.8	4.3	4.9	3.5
Apparel and services	5.0	6.8	5.6	5.1	4.7	4.6	4.3	4.7	3.6
Transportation	18.5	20.2	20.2	17.9	19.3	18.7	15.6	16.7	13.7
Vehicle purchases (net outlay)	7.9	9.4	9.3	7.5	8.2	7.3	6.1	6.6	5.2
Gasoline and motor oil	3.2	3.8	3.2	3.2	3.2	3.3	2.7	2.9	2.3
Other vehicle expenses	6.4	5.9	6.6	6.3	6.8	6.6	5.6	5.9	5.2
Public transportation	1.1	1.2	1.1	.9	1.2	1.4	1.2	1.4	1.1
Health care	5.3	2.3	3.5	4.0	4.3	6.1	11.7	10.4	13.8
Entertainment	5.2	5.7	5.3	5.3	5.3	5.3	4.5	4.7	4.2
Personal care products and services	1.5	1.6	1.5	1.5	1.4	1.5	1.8	1.8	1.9
Reading	.5	.3	.4	.4	.5	.6	.7	.7	.7
Education	1.6	6.0	1.4	1.5	2.4	.8	.6	.8	.3
Tobacco products and smoking supplies	.8	1.1	.7	.8	.7	.8	.6	.8	.4
Miscellaneous	2.4	1.5	2.2	2.4	2.4	3.0	2.5	2.7	2.3
Cash contributions	2.9	.9	1.4	2.3	3.2	3.4	5.4	4.3	7.3
Personal insurance and pensions	9.3	5.1	9.6	10.7	11.0	9.6	3.9	4.9	2.3
Life and other personal insurance	1.1	.3	.7	.9	1.3	1.5	1.4	1.5	1.2
Pensions and Social Security	8.2	4.8	8.9	9.7	9.7	8.2	2.6	3.4	1.1

[1] Components of income and taxes are derived from "complete income reporters" only; see glossary.
[2] Value less than 0.05.

186

Table 40. **Shares of average annual expenditures and characteristics of all consumer units classified by composition of the consumer unit, Consumer Expenditure Survey, 1987 and 1997**

			Husband and wife consumer units					One parent, at least one child under 18	Single person and other consumer units
Item	Total husband and wife consumer units	Husband and wife only	Husband and wife with children				Other husband and wife consumer units		
			Total husband and wife with children	Oldest child under 6	Oldest child 6 to 17	Oldest child 18 or over			
1987									
Number of consumer units (in thousands)	52,110	20,445	28,082	5,937	14,296	7,849	3,584	5,840	36,200
Consumer unit characteristics:									
Income before taxes [1]	$36,114	$32,307	$39,120	$35,505	$37,263	$45,238	$35,568	$14,737	$17,237
Age of reference person	47.0	55.3	40.7	30.5	38.5	52.4	48.8	35.0	49.1
Average number in consumer unit:									
Persons	3.2	2.0	3.9	3.4	4.2	3.9	4.9	3.0	1.5
Children under 18	.9	n.a.	1.6	1.5	2.2	.6	1.4	1.8	.2
Persons 65 and over	.3	.6	.1	(²)	(²)	.2	.5	(²)	.3
Earners	1.7	1.2	2.1	1.6	1.9	2.7	2.4	.9	.9
Vehicles	2.6	2.3	2.9	2.2	2.7	3.4	2.9	1.0	1.2
Percent homeowner	79.0	79.0	77.5	62.0	77.0	90.0	78.0	33.0	44.0
Average annual expenditures	$30,659	$26,541	$33,578	$29,414	$32,899	$37,966	$32,010	$16,521	$16,590
Percent distribution	100.0	100.0	100.0	100.0	100.0	100.0	100.0	100.0	100.0
Food	14.9	14.2	15.3	13.0	15.8	15.8	17.0	17.8	14.5
Food at home	8.7	7.8	9.0	8.3	9.2	9.1	11.0	11.3	7.7
Cereals and bakery products	1.2	1.1	1.3	1.1	1.4	1.3	1.5	1.6	1.1
Meats, poultry, fish, and eggs	2.4	2.2	2.5	2.2	2.4	2.6	3.2	3.3	2.0
Dairy products	1.1	1.0	1.2	1.1	1.3	1.2	1.4	1.5	1.0
Fruits and vegetables	1.4	1.4	1.4	1.3	1.4	1.5	1.9	1.8	1.4
Other food at home	2.3	2.1	2.5	2.5	2.6	2.3	2.9	3.0	2.1
Food away from home	6.2	6.3	6.3	4.7	6.6	6.7	6.0	6.4	6.8
Alcoholic beverages	1.0	1.1	.9	.8	.9	1.0	.9	1.0	1.8
Housing	29.3	29.5	29.2	34.5	30.3	24.1	29.6	34.9	32.6
Shelter	15.2	15.4	15.1	18.5	16.0	11.4	15.5	19.7	19.1
Owned dwellings	10.9	10.5	11.0	12.3	12.1	8.6	11.3	6.9	7.2
Rented dwellings	3.1	3.4	2.9	5.4	3.0	1.2	3.1	12.2	11.0
Other lodging	1.2	1.5	1.2	.9	1.0	1.5	1.2	.7	.9
Utilities, fuels, and public services	6.6	6.8	6.4	6.2	6.5	6.4	7.4	8.4	7.3
Household operations	1.6	1.0	1.9	3.9	1.9	.8	1.3	2.2	1.2
Housekeeping supplies	1.4	1.5	1.4	1.4	1.4	1.3	1.4	1.5	1.4
Household furnishings and equipment	4.5	4.8	4.4	4.5	4.4	4.3	4.0	3.1	3.6
Apparel and services	5.7	5.3	5.9	5.7	6.2	5.6	6.2	6.9	6.3
Transportation	19.5	18.8	19.9	19.0	18.2	23.1	18.6	17.2	17.5
Vehicle purchases	8.7	7.9	9.3	9.3	8.3	10.9	7.8	8.5	7.1
Gasoline and motor oil	3.8	3.6	3.8	3.3	3.7	4.2	3.9	3.2	3.4
Other vehicle expenses	6.0	5.9	6.0	5.6	5.6	7.0	5.8	4.7	5.5
Public transportation	1.0	1.3	.8	.8	.6	1.0	1.1	.8	1.5
Health care	4.7	6.1	3.9	3.9	3.9	4.0	5.1	3.0	4.7
Entertainment	5.0	4.6	5.2	5.0	5.6	4.8	4.8	4.5	4.7
Personal care products and services	1.3	1.4	1.3	1.1	1.2	1.5	1.2	1.8	1.4
Reading	.6	.6	.5	.5	.5	.5	.5	.5	.7
Education	1.4	.9	1.7	.5	1.5	2.7	1.3	.9	1.5
Tobacco products and smoking supplies	.9	.9	.9	.8	.9	1.0	1.3	1.2	1.0
Miscellaneous	2.9	3.0	2.6	2.8	2.6	2.8	3.1	2.7	3.3
Cash contributions	3.1	4.3	2.6	2.2	2.4	3.2	1.8	1.9	3.0
Personal insurance and pensions	9.7	9.5	10.0	10.1	10.0	10.0	8.6	5.9	7.3
Life and other personal insurance	1.4	1.4	1.4	1.1	1.5	1.3	1.5	.8	.7
Pensions and Social Security	8.3	8.0	8.6	9.0	8.5	8.6	7.1	5.1	6.5

See footnotes at end of table.

187

Table 40. **Shares of average annual expenditures and characteristics of all consumer units classified by composition of the consumer unit, Consumer Expenditure Survey, 1987 and 1997—Continued**

Item	Total husband and wife consumer units	Husband and wife only	Husband and wife with children — Total husband and wife with children	Oldest child under 6	Oldest child 6 to 17	Oldest child 18 or over	Other husband and wife consumer units	One parent, at least one child under 18	Single person and other consumer units
1997									
Number of consumer units (in thousands)	55,205	22,531	28,382	5,431	15,360	7,591	4,291	6,626	43,745
Consumer unit characteristics									
Income before taxes [1]	$52,981	$47,475	$57,598	$57,063	$56,673	$59,938	$51,038	$24,185	$25,811
Age of reference person	48.2	56.6	41.5	32.0	39.9	51.4	47.9	36.8	48.9
Average number in consumer unit:									
Persons	3.2	2.0	4.0	3.5	4.2	3.9	4.8	3	1.6
Children under 18	.9	n.a.	1.6	1.5	2.2	.6	1.4	1.8	.2
Persons 65 and over	.3	.7	.1	(²)	(²)	.2	.5	(²)	.3
Earners	1.7	1.2	2.0	1.7	1.9	2.6	2.3	1.0	.9
Vehicles	2.6	2.4	2.7	2.2	2.6	3.4	2.7	1.2	1.3
Percent homeowner	80	83	78	66	77	88	75	37	47
Average annual expenditures	$44,101	$39,515	$47,716	$45,723	$47,124	$50,485	$44,311	$26,352	$24,160
Percent distribution	100.0	100.0	100.0	100.0	100.0	100.0	100.0	100.0	100.0
Food	13.8	13.3	13.9	12.3	14.4	14.2	15.9	15.4	13.1
Food at home	8.4	7.6	8.6	8.0	8.8	8.6	10.6	10.5	7.4
Cereals and bakery products	1.3	1.1	1.4	1.2	1.4	1.4	1.7	1.6	1.2
Meats, poultry, fish, and eggs	2.1	1.9	2.2	1.9	2.2	2.3	3.1	2.9	1.9
Dairy products	.9	.8	1.0	.9	1.0	.9	1.1	1.1	.8
Fruits and vegetables	1.4	1.3	1.3	1.2	1.3	1.4	1.7	1.7	1.3
Other food at home	2.6	2.4	2.7	2.7	2.8	2.6	3.1	3.1	2.3
Food away from home	5.5	5.7	5.3	4.3	5.5	5.6	5.2	4.9	5.6
Alcoholic beverages	.8	1.0	.6	.6	.6	.6	.7	.5	1.2
Housing	31.1	31.0	31.2	34.9	32.0	27.2	31.1	37.3	34.6
Shelter	17.0	16.5	17.5	19.1	18.4	14.6	15.7	20.9	20.8
Owned dwellings	12.5	11.9	13.2	13.8	14.0	11.2	10.4	8.9	9.1
Rented dwellings	3.1	2.9	3.0	4.8	3.2	1.7	4.3	11.3	10.8
Other lodging	1.4	1.7	1.2	.6	1.2	1.7	1.0	.7	.9
Utilities, fuels, and public services	6.5	6.5	6.4	5.6	6.5	6.7	7.5	8.6	7.6
Household operations	1.6	1.1	2.0	4.7	1.8	.7	1.6	2.5	1.3
Housekeeping supplies	1.4	1.4	1.3	1.4	1.3	1.4	1.3	1.3	1.1
Household furnishings and equipment	4.6	5.5	4.0	4.0	4.0	3.8	5.0	4.0	3.8
Apparel and services	5.0	4.6	5.3	4.9	5.7	5.0	5.2	5.8	4.5
Transportation	19.2	18.6	19.5	20.6	17.9	21.9	19.4	15.9	17.7
Vehicle purchases (net outlay)	8.1	8.0	8.3	10.2	7.3	9.0	7.8	6.6	7.5
Gasoline and motor oil	3.2	3.0	3.3	2.9	3.2	3.8	3.7	2.9	3.0
Other vehicle expenses	6.7	6.2	6.9	6.6	6.5	7.9	6.9	5.6	6.0
Public transportation	1.1	1.3	1.0	.9	.9	1.2	1.0	.9	1.2
Health care	5.3	6.8	4.4	3.7	4.3	5.0	5.4	4.2	5.4
Entertainment	5.5	5.6	5.4	4.5	5.7	5.7	4.7	4.7	4.7
Personal care products and services	1.5	1.5	1.4	1.3	1.4	1.5	1.6	1.8	1.5
Reading	.5	.6	.4	.4	.4	.4	.3	.3	.5
Education	1.6	1.0	1.9	.6	1.8	3.0	1.3	2.2	1.8
Tobacco products and smoking supplies	.7	.6	.6	.5	.6	.7	1.0	.7	1.0
Miscellaneous	2.2	2.3	2.1	2.3	1.9	2.4	2.2	3.1	2.9
Cash contributions	2.8	3.5	2.3	2.3	2.3	2.3	2.2	1.6	3.4
Personal insurance and pensions	10.1	9.5	10.7	11.2	10.9	10.0	9.1	6.4	7.8
Life and other personal insurance	1.2	1.3	1.2	1.0	1.3	1.2	1.2	.7	.8
Pensions and Social Security	8.9	8.2	9.5	10.2	9.7	8.8	7.9	5.8	6.9

[1] Components of income and taxes are derived from "complete income reporters" only; see glossary.
[2] Value less than 0.05.
n.a. Not applicable.

Table 41. Shares of average annual expenditures and characteristics of all consumer units classified by region of residence, Consumer Expenditure Survey, 1987 and 1997

Item	All consumer units	Northeast	Midwest	South	West
1987					
Number of consumer units (in thousands)	94,150	19,731	23,966	31,303	19,151
Consumer unit characteristics:					
Income before taxes [1]	$27,326	$27,494	$25,772	$26,479	$30,373
Age of reference person	47.0	49.1	46.9	46.6	45.8
Average number in consumer unit:					
Persons	2.6	2.5	2.5	2.6	2.6
Children under 18	.7	.6	.7	.7	.7
Persons 65 and over	.3	.4	.3	.3	.3
Earners	1.4	1.3	1.4	1.4	1.4
Vehicles	2.0	1.6	2.1	2	2.2
Percent homeowner	63	61	66	63	57
Average annual expenditures	$24,414	$25,079	$23,021	$23,292	$27,309
Percent distribution:	100.0	100.0	100.0	100.0	100.0
Food	15.0	15.6	15.0	14.8	14.7
Food at home	8.6	8.8	8.6	8.4	8.7
Cereals and bakery products	1.2	1.3	1.2	1.2	1.2
Meats, poultry, fish, and eggs	2.3	2.6	2.3	2.3	2.2
Dairy products	1.1	1.2	1.1	1.1	1.2
Fruits and vegetables	1.5	1.5	1.4	1.4	1.6
Other food at home	2.3	2.1	2.4	2.4	2.4
Food away from home	6.4	6.8	6.4	6.4	6.0
Alcoholic beverages	1.2	1.4	1.1	1.0	1.3
Housing	30.4	31.7	29.3	29.3	31.7
Shelter	16.4	17.7	14.8	14.9	18.8
Owned dwellings	9.7	10.4	9.3	9.0	10.6
Rented dwellings	5.5	5.8	4.4	4.9	7.2
Other lodging	1.1	1.5	1.1	1.0	1.1
Utilities, fuels, and public services	6.8	7.0	7.3	7.4	5.4
Household operations	1.5	1.2	1.5	1.7	1.6
Housekeeping supplies	1.4	1.4	1.4	1.4	1.3
Household furnishings and equipment	4.2	4.4	4.3	3.8	4.6
Apparel and services	5.9	6.8	5.7	5.9	5.3
Transportation	18.8	17.8	19.5	19.7	17.9
Vehicle purchases	8.3	7.6	8.9	9.0	7.2
Gasoline and motor oil	3.6	3.1	3.8	4.0	3.4
Other vehicle expenses	5.8	5.6	5.9	5.8	6.0
Public transportation	1.1	1.5	1.0	0.9	1.3
Health care	4.6	4.2	4.8	5.2	4.2
Entertainment	4.9	4.6	5.0	4.7	5.4
Personal care products and services	1.4	1.4	1.3	1.4	1.3
Reading	.6	.7	.6	.5	.6
Education	1.4	1.9	1.6	1.1	1.0
Tobacco products and smoking supplies	1.0	.9	1.1	1.0	.7
Miscellaneous	2.9	2.6	2.8	3.0	3.3
Cash contributions	3.0	2.3	3.2	3.2	3.4
Personal insurance and pensions	8.9	8.2	9.0	9.1	9.2
Life and other personal insurance	1.2	1.0	1.3	1.4	.9
Pensions and Social Security	7.7	7.2	7.6	7.7	8.3

See footnote at end of table.

189

Table 41. Shares of average annual expenditures and characteristics of all consumer units classified by region of residence, Consumer Expenditure Survey, 1987 and 1997—Continued

Item	All consumer units	Northeast	Midwest	South	West
1997					
Number of consumer units (in thousands)	105,576	21,090	25,228	36,832	22,426
Consumer unit characteristics:					
Income before taxes [1]	$39,926	$43,336	$39,222	$35,691	$44,368
Age of reference person	47.7	48.1	48.8	47.7	46.2
Average number in consumer unit::					
Persons	2.5	2.5	2.5	2.5	2.7
Children under 18	.7	.6	.7	.7	.8
Persons 65 and over	.3	.3	.3	.3	.3
Earners	1.3	1.3	1.4	1.3	1.4
Vehicles	2.0	1.6	2.2	1.9	2.1
Percent homeowner	64	59	69	66	58
Average annual expenditures..........................	$34,819	$36,070	$33,791	$32,226	$39,037
Percent distribution:	100.0	100.0	100.0	100.0	100.0
Food	13.8	14.9	13.7	13.7	13.0
Food at home	8.3	8.2	8.1	8.6	8.0
Cereals and bakery products	1.3	1.4	1.3	1.3	1.2
Meats, poultry, fish, and eggs	2.1	2.2	2.0	2.3	2.0
Dairy products	.9	.9	.9	.9	.9
Fruits and vegetables	1.4	1.5	1.3	1.4	1.4
Other food at home	2.6	2.3	2.6	2.7	2.5
Food away from home	5.5	6.6	5.6	5.1	5.0
Alcoholic beverages	.9	1.1	.9	.7	1.0
Housing	32.4	34.6	31.2	30.6	34.0
Shelter	18.2	20.9	16.7	15.7	20.7
Owned dwellings	11.3	13.0	11.2	9.5	12.3
Rented dwellings	5.7	6.4	4.4	5.3	7.0
Other lodging	1.2	1.5	1.2	1.0	1.4
Utilities, fuels, and public services	6.9	6.9	7.3	7.6	5.7
Household operations	1.6	1.3	1.4	1.7	1.9
Housekeeping supplies	1.3	1.2	1.4	1.3	1.3
Household furnishings and equipment	4.3	4.4	4.4	4.3	4.4
Apparel and services	5.0	5.3	5.1	5.0	4.5
Transportation	18.5	16.2	18.8	20.1	18.2
Vehicle purchases (net outlay)	7.9	5.7	8.2	9.5	7.2
Gasoline and motor oil	3.2	2.7	3.3	3.5	3.0
Other vehicle expenses	6.4	6.2	6.3	6.4	6.7
Public transportation	1.1	1.6	1.0	.8	1.3
Health care	5.3	4.7	5.6	5.9	4.6
Entertainment	5.2	4.9	5.7	4.8	5.5
Personal care products and services	1.5	1.4	1.5	1.7	1.4
Reading	.5	.5	.5	.4	.5
Education	1.6	2.1	1.5	1.4	1.7
Tobacco products and smoking supplies	.8	.7	.9	.8	.6
Miscellaneous	2.4	2.3	2.4	2.5	2.5
Cash contributions	2.9	2.1	2.9	3.3	2.9
Personal insurance and pensions	9.3	9.1	9.3	8.9	9.8
Life and other personal insurance	1.1	1.1	1.1	1.3	.8
Pensions and Social Security	8.2	8.1	8.2	7.6	9.0

[1] Components of income and taxes are derived from "complete income reporters" only; see glossary.

Table 42. Shares of average annual expenditures and characteristics of all consumer units classified by origin of the reference person, Consumer Expenditure Survey, 1987 and 1997

Item	All consumer units	Hispanic	Non-Hispanic Total Non-Hispanic	Non-Hispanic Non-Hispanic less Afro-American	Non-Hispanic Afro-American
1987					
Number of consumer units (in thousands)	94,150	4,954	89,196	80,421	8,774
Consumer unit characteristics:					
Income before taxes [1]	$27,326	$21,897	$27,635	$28,750	$17,121
Age of reference person	47.0	41.0	47.4	47.6	45.7
Average number in consumer unit:					
Persons	2.6	1.3	2.5	.6	2.8
Children under 18	.7	3.4	.7	2.5	1.0
Persons 65 and over	.3	.1	1.4	1.4	.2
Earners	1.4	1.5	.3	.3	1.2
Vehicles	2.0	1.6	2.0	2.1	1.2
Percent homeowner	63	39	64	66	45
Average annual expenditures	$24,413	$20,890	$24,609	$25,515	$16,361
Percent distribution	100.0	100.0	100.0	100.0	100.0
Food	15.0	17.5	14.9	14.8	16.2
Food at home	8.6	11.4	8.5	8.3	11.1
Cereals and bakery products	1.2	1.5	1.2	1.2	1.5
Meats, poultry, fish, and eggs	2.3	3.4	2.3	2.2	3.9
Dairy products	1.1	1.4	1.1	1.1	1.2
Fruits and vegetables	1.5	2.1	1.4	1.4	1.9
Other food at home	2.3	3.0	2.4	2.4	2.6
Food away from home	6.4	6.1	6.4	6.5	5.1
Alcoholic beverages	1.2	1.2	1.2	1.2	.9
Housing	30.4	32.4	30.3	30.1	32.3
Shelter	16.4	19.3	16.2	16.2	16.8
Owned dwellings	9.7	8.2	9.8	10.0	6.8
Rented dwellings	5.5	10.7	5.3	5.0	9.6
Other lodging	1.1	.4	1.2	1.2	.4
Utilities, fuels, and public services	6.8	6.9	6.8	6.6	9.8
Household operations	1.5	1.0	1.5	1.6	1.2
Housekeeping supplies	1.4	1.8	1.4	1.4	1.3
Household furnishings and equipment	4.2	3.4	4.3	4.4	3.1
Apparel and services	5.9	6.4	5.9	5.8	7.9
Transportation	18.8	19.3	18.8	18.8	18.8
Vehicle purchases (net outlay)	8.3	8.2	8.3	8.3	7.7
Gasoline and motor oil	3.6	4.1	3.6	3.6	4.0
Other vehicle expenses	5.8	5.8	5.8	5.8	5.9
Public transportation	1.1	1.2	1.1	1.1	1.2
Health care	4.6	3.5	4.7	4.8	3.8
Entertainment	4.9	3.9	4.9	5.1	3.2
Personal care products and services	1.4	1.3	1.4	1.3	1.7
Reading	.6	.4	.6	.6	.4
Education	1.4	1.6	1.4	1.4	1.0
Tobacco products and smoking supplies	1.0	.7	1.0	1.0	1.1
Miscellaneous	2.9	2.3	3.0	2.9	3.2
Cash contributions	3.0	1.9	3.1	3.2	1.9
Personal insurance and pensions	8.9	7.7	9.0	9.1	7.5
Life and other personal insurance	1.2	.6	1.2	1.2	1.6
Pensions and Social Security	7.7	7.0	7.7	7.9	5.8

See footnote at end of table.

Table 42. Shares of average annual expenditures and characteristics of all consumer units classified by origin of the reference person, Consumer Expenditure Survey, 1987 and 1997—Continued

Item	All consumer units	Hispanic	Non-Hispanic		
			Total Non-Hispanic	Non-Hispanic less Afro-American	Afro-American
1997					
Number of consumer units (in thousands)	105,576	8,905	96,670	86,130	10,540
Consumer unit characteristics:					
Income before taxes [1]	$39,926	$29,976	$40,907	$42,381	$28,323
Age of reference person	47.7	42.0	48.3	48.6	45.0
Average number in consumer unit:					
Persons	2.5	3.4	2.4	2.4	2.7
Children under 18	.7	1.3	.6	.6	1.0
Persons 65 and over	.3	.2	.3	.3	.2
Earners	1.3	1.6	1.3	1.3	1.2
Vehicles	2.0	1.7	2.0	2.1	1.2
Percent homeowner	64	47	65	68	44
Average annual expenditures	$34,819	$29,333	$35,325	$36,568	$25,332
Percent distribution	100.0	100.0	100.0	100.0	100.0
Food	13.8	16.6	13.6	13.6	14.1
Food at home	8.3	11.5	8.0	7.9	10.0
Cereals and bakery products	1.3	1.6	1.3	1.3	1.5
Meats, poultry, fish, and eggs	2.1	3.6	2.0	1.9	3.5
Dairy products	.9	1.2	.9	.9	.8
Fruits and vegetables	1.4	2.1	1.3	1.3	1.6
Other food at home	2.6	3.0	2.5	2.5	2.6
Food away from home	5.5	5.1	5.5	5.7	4.1
Alcoholic beverages	.9	.7	.9	.9	.5
Housing	32.4	33.8	32.3	32.0	35.0
Shelter	18.2	19.8	18.1	18.0	19.4
Owned dwellings	11.3	9.1	11.5	11.7	8.4
Rented dwellings	5.7	10.1	5.4	4.9	10.4
Other lodging	1.2	.5	1.3	1.3	.6
Utilities, fuels, and public services	6.9	7.4	6.9	6.6	9.8
Household operations	1.6	1.1	1.6	1.6	1.4
Housekeeping supplies	1.3	1.4	1.3	1.3	1.1
Household furnishings and equipment	4.3	4.2	4.4	4.5	3.2
Apparel and services	5.0	6.7	4.8	4.7	6.5
Transportation	18.5	19.0	18.5	18.4	19.3
Vehicle purchases (net outlay)	7.9	8.1	7.8	7.8	8.6
Gasoline and motor oil	3.2	3.7	3.1	3.1	3.1
Other vehicle expenses	6.4	6.1	6.4	6.4	6.5
Public transportation	1.1	1.2	1.1	1.1	1.0
Health care	5.3	4.0	5.4	5.5	4.1
Entertainment	5.2	3.9	5.3	5.5	3.4
Personal care products and services	1.5	1.6	1.5	1.4	2.5
Reading	.5	.2	.5	.5	.3
Education	1.6	1.6	1.6	1.7	.9
Tobacco products and smoking supplies	.8	.4	.8	.8	.7
Miscellaneous	2.4	2.4	2.4	2.5	2.2
Cash contributions	2.9	1.4	3.0	3.0	2.5
Personal insurance and pensions	9.3	7.8	9.4	9.5	8.1
Life and other personal insurance	1.1	.7	1.1	1.1	1.3
Pensions and Social Security	8.2	7.1	8.2	8.4	6.8

[1] Components of income and taxes are derived from "complete income reporters" only: see glossary.

Table 43. **Number of earners in families by type of family, selected years, 1990-98**

(In thousands)

Characteristic	1990	1994	1995	1996	1997	1998
Total, all families	66,623	69,211	69,971	70,174	70,840	71,443
Married-couple families	52,385	53,246	53,927	53,621	53,654	54,361
No earners	6,812	7,280	7,227	7,278	7,148	7,289
One earner	11,748	11,842	11,772	11,739	11,556	11,728
Husband	9,212	8,745	8,719	8,821	8,671	8,792
Wife	1,840	2,411	2,372	2,253	2,214	2,302
Other family member	695	687	681	664	671	634
Two earners	26,011	26,957	27,472	27,361	27,474	27,935
Husband and wife	23,929	24,806	25,377	25,478	25,536	25,959
Husband and other family member	1,657	1,540	1,533	1,365	1,443	1,412
Husband is not an earner	425	612	562	518	496	564
Three earners or more	7,815	7,166	7,455	7,243	7,476	7,409
Husband and wife	6,950	6,496	6,748	6,582	6,870	6,805
Husband is an earner, not wife	716	511	516	514	456	441
Families maintained by women[1]	11,309	12,974	12,768	12,998	13,269	13,112
No earner	2,510	3,111	2,855	2,679	2,586	2,342
One earner	5,530	6,495	6,581	6,868	7,112	7,146
Householder	4,468	5,367	5,495	5,627	5,906	5,903
Other family member	1,063	1,128	1,086	1,211	1,205	1,243
Two earners or more	3,268	3,368	3,332	3,452	3,572	3,623
Householder and other family member(s)	2,903	3,049	3,044	3,156	3,341	3,332
Householder is not an earner	365	319	289	296	230	291
Families maintained by men[1]	2,929	2,992	3,276	3,555	3,916	3,970
No earner	281	332	382	357	359	346
One earner	1,376	1,615	1,705	1,821	1,982	2,106
Householder	1,127	1,372	1,437	1,568	1,683	1,806
Other family member	249	242	268	253	298	301
Two earners or more	1,272	1,045	1,189	1,377	1,576	1,518
Householder and other family member(s)	1,201	983	1,118	1,278	1,454	1,413
Householder is not an earner	72	63	71	98	122	105

[1] Families maintained by widowed, divorced, separated, or single persons.

NOTE: Data on the number and type of families are collected in March of the subsequent year. Earner status refers to the preceding calendar year. The comparability of historical labor force data has been affected at various times by methodological and conceptual changes. For an explanation, see the Explanatory Notes and Estimates of Error section of *Employment and Earnings*, a monthly periodical published by the Bureau of Labor Statistics.

Table 44. Employment Cost Index for benefit costs, annual averages[1] 1980-98

Year	Civilian workers	State and local government workers	Private industry workers						
			All private industry workers	White-collar workers	Blue-collar workers	Goods-producing workers	Service-producing workers	Manufac-turing workers	Nonman-ufacturing workers
1980	–	–	57.3	56.5	58.6	58.4	56.4	57.8	57.0
1981	–	–	64.7	63.8	66.1	66.2	63.3	65.6	64.1
1982	68.4	–	69.4	68.2	71.3	71.5	67.5	70.7	68.6
1983	74.0	–	75.1	73.7	77.1	77.2	73.2	76.4	74.3
1984	79.3	–	80.3	79.4	81.7	81.8	79.0	81.1	79.8
1985	83.1	–	83.8	83.3	84.5	85.1	82.5	84.6	83.2
1986	86.2	–	86.6	86.4	87.0	87.6	85.7	86.9	86.5
1987	89.2	–	89.3	89.3	89.5	89.8	89.0	88.6	89.9
1988	95.0	–	95.1	94.5	96.0	96.0	94.3	95.3	95.0
1989	100.9	–	100.6	100.6	100.7	100.7	100.6	100.7	100.6
1990	108.0	110.0	107.5	107.8	107.2	107.9	107.2	107.6	107.5
1991	114.4	115.6	114.1	114.4	113.6	114.6	113.7	114.0	114.2
1992	120.5	120.9	120.4	120.2	120.5	121.5	119.5	120.9	120.2
1993	126.7	125.5	127.0	126.3	127.5	129.2	125.1	128.8	125.9
1994	131.5	129.3	132.1	132.0	131.8	134.1	130.3	133.3	131.3
1995	134.8	132.7	135.3	132.1	133.9	136.3	134.2	135.7	134.8
1996	137.2	135.7	137.7	138.8	136.1	138.7	136.6	138.7	137.0
1997	139.9	137.9	140.5	141.9	138.2	140.9	139.7	141.0	140.0
1998	143.4	141.2	144.0	146.0	140.5	142.5	144.2	142.3	144.3

[1] The annual average is the average for the four quarters of the year.

Dash indicates data not available.

Table 45. Percent of full-time employees participating in employer-provided benefit plans and in selected features within plans, medium and large private establishments, selected years 1984-97

Item	1984	1986	1988	1989	1991	1993	1995	1997
Scope of survey (in 000's)	21,013	21,303	31,059	32,428	31,163	28,728	33,374	38,409
Number of employees (in 000's):								
With medical care	20,383	20,238	27,953	29,834	25,865	23,519	25,546	29,340
With life insurance	20,172	20,451	28,574	30,482	29,293	26,175	29,078	33,495
With defined benefit plan	17,231	16,190	19,567	20,430	18,386	16,015	17,417	19,202
Time-off plans								
Participants with:								
Paid lunch time	9	10	11	10	8	9	–	–
Average minutes per day	26	27	29	26	30	29	–	–
Paid rest time	73	72	72	71	67	68	–	–
Average minutes per day	26	26	26	26	28	26	–	–
Paid funeral leave	–	88	85	84	80	83	80	81
Average days per								
occurrence	–	3.2	3.2	3.3	3.3	3.0	3.3	3.7
Paid holidays	99	99	96	97	92	91	89	89
Average days per year[1]	9.8	10.0	9.4	9.2	10.2	9.4	9.1	9.3
Paid personal leave	23	25	24	22	21	21	22	20
Average days per year	3.6	3.7	3.3	3.1	3.3	3.1	3.3	3.5
Paid vacations...........................	99	100	98	97	96	97	96	95
Paid sick leave[2]	67	70	69	68	67	65	58	56
Unpaid maternity leave	–	–	33	37	37	60	–	–
Unpaid paternity leave	–	–	16	18	26	53	–	–
Unpaid family leave	–	–	–	–	–	–	84	93
Insurance plans								
Participants in medical								
care plans	97	95	90	92	83	82	77	76
Percent of participants with								
Coverage for:								
Home health care	46	66	76	75	81	86	78	85
Extended care facilities	62	70	79	80	80	82	73	78
Physical exams	8	18	28	28	30	42	56	63
Percent of participants with								
employee contribution								
required for								
Self coverage	36	43	44	47	51	61	67	69
Average monthly								
contribution	$11.93	$12.80	$19.29	$25.31	$26.60	$31.55	$33.92	$39.14
Family coverage	58	63	64	66	69	76	78	80
Average monthly								
contribution	$35.93	$41.40	$60.07	$72.10	$96.97	$107.42	$118.33	$130.07
Participants in life insurance								
plans	96	96	92	94	94	91	87	87
Percent of participants with:								
Accidental death and								
dismemberment insurance ..	74	72	78	71	71	76	77	74
Survivor income benefits	–	10	8	7	6	5	7	6
Retiree protection available ...	64	59	49	42	44	41	37	33
Participants in long-term disability								
insurance plans	47	48	42	45	40	41	42	43
Participants in sickness and								
accident insurance plans	51	49	46	43	45	44	–	–
Participants in short-term								
disability plans[2].........................	–	–	–	–	–	–	53	55
Retirement plans								
Participants in defined benefit								
pension plans	82	76	63	63	59	56	52	50
Percent of participants with:								
Normal retirement prior to								
age 65	63	64	59	62	55	52	52	52
Early retirement available	97	98	98	97	98	95	96	95
Ad hoc pension increase in								
last 5 years	47	35	26	22	7	6	4	10
Terminal earnings formula	54	57	55	64	56	61	58	56
Benefit coordinated with								
Social Security	56	62	62	63	54	48	51	49
Participants in defined								
contributions plans	–	60	45	48	48	49	55	57
Participants in plans with tax								
deferred savings arrangements ..	–	33	36	41	44	43	54	55
Other benefits								
Employees eligible for:								
Flexible benefits plans	–	2	5	9	10	12	12	13
Reimbursement accounts[3]	–	5	12	23	36	52	38	32
Premium conversion plans[4]	–	–	–	–	–	–	5	7

[1] Methods used to calculate the average number of paid holidays were revised in 1995 to count partial days more precisely. Average holidays for 1995 and 1997 are not comporable to those reported in 1991 and 1993.
[2] See footnote 1, table 48.
[3] Prior to 1995, reimbursement accounts that were part of flexible benefit plans were tabulated separately.
[4] Included in reimbursement accounts prior to 1995.

NOTE: Dash indicates data not available.

195

Table 46. **Percent of full-time employees participating in employer-provided benefit plans and in selected features within plans, small private establishments and State and local governments, selected years 1987-96**

Item	Small private establishments			State and local governments governments			
	1992	1994	1996	1987	1990	1992	1994
Scope of survey (in 000's)	34,360	35,910	39,816	10,321	12,972	12,466	12,907
Number of employees (in 000's):							
With medical care	24,396	23,536	25,599	9,599	12,064	11,219	11,192
With life insurance	21,990	21,955	24,635	8,773	11,415	11,095	11,194
With defined benefit plan	7,559	5,480	5,883	9,599	11,675	10,845	11,708
Time-off plans							
Participants with:							
Paid lunch time	9	–	–	17	11	10	–
Average minutes per day	37	–	–	34	36	34	–
Paid rest time	49	–	–	58	56	53	–
Average minutes per day	26	–	–	29	29	29	–
Paid funeral leave	50	50	51	56	63	65	62
Average days pe occurrence	3.0	3.1	3.0	3.7	3.7	3.7	3.7
Paid holidays	82	82	80	81	74	75	73
Average days per year[1]	9.2	7.5	7.6	10.9	13.6	14.2	11.5
Paid personal leave	12	13	14	38	39	38	38
Average days per year	2.6	2.6	3.0	2.7	2.9	2.9	3.0
Paid vacations	88	88	86	72	67	67	66
Paid sick leave[2]	53	50	50	97	95	95	94
Unpaid leave	18	–	–	57	51	59	–
Unpaid paternity leave	8	–	–	30	33	44	–
Unpaid family leave	–	47	48	–	–	–	93
Insurance plans							
Participants in medicalcare plans	71	66	64	93	93	90	87
Percent of participants with coverage for:							
Home health care	80	–	–	76	82	87	84
Extended care facilities	84	–	–	78	79	84	81
Physical exam	28	–	–	36	36	47	55
Percent of participants with employee contribution required for:							
Self coverage	47	52	52	35	38	43	47
Average monthly contribution	$36.51	$40.97	$42.63	$15.74	$25.53	$28.97	$30.20
Family coverage	73	76	75	71	65	72	71
Average monthly contribution	$150.54	$159.63	$181.53	$71.89	$117.59	$139.23	$149.70
Participants in life insurance plans	64	61	62	85	88	89	87
Percent of participants with:							
Accidental death and dismemberment insurance	76	79	77	67	67	74	64
Survivor income benefits	1	2	1	1	1	1	2
Retiree protection available	25	20	13	55	45	46	46
Participants in long-term disability insurance plans	23	20	22	31	27	28	30
Participants in sickness and accident insurance plans	26	26	–	14	21	22	21
Participants in short-term disability plans[2]	–	–	29	–	–	–	–
Retirement plans							
Participants in defined benefit pension plans	22	15	15	93	90	87	91
Percent of participants with:							
Normal retirement prior to age 65	50	–	47	92	89	92	92
Early retirement available	95	–	92	90	88	89	87
Ad hoc pension increase in last 5 years	4	–	–	33	16	10	13
Terminal earnings formula	54	–	53	100	100	100	99
Benefit coordinated with Social Security	46	–	44	18	8	10	49
Participants in defined contributions plans	33	34	38	9	9	9	9
Participants in plans with tax deferred savings arrangements	24	23	28	28	45	45	24
Other Benefits							
Employees eligible for:							
Flexible benefits plans	2	3	4	5	5	5	5
Reimbursement accounts[3]	14	19	12	5	31	50	64
Premium conversion plans[4]	–	–	7	–	–	–	–

[1] Methods used to calculate the average number of paid holidays were revised in 1994 to count partial days more precisely. Average holidays for 1994 are not comparable to those reported in 1990 and 1992.
[2] See footnote 1, table 48.
[3] Prior to 1996, reimbursement accounts that were part of flexible benefit plans were tabulated separately.
[4] Included in reimbursement accounts prior to 1996.

NOTE: Dash indicates data not available.

Table 47. **Percent of employees participating in or eligible for selected benefits by private and public sectors and full- and part-time status, United States, 1994-95**

Item	All employees	Private sector employees	Public sector employees	Full-time employees	Part-time employees
Scope of survey (in 000s)	103,721	88,828	14,893	82,190	21,531
Participants with:					
Paid:					
Holidays	73	74	68	84	32
Vacations	77	80	60	88	36
Personal leave	18	15	35	20	8
Funeral leave	56	55	58	64	24
Jury duty leave	66	62	88	75	33
Sick leave[1]	50	44	86	59	15
Unpaid:					
Family leave	62	58	89	69	36
Short-term disability coverage[1]	33	35	20	38	16
Long-term disability insurance	25	25	27	31	3
Medical care	61	58	79	73	13
Dental care	37	34	58	45	9
Life insurance	63	60	80	76	13
All retirement[2]	57	51	91	66	23
Defined benefit pension	36	28	86	42	15
Defined contribution[3]	33	37	9	39	12
Types of plans:					
Savings and thrift	21	24	2	24	6
Deferred profit sharing	10	11	-	11	4
Employee stock ownership	2	3	-	3	-
Money purchase pension	5	5	6	6	2
Employees eligible for:					
Flexible benefits plans	6	6	5	7	2
Reimbursement accounts	-	-	-	-	-
Severance pay	22	21	27	26	7
Supplemental unemployment benefits	1	2	(⁴)	2	(⁴)
Employer assistance for child care	5	4	9	5	3
Long-term care insurance	3	3	3	3	2
Wellness programs	19	16	32	22	7
Employee assistance programs	36	31	65	41	19
Job-related travel accident assistance	22	23	13	24	12
Nonproduction bonuses	37	38	31	42	19
Job-related educational assistance	46	44	60	53	24
Non-job-related educational assistance	11	10	18	13	5

[1] The definitions for paid sick leave and short-term-disability (previously sickness and accident insurance) were changed for the 1996 survey. Paid sick leave now only includes plans that either specify a maximum number of days per year or unlimited days. Short-term disability now includes all insured, self-insured, and State-mandated plans available on a per disability basis as well as the unfunded per disability plans previously reported as sick leave. Sickness and accident insurance, reported in years prior to this survey, only included insured, self-insured, and State-mandated plans providing per disability benefits at less than full pay.

[2] Includes defined benefit pension and defined contribution retirement plans. The total is less than the sum of the individuals items because some employees participated in more than one plan.

[3] The total is less than the sum of the individuals items because some employees participated in more than one plan.

[4] Less than 0.5 percent.

NOTE: Dash indicates no data available or no employees in this category.

197

Table 48. **Fatal occupational injuries and employment by event or exposure, 1992-97**

Event or exposure[1]	Fatalities			
	1992-96 average	1996[2]	1997	
		Number	Number	Percent
Total	6,331	6,202	6,218	100
Transportation incidents	2,587	2,601	2,599	42
Highway	1,287	1,346	1,387	22
Collision between vehicles, mobile equipment	640	667	639	10
Moving in same direction	104	96	103	2
Moving in opposite directions, oncoming	228	220	229	4
Moving in intersection	125	153	142	2
Vehicle struck stationary object or equipment	231	243	280	5
Noncollision	343	352	384	6
Jackknifed or overturned—no collision	250	266	295	5
Nonhighway (farm, industrial premises)	400	374	377	6
Overturned	213	206	216	3
Aircraft	334	324	261	4
Worker struck by a vehicle	369	353	367	6
Water vehicle	106	119	109	2
Railway	78	74	93	1
Assaults and violent acts	1,275	1,165	1,103	18
Homicides	1,032	927	856	14
Shooting	839	761	705	11
Stabbing	78	80	73	1
Other, including bombing	115	86	78	1
Self-inflicted injuries	213	204	212	3
Contact with objects and equipment	998	1,010	1,034	17
Struck by object	568	582	578	9
Struck by falling object	365	403	384	6
Struck by flying object	69	58	53	1
Caught in or compressed by equipment or objects	289	285	320	5
Caught in running equipment or machinery	147	146	189	3
Caught in or crushed in collapsing materials	122	131	118	2
Falls	645	691	715	11
Fall to lower level	562	610	652	10
Fall from ladder	87	97	116	2
Fall from roof	130	149	154	2
Fall from scaffold	79	88	87	1
Fall on same level	56	52	44	1
Exposure to harmful substances or environments	596	533	550	9
Contact with electric current	327	281	297	5
Contact with overhead powerlines	128	116	138	2
Contact with temperature extremes	42	33	40	1
Exposure to caustic, noxious, or allergenic substance	121	123	123	2
Inhalation of substances	75	76	59	1
Oxygen deficiency	105	95	87	1
Drowning, submersion	81	70	70	1
Fires and explosions	193	185	196	3
Other events or exposures[3]	37	17	21	—

[1] Based on the 1992 BLS Occupational Injury and Illness Classification Structures.
[2] The BLS news release issued August 7,1997, reported a total of 6,112 fatal work injuries for calendar year 1996. Since then, an additional 90 job-related fatalities were identified, bringing the total job-related fatality count for 1996 to 6,202.
[3] Includes the category "Bodily reaction and exertion."

NOTE: Totals for major categories may include subcategories not shown separately. Percentages may not add to totals because of rounding. Dashes indicate less than 0.5 percent or data that are not available or that do not meet publication criteria.

SOURCE: Bureau of Labor Statistics, U.S. Department of Labor, in cooperation with State and Federal agencies, Census of Fatal Occupational Injuries, 1992-1997.

Table 49. Number, percent distribution, employment, and rate of fatal occupational injuries by occupation, 1997

Occupation[1]	Fatalities		Employ-ment[2] (in thousands)	Fatalities Per 100,000 employed[3]
	Number	Percent		
Total	6,218	100	130,810	4.7
Managerial and professional specialty	667	11	37,686	1.8
Executive, administrative, and managerial	417	7	18,440	2.3
Professional specialty	250	4	19,245	1.3
Technical, sales, and administrative support	733	12	38,309	1.9
Technicians and related support occupations	172	3	4,214	4.1
Airplane pilots and navigators	100	2	120	83.3
Sales occupations	458	7	15,734	2.9
Supervisors and proprietors, sales occupations	223	4	4,635	4.8
Sales workers, retail and personal services	182	3	6,887	2.6
Cashiers	84	1	3,007	2.8
Administrative support occupations, including clerical	103	2	18,361	.6
Service occupations.	492	8	17,537	2.8
Protective service occupations	283	5	2,300	12.3
Firefighting and fire prevention occupations, including supervisors	49	1	268	18.3
Police and detectives, including supervisors	156	3	1,113	14.0
Guards, including supervisors	78	1	920	8.5
Farming, forestry, and fishing	923	15	3,503	25.9
Farm ooccupations	615	10	2,177	27.5
Forestry and logging occupations	128	2	108	118.5
Timber cutting and logging occupations	110	2	79	139.2
Fishers, hunters, and trappers	60	1	49	122.4
Fishers, including vessel captains and officers	58	1	47	123.4
Precision production, craft, and repair	1,094	18	14,124	7.7
Mechanics and repairers	325	5	4,675	7.0
Construction trades	593	10	5,378	11.0
Carpenters	98	2	1,335	7.3
Electricians	94	2	774	12.1
Painters	39	1	545	7.2
Roofers	55	1	200	27.5
Structural metal workers	45	1	66	68.2
Operators, fabricators, and laborers	2,161	35	18,399	11.7
Machine operators, assemblers, and inspectors	221	4	7,962	2.8
Transportation and material moving occupations	1,271	20	5,389	23.6
Motor vehicle operators	1,026	17	4,089	25.1
Truck drivers	857	14	3,075	27.9
Driver-sales workers	44	1	150	29.3
Taxicab drivers and chauffeurs	100	2	248	40.3
Material moving equipment operators	169	3	1,125	15.0
Handlers, equipment cleaners, helpers, and laborers	669	11	5,048	13.2
Construction laborers	333	5	811	41.1
Laborers, except construction	208	3	1,323	15.6
Military[4]	94	2	1,252	7.5

[1] Based on the 1990 Occupational Classification System developed by the Bureau of the Census.

[2] The employment figures, except for military, are annual average estimates of employed civilians, 16 years of age and older, from the Current Population Survey (CPS), 1997. The resident military figure, derived from resident and civilian population data from the Bureau of the Census, was added to the CPS employment total.

[3] The rate represents the number of fatal occupational injuries per 100,000 employed workers and was calculated as follows: (N/W) x 100,000, where N = the number of fatal work injuries, and W = the number of employed workers. There were 21 fatally injured workers under the age of 16 years that were not included in the rate calculations to maintain consistency with the CPS employment.

[4] Resident armed forces.

NOTE: Totals for major categories may include subcategories not shown separately. Percentages may not add to totals because of rounding. There were 64 fatalities for which there was insufficient information to determine an occupation classification.

SOURCE: Bureau of Labor Statistics, U.S. Department of Labor, in cooperation with State and Federal agencies, Census of Fatal Occupational Injuries, 1997.

Table 50. Number, percent distribution, employment, and rate of fatal occupational injuries by Industry, 1997

Industry	SIC code[1]	Fatalities		Employ-ment[2] (in thousands)	Fatalities Per 100,000 employed[3]
		Number	Percent		
Total		6,218	100	130,810	4.7
Private industry		5,594	90	111,417	5.0
Agriculture, forestry, and fishing		830	13	3,479	23.4
Agricultural production - crops	01	373	6	985	36.8
Agricultural production - livestock	02	182	3	1,205	14.8
Agricultural services.......................................	07	176	3	1,199	14.7
Mining		158	3	632	25.0
Coal mining	12	32	1	84	38.1
Oil and gas extraction	13	85	1	369	23.0
Construction..		1,107	18	7,844	14.1
General building contractors	15	194	3	—	—
Heavy construction, except building	16	252	4	—	—
Special trades contractors	17	648	10	—	—
Manufacturing		743	12	20, 765	3.6
Food and kindred products	20	78	1	1,697	4.6
Lumber and wood products...........................	24	199	3	817	24.4
Transportation and public utilities		1,002	16	7,594	13.2
Local and interurban passenger transportation	41	106	2	551	19.2
Trucking and warehousing	42	569	9	2,560	22.2
Transportation by air......................................	45	83	1	822	10.1
Electric, gas, and sanitary services	49	89	1	1,060	8.4
Wholesale trade		241	4	4,896	4.9
Retail trade		665	11	21,782	3.0
Food stores...	54	189	3	3,643	5.1
Automotive dealers and service stations.....................	55	115	2	2,217	5.2
Eating and drinking places	58	150	2	6,581	2.3
Finance, insurance, and real estate		97	2	8,080	1.2
Services		722	12	36,346	2.0
Business services	73	181	3	6,024	3.0
Automotive repair, services, and parking	75	109	2	1,623	6.7
Government[4]..		624	10	19,393	3.2
Federal (including resident armed forces)		162	3	4,461	3.6
State		127	2	5,031	2.5
Local.		331	5	9,901	3.3
Police protection	9221	113	2	—	—

[1] Standard Industrial Classification Manual, 1987 Edition.

[2] The employment is an annual average of employed civilians 16 years of age and older, plus resident armed forces, from the Current Population Survey, 1996.

[3] The rate represents the number of fatal occupational injuries per 100,000 employed workers and was calculated as follows: (N/W) x 100,000, where N = the number of fatal work injuries, and W = the number of employed workers. There were 21 fatally injured workers under the age of 16 years that were not included in the rate calculations to maintain consistency with the CPS employment.

[4] Includes fatalities to workers employed by governmental organizations regardless of industry.

NOTE: Totals for major categories may include subcategories not shown separately. Percentages may not add to totals because of rounding. There were 31 fatalities for which there was insufficient information to determine a specific industry classification, though a distinction between private sector and government was made for each.

Dashes indicate data that are not available or that do not meet publication criteria.

SOURCE: Bureau of Labor Statistics, U.S. Department of Labor, in cooperation with State and Federal agencies, Census of Fatal Occupational Injuries, 1997.

Table 51. **Number, percent distribution, employment, and rate of fatal occupational injuries by selected worker characteristics, 1997**

Characteristics	Fatalities		Employ-ment[1] (in thousands)	Fatalities Per 100,000 employed[2]
	Number	Percent		
Total	6,218	100	130,810	4.7
Employee status				
Wage and salary workers	4,959	80	120,126	4.1
Self-employed[3]	1,259	20	10,684	11.6
Sex				
Men	5,743	92	70,769	8.1
Women	475	8	60,041	.8
Age[4]				
Under 16 years	21	—	—	—
16 to 17 years	41	1	2,650	1.5
18 to 19 years	113	2	4,102	2.8
20 to 24 years	503	8	12,758	3.9
25 to 34 years	1,319	21	32,288	4.1
35 to 44 years	1,520	24	36,174	4.2
45 to 54 years	1,298	21	26,780	4.8
55 to 64 years	870	14	12,297	7.1
65 years and over	519	8	3,761	13.8
Race				
White	5,098	82	110,819	4.6
Black	676	11	14,211	4.8
Asian or Pacific Islander	189	3	—	—
American Indian, Aleut, Eskimo	35	1	—	—
Other or not reported	220	4	—	—
Hispanic origin				
Hispanic[5]	656	11	12,813	5.1

[1] The employment is an annual average of employed civilians 16 years of age and older, plus resident armed forces, from the Current Population Survey, 1997.

[2] The rate represents the number of fatal occupational injuries per 100,000 employed workers and was calculated as follows: (N/W) x 100,000, where N = the number of fatal work injuries, and W = the number of employed workers. There were 21 fatally injured workers under the age of 16 years that were not included in the rate calculations to maintain consistency with the CPS employment.

[3] Includes paid and unpaid family workers and may include owners of incorporated businesses or members of partnerships.

[4] There were 14 fatalities for which age was not reported.

[5] Persons identified as Hispanic may be of any race. Hispanic employment does not include resident armed forces.

NOTE: Totals may include subcategories not shown separately. Percentages may not add to totals because of rounding. Dashes indicate less than 0.5 percent or data that are not available or that do not meet publication criteria.

SOURCE: Bureau of Labor Statistics, U.S. Department of Labor, in cooperation with State and Federal agencies, Census of Fatal Occupational Injuries, 1997.

Table 52. **Number of nonfatal occupational injury and illness cases involving days away from work[1] by selected occupation and industry division, 1996**

(In thousands)

Occupation	Private industry[2]	Goods producing				Service producing				
		Agriculture, forestry, and fishing[2]	Mining	Construction	Manufacturing	Transportation and public utilities[2]	Wholesale trade	Retail trade	Finance, insurance, and real estate	Services
Total	1,880.5	38.3	15.1	182.3	462.2	224.0	144.7	322.0	42.8	449.0
Truckdrivers	152.8	1.3	1.0	5.0	13.1	80.8	26.8	14.5	.2	10.0
Laborers, nonconstruction	108.5	1.2	1.6	-	37.7	6.9	29.1	16.7	1.9	13.5
Nursing aides, orderlies	93.6	-	(4)	-	-	-	-	-	.5	93.1
Janitors and cleaners	46.9	.5	(4)	.3	7.3	1.2	1.2	6.7	6.5	23.3
Assemblers	44.0	.1	-	.6	39.2	.1	1.5	.7	-	1.7
Construction laborers	43.7	-	-	42.9	.2	.3	-	-	.1	.2
Carpenters	33.5	-	(4)	25.9	3.1	.1	.6	1.9	.4	1.5
Stock handlers and baggers	31.9	.1	(4)	(4)	2.0	.3	3.2	25.7	-	.6
Cashiers	30.9	-	-	-	.1	.1	.4	27.7	.2	2.4
Cooks	30.7	-	-	.3	.2	.1	.1	19.6	.2	10.1
Miscellaneous food preparation	28.9	-	-	-	.2	(4)	-	20.6	.2	7.8
Registered nurses	28.9	-	-	-	(4)	(4)	-	-	(4)	28.7
Maids and housemen	27.2	-	(4)	-	.1	.1	-	.1	1.1	25.8
Supervisors and proprietors	26.9	-	-	.2	.4	.1	2.6	21.9	.5	1.4
Welders and cutters	26.1	.1	.3	3.0	18.2	.9	2.3	-	-	1.4
Sales workers, other commodities	25.2	-	-	-	.2	.1	2.0	20.7	.3	1.8
Mechanics, automobile	21.0	-	-	.1	.4	.6	1.4	11.7	(4)	6.8
Shipping and receiving clerks	19.8	.1	-	.1	6.5	5.8	2.2	4.2	(4)	.9
Groundskeepers and gardeners, except farm	18.5	8.6	-	.2	.2	.4	.2	1.0	1.9	5.9
Driver-sales workers	17.5	-	-	.1	4.1	.6	8.6	2.9	-	1.3
Farm workers	16.0	14.0	.2	-	.3	.8	.6	-	(4)	-
Electricians	15.2	-	.4	10.4	2.5	.6	.1	-	(4)	1.0
Health aides, except nursing	14.8	-	-	-	-	-	-	-	.1	14.6
Plumbers and pipefitters	13.4	.1	-	9.4	1.9	.4	.8	.2	.1	.5
Industrial truck operators	13.2	.3	.4	.3	6.7	1.7	2.3	1.2	-	.3
Guards and police, except public	13.1	-	(4)	-	.5	1.5	.2	1.5	.7	8.7
Packaging, filling machine operators	12.9	.1	-	-	11.4	-	1.1	.1	-	.1
Waiters and waitresses	12.5	-	-	-	(4)	.1	-	8.6	.1	3.7
Stock and inventory clerks	12.4	-	-	.1	2.5	.8	1.5	5.3	.1	2.1
Supervisors, production workers	12.2	.1	.1	-	8.7	.5	1.4	.6	.1	.6
Repairers, industrial machinery	11.9	-	1.4	.1	9.1	.3	.5	.1	(4)	.4
Licensed practical nurses	11.8	-	-	-	(4)	-	-	-	0.1	11.7

[1] Days-away-from-work cases include those which result in days away from work with or without restricted work activity.

[2] Excludes farms with fewer than 11 employees.

[3] Data conforming to OSHA definitions for mining operators in coal, metal, and nonmetal mining and for employers in railroad transportation are provided to BLS by the Mine Safety and Health Administration, U.S. Department of Labor; and by the Federal Railroad Administration, U.S. Department of Transportation. Independent mining contractors are excluded from the coal, metal, and nonmetal industries.

[4] Less than 0.1.

NOTE: Dashes indicate data that are not available. Because of rounding and nonclassifiable responses, data may not sum to the totals.

SOURCE: Bureau of Labor Statistics, U.S. Department of Labor

Table 53. **Percent distribution of nonfatal occupational injuries and illnesses involving days away from work[1] by selected worker characteristics and a number of days away from work, 1996**

Characteristic	Total cases	Percent of cases involving							Median days away from work
		1 day	2 days	3 to 5 days	6 to 10 days	11 to 20 days	21 to 30 days	31 days or more	
Total [1,880,500 cases]	100.0	16.7	13.1	20.6	13.2	11.7	6.2	18.5	5
Sex:									
Men	100.0	16.6	12.8	20.0	13.1	11.8	6.4	19.1	6
Women..	100.0	16.8	13.5	21.8	13.4	11.5	5.9	17.1	5
Age (in years)[2]:									
14 to 15..	100.0	22.4	36.6	15.1	6.3	3.6	11.2	4.9	2
16 to 19..	100.0	21.5	16.8	23.0	15.0	8.9	4.2	10.7	4
20 to 24..	100.0	20.9	14.4	24.3	12.9	10.7	5.0	11.7	4
25 to 34..	100.0	18.5	14.0	21.1	13.0	11.3	6.1	15.9	5
35 to 44..	100.0	16.0	12.5	20.1	13.4	11.9	6.3	20.0	6
45 to 54..	100.0	12.7	10.8	18.9	13.2	12.6	7.4	24.5	8
55 to 64..	100.0	11.8	10.9	16.9	13.4	14.1	7.4	25.5	9
65 and over	100.0	9.6	11.1	17.2	13.2	11.9	7.1	29.9	10
Occupation:									
Managerial and professional specialty	100.0	20.1	16.3	23.5	12.6	9.4	4.6	13.4	4
Technical, sales, and administrative support	100.0	17.8	13.5	20.9	13.1	11.4	6.2	17.0	5
Service	100.0	15.8	13.8	24.1	13.8	11.9	5.8	14.8	5
Farming, forestry, and fishing	100.0	17.4	13.7	21.4	15.7	10.0	7.2	14.7	5
Precision production, craft, and repair	100.0	16.4	12.3	18.9	13.0	11.6	6.7	21.1	6
Operators, fabricators, and laborers ...	100.0	16.2	12.4	19.3	13.0	12.1	6.5	20.5	6
Length of service with employer:									
Less than 3 months	100.0	17.5	13.8	23.1	13.2	10.5	5.7	16.3	5
3 to 11 months	100.0	18.7	14.5	21.6	12.7	10.8	5.1	16.7	5
1 to 5 years	100.0	17.5	13.3	20.9	13.5	11.2	6.2	17.3	5
More than 5 years	100.0	14.0	11.7	18.7	13.3	13.1	7.2	22.0	7
Race or ethnic origin:									
White, non-Hispanic	100.0	17.0	13.5	20.3	13.1	11.6	6.3	18.2	5
Black, non-Hispanic	100.0	16.7	13.2	22.2	12.3	11.7	5.6	18.3	5
Hispanic	100.0	15.4	11.7	20.6	14.6	11.4	6.6	19.7	6
Asian or Pacific Islander	100.0	19.2	13.6	20.0	13.3	10.5	6.4	17.0	5
American Indian or Alaskan Native	100.0	20.0	13.5	23.3	11.7	11.1	5.8	14.5	4

[1] Days-away-from-work cases include those which result in days away from work with or without restricted work activity.
[2] Information is not shown separately in this release for injured workers under age 14; they accounted for fewer than 50 cases.

NOTE: Because of rounding, percentages may not add to 100.

SOURCE: Bureau of Labor Statistics, U.S. Department of Labor

Table 54. Incidence rates and number of cases of nonfatal occupational injuries and illnesses, private industry, 1973-97

Year[1]	Injury incidence rate[2]				Number (In thousands)			
	Total cases	Lost workday cases		Cases without lost workdays	Total cases	Lost workday cases		Cases without lost workdays
		Total[3]	With days away from work[4]			Total[3]	With days away from work[4]	
1973	11.0	3.4	-	7.5	6,078.7	1,908.0	-	4,165.0
1974	10.4	3.5	-	6.9	5,915.8	2,001.8	-	3,908.1
1975	9.1	3.3	3.2	5.8	4,983.1	1,825.2	1,730.5	3,152.6
1976	9.2	3.5	3.3	5.7	5,163.7	1,978.8	1,875.4	3,180.4
1977	9.3	3.8	3.6	5.5	5,460.3	2,203.6	2,092.1	3,250.6
1978[5]	9.4	4.1	3.8	5.3	5,799.4	2,492.0	2,327.5	3,302.0
1979[5]	9.5	4.3	4.0	5.2	6,105.7	2,757.7	2,553.5	3,342.3
1980	8.7	4.0	3.7	4.7	5,605.8	2,539.9	2,353.8	3,060.4
1981	8.3	3.8	3.5	4.5	5,404.4	2,457.5	2,269.2	2,941.8
1982	7.7	3.5	3.2	4.2	4,856.4	2,182.4	2,016.2	2,668.6
1983[5]	7.6	3.4	3.2	4.2	4,854.1	2,182.7	2,014.2	2,667.6
1984[5]	8.0	3.7	3.4	4.3	5,419.7	2,501.5	2,303.7	2,913.4
1985	7.9	3.6	3.3	4.3	5,507.2	2,537.0	2,319.2	2,965.9
1986	7.9	3.6	3.3	4.3	5,629.0	2,590.3	2,356.9	3,034.6
1987	8.3	3.8	3.4	4.4	6,035.9	2,801.6	2,483.9	3,230.6
1988	8.6	4.0	3.5	4.6	6,440.4	2,977.8	2,585.8	3,458.7
1989	8.6	4.0	3.4	4.6	6,576.3	3,073.9	2,624.2	3,497.9
1990	8.8	4.1	3.4	4.7	6,753.0	3,123.8	2,613.5	3,625.6
1991	8.4	3.9	3.2	4.5	6,345.7	2,944.2	2,398.4	3,398.3
1992[6]	8.9	3.9	3.0	5.0	6,799.4	2,953.4	2,331.1	3,846.0
1993[6]	8.5	3.8	2.9	4.8	6,737.4	2,967.4	2,252.5	3,770.0
1994[6]	8.4	3.8	2.8	4.6	6,766.9	3,061.0	2,236.6	3,705.9
1995[6]	8.1	3.6	2.5	4.4	6,575.4	2,972.1	2,040.9	3,603.2
1996[6]	7.4	3.4	2.2	4.1	6,238.9	2,832.5	1,880.6	3,406.4
1997[6]	7.1	3.3	2.1	3.8	6,145.6	2,866.2	1,833.4	3,279.4

[1] Data for 1973-75 are based on the Standard Industrial Classification Manual, 1967 Edition; data for 1976-87 are based on the Standard Industrial Classification Manual, 1972 Edition; and data for 1988-96 are based on the *Standard Industrial Classification Manual, 1987 Edition.*

[2] The incidence rates represent the number of injuries and illnesses per 100 full-time workers and were calculated as: (N/EH) X 200,000, where:

N = number of injuries and illnesses
EH = total hours worked by all employees during the calendar year
200,000 = base for 100 equivalent full-time workers (working 40 hours per week, 50 weeks per year).

[3] Total includes cases involving restricted work activity only in addition to days-away-from-work cases with or without restricted work activity.

[4] Days-away-from-work cases include those which result in days away from work with or without restricted work activity.

[5] To maintain historical comparability with the rest of the series, data for small nonfarm employers in low-risk industries who were not surveyed were imputed and included in the survey estimates.

[6] Data for 1992-96 excluded fatal work-related injuries and illnesses.

NOTE: Because of rounding, components may not add to totals. Data for 1976-97 exclude farms with fewer than 11 employees.
- Indicates data not available

SOURCE: Bureau of Labor Statistics, U.S. Department of Labor

Table 55. **Unemployment for selected demographic groups, annual averages, 1948-98**

(In thousands)

Year	Total unem- ployed	Men Total	Men 16 to 19 years	Men 20 years and over	Women Total	Women 16 to 19 years	Women 20 years and over	White	Black	Married men, spouse pre- sent	Women who main- tain families
1948	2,276	1,559	256	1,305	717	153	564	–	–	–	–
1949	3,637	2,572	353	2,219	1,065	223	841	–	–	–	–
1950	3,288	2,239	318	1,922	1,049	195	854	–	–	–	–
1951	2,055	1,221	191	1,029	834	145	689	–	–	–	–
1952	1,883	1,185	205	980	698	140	559	–	–	–	–
1953[1]	1,834	1,202	184	1,019	632	123	510	–	–	–	–
1954	3,532	2,344	310	2,035	1,188	191	997	2,859	–	–	–
1955	2,852	1,854	274	1,580	998	176	823	2,252	–	972	–
1956	2,750	1,711	269	1,442	1,039	209	832	2,159	–	905	–
1957	2,859	1,841	300	1,541	1,018	197	821	2,289	–	982	–
1958	4,602	3,098	416	2,681	1,504	262	1,242	3,680	–	1,799	–
1959	3.740	2,420	398	2,022	1,320	256	1,063	2,946	–	1,296	–
1960[1]	3,852	2,486	426	2,060	1,366	286	1,080	3,065	–	1,334	–
1961	4,714	2,997	479	2,518	1,717	349	1,368	3,743	–	1,676	–
1962[1]	3,911	2,423	408	2,016	1,488	313	1,175	3,052	–	1,300	–
1963	4,070	2,472	501	1,971	1,598	383	1,216	3,208	–	1,235	–
1964	3,786	2,205	487	1,718	1,581	385	1,195	2,999	–	1,039	–
1965	3,366	1,914	479	1,435	1,452	395	1,056	2,691	–	883	–
1966	2,875	1,551	432	1,120	1,324	405	921	2,255	–	706	–
1967	2,975	1,508	448	1,060	1,468	391	1,078	2,338	–	685	70
1968	2,817	1,419	426	993	1,397	412	985	2,226	–	620	124
1969	2,832	1,403	440	963	1,429	413	1,015	2,260	–	582	130
1970	4,093	2,238	599	1,638	1,855	506	1,349	3,339	–	1,002	161
1971	5,016	2,789	693	2,097	2,227	568	1,658	4,085	–	1,255	236
1972[1]	4,882	2,659	711	1,948	2,222	598	1,625	3,906	906	1,100	245
1973[1]	4,365	2,275	653	1,624	2,089	583	1,507	3,442	846	916	249
1974	5,156	2,714	757	1,957	2,441	665	1,777	4,097	965	1,087	266
1975	7,929	4,442	966	3,476	3,486	802	2,684	6,421	1,369	2,063	401
1976	7,406	4,036	939	3,098	3,369	780	2,588	5,914	1,334	1,709	428
1977	6,991	4,004	874	2,794	3,324	789	2,535	5,441	1,393	1,462	422
1978[1]	6,202	3,142	813	2,328	3,061	769	2,292	4,698	1,330	1,135	417
1979	6,137	3,120	811	2,308	3,018	743	2,276	4,664	1,319	1,134	425
1980	7,637	4,267	913	3,353	3,370	755	2,615	5,884	1,553	1,709	482
1981	8,273	4,577	962	3,615	3,696	800	2,895	6,343	1,731	1,766	579
1982	10,678	6,179	1,090	5,089	4,499	886	3,613	8,241	2,142	2,632	675
1983	10,717	6,260	1,003	5,257	4,457	825	3,632	8,128	2,272	2,634	706
1984	8,539	4,744	812	3,932	3,794	687	3,107	6,372	1,914	1,896	627
1985	8,312	4,521	806	3,715	3,791	661	3,129	6,191	1,864	1,767	651
1986[1]	8,237	4,530	779	3,751	3,707	675	3,032	6,140	1,840	1,819	632
1987	7,425	4,101	732	3,369	3,324	616	2,709	5,501	1,684	1,625	613
1988	6,701	3,655	667	2,987	3,046	558	2,487	4,944	1,547	1,360	547
1989	6,528	3,525	658	2,867	3,003	536	2,467	4,770	1,544	1,276	558
1990[1]	7,047	3,906	667	3,239	3,140	544	2,596	5,186	1,565	1,446	580
1991	8,628	4,946	751	4,195	3,683	608	3,074	6,560	1,723	1,875	663
1992	9,613	5,523	806	4,717	4,090	621	3,469	7,169	2,011	2,150	737
1993	8,940	5,055	768	4,287	3,885	597	3,288	6,655	1,844	1,899	731
1994[1]	7,996	4,367	740	3,627	3,629	580	3,049	5,892	1,666	1,592	692
1995	7,404	3,983	744	3,239	3,421	602	2,819	5,459	1,538	1,424	624
1996	7,236	3,880	733	3,146	3,356	573	2,783	5,300	1,592	1,322	658
1997[1]	6,739	3,577	694	2,882	3,162	577	2,585	4,836	1,560	1,167	684
1998[1]	6,210	3,266	686	2,580	2,944	519	2,424	4,484	1,426	1,034	612

[1] The comparability of historical labor force data has been affected at various times by methodological and conceptual changes. For an explanation, see the Explanatory Notes and Estimates of Error section of *Employment and Earnings*, a monthly periodical published by the Bureau of Labor Statistics.

Dash indicates data not available.

Table 56. **Unemployment rates for selected demographic groups, annual averages, 1948-98**

(Percent)

Year	Total all workers	Men			Women			White	Black	Married men, spouse present	Women who maintain families
		Total	16 to 19 years	20 years and over	Total	16 to 19 years	20 years and over				
1948	3.8	3.6	9.8	3.2	4.1	8.3	3.6	–	–	–	–
1949	5.9	5.9	14.3	5.4	6.0	12.3	5.3	–	–	–	–
1950	5.3	5.1	12.7	4.7	5.7	11.4	5.1	–	–	–	–
1951	3.3	2.8	8.1	2.5	4.4	8.3	4.0	–	–	–	–
1952	3.0	2.8	8.9	2.4	3.6	8.0	3.2	–	–	–	–
1953[1]	2.9	2.8	7.9	2.5	3.3	7.2	2.9	–	–	–	–
1954	5.5	5.3	13.5	4.9	6.0	11.4	5.5	5.0	–	–	–
1955	4.4	4.2	11.6	3.8	4.9	10.2	4.4	3.9	–	2.6	–
1956	4.1	3.8	11.1	3.4	4.8	11.2	4.2	3.6	–	2.3	–
1957	4.3	4.1	12.4	3.6	4.7	10.6	4.1	3.8	–	2.8	–
1958	6.8	6.8	17.1	6.2	6.8	14.3	6.1	6.1	–	5.1	–
1959	5.5	5.2	15.3	4.7	5.9	13.5	5.2	4.8	–	3.6	–
1960[1]	5.5	5.4	15.3	4.7	5.9	13.9	5.1	5.0	–	3.7	–
1961	6.7	6.4	17.1	5.7	7.2	16.3	6.3	6.0	–	4.6	–
1962[1]	5.5	5.2	14.7	4.6	6.2	14.6	5.4	4.9	–	3.6	–
1963	5.7	5.2	17.2	4.5	6.5	17.2	5.4	5.0	–	3.4	–
1964	5.2	4.6	15.8	3.9	6.2	16.6	5.2	4.6	–	2.8	–
1965	4.5	4.0	14.1	3.2	5.5	15.7	4.5	4.1	–	2.4	–
1966	3.8	3.2	11.7	2.5	4.8	14.1	3.8	3.4	–	1.9	–
1967	3.8	3.1	12.3	2.3	5.2	13.5	4.2	3.4	–	1.8	4.9
1968	3.6	2.9	11.6	2.2	4.8	14.0	3.8	3.2	–	1.6	4.4
1969	3.5	2.8	11.4	2.1	4.7	13.3	3.7	3.1	–	1.5	4.4
1970	4.9	4.4	15.0	3.5	5.9	15.6	4.8	4.5	–	2.6	5.4
1971	5.9	5.3	16.6	4.4	6.9	17.2	5.7	5.4	–	3.2	7.3
1972[1]	5.6	5.0	15.9	4.0	6.6	16.7	5.4	5.1	10.4	2.8	7.2
1973[1]	4.9	4.2	13.9	3.3	6.0	15.3	4.9	4.3	9.4	2.3	7.1
1974	5.6	4.9	15.6	3.8	6.7	16.6	5.5	5.0	10.5	2.7	7.0
1975	8.5	7.9	20.1	6.8	9.3	19.7	8.0	7.8	14.8	5.1	10.0
1976	7.7	7.1	19.2	5.9	8.6	18.7	7.4	7.0	14.0	4.2	10.1
1977	7.1	6.3	17.3	5.2	8.2	18.3	7.0	6.2	14.0	3.6	9.4
1978[1]	6.1	5.3	15.8	4.3	7.2	17.1	6.0	5.2	12.8	2.8	8.5
1979	5.8	5.1	15.9	4.2	6.8	16.4	5.7	5.1	12.3	2.8	8.3
1980	7.1	6.9	18.3	5.9	7.4	17.2	6.4	6.3	14.3	4.2	9.2
1981	7.6	7.4	20.1	6.3	7.9	19.0	6.8	6.7	15.6	4.3	10.4
1982	9.7	9.9	24.4	8.8	9.4	21.9	8.3	8.6	18.9	6.5	11.7
1983	9.6	9.9	23.3	8.9	9.2	21.3	8.1	8.4	19.5	6.5	12.2
1984	7.5	7.4	19.6	6.6	7.6	18.0	6.8	6.5	15.9	4.6	10.3
1985	7.2	7.0	19.5	6.2	7.4	17.6	6.6	6.2	15.1	4.3	10.4
1986[1]	7.0	6.9	19.0	6.1	7.1	17.6	6.2	6.0	14.5	4.4	9.8
1987	6.2	6.2	17.8	5.4	6.2	15.9	5.4	5.3	13.0	3.9	9.2
1988	5.5	5.5	16.0	4.8	5.6	14.4	4.9	4.7	11.7	3.3	8.1
1989	5.3	5.2	15.9	4.5	5.4	14.0	4.7	4.5	11.4	3.0	8.1
1990[1]	5.6	5.7	16.3	5.0	5.5	14.7	4.9	4.8	11.4	3.4	8.3
1991	6.8	7.2	19.8	6.4	6.4	17.5	5.7	6.1	12.5	4.4	9.3
1992	7.5	7.9	21.5	7.1	7.0	18.6	6.3	6.6	14.2	5.1	10.0
1993	6.9	7.2	20.4	6.4	6.6	17.5	5.9	6.1	13.0	4.4	9.7
1994[1]	6.1	6.2	19.0	5.4	6.0	16.2	5.4	5.3	11.5	3.7	8.9
1995	5.6	5.6	18.4	4.8	5.6	16.1	4.9	4.9	10.4	3.3	8.0
1996	5.4	5.4	18.1	4.6	5.4	15.2	4.8	4.7	10.5	3.0	8.2
1997[1]	4.9	4.9	16.9	4.2	5.0	15.0	4.4	4.2	10.0	2.7	8.1
1998[1]	4.5	4.4	16.2	3.7	4.6	12.9	4.1	3.9	8.9	2.4	7.2

[1] The comparability of historical labor force data has been affected at various times by methodological and conceptual changes. For an explanation, see the Explanatory Notes and Estimates of Error section of *Employment and Earnings*, a monthly periodical published by the Bureau of Labor Statistics.

Dash indicates data not available.

Table 57. Unemployed persons by duration and reason, annual averages, 1948-98

(Numbers in thousands)

Year	Total unem- ployed	Duration of unemployment						Reason for unemployment			
		Less than 5 weeks	5 to14 weeks	15 to 26 weeks	27 weeks and over	Mean dura- tion (weeks)	Median dura- tion (weeks)	Job losers[1]	Job leavers	Reen- trants	New entrants
1948	2,276	1,300	669	193	116	8.6	–	–	–	–	–
1949	3,637	1,756	1,194	428	256	10.0	–	–	–	–	–
1950	3,288	1,450	1,055	425	357	12.1	–	–	–	–	–
1951	2,055	1,177	574	166	137	9.7	–	–	–	–	–
1952	1,883	1,135	516	148	84	8.4	–	–	–	–	–
1953[2]	1,834	1,142	482	132	78	8.0	–	–	–	–	–
1954	3,532	1,605	1,116	495	317	11.8	–	–	–	–	–
1955	2,852	1,335	815	366	336	13.0	–	–	–	–	–
1956	2,750	1,412	805	301	232	11.3	–	–	–	–	–
1957	2,859	1,408	891	321	239	10.5	–	–	–	–	–
1958	4,602	1,753	1,396	785	667	13.9	–	–	–	–	–
1959	3,740	1,585	1,114	469	571	14.4	–	–	–	–	–
1960[2]	3,852	1,719	1,176	503	454	12.8	–	–	–	–	–
1961	4,714	1,806	1,376	728	804	15.6	–	–	–	–	–
1962[2]	3,911	1,663	1,134	534	585	14.7	–	–	–	–	–
1963	4,070	1,751	1,231	535	553	14.0	–	–	–	–	–
1964	3,786	1,697	1,117	491	482	13.3	–	–	–	–	–
1965	3,366	1,628	983	404	351	11.8	–	–	–	–	–
1966	2,875	1,573	779	287	239	10.4	–	–	–	–	–
1967	2,975	1,634	893	271	177	8.7	2.3	1,229	438	945	396
1968	2,817	1,594	810	256	156	8.4	4.5	1,070	431	909	407
1969	2,832	1,629	827	242	133	7.8	4.4	1,017	436	965	413
1970	4,093	2,139	1,290	428	235	8.6	4.9	1,811	550	1,228	504
1971	5,016	2,245	1,585	668	519	11.3	6.3	2,323	590	1,472	630
1972[2]	4,882	2,242	1,472	601	566	12.0	6.2	2,108	641	1,456	677
1973[2]	4,365	2,224	1,314	483	343	10.0	5.2	1,694	683	1,340	649
1974	5,156	2,604	1,597	574	381	9.8	5.2	2,242	768	1,463	681
1975	7,929	2,940	2,484	1,303	1,203	14.2	8.4	4,386	827	1,892	823
1976	7,406	2,844	2,196	1,018	1,348	15.8	8.2	3,679	903	1,928	895
1977	6,991	2,919	2,132	913	1,028	14.3	7.0	3,166	909	1,963	953
1978[2]	6,202	2,865	1,923	766	648	11.9	5.9	2,585	874	1,857	885
1979	6,137	2,950	1,946	706	535	10.8	5.4	2,635	880	1,806	817
1980	7,637	3,295	2,470	1,052	820	11.9	6.5	3,947	891	1,927	872
1981	8,273	3,449	2,539	1,122	1,162	13.7	6.9	4,267	923	2,102	981
1982	10,678	3,883	3,311	1,708	1,776	15.6	8.7	6,268	840	2,384	1,185
1983	10,717	3,570	2,937	1,652	2,559	20.0	10.1	6,258	830	2,412	1,216
1984	8,539	3,350	2,451	1,104	1,634	18.2	7.9	4,421	823	2,184	1,110
1985	8,312	3,498	2,509	1,025	1,280	15.6	6.8	4,139	877	2,256	1,039
1986[2]	8,237	3,448	2,557	1,045	1,187	15.0	6.9	4,033	1,015	2,160	1,029
1987	7,425	3,246	2,196	943	1,040	14.5	6.5	3,566	965	1,974	920
1988	6,701	3,084	2,007	801	809	13.5	5.9	3,092	983	1,809	816
1989	6,528	3,174	1,978	730	646	11.9	4.8	2,983	1,024	1,843	677
1990[2]	7,047	3,265	2,257	822	703	12.0	5.3	3,387	1,041	1,930	688
1991	8,628	3,480	2,791	1,246	1,111	13.7	6.8	4,694	1,004	2,139	792
1992	9,613	3,376	2,830	1,453	1,954	17.7	8.7	5,389	1,002	2,285	937
1993	8,940	3,262	2,584	1,297	1,798	18.0	8.3	4,848	976	2,198	919
1994[2]	7,996	2,728	2,408	1,237	1,623	18.8	9.2	3,815	791	2,786	604
1995	7,404	2,700	2,342	1,085	1,278	16.6	8.3	3,476	824	2,525	579
1996	7,236	2,633	2,287	1,053	1,262	16.7	8.3	3,370	774	2,512	580
1997[2]	6,739	2,538	2,138	995	1,067	15.8	8.0	3,037	795	2,338	569
1998[2]	6,210	2,622	1,950	763	875	14.5	6.7	2,822	734	2,132	520

[1] Beginning January 1994 includes persons who completed temporary jobs.

[2] The comparability of historical labor force data has been affected at various times by methodological and conceptual changes. For an explanation, see the Explanatory Notes and Estimates of Error section of *Employment and Earnings*, a monthly periodical published by the Bureau of Labor Statistics.

Dash indicates data not available.

Table 58. **Unemployment rates of persons 25 to 64 years of age by educational attainment and sex, March 1970-98**

(Percent)

Year	Less than 4 years of high school	4 years of high school, only	College	
			1 to 3 years	4 years or more
TOTAL				
1970	4.6	2.9	2.9	1.3
1971	6.4	4.0	3.7	2.0
1972[1]	5.8	3.9	3.5	2.0
1973[1]	5.4	3.3	2.9	1.7
1974	5.3	3.4	3.4	1.7
1975	10.7	6.9	5.5	2.5
1976	8.6	6.1	5.2	2.4
1977	9.0	5.6	5.0	2.8
1978[1]	7.4	4.5	3.3	2.2
1979	7.2	4.4	3.5	2.1
1980	8.4	5.1	4.3	1.9
1981	10.1	6.2	4.5	2.2
1982	12.5	8.5	6.4	3.0
1983	15.8	10.0	7.3	3.5
1984	12.1	7.2	5.3	2.7
1985	11.4	6.9	4.7	2.4
1986[1]	11.6	6.9	4.7	2.3
1987	11.1	6.3	4.5	2.3
1988	9.4	5.4	3.7	1.7
1989	8.9	4.8	3.4	2.2
1990[1]	9.6	4.9	3.7	1.9
1991	12.3	6.7	5.0	2.9
1992	13.5	7.7	5.9	2.9
1993	13.0	7.3	5.5	3.2
1994[1]	12.6	6.7	5.0	2.9
1995	10.0	5.2	4.5	2.5
1996	10.9	5.5	4.1	2.2
1997[1]	10.4	5.1	3.8	2.0
1998[1]	8.5	4.8	3.6	1.8
Men				
1970	4.0	2.4	2.7	1.1
1971	6.0	3.6	3.5	1.8
1972[1]	5.4	3.6	3.1	1.9
1973[1]	5.0	2.8	2.8	1.6
1974	4.7	3.1	2.9	1.5
1975	10.5	6.7	5.1	2.2
1976	8.3	5.8	5.1	2.2
1977	8.6	5.1	4.5	2.4
1978[1]	7.1	4.2	3.1	1.9
1979	6.6	4.2	3.2	1.7
1980	8.2	5.3	4.4	1.7
1981	10.2	6.6	4.4	1.9
1982	12.7	9.3	6.8	2.9
1983	16.1	11.9	8.4	3.4
1984	12.3	8.1	5.2	2.7
1985	11.2	7.2	4.5	2.4
1986[1]	11.7	7.4	4.7	2.3
1987	11.2	6.7	5.0	2.5
1988	10.0	6.2	3.9	1.0
1989	9.4	5.4	3.2	2.3
1990[1]	9.6	5.3	3.9	2.1
1991	13.4	7.7	5.2	3.2
1992	14.8	8.8	6.4	3.2
1993	14.1	8.7	6.3	3.4
1994[1]	12.8	7.2	5.3	2.9
1995	10.9	5.7	4.4	2.6
1996[1]	11.0	6.4	4.5	2.3
1997[1]	9.9	5.6	4.0	2.1
1998[1]	8.0	5.1	3.7	1.7

See footnote at end of table.

Table 58. **Unemployment rates of persons 25 to 64 years of age by educational attainment and sex, March 1970-98—Continued**

(Percent)

Year	Less than 4 years of high school	4 years of high school, only	College	
			1 to 3 years	4 years or more
Women				
1970	5.7	3.6	3.1	1.9
1971	7.2	4.5	4.3	2.4
1972[1]	6.6	4.3	4.2	2.3
1973[1]	6.2	3.9	3.0	2.1
1974	6.4	3.8	4.4	2.1
1975	10.5	7.1	6.3	3.4
1976	9.2	6.5	5.5	2.7
1977	9.7	6.2	5.7	3.6
1978[1]	7.9	4.9	3.6	2.6
1979	8.3	4.7	3.8	2.8
1980	8.9	5.0	4.1	2.2
1981	10.0	5.8	4.6	2.7
1982	12.2	7.8	5.3	3.3
1983	15.3	8.0	6.0	3.7
1984	11.7	6.3	5.3	2.7
1985	11.7	6.5	4.8	2.5
1986[1]	11.4	6.3	4.8	2.4
1987	10.9	5.8	4.0	2.1
1988	8.5	4.6	3.4	1.9
1989	8.1	4.2	3.7	2.0
1990[1]	9.5	4.6	3.5	1.7
1991	10.7	5.5	4.8	2.5
1992	11.4	6.5	5.3	2.5
1993	11.2	5.8	4.6	2.9
1994[1]	12.4	6.2	4.7	2.9
1995	8.6	4.6	4.5	2.4
1996	10.7	4.4	3.8	2.1
1997[1]	11.3	4.5	3.6	2.0
1998[1]	9.3	4.4	3.5	1.9

[1] Data on educational attainment, beginning in 1992, reflect degrees or diplomas received rather than years of school completed and are not strictly comparable with data for prior years. In addition, the comparability of historical labor force data has been affected at various times by methodological and conceptual changes. For an explanation, see the Explanatory Notes and Estimates of Error section of *Employment and Earnings*, a monthly periodical published by the Bureau of Labor Statistics.

Table 59. **Civilian unemployment rates, approximating U.S. concepts, 10 countries, 1959-98**

Year	United States	Canada	Australia	Japan	France	Germany ([1])	Italy	Nether- lands	Sweden	United Kingdom
1959	5.5	5.6	[2]2.1	2.3	1.6	2.0	4.8	–	[3]1.7	2.8
1960	5.5	6.5	[2]1.6	1.7	1.5	1.1	3.7	–	[3]1.7	2.2
1961	6.7	6.7	[2]3.0	1.5	1.2	.6	3.2	–	1.5	2.0
1962	5.5	5.5	[2]2.9	1.3	1.4	.6	2.8	–	1.5	2.7
1963	5.7	5.2	[2]2.3	1.3	1.6	.5	2.4	–	1.7	3.3
1964	5.2	4.4	1.4	1.2	1.2	.4	2.7	–	1.6	2.5
1965	4.5	3.6	1.3	1.2	1.6	.3	3.5	–	1.2	2.1
1966	3.8	3.4	1.6	1.4	1.6	.3	3.7	–	1.6	2.3
1967	3.8	3.8	1.9	1.3	2.1	1.3	3.4	–	2.1	3.3
1968	3.6	4.5	1.8	1.2	2.7	1.1	3.5	–	2.2	3.2
1969	3.5	4.4	1.8	1.1	2.3	.6	3.5	–	1.9	3.1
1970	4.9	5.7	1.6	1.2	2.5	.5	3.2	–	1.5	3.1
1971	5.9	6.2	1.9	1.3	2.8	.6	3.3	–	2.6	3.9
1972	5.6	6.2	2.6	1.4	2.9	.7	3.8	–	2.7	4.2
1973	4.9	5.5	2.3	1.3	2.8	.7	3.7	3.1	2.5	3.2
1974	5.6	5.3	2.7	1.4	2.9	1.6	3.1	3.6	2.0	3.1
1975	8.5	6.9	4.9	1.9	4.2	3.4	3.4	5.1	1.6	4.6
1976	7.7	7.2	4.8	2.0	4.6	3.4	3.9	5.4	1.6	5.9
1977	7.1	8.1	5.6	2.0	5.2	3.4	4.1	4.9	1.8	6.4
1978	6.1	8.4	6.3	2.3	5.4	3.3	4.1	5.1	2.2	6.3
1979	5.8	7.5	6.3	2.1	6.1	2.9	4.4	5.1	2.1	5.4
1980	7.1	7.5	6.1	2.0	6.5	2.8	4.4	6.0	2.0	7.0
1981	7.6	7.6	5.8	2.2	7.6	4.0	4.9	8.9	2.5	10.5
1982	9.7	11.0	7.2	2.4	8.3	5.6	5.4	10.2	3.1	11.3
1983	9.6	11.9	10.0	2.7	8.6	[4]6.9	5.9	[4]11.4	3.5	11.8
1984	7.5	11.3	9.0	2.8	10.0	7.1	5.9	11.5	3.1	11.7
1985	7.2	10.5	8.3	2.6	10.5	7.2	6.0	9.6	2.8	11.2
1986	7.0	9.6	8.1	2.8	10.6	6.6	[4]7.5	10.0	2.6	11.2
1987	6.2	8.9	8.1	2.9	10.8	6.3	7.9	10.0	[4]2.2	10.3
1988	5.5	7.8	7.2	2.5	10.3	6.3	7.9	[4]7.6	1.9	8.6
1989	5.3	7.5	6.2	2.3	9.6	5.7	7.8	7.0	1.6	7.2
1990	[4]5.6	8.1	6.9	2.1	9.1	5.0	7.0	6.2	1.8	6.9
1991	6.8	10.4	9.6	2.1	9.6	4.3[P]	[4]6.9	5.9	3.1	8.8
1992	7.5	11.3	10.8	2.2	[4]10.4	4.6[P]	7.3	5.6	5.6	10.1
1993	6.9	11.2	10.9	2.5	11.8	5.7[P]	[4]10.2	6.6	9.3	10.5
1994	[4]6.1	10.4	9.7	2.9	12.3	6.5[P]	11.3	7.2	9.6	9.7
1995	5.6	9.5	8.5	3.2	11.8	6.5[P]	12.0	7.0	9.1	8.7
1996	5.4	9.7	8.6	3.4	12.5	7.2[P]	12.1	6.4	9.9	8.2
1997	4.9	9.2	8.6	3.4	12.4	7.8[P]	12.3	5.2	10.1	7.0
1998	4.5	8.3	8.0	4.1[P]	11.8[P]	7.5[P]	12.3	–	8.4	6.3[P]

[1] Former West Germany.

[2] The Australian labor force survey was initiated in 1964. Unemployment rates for 1959-63 are estimates made by an Australian researcher.

[3] The Swedish labor force survey was initiated in 1961. The figures for 1959-60 are estimates made by the Organization for Economic Cooperation and Development.

[4] There are breaks in the series for the United States (1990, 1994), France (1992), Germany (1983), Italy (1986, 1991, 1993), the Netherlands (1983, 1988), and Sweden (1987):
The United States (1990): The impact was to raise the unemployment rate by 0.1 percentage point.
The United States (1994): The impact was to raise the unemployment rate by 0.1 percentage point.
France (1992): The impact was to lower the unemployment rate by 0.1 percentage point.
Germany (1983): The impact was to lower the unemployment rate by 0.3 percentage point.
Italy (1986): The impact was to raise the unemployment rate by 1.2 percentage points.
Italy (1991): The impact was to raise the unemployment rate by approximately 0.3 percentage point.
Italy (1993): The impact was to raise the unemployment rate by approximately 1.1 percentage points.
Netherlands (1983): The impact was to lower the unemployment rate by about 2 percentage points.
Netherlands (1988): The impact was to lower the unemployment rate by 1.7 percentage points.
Sweden (1987): The net impact of the break and the BLS adjustment for students seeking work lowered the unemployment rate by 0.1 percentage point.

p = preliminary.

Dash indicates data not available.

Table 60. **Consumer price indexes, 16 countries, 1950-97**

(Indexes: 1982-84=100)

Year	United States [1]	Canada [2]	Japan [3]	Australia II	Austria I	Belgium [4]	Denmark [5]	France [6]
1950	24.1	21.6	14.8	12.6	–	24.0	12.3	11.1
1955	26.8	24.4	20.2	18.9	–	26.6	15.0	14.5
1956	27.2	24.8	20.3	20.1	–	27.4	15.8	14.8
1957	28.1	25.6	20.9	20.7	–	28.2	16.1	15.3
1958	28.9	26.3	20.8	20.9	–	28.6	16.3	17.6
1959	29.1	26.6	21.1	21.3	–	29.0	16.5	18.7
1960	29.6	26.9	21.8	22.1	32.6	29.1	16.7	19.4
1961	29.9	27.1	23.0	22.7	33.8	29.3	17.4	20.0
1962	30.2	27.4	24.6	22.6	35.3	29.8	18.8	21.0
1963	30.6	27.9	26.4	22.4	36.2	30.4	19.8	22.0
1964	31.0	28.4	27.4	23.2	37.6	31.7	20.5	22.7
1965	31.5	29.1	29.5	24.2	39.5	32.9	21.8	23.3
1966	32.4	30.2	31.0	24.9	40.3	34.3	23.3	23.9
1967	33.4	31.3	32.3	25.7	41.9	35.3	25.0	24.6
1968	34.8	32.5	34.0	26.3	43.1	36.3	27.0	25.7
1969	36.7	34.0	35.8	27.1	44.4	37.6	27.9	27.3
1970	38.8	35.1	38.5	28.2	46.4	39.1	29.8	28.8
1971	40.5	36.2	40.9	29.9	48.5	40.8	31.5	30.3
1972	41.8	37.9	42.9	31.6	51.6	43.0	33.6	32.2
1973	44.4	40.7	47.9	34.6	55.5	46.0	36.7	34.6
1974	49.3	45.2	59.1	39.9	60.8	51.9	42.3	39.3
1975	53.8	50.1	66.0	45.9	65.9	58.5	46.4	43.9
1976	56.9	53.8	72.2	52.1	70.8	63.8	50.5	48.2
1977	60.6	58.1	78.1	58.5	74.6	68.4	56.1	52.7
1978	65.2	63.3	81.4	63.1	77.3	71.4	61.8	57.5
1979	72.6	69.1	84.4	68.8	80.2	74.6	67.7	63.6
1980	82.4	76.1	90.9	75.8	85.3	79.6	76.1	72.3
1981	90.9	85.6	95.4	83.2	91.1	85.6	85.0	82.0
1982	96.5	94.9	98.0	92.4	96.0	93.1	93.6	91.7
1983	99.6	100.4	99.8	101.8	99.2	100.3	100.0	100.5
1984	103.9	104.7	102.1	105.8	104.8	106.6	106.4	107.9
1985	107.6	108.9	104.2	112.9	108.2	111.8	111.4	114.2
1986	109.6	113.4	104.8	123.2	110.0	113.3	115.4	117.2
1987	113.6	118.4	104.9	133.6	111.6	115.0	120.0	120.9
1988	118.3	123.2	105.7	143.3	113.8	116.4	125.5	124.2
1989	124.0	129.3	108.1	154.1	116.6	120.0	131.5	128.6
1990	130.7	135.5	111.4	165.3	120.5	124.1	135.0	132.8
1991	136.2	143.1	115.1	170.7	124.5	128.3	138.2	137.1
1992	140.3	145.3	117.0	172.4	129.5	131.4	141.1	140.4
1993	144.5	147.9	118.6	175.5	134.1	135.0	142.9	143.3
1994	148.2	148.2	119.4	178.8	138.2	138.2	145.8	145.7
1995	152.4	151.4	119.2	187.1	141.3	140.2	148.8	148.2
1996	156.9	153.8	119.4	192.0	143.9	143.1	151.9	151.2
1997	160.5	156.2	121.5	192.5	145.8	145.4	155.3	153.0

See footnotes at end of table.

211

Table 60. **Consumer price indexes, 16 countries, 1950-97—Continued**

(Indexes: 1982-84=100)

Year	Germany I[7]	Italy I[8]	Nether-lands II[9]	Norway I[10]	Spain II[9]	Sweden I	Switzer-land I[11]	United Kingdom I[12]
1950	33.9	8.8	21.1	13.6	5.5	13.3	33.2	9.8
1955	37.3	10.8	24.9	18.4	6.3	17.5	36.0	12.8
1956	38.3	11.1	25.1	19.1	6.7	18.4	36.6	13.5
1957	39.1	11.3	26.8	19.6	7.4	19.2	37.3	14.0
1958	39.9	11.6	27.2	20.6	8.4	20.0	38.0	14.4
1959	40.3	11.6	27.5	21.0	9.0	20.2	37.7	14.5
1960	40.9	11.8	28.2	21.1	9.1	21.0	38.2	14.6
1961	41.9	12.1	28.5	21.6	9.2	21.5	39.0	15.1
1962	43.1	12.6	29.2	22.8	9.7	22.5	40.6	15.8
1963	44.4	13.6	30.2	23.4	10.6	23.2	42.0	16.1
1964	45.4	14.4	31.9	24.7	11.3	23.9	43.3	16.6
1965	46.9	15.0	33.2	25.7	12.8	25.1	44.8	17.4
1966	48.6	15.4	35.1	26.6	13.6	26.8	46.9	18.1
1967	49.4	15.9	36.4	27.8	14.5	27.9	48.8	18.5
1968	50.2	16.1	37.7	28.7	15.2	28.4	50.0	19.4
1969	51.1	16.5	40.5	29.6	15.5	29.2	51.3	20.5
1970	52.8	17.3	42.3	32.8	16.4	31.2	53.1	21.8
1971	55.6	18.2	45.5	34.8	17.7	33.6	56.6	23.8
1972	58.7	19.2	49.1	37.3	19.2	35.6	60.4	25.5
1973	62.8	21.3	53.0	40.1	21.4	38.0	65.7	27.9
1974	67.2	25.4	58.1	43.8	24.8	41.7	72.1	32.3
1975	71.2	29.7	64.0	49.0	29.0	45.8	76.9	40.1
1976	74.2	34.6	69.7	53.5	34.1	50.5	78.2	46.8
1977	77.0	41.0	74.3	58.3	42.4	56.3	79.2	54.2
1978	79.0	46.0	77.4	63.1	50.8	61.9	80.1	58.7
1979	82.3	52.8	80.6	66.1	58.8	66.4	83.0	66.6
1980	86.7	64.0	85.9	73.3	67.9	75.5	86.3	78.5
1981	92.2	75.4	91.7	83.3	77.8	84.6	91.9	87.9
1982	97.1	87.8	97.1	92.7	89.0	91.8	97.1	95.4
1983	100.3	100.7	99.8	100.5	99.9	100.1	100.0	99.8
1984	102.7	111.5	103.1	106.8	111.1	108.1	102.9	104.8
1985	104.8	121.8	105.4	112.9	120.9	116.1	106.4	111.1
1986	104.7	129.0	105.6	121.0	131.5	121.0	107.2	114.9
1987	104.9	135.1	105.0	131.9	138.5	126.0	108.8	119.7
1988	106.3	141.9	105.8	140.4	145.1	133.4	110.8	125.6
1989	109.2	150.8	107.1	146.8	155.0	142.0	114.3	135.4
1990	112.1	160.5	109.6	152.8	165.4	156.8	120.5	148.2
1991	116.0	170.6	113.0	158.0	175.2	171.5	127.5	156.9
1992	120.6	179.3	116.5	161.7	185.6	175.3	132.7	162.7
1993	125.7	187.3	119.5	165.4	194.1	183.5	137.0	165.3
1994	129.1	194.9	122.8	167.7	203.3	187.5	138.2	169.3
1995	131.3	205.0	125.0	171.8	212.8	192.3	140.6	175.2
1996	133.1	212.8	127.3	174.0	220.3	193.2	141.7	179.4
1997	135.5	217.0	130.1	178.5	224.8	194.2	142.4	185.1

I = All Households Index, II = Worker Households Index

[1] All urban households from 1978; urban worker households prior to 1978.
[2] All households from January 1995; all urban households from September 1978 to December 1994; and middle income urban households prior to September 1978.
[3] Excluding agricultural and single person households.
[4] Excluding rent and several other services prior to 1976.
[5] Excluding rent prior to 1964.
[6] Paris only prior to 1962. All urban households from 1993; urban worker households for 1962 through 1992.
[7] Refers to the former West Germany. Middle income worker households prior to 1962.
[8] Middle income worker households prior to 1955.
[9] Middle income worker households.
[10] Urban worker households prior to 1960.
[11] All urban households from May 1993; urban worker households through April 1993.
[12] Excluding pensioner and high income households.
Dash indicates data not available.

Table 61. **Hourly compensation costs in U.S. dollars for production workers in manufacturing, 29 countries or areas, 1975-97**

Year	United States	Canada	Mexico	Australia[1]	Hong Kong SAR[2]	Israel	Japan	Korea	New Zealand	Singapore
1975	$6.36	$5.96	$1.47	$5.62	$0.76	$2.25	$3.00	$0.32	$3.21	$0.84
1976	6.92	7.06	1.64	6.22	.87	2.38	3.25	.42	3.00	.86
1977	7.59	7.35	1.34	6.29	1.03	2.68	3.96	.56	3.37	.91
1978	8.28	7.42	1.62	7.00	1.18	2.57	5.45	.76	4.14	1.05
1979	9.04	7.87	1.91	7.47	1.31	3.30	5.40	1.01	4.71	1.26
1980	9.87	8.67	2.21	8.47	1.51	3.79	5.52	.96	5.33	1.49
1981	10.87	9.55	2.82	9.80	1.55	4.18	6.08	1.02	5.69	1.80
1982	11.68	10.44	1.97	9.98	1.66	4.43	5.60	1.09	5.62	1.96
1983	12.14	11.13	1.42	9.31	1.51	4.88	6.03	1.15	5.19	2.21
1984	12.55	11.14	1.56	9.83	1.58	4.65	6.23	1.20	4.65	2.46
1985	13.01	10.94	1.59	8.20	1.73	4.06	6.34	1.23	4.47	2.47
1986	13.26	11.10	1.09	8.54	1.88	5.20	9.22	1.31	5.50	2.23
1987	13.52	12.04	1.04	9.46	2.09	6.34	10.79	1.59	6.77	2.31
1988	13.91	13.50	1.25	11.35	2.40	7.67	12.63	2.20	8.19	2.67
1989	14.32	14.77	1.43	12.41	2.79	7.69	12.53	3.17	7.80	3.15
1990	14.91	15.84	1.58	13.07	3.20	8.55	12.80	3.71	8.33	3.78
1991	15.58	17.16	1.84	13.53	3.58	8.79	14.67	4.61	8.36	4.35
1992	16.09	17.03	2.17	13.02	3.92	9.09	16.38	5.22	7.91	4.95
1993	16.51	16.43	2.40	12.49	4.29	8.82	19.21	5.64	8.01	5.25
1994	16.87	15.85	2.47	14.02	4.61	9.19	21.35	6.40	8.93	6.29
1995	17.19	16.04	1.51	15.05	4.82	10.54	23.82	7.29	10.11	7.33
1996	17.70	16.66	1.54	16.52	5.14	10.99	20.91	8.09	11.03	8.32
1997	18.24	16.55	1.75	16.00	5.42	12.05	19.37	7.22	11.02	8.24

Year	Sri Lanka	Taiwan	Austria[3]	Belgium	Denmark	Finland[4]	France	Germany[5]	Greece	Ireland
1975	$0.28	$0.40	$4.51	$6.41	$6.28	$4.61	$4.52	$6.31	$1.69	$3.03
1976	.24	.46	4.78	6.90	6.63	5.19	4.70	6.68	1.92	2.86
1977	.32	.53	5.67	8.29	7.25	5.58	5.21	7.81	2.29	3.12
1978	.26	.62	6.91	10.14	8.98	5.88	6.43	9.58	2.84	3.97
1979	.23	.79	7.96	11.82	10.53	7.51	7.69	11.21	3.37	4.85
1980	.22	1.00	8.88	13.11	10.83	8.24	8.94	12.25	3.73	5.95
1981	.21	1.21	7.78	11.31	9.41	8.04	8.02	10.45	3.66	5.59
1982	.24	1.24	7.78	9.49	8.87	8.03	7.85	10.28	4.12	5.71
1983	.25	1.29	7.81	9.08	8.69	7.54	7.74	10.19	3.78	5.67
1984	.25	1.42	7.35	8.63	8.03	7.77	7.29	9.37	3.74	5.59
1985	.28	1.50	7.58	8.97	8.13	8.16	7.52	9.53	3.66	5.92
1986	.29	1.73	10.73	12.43	11.07	10.71	10.28	13.34	4.07	8.02
1987	.30	2.26	13.67	15.25	14.61	13.44	12.29	16.91	4.61	9.31
1988	.31	2.81	14.52	15.82	15.19	15.70	12.95	18.16	5.22	10.00
1989	.31	3.52	14.16	15.48	14.53	16.85	12.65	17.66	5.49	9.61
1990	.35	3.93	17.75	19.17	18.04	21.03	15.49	21.88	6.76	11.66
1991	.40	4.36	18.09	19.75	18.39	21.25	15.65	22.63	6.95	11.91
1992	.40	5.09	20.29	22.05	20.20	19.92	17.46	25.38	7.60	13.12
1993	.42	5.23	20.16	21.44	19.11	16.63	16.79	25.32	7.23	11.89
1994	.45	5.55	21.51	23.07	20.30	19.06	17.63	27.03	7.73	12.39
1995	.48	5.92	25.21	26.65	24.07	24.14	20.01	32.22	9.17	13.57
1996	.48	5.93	24.66	25.89	24.11	23.56	19.92	31.79	9.59	13.85
1997	–	5.89	21.92	22.82	22.02	21.44	17.97	28.28	–	13.57

See footnotes at end of table.

213

Table 61. Hourly compensation costs in U.S. dollars for production workers in manufacturing, 29 countries or areas, 1975-97—Continued

Year	Italy	Luxem-bourg	Nether-lands	Norway	Portugal	Spain	Sweden	Switzer-land	United King-dom
1975	$4.67	$6.50	$6.58	$6.77	$1.58	$2.53	$7.18	$6.09	$3.37
1976	4.34	6.99	6.90	7.52	1.66	2.86	8.25	6.45	3.21
1977	4.99	8.06	8.02	8.56	1.58	3.18	8.88	6.88	3.45
1978	5.83	9.86	9.98	9.51	1.63	3.88	9.65	9.59	4.41
1979	7.06	11.12	11.41	10.28	1.68	5.31	11.33	10.56	5.70
1980	8.15	12.03	12.06	11.59	2.06	5.89	12.51	11.09	7.56
1981	7.57	9.85	9.91	11.01	2.04	5.55	11.80	10.14	7.31
1982	7.44	8.61	9.78	10.83	1.88	5.28	10.07	10.42	6.92
1983	7.70	8.15	9.49	10.32	1.62	4.56	8.89	10.46	6.49
1984	7.35	7.79	8.70	10.07	1.45	4.47	9.17	9.64	6.04
1985	7.63	7.81	8.75	10.37	1.53	4.66	9.66	9.66	6.27
1986	10.47	10.86	12.22	13.24	2.08	6.25	12.43	13.76	7.66
1987	13.02	13.35	15.14	16.79	2.52	7.63	15.12	17.08	9.09
1988	13.98	14.22	15.83	18.45	2.78	8.55	16.82	18.01	10.61
1989	14.40	13.92	15.00	18.29	2.97	8.96	17.52	16.73	10.56
1990	17.45	16.74	18.06	21.47	3.77	11.38	20.93	20.86	12.70
1991	18.32	17.14	18.13	21.63	4.24	12.29	22.15	21.69	13.74
1992	19.35	19.10	20.10	23.03	5.17	13.50	24.59	23.23	14.37
1993	15.80	18.74	20.08	20.21	4.50	11.62	17.59	22.63	12.41
1994	15.89	20.33	20.80	20.97	4.60	11.54	18.62	24.91	12.80
1995	16.21	23.35	24.02	24.38	5.37	12.88	21.44	29.30	13.67
1996	17.73	22.55	23.08	25.05	5.58	13.51	24.37	28.34	14.13
1997	16.74	–	20.61	23.72	5.29	12.16	22.24	24.19	15.47

[1] Production and nonproduction workers other than those in managerial, executive, professional, and higher supervisory positions.

[2] Hong Kong Special Administrative Region of China. Average of selected manufacturing industries.

[3] Excludes handicraft manufacturers, printing and publishing, and miscellaneous manufacturing.

[4] Including mining and electrical power plants.

[5] Former West Germany. Excluding handicraft manufacturers.

Dash indicates data not available.

214

Table 62. **Output per hour, hourly compensation, and unit labor costs in manufacturing, 12 countries, 1950-97**

(Indexes: 1992=100)

Year	United States	Canada	Japan	Belgium	Den-mark	France	Ger-many	Italy	Nether-lands	Norway	Sweden	United Kingdom
					Output per hour							
1950	–	28.0	–	–	22.6	13.9	13.2	11.2	12.3	24.5	19.7	24.7
1955	–	34.3	8.7	–	24.6	17.6	19.7	15.6	15.4	28.5	21.6	26.6
1960	–	40.7	14.0	17.9	29.9	23.0	29.2	19.6	19.5	36.7	27.6	30.2
1961	–	42.9	15.8	18.1	31.6	24.5	30.6	21.2	20.6	38.0	29.0	30.2
1962	–	46.3	16.6	19.0	33.2	26.1	32.7	23.4	21.2	38.0	31.3	30.9
1963	–	48.1	18.0	19.8	34.3	27.5	34.1	24.1	21.9	40.0	33.1	32.5
1964	–	50.4	20.4	21.0	37.1	29.7	37.0	24.3	23.9	42.2	36.0	34.7
1965	–	52.9	21.2	22.1	38.9	31.8	39.3	27.1	25.4	44.7	38.7	35.7
1966	–	53.7	23.3	23.6	40.8	34.4	40.9	29.4	27.0	46.6	40.3	36.9
1967	–	54.3	26.3	24.9	43.8	36.5	43.4	30.9	28.9	48.3	43.7	38.6
1968	–	57.6	29.5	27.1	47.8	40.3	47.1	33.3	32.3	51.3	47.8	41.4
1969	–	60.5	33.8	29.6	49.8	42.9	50.4	34.5	35.3	56.1	51.5	42.4
1970	–	59.2	38.0	32.7	52.7	45.5	52.1	36.8	38.6	57.8	52.8	43.3
1971	–	62.7	40.2	34.6	56.3	48.2	54.1	37.4	40.9	60.1	55.1	45.4
1972	–	65.6	44.1	38.6	60.8	50.4	57.4	40.5	44.1	63.6	57.9	47.9
1973	–	69.6	48.1	42.7	66.9	53.9	61.1	43.9	48.8	67.6	62.1	51.4
1974	–	70.8	49.3	45.0	69.1	55.1	63.3	46.7	52.4	70.6	64.8	52.2
1975	–	68.1	50.7	46.8	76.1	57.0	65.9	45.2	51.6	69.7	65.8	51.1
1976	–	73.0	53.8	51.6	78.8	60.5	70.7	51.4	57.1	71.9	66.8	53.3
1977	70.6	77.1	55.9	54.1	80.4	64.1	73.0	52.4	61.8	71.5	65.8	53.8
1978	71.1	78.4	58.1	57.4	81.6	67.0	75.4	55.8	65.9	72.8	67.6	54.5
1979	72.1	78.3	62.9	60.6	85.6	70.1	78.8	61.2	69.2	78.1	72.9	55.0
1980	71.9	75.2	63.9	64.5	90.3	70.5	77.3	64.0	69.8	76.7	74.0	54.4
1981	75.5	77.0	66.0	68.9	91.8	72.6	78.9	65.5	71.4	76.5	73.5	57.2
1982	77.8	75.2	68.7	73.0	92.1	77.7	78.6	66.6	72.7	79.7	76.7	60.3
1983	81.4	79.7	69.6	80.6	96.6	79.4	82.6	70.2	78.4	82.4	81.8	65.0
1984	84.6	86.5	71.9	84.6	96.1	80.7	85.5	77.1	86.1	87.4	85.6	68.5
1985	87.8	89.7	77.3	86.6	96.7	83.8	88.9	81.5	89.7	90.2	87.1	71.1
1986	88.3	89.2	76.9	87.8	91.1	85.2	89.6	82.6	91.0	89.0	88.5	73.9
1987	94.4	91.1	81.2	88.9	90.6	86.7	88.4	85.0	91.7	93.3	90.1	78.1
1988	98.0	91.0	84.8	92.0	94.1	92.7	91.6	86.6	93.8	92.1	90.8	82.6
1989	97.1	92.4	89.5	96.9	99.6	97.4	94.5	89.4	97.2	94.6	93.8	86.2
1990	97.8	95.2	95.4	96.9	99.1	99.1	99.0	92.8	98.6	96.6	95.0	89.2
1991	98.3	95.0	99.4	99.1	99.6	98.7	101.9	95.3	99.6	97.5	95.0	93.9
1992	100.0	100.0	100.0	100.0	100.0	100.0	100.0	100.0	100.0	100.0	100.0	100.0
1993	102.1	103.3	100.5	104.1	104.5	101.8	100.6	104.5	101.9	100.6	106.7	105.6
1994	108.3	105.7	101.8	110.0	–	110.4	107.9	107.4	114.2	101.4	116.1	109.2
1995	114.9	108.4	109.3	108.9	–	114.3	111.2	113.9	119.9	102.0	122.4	107.4
1996	117.3	106.6	111.9	110.0	–	117.9	115.1	114.4	124.4	102.6	125.4	106.1
1997	122.3	109.6	117.4	116.7	–	125.9	121.8	117.4	130.2	103.2	133.6	106.6

See footnotes at end of table.

Table 62. **Output per hour, hourly compensation, and unit labor costs in manufacturing, 12 countries, 1950-97—Continued**

(Indexes: 1992=100)

Year	United States	Canada[1]	Japan	Belgium	Den-mark	France[1]	Ger-many	Italy	Nether-lands	Norway	Sweden[1]	United Kingdom[1]
	Hourly compensation in national currency											
1950	8.7	5.7	_	_	2.5	1.6	3.4	0.8	3.1	2.2	1.9	1.6
1955	11.7	8.1	3.1	_	3.4	2.9	5.0	1.2	4.6	3.4	3.0	2.3
1960	14.9	10.4	4.3	5.6	4.6	4.3	8.2	1.6	6.4	4.7	4.1	3.1
1961	15.4	10.7	5.0	5.9	5.2	4.8	9.1	1.7	7.3	5.2	4.5	3.3
1962	15.9	11.1	5.7	6.3	5.6	5.3	10.3	2.0	7.8	5.7	5.0	3.4
1963	16.4	11.6	6.4	7.0	6.1	5.7	11.0	2.4	8.6	6.1	5.6	3.6
1964	17.1	12.1	7.2	7.9	6.6	6.2	11.9	2.6	10.0	6.5	6.1	3.8
1965	17.5	12.8	8.1	8.8	7.4	6.8	13.1	2.8	11.2	7.2	6.7	4.2
1966	18.3	13.7	9.0	9.7	8.4	7.2	14.3	2.9	12.6	7.8	7.3	4.5
1967	19.3	14.5	10.0	10.6	9.4	7.7	15.0	3.2	13.9	8.7	8.1	4.7
1968	20.7	15.4	11.7	11.3	10.3	8.7	16.2	3.5	15.5	9.6	8.8	5.0
1969	22.2	16.6	13.8	12.4	11.6	9.3	17.7	3.8	17.6	10.6	9.6	5.5
1970	23.8	17.8	16.5	14.1	13.3	10.5	20.8	4.6	20.3	11.8	10.8	6.3
1971	25.3	18.9	19.0	16.2	15.2	11.7	23.3	5.3	23.3	13.5	12.1	7.2
1972	26.6	20.2	21.9	18.7	16.9	13.0	25.8	6.0	26.7	15.1	13.5	8.3
1973	28.7	22.0	26.8	21.7	20.5	14.9	29.1	7.0	31.8	17.0	15.2	9.5
1974	31.8	25.5	35.1	26.4	24.8	17.7	33.1	9.2	38.0	19.9	17.8	11.4
1975	35.7	29.2	40.9	32.0	29.6	21.6	36.5	11.6	43.4	23.8	21.9	15.1
1976	38.7	33.4	44.0	36.3	33.0	24.7	39.3	14.4	48.4	27.5	25.6	17.5
1977	42.0	37.0	48.6	40.5	36.5	28.1	43.0	17.1	52.8	30.9	28.0	19.8
1978	45.4	39.8	51.8	43.7	40.2	31.6	46.3	19.7	57.2	34.1	31.2	23.1
1979	49.9	43.2	55.1	47.5	45.0	35.9	49.7	23.8	61.4	35.8	33.6	27.4
1980	55.8	47.7	58.6	52.7	49.6	41.3	53.9	27.9	64.7	39.0	37.4	33.1
1981	61.3	53.3	62.7	58.5	54.6	47.9	57.3	33.8	67.6	43.3	41.3	38.4
1982	67.3	59.9	64.8	61.0	59.5	56.9	60.4	39.8	71.7	48.2	44.3	42.3
1983	69.1	63.7	67.6	64.7	63.6	62.7	63.4	46.6	74.9	52.9	48.8	45.4
1984	71.5	66.1	69.7	70.1	67.2	68.1	66.4	53.5	77.8	57.9	53.0	49.0
1985	75.3	69.9	72.5	74.5	71.7	73.7	70.2	60.1	81.9	63.4	58.4	53.6
1986	78.7	72.5	76.1	77.6	73.2	76.8	73.1	62.6	85.1	69.1	63.1	58.2
1987	80.9	75.3	77.9	79.3	80.1	79.7	76.6	66.1	87.8	78.5	67.3	64.7
1988	84.2	77.9	79.2	81.0	82.9	82.7	79.6	68.7	87.7	83.3	71.7	68.9
1989	86.9	82.5	84.2	85.2	87.7	87.2	83.4	75.5	88.5	87.2	79.4	73.6
1990	91.0	89.5	90.7	89.9	92.7	91.8	89.4	84.0	90.8	92.3	87.6	82.2
1991	95.8	94.7	95.9	95.5	95.9	96.3	95.1	93.1	95.2	97.5	95.4	92.1
1992	100.0	100.0	100.0	100.0	100.0	100.0	100.0	100.0	100.0	100.0	100.0	100.0
1993	102.9	99.8	104.6	104.9	104.6	103.6	105.9	107.1	103.7	101.5	98.0	105.9
1994	105.8	100.4	106.7	108.4	_	106.2	111.7	106.6	108.2	104.4	101.1	109.2
1995	108.3	103.7	109.5	111.6	_	107.7	117.7	112.3	110.6	109.2	106.2	110.9
1996	110.7	106.0	110.5	114.1	_	109.4	123.7	119.4	113.9	114.4	113.4	112.2
1997	115.3	108.8	114.0	116.5	_	112.6	126.6	125.2	117.0	119.6	118.3	116.8

See footnotes at end of table.

Table 62. **Output per hour, hourly compensation, and unit labor costs in manufacturing, 12 countries, 1950-97—Continued**

(Indexes: 1992=100)

Year	United States	Canada[1]	Japan	Belgium	Den-mark	France[1]	Ger-many	Italy	Nether-lands	Norway	Sweden[1]	United Kingdom[1]
	Hourly compensation in U.S. dollars											
1950	8.7	6.3	—	—	2.2	2.5	1.3	1.6	1.4	1.9	2.1	2.5
1955	11.7	9.9	1.1	—	3.0	4.3	1.9	2.3	2.1	2.9	3.3	3.6
1960	14.9	13.0	1.5	3.6	4.0	4.7	3.1	3.1	3.0	4.1	4.7	4.9
1961	15.4	12.7	1.8	3.8	4.5	5.1	3.6	3.4	3.6	4.5	5.1	5.2
1962	15.9	12.5	2.0	4.1	4.9	5.7	4.0	4.1	3.8	4.9	5.7	5.5
1963	16.4	13.0	2.3	4.5	5.4	6.2	4.3	4.8	4.2	5.3	6.3	5.7
1964	17.1	13.5	2.5	5.1	5.8	6.7	4.7	5.1	4.9	5.6	6.9	6.0
1965	17.5	14.3	2.8	5.7	6.4	7.3	5.1	5.5	5.5	6.2	7.6	6.6
1966	18.3	15.4	3.1	6.3	7.3	7.7	5.6	5.8	6.1	6.8	8.3	7.2
1967	19.3	16.2	3.5	6.9	8.1	8.3	5.9	6.4	6.8	7.6	9.2	7.3
1968	20.7	17.3	4.1	7.3	8.3	9.3	6.3	6.8	7.5	8.4	10.0	6.8
1969	22.2	18.7	4.9	8.0	9.3	9.5	7.0	7.5	8.5	9.2	10.8	7.4
1970	23.8	20.6	5.8	9.1	10.7	10.0	8.9	9.1	9.9	10.3	12.1	8.5
1971	25.3	22.6	6.9	10.7	12.4	11.3	10.5	10.6	11.7	11.9	13.8	9.9
1972	26.6	24.7	9.2	13.6	14.7	13.6	12.6	12.6	14.6	14.2	16.6	11.7
1973	28.7	26.5	12.5	17.9	20.5	17.7	17.2	14.9	20.1	18.4	20.3	13.1
1974	31.8	31.5	15.3	21.8	24.6	19.4	20.0	17.4	24.9	22.4	23.5	15.0
1975	35.7	34.7	17.5	28.0	31.1	26.6	23.2	21.9	30.2	28.4	30.8	19.0
1976	38.7	40.9	18.8	30.2	32.9	27.4	24.4	21.4	32.2	31.3	34.2	17.9
1977	42.0	42.1	23.0	36.3	36.7	30.2	28.9	23.8	37.9	36.0	36.5	19.5
1978	45.4	42.2	31.5	44.7	44.1	37.2	36.0	28.5	46.5	40.4	40.2	25.1
1979	49.9	44.6	32.0	52.1	51.6	44.6	42.4	35.3	53.8	43.9	45.7	33.0
1980	55.8	49.3	32.9	58.0	53.2	51.8	46.3	40.3	57.3	49.0	51.5	43.6
1981	61.3	53.7	36.1	50.8	46.2	46.6	39.7	36.6	47.8	46.9	47.5	44.0
1982	67.3	58.6	33.5	42.9	43.0	45.7	38.9	36.2	47.2	46.4	41.1	41.9
1983	69.1	62.5	36.1	40.7	42.0	43.6	38.7	37.8	46.2	45.0	37.1	38.9
1984	71.5	61.7	37.2	39.0	39.2	41.3	36.4	37.5	42.6	44.1	37.3	37.1
1985	75.3	61.8	38.5	40.4	40.9	43.5	37.3	38.8	43.4	45.8	39.5	39.4
1986	78.7	63.0	57.3	55.8	54.6	58.7	52.6	51.7	61.1	58.1	51.6	48.4
1987	80.9	68.7	68.3	68.3	70.6	70.2	66.5	62.8	76.2	72.3	61.8	60.0
1988	84.2	76.5	78.4	70.8	74.3	73.5	70.8	65.0	78.0	79.3	68.1	69.5
1989	86.9	84.2	77.3	69.5	72.3	72.3	69.3	67.8	73.4	78.4	71.7	68.3
1990	91.0	92.7	79.3	86.4	90.4	89.2	86.4	86.3	87.7	91.7	86.2	83.0
1991	95.8	99.9	90.3	89.7	90.5	90.3	89.4	92.5	89.4	93.3	91.8	92.1
1992	100.0	100.0	100.0	100.0	100.0	100.0	100.0	100.0	100.0	100.0	100.0	100.0
1993	102.9	93.5	119.3	97.6	97.4	96.8	100.0	83.9	98.1	88.8	73.3	90.0
1994	105.8	88.8	132.4	104.3	—	101.4	107.6	81.5	104.6	92.0	76.3	94.7
1995	108.3	91.3	147.7	121.8	—	114.3	128.3	84.9	121.2	107.1	86.6	99.1
1996	110.7	93.9	128.8	118.4	—	113.2	128.4	95.4	118.8	110.0	98.5	99.2
1997	115.3	94.9	119.4	104.6	—	102.1	114.0	90.6	105.4	104.9	90.1	108.3

See footnotes at end of table.

217

Table 62. **Output per hour, hourly compensation, and unit labor costs in manufacturing, 12 countries, 1950-97—Continued**

(Indexes: 1992=100)

Year	United States	Canada[1]	Japan	Belgium	Den-mark	France[1]	Ger-many	Italy	Nether-lands	Norway	Sweden[1]	United Kingdom[1]
	Unit labor costs in national currency											
1950	–	20.3	–	–	11.0	11.7	25.6	7.4	25.5	9.0	9.5	6.5
1955	_	23.5	36.1	_	13.8	16.3	25.5	7.6	29.7	11.8	13.7	8.6
1960	_	25.6	30.9	31.2	15.4	18.7	28.0	8.0	33.0	12.9	14.9	10.1
1961	_	24.9	31.8	32.6	16.3	19.4	29.9	8.2	35.7	13.6	15.6	10.8
1962	_	24.0	34.6	33.3	17.0	20.2	31.6	8.7	37.0	15.0	16.1	11.1
1993	_	24.1	35.7	35.5	17.9	20.9	32.3	10.1	39.4	15.2	16.8	11.0
1964	_	24.0	35.4	37.7	17.9	21.0	32.3	10.6	41.9	15.4	16.9	11.0
1965	_	24.2	38.3	39.8	18.9	21.3	33.4	10.2	44.2	16.0	17.3	11.7
1966	_	25.6	38.5	41.1	20.5	20.8	34.8	10.0	46.5	16.8	18.2	12.3
1967	_	26.7	38.1	42.5	21.4	21.1	34.6	10.5	48.2	18.1	18.6	12.1
1968	_	26.8	39.6	41.8	21.6	21.7	34.4	10.4	48.0	18.8	18.5	12.1
1969	_	27.5	41.0	41.9	23.4	21.7	35.1	11.0	49.8	19.0	18.7	12.9
1970	_	30.0	43.3	43.2	25.2	23.0	39.9	12.6	52.7	20.4	20.5	14.6
1971	_	30.2	47.3	46.7	27.1	24.4	43.0	14.3	56.9	22.5	22.0	15.8
1972	_	30.8	49.6	48.4	27.8	25.7	44.8	14.8	60.5	23.7	23.4	17.3
1973	_	31.6	55.7	50.8	30.6	27.6	47.6	16.0	65.1	25.1	24.4	18.4
1974	_	36.0	71.1	58.6	35.9	32.0	52.3	19.7	72.5	28.2	27.5	21.8
1975	_	42.9	80.6	68.3	38.9	37.8	55.3	25.7	84.1	34.2	33.3	29.5
1976	_	45.7	81.9	70.3	41.8	40.8	55.6	28.1	84.7	38.3	38.3	32.8
1977	59.6	48.0	86.8	74.8	45.4	43.8	59.0	32.6	85.5	43.2	42.6	36.8
1978	63.8	50.7	89.1	76.0	49.3	47.2	61.4	35.2	86.7	46.8	46.2	42.3
1979	69.1	55.2	87.5	78.5	52.5	51.1	63.1	39.0	88.8	45.8	46.2	49.9
1980	77.6	63.4	91.7	81.7	55.0	58.6	69.6	43.7	92.7	50.8	50.6	60.9
1981	81.3	69.2	95.1	84.9	59.5	66.0	72.6	51.6	94.8	56.6	56.1	67.2
1982	86.5	79.6	95.8	83.6	64.6	73.2	76.9	59.8	98.8	60.5	57.8	70.1
1983	84.9	79.9	97.2	80.3	65.8	79.0	76.7	66.4	95.6	64.2	59.7	69.8
1984	84.4	76.4	96.8	82.8	69.9	84.4	77.6	69.4	90.3	66.3	61.9	71.5
1985	85.8	77.9	93.8	86.1	74.2	88.0	78.9	73.8	91.3	70.2	67.1	75.4
1986	89.1	81.3	99.0	88.3	80.4	90.2	81.6	75.8	93.5	77.7	71.3	78.8
1987	85.7	82.6	96.0	89.3	88.4	92.0	86.7	77.8	95.8	84.1	74.7	82.8
1988	85.9	85.6	93.4	88.0	88.2	89.3	86.9	79.4	93.5	90.4	79.0	83.4
1989	89.5	89.3	94.0	87.9	88.1	89.5	88.3	84.4	91.1	92.2	84.7	85.5
1990	93.1	94.0	95.0	92.7	93.6	92.6	90.3	90.5	92.1	95.6	92.3	92.1
1991	97.5	99.7	96.5	96.3	96.3	97.6	93.3	97.7	95.6	100.0	100.4	98.1
1992	100.0	100.0	100.0	100.0	100.0	100.0	100.0	100.0	100.0	100.0	100.0	100.0
1993	100.8	96.6	104.1	100.8	100.1	101.8	105.3	102.5	101.8	100.9	91.8	100.3
1994	97.7	95.0	104.9	98.6	93.0	96.2	103.6	99.2	94.8	102.9	87.0	100.1
1995	94.3	95.7	100.1	102.5	93.4	94.2	105.9	98.6	92.3	107.1	86.8	103.3
1996	94.3	99.4	98.8	103.7	92.3	92.8	107.5	104.4	91.5	111.5	90.4	105.8
1997	94.3	99.3	97.1	99.8	95.3	89.4	103.9	106.6	89.9	115.9	88.5	109.5

See footnotes at end of table.

Table 62. Output per hour, hourly compensation, and unit labor costs in manufacturing, 12 countries, 1950-97—Continued

(Indexes: 1992=100)

Year	United States	Canada[1]	Japan	Belgium	Den-mark	France[1]	Ger-many	Italy	Nether-lands	Norway	Sweden[1]	United Kingdom[1]
					Unit labor costs in U.S. dollars							
1950	–	22.4	–	–	9.6	17.7	9.5	14.6	11.8	7.8	10.7	10.3
1955	–	28.8	12.7	–	12.0	24.6	9.5	15.0	13.7	10.2	15.5	13.6
1960	–	31.9	10.9	20.1	13.5	20.2	10.5	15.9	15.4	11.3	16.8	16.1
1961	–	29.7	11.2	21.0	14.3	21.0	11.6	16.2	17.3	11.9	17.6	17.2
1962	–	27.1	12.1	21.5	14.9	21.8	12.3	17.3	18.1	13.0	18.2	17.7
1963	–	26.9	12.5	22.9	15.7	22.5	12.7	19.9	19.2	13.2	18.9	17.5
1964	–	26.9	12.4	24.3	15.6	22.7	12.7	20.9	20.4	13.3	19.1	17.4
1965	–	27.1	13.4	25.7	16.5	23.0	13.1	20.1	21.6	13.9	19.6	18.6
1966	–	28.7	13.5	26.5	17.9	22.5	13.6	19.7	22.6	14.6	20.5	19.4
1967	–	29.9	13.3	27.5	18.5	22.7	13.6	20.7	23.5	15.7	21.0	18.8
1968	–	30.0	13.9	26.9	17.4	23.2	13.4	20.5	23.3	16.4	20.9	16.4
1969	–	30.9	14.5	26.9	18.8	22.1	14.0	21.6	24.1	16.5	21.0	17.4
1970	–	34.8	15.3	28.0	20.3	22.0	17.1	24.7	25.6	17.8	23.0	19.7
1971	–	36.1	17.3	30.9	22.1	23.4	19.3	28.5	28.7	19.9	25.1	21.9
1972	–	37.6	20.8	35.3	24.1	27.0	22.0	31.2	33.1	22.3	28.7	24.5
1973	–	38.1	26.1	42.1	30.7	32.9	28.1	34.0	41.2	27.2	32.7	25.5
1974	–	44.5	30.9	48.4	35.6	35.1	31.7	37.3	47.5	31.7	36.2	28.8
1975	–	51.0	34.5	59.8	40.9	46.7	35.2	48.6	58.6	40.7	46.8	37.2
1976	–	56.0	35.0	58.6	41.8	45.3	34.5	41.7	56.4	43.6	51.3	33.6
1977	59.6	54.6	41.1	67.1	45.7	47.2	39.7	45.5	61.2	50.4	55.5	36.3
1978	63.8	53.8	54.2	77.7	54.1	55.6	47.8	51.1	70.6	55.5	59.5	45.9
1979	69.1	56.9	50.9	86.0	60.3	63.6	53.8	57.8	77.9	56.2	62.8	60.0
1980	77.6	65.6	51.5	90.0	58.9	73.5	59.9	62.9	82.1	63.9	69.6	80.1
1981	81.3	69.7	54.6	73.7	50.4	64.2	50.3	55.9	67.0	61.3	64.6	77.0
1982	86.5	77.9	48.8	58.7	46.7	58.9	49.5	54.4	65.0	58.3	53.6	69.4
1983	84.9	78.4	51.8	50.5	43.4	54.9	46.9	53.8	58.9	54.7	45.3	59.9
1984	84.4	71.3	51.7	46.1	40.8	51.2	42.6	48.7	49.5	50.5	43.6	54.1
1985	85.8	68.9	49.9	46.6	42.3	51.9	41.9	47.6	48.4	50.8	45.4	55.4
1986	89.1	70.7	74.5	63.6	60.0	69.0	58.7	62.6	67.1	65.3	58.3	65.5
1987	85.7	75.3	84.2	76.8	77.9	81.0	75.3	73.9	83.1	77.5	68.5	76.9
1988	85.9	84.1	92.4	76.9	79.0	79.3	77.2	75.1	83.1	86.1	75.0	84.1
1989	89.5	91.1	86.3	71.7	72.6	74.3	73.3	75.8	75.5	82.9	76.4	79.3
1990	93.1	97.3	83.1	89.2	91.3	90.0	87.3	93.0	88.9	95.0	90.8	93.0
1991	97.5	105.1	90.9	90.6	90.8	91.5	87.8	97.0	89.8	95.7	96.6	98.2
1992	100.0	100.0	100.0	100.0	100.0	100.0	100.0	100.0	100.0	100.0	100.0	100.0
1993	100.8	90.5	118.8	93.7	93.2	95.1	99.4	80.3	96.3	88.3	68.6	85.3
1994	97.7	84.0	130.1	94.8	88.3	91.8	99.8	75.8	91.6	90.7	65.7	86.8
1995	94.3	84.2	135.1	111.8	100.7	100.0	115.5	74.6	101.2	105.0	70.8	92.3
1996	94.3	88.1	115.1	107.6	96.1	96.1	111.6	83.4	95.4	107.3	78.5	93.4
1997	94.3	86.7	101.7	89.6	87.0	81.1	93.5	77.1	81.0	101.6	67.5	101.5

[1]Compensation adjusted to include changes in employment taxes that are not compensation to employees, but are labor costs to employers.

Dash indicates data not available.

NOTE: The data relate to employees (wage and salary earners) in Belgium, Denmark, Italy, the Netherlands, and the United Kingdom, and to all employed persons (employees and self-employed workers) in the other countries.